Divided We Fall
How Disunity Leads to Defeat

James Rothrock
Lt. Col. USAF (Ret)

Bloomington, IN  Milton Keynes, UK
authorHOUSE

AuthorHouse™
1663 Liberty Drive, Suite 200
Bloomington, IN 47403
www.authorhouse.com
Phone: 1-800-839-8640

AuthorHouse™ *UK Ltd.*
500 Avebury Boulevard
Central Milton Keynes, MK9 2BE
www.authorhouse.co.uk
Phone: 08001974150

Cover design by April Mostek

© 2006 James Rothrock Lt. Col. USAF (Ret). All rights reserved.

No part of this book may be reproduced, stored in a retrieval system, or transmitted by any means without the written permission of the author.

First published by AuthorHouse 5/3/2006

ISBN: 1-4259-1107-2 (sc)
ISBN: 1-4259-1108-0 (dj)

Library of Congress Control Number: 2006900042

Printed in the United States of America
Bloomington, Indiana

This book is printed on acid-free paper.

Acknowledgements

The Vietnam Center and Archive at Texas Tech University has been a major resource in the preparation of this book. The Vietnam Archive at Texas Tech is recognized as having the largest and most comprehensive assortment of documents about every aspect of the Vietnam War. I am forever grateful to the entire staff at the Vietnam Center for their legendary support and service.

I also owe a debt of gratitude to the librarians at Hurlburt Field, Florida, Fort Carson, Colorado and the Air Force Academy for their help in acquiring research materials.

A special thanks to the freedom of information administrators at CIA and FBI headquarters who were exceptionally helpful and cooperative in aiding my research.

—James Rothrock
December 1, 2005

*For those who gave their all
and all those who served with honor*

Contents

Acknowledgements v

Preface ix

Chapter One   The Second Front 1

Chapter Two   Why Vietnam 10

Chapter Three   Hanoi's Grand Facade 46

Chapter Four   The Rise of the Second Front 80

Chapter Five   From Hanoi with Love 128

Chapter Six   The Collaborators 154

Chapter Seven   Band of Traitors 182

Chapter Eight   Assault on the Troops 216

Chapter Nine   Sabotaging the War Effort 242

Chapter Ten   Peace Initiatives 263

Chapter Eleven   Sellout 297

Chapter Twelve   Prolonging the War 319

Chapter Thirteen   Aftermath 341

Chapter Fourteen   The Antiwar Legacy 350

Appendixes:

A   NSAM No. 52, May 11, 1961 355

B   NSAM No. 111, November 22, 1961 359

C   NSAM No. 273, November 26, 1963 363

D   Address by President Johnson, April 7, 1965 367

E	Chronology of Second Tonkin Gulf Incident	378
F	President's Message to Congress, August 5, 1964	383
G	Gulf of Tonkin Resolution	386
H	State Department White Paper, February 27, 1965	388
I	Statement by Secretary of Defense Robert S. McNamara	393
J	CIA Memo: International Communist Aid to North Vietnam	410
K	MACV Policy on Handling Prisoners of War	421
L	Messages from Communist Officials	427
M	List of Broadcasts from Hanoi	435
N	Military Buildup Committee	438

Glossary 451

Notes 454

Bibliography 489

Index 509

Preface

Then join hand in hand, brave Americans all! By uniting we stand, by dividing we fall.

—John Dickinson

Historians have suggested many reasons for America's defeat in Vietnam. The premise of this book is that disunity on the home front was the most significant and influential factor leading to our downfall in Vietnam. The disunity in America was incited and fueled by the antiwar movement. This movement, collectively consisting of the antiwar factions, the media, academia and congressional doves, gave rise to the "second front" which became a major weapon in Hanoi's arsenal. This second front was ever present in the minds of North Vietnam's leaders. It played a major role in Hanoi's strategy and was valued as the equivalent of several army divisions.

The disunity fostered by the antiwar movement emboldened our enemies and encouraged them to hold out in the face of battlefield defeats. The purpose of this book is to reveal the full impact of the second front, how it influenced the conduct of the war and most importantly, its effect on the outcome of the war. Above all, it is meant to show how the most powerful nation in the world can go down in defeat when its people are divided.

The most important lesson of the Vietnam War is that *disunity on the home front leads to defeat abroad.* France found this out when the will of its people gave way, and it was forced to leave Indochina in defeat. The divisions over the war in Iraq are a strong indication that we have not learned the lessons of Vietnam. If disunity is ever allowed to prevail as it did during the Vietnam War, there will be more defeats on the horizon for the United States.

Several years have been devoted to gathering information for this book, including information obtained under the Freedom of Information Act; declassified CIA, FBI, State Department, US Information Agency, and Department of Defense files; Presidential libraries; Congressional Records; captured enemy documents; intercepts of enemy radio broadcasts; numerous books, periodicals and newspaper files; and the review of several thousand documents held by Texas Tech University's Vietnam Center. The most irrefutable source concerning the impact of the antiwar movement on North Vietnam's war strategy comes from a conversation I had with the former North Vietnamese Army Colonel, Bui Tin, in October of 2003. Colonel Tin was once on Ho Chi Minh's personal staff; he rose to key positions in the North Vietnamese Army and Communist Party of Vietnam; and he was the senior North Vietnamese officer present in Saigon who accepted the surrender of South Vietnam.

Recently, the thesis of this work was validated by a well known American statesman, Henry Kissinger, former Secretary of State, National Security Adviser to presidents Nixon and Ford and US negotiator at the Paris peace talks to end the war in Vietnam. On August 25, 2005 he made this statement of historical significance on CNN: "In Vietnam we defeated ourselves with domestic divisions."

—James Rothrock
December 1, 2005

Chapter One

The Second Front

A nation can survive its fools and even the ambitious, but it cannot survive treason from within.

—Cicero

The war in Vietnam was not fought solely in the jungles and rice paddies of Vietnam. While the battles raged there, another war was being waged in our own backyard and in the world arena. This "second front" was a crucial element of Hanoi's war fighting strategy. It was being fought on the streets and campuses of the United States and in the major cities around the world. This was not the usual kind of war. It was political warfare—a war for the hearts and minds of the American people and world opinion. Victory was measured by Hanoi's success in weakening the resolve of the American people to continue support of the war and in turning world opinion against the United States. There were no guns or bombs in this type of warfare, only a very aggressive and clever propaganda campaign. The cornerstone of this "second front" was the antiwar movement in the United States. It became a major weapon in Hanoi's arsenal for winning the war.

In a TOP SECRET (declassified) memorandum for the president on November 16, 1967, the Under Secretary of State, Nicholas Katzenbach, advised President Johnson of certain fundamental premises he saw about the war in Vietnam:

1. The war is being actively fought on two fronts: One, in Vietnam with our military and civilian efforts; the

other, in the United States with our efforts to maintain whatever level of popular and Congressional support is necessary to continue our efforts.

2. Hanoi's strategy is based on winning the war in the United States, not in Vietnam where our military might obviously forecloses that possibility.

3. The war can be lost in the United States. There is considerable justification for Hanoi's belief that public and Congressional opinion will not permit the United States to keep meeting immense costs in men, money, and—above all—severe internal divisions for many more months without an end visibly in sight.[1]

In his essay, *How Political Warfare Caused America to Snatch Defeat from the Jaws of Victory in Vietnam*, Robert Turner, Associate Director, Center for National Security Law, wrote: "If not unique, the Vietnam War was at least unusual because of the importance played by political warfare in determining the final outcome. Indeed, it can be credibly argued that the outcome was determined less by military operations in Indochina than by misperceptions of the conflict in the United States and around the world and the resulting political crisis within the United States."[2] He went on to point out that the North Vietnamese Army and so-called Viet Cong did not win a single major battle with US forces, nor did they win the war militarily while the United States was involved. However, in Turner's view, there was no doubt about the reason for the final outcome. He reasoned, "[North Vietnam] did ultimately win the most important struggle—the battle to decide whether the United States had the political *will* to persevere in its efforts to prevent a Communist victory in Indochina."[3] He notes that reliance on "political warfare was Hanoi's game plan from the start."[4]

A 1965 *U.S. News and World Report* article citing officials and observers on the scene in Saigon, reported that the leaders in Hanoi knew that France was defeated in the Indochina war not on the battlefield but at home where they lost the will to fight. The article warned that Hanoi was counting on the same thing happening in the United States: "There is an agreement among most thoughtful observers here [Saigon] that the Communists are greatly impressed by the antidraft and antiwar demonstrations in the U.S. and that they are counting on those demonstrations to affect the U.S. will to fight."[5]

In an interview with *The Wall Street Journal* columnist, Stephen Young, on August 3, 1995, the former North Vietnamese Army Colonel Bui Tin was asked how Hanoi intended to defeat the Americans. He responded, "By fighting a long war which would break their will to help South Vietnam." He added, "Ho Chi Minh said, 'We don't need to win military victories, we only need to hit them [Americans] until they give up and get out.'"[6]

In a conversation with Colonel Bui Tin in October of 2003, the author asked the Colonel about the importance of the antiwar movement in the United States to North Vietnam's strategy. Colonel Bui Tin was emphatic about the enormous effect the movement had on their strategy and plans. He explained that the leaders in Hanoi paid close attention every day to what was happening with the antiwar movement in America. He went on to say that Hanoi placed great value and appreciation in the antiwar movement and considered it the equivalent of several army divisions fighting on their side.[7]

Patrick J. Honey, an authority on Vietnamese affairs, reported in 1971 that "politically, things are going Hanoi's way in view of the antiwar movement in the United States....The disintegration of America's determination to continue the war marks a great breakthrough for Hanoi....[The] weariness of war in the U.S. is more valuable to Hanoi than the sending of 15 extra Red Divisions to fight on the ground."[8]

In essence, the antiwar movement in the United States became a "second front" for North Vietnam. Commentary on February 2, 1967 in *Nhan-Dan*, the official voice of the Lao Dong Communist Party in Hanoi, left no doubt about the effect of the antiwar movement: "The American people's movement of the protest against the US aggressive war in Vietnam has actually become a 'second front' against US imperialism right in the United States. It is certain that the stormy struggle of the American people for an end to the cruel and savage war of the Johnson clique in Vietnam will continue surging up vigorously. The flames of this struggle are burning under the feet of the US imperialists right at their principal base."[9]

The aid and encouragement that Hanoi received from the antiwar activists raises daunting questions about the motives and agenda of the activists. Were they so uninformed that they did not know they were aiding the enemy who was killing our troops while they were in the streets demonstrating and waving the Viet Cong flag? Didn't they care? Did they hate their own country so much that they wanted the other side to win? Or were they simply naïve, unwitting pawns? Granted, there were probably some true pacifists who opposed war for any reason; however, there were far too many intellectuals, professors, students and congressmen who were not pacifists, yet they supported and led the antiwar movement. Some of the younger activists might qualify as unwitting pawns, but those who were out in front promoting and leading the protests cannot hide behind the cloak of naïveté or ignorance. They have blood on their hands.

On August 7, 1967, Walt Rostow, Special Assistant for National Security Affairs to President Johnson, 1966-1969, reported to the president: "All evidence we have indicates that Hanoi does not now expect to win the war in the South on the battlefield. They are hanging on hoping that there will be a break in the will of the U.S. to continue the war."[10]

Dean Rusk, the Secretary of State during most of the Kennedy and Johnson administrations, made the case for showing a strong, united front to Hanoi. He held that "had North Vietnam been convinced that the United States was unequivocally committed to South Vietnam and that we were going to see it through, Hanoi might have decided to negotiate a settlement on terms less than the reunification of all of Vietnam by force. But instead the North Vietnamese judged that if they stayed with it, American public support for the war would collapse and then they could win on the home front in the United States what they couldn't win on the ground in Vietnam."[11]

From 1966 forward, Hanoi began to see thousands of antiwar demonstrators in the streets of America calling for an end to the war and congressional doves threatening to cut off all funds for the war. Our negotiating leverage wilted and Hanoi's incentive to negotiate was severely diminished. All that the leaders in Hanoi had to do was sit back and wait. They did just that, and the war was prolonged far beyond its logical conclusion. Dean Rusk spoke with conviction on this subject, "Americans opposed to the war, whatever their motivations, however sincerely they may have wanted peace, in effect said to Hanoi, 'now, just hang in there, fellows, and you will get what you want politically even though you cannot win it militarily.'"[12]

Douglas Pike, who spent many years in the United States Foreign Service at posts in Saigon, is one of the foremost experts on North Vietnam's political strategy. In his book, *PAVN: People's Army of Vietnam,* he describes the Maoist military strategy that was the pattern used by the Viet-Minh in their war with France and the struggle against South Vietnam and the United States. That strategy relied on two inseparable tracks, the armed struggle (armed *dau tranh*) and the political struggle (political *dau tranh*). Although the balance between the two tracks varied depending on the stage of the conflict, the two were molded into a single, integrated instrument of war. During the involvement of the United States in the war in Vietnam, North Vietnam's activity in the political *dau tranh* far exceeded that of armed *dau tranh*.[13] This reflects the importance that North Vietnam placed on political warfare.

Douglas Pike identified three action programs that made up the political *dau tranh* program. They include the *dich van* program which applied to action among the people controlled by their enemy, including the South Vietnamese and Americans; the *binh van* program which was aimed at the enemy military and civil servants with the goal of destroying and weakening enemy armed forces and government by nonmilitary means; and the *dan van* program which included action among the people who were under the control of the North Vietnamese and so-called Viet Cong in liberated (captured) zones. In addition to actions to undermine the government of South Vietnam, the *dish van* program was directed at the world arena, particularly the United States. The objective of this strategy as applied to the United States was "to do battle with America on its home ground, not with guns but with weapons of perceptional obfuscation...."[14]

As defined by Douglas Pike, "The *dish van* program among Americans operated on two levels: strategic, to shape perception by the Americans so as to convince them victory in Vietnam was impossible, and, therefore, undermine the war at home and American diplomacy worldwide; and tactical, that is, power nullification, to limit American response in Vietnam by inhibiting full use of American capability there."[15] Pike makes the case that the program of political warfare was successful in shaping many false perceptions throughout the world and especially the United States. He contends that "certainly the *dish van* program's vilification of the American air war succeeded in the United States to the extent of causing many people to believe that the air strikes somehow were more brutal and horrible than they were....It created myths that defy elementary logic, yet they endure and threaten to become the orthodoxy of history."[16] Many of these myths will be exposed in forthcoming chapters.

The significance of Hanoi's reliance on the *dish van* program can be seen in the report by General Phillip B. Davidson in his book, *Vietnam at War,* in which he describes how Hanoi saw its defeat during the Tet offensive in 1968 turned into a psychological victory over the United States. "It [Hanoi] saw that Indochina War II could be won in the United States through the news media, academia, the antiwar dissenters, and Congress itself. In mid-1968 Hanoi began an intensive and calculated program within the United States to undermine American public support for the war."[17]

The enormity of the political warfare program pursued by North Vietnam is outlined in a SECRET enemy document captured on March 10, 1967 by U.S. Army units during Operation Junction City in Tay Ninh Province. This document, *Report on Propaganda and Foreign Affairs,* was prepared June 15, 1966 by the Subcommittee for Foreign Activities of COSVN (Central Office for South Vietnam, North Vietnam's highest echelon in South Vietnam). It provides a detailed account of the organizational structure, mission, programs, operations and direction of propaganda activities around the world. The report makes it clear that the majority of propaganda and diplomatic activities in the South were controlled and directed by North Vietnam's Central Committee in Hanoi (Lao Dong Communist Party).[18] In view of the importance of this report in showing the emphasis North Vietnam placed on the political struggle (*dish van*), significant excerpts of this report are highlighted below.

> *In capitalist countries, such as the United States, we always keep abreast of the American people's opinions and try to motivate youths, intellectuals and religious sects to protest the war of aggression waged by their government in Vietnam. At the same time, we motivate families of the US troops dispatched to Vietnam to protest this sending of troops.* [Emphasis added] *In addition, we actively support the anti-American movements in the US satellite countries which also have troops in SVN, such as the Philippines, South Korea, etc...while we have highly appreciated movements against the US imperialists' warmongering and aggressive policy*

and for peace, democracy, and support to Vietnam, launched by the peoples of the political parties of Japan, France, Great Britain, and a number of North European countries....

We succeeded in condemning the US war of aggression and unmasking the United States' new kind of colonialism and their fascist dictatorial regime in Saigon. We frustrated the enemy's distorted propaganda effort and false attempt to establish peace in Vietnam....

To introduce our movement to the world we have clearly pointed out the just cause of our struggle and make it clear that the southern revolution is an integral part of the national liberation movements in the world....

Based on the COSVN resolution concerning revolutionary tasks in South Vietnam in 1966, the general policy on information and propaganda activities and foreign affairs is designed to serve strategic objectives of the Party, which are as follows:

> Strive to enlist support and assistance from the socialist camp, the peoples of the world, the Americans, the Khmer peoples, the Laotians, the neutralist government of Cambodia and Laos.
>
> Concentrate all efforts on denouncing the US aggression in Vietnam.
>
> Denounce the inhumane acts perpetrated by the Americans, such as the use of chemicals, gas, artillery and airstrikes to decimate our people. Lay bare the US deceitful peace offensive. Play up our just cause and the prospect of inevitable victory. *Enlist the sympathy and support of the socialist camp, the peoples of the world, including the people of the United*

States of America. [Emphasis added] Isolate the Americans and their lackeys....

Make every effort to persuade the people of America and its satellites to support us, to oppose the US Government's aggressive policy, and to exploit the anti-war spirit of American and satellite soldiers in the South....[Emphasis added]

Make sweeping efforts to enlist support from various peoples all over the world fighting for the same cause like us (national liberation, peace and democracy) with a view to forming a front of unified action against the imperialists and colonialists whose leaders are the US. Emphasis is to be laid on strengthening the Indo-Chinese People's Front against the Americans....

Pay attention to the propaganda task. *Motivate the American people against the* [US] *crimes, and request an end to the war of aggression in South Vietnam. An effort should be made to motivate the soldiers' dependents to launch anti-war demonstrations and request repatriation....*[Emphasis added]

In imperialist countries such as the USA, England, a number of countries in northwestern Europe, and US satellite countries having soldiers fighting in Vietnam, we must use all the available means of propaganda to kindle a widespread anti-war movement among the people. [Emphasis added] At the same time, we must try to create pressure on the ruling circles of the above countries to request the US to halt its war of aggression in Vietnam.[19]

The forgoing excerpts clearly reflect North Vietnam's efforts to incite and enlist the American people to support its cause. The growth and proliferation of the antiwar movement in the United States in the 1960s and early 1970s attests to the success of this program. The bulk of this book will be devoted to unmasking the legacy of the antiwar movement:

- How the movement subverted America's war effort and contributed to our eventual defeat.
- How it encouraged the enemy to hold out in the face of numerous battlefield defeats, prolonging the war by several years during which thousands of Americans, South Vietnamese, Laotians, Cambodians and North Vietnamese lost their lives needlessly.
- How it undermined our negotiating leverage by demanding unilateral concessions and acceptance of the enemy's terms to end the war.
- How it impaired the prosecution of the war and increased the risks for our troops by massive opposition to our strikes on enemy sanctuaries and staging bases in Laos and Cambodia.
- How it caused our prisoners held by North Vietnam to suffer physical and psychological torture.
- How it undermined the morale and discipline of our troops.
- How it sapped the morale of the South Vietnamese government and people and subverted their confidence in the United States.
- How it had an adverse impact on our presidential policy decisions and congressional support of the war.
- How it boosted the morale of the enemy and aided Hanoi's propaganda war around the world.

As a prelude to delving into the legacy of the antiwar movement, it is noteworthy to review why six former presidents of the United States saw that it was in our national interests to aid Vietnam and other nations of Southeast Asia in their fight against Communist aggression. The big lie that the war was an internal insurgency within South Vietnam, a myth fabricated by North Vietnam and espoused by the antiwar activists in the United States, will be exposed.

Chapter Two

Why Vietnam

Let every nation know, whether it wishes us well or ill, that we shall pay any price, bear any burden, meet any hardship, support any friend, oppose any foe to assure the survival and the success of liberty.

—John F. Kennedy

Six American presidents saw that the defense of Indochina (Vietnam, Laos and Cambodia) against a growing communist threat was of vital importance to the national security of the United States. They envisioned the whole of Southeast Asia in the balance. As early as 1950, the United States began to aid the people of Indochina in their efforts to counter the growing communist insurgency. Vietnam was seen as pivotal to the defense of the region, and the presidents of that era committed the United States to aiding South Vietnam in its struggle for freedom and independence.[1] Their reasons have been lost with time or misrepresented so extensively that today the common belief is that our involvement in Vietnam was a mistake. It is illogical to conclude that all six presidents and their advisors had it wrong. In any study of the Vietnam War it is essential to look at the reasons these prominent leaders of our country felt strongly enough about defending South Vietnam to sacrifice the lives of thousands of our young men and women. The agony of such a decision had to be weighed against an unwavering belief that the cause of defending a small nation in the path of aggression was of great importance to our national interests.

These six presidents lived during a period in our history when the initial conquests by Nazi Germany in the 1930's were allowed to go unchallenged. The disastrous consequences of such appeasement were indelibly impressed on their minds. They learned that allowing even the smallest state to be swallowed up by a belligerent neighbor would only feed the aggressor's appetite and lead to more aggression. In 1938 on the eve of Hitler's annexation of Czechoslovakia, Winston Churchill warned, "It is not Czechoslovakia alone which is menaced, but also the freedom and democracy of all nations. The belief that security can be obtained by throwing a small state to the wolves is a fatal delusion."[2] This might well have been weighing on the minds of those in the White House when they made their decision to aid South Vietnam.

While each of our presidents agonized over the decision to go to war, the leaders of the Communist party in Vietnam did not have to labor over such choices. Their plan for the people of Indochina was spelled out before any of the six American presidents were in office: "Their long range objective was coolly stated in 1927 by the Moscow-trained secret agent Nguyen Van Thanh, alias 'Nguyen Ai Quoc' – who, under the alias 'Ho Chi Minh, achieved the first part of his goal when he became ruler of Communist North Vietnam."[3] He vowed, "I intend to form an Indochinese national revolutionary movement whose leaders will bring its members step by step to orthodox Communism."[4] This was what was in store for all of Indochina: Vietnam, Cambodia, and Laos. It is worthwhile to look at how one man of seemingly slight stature, Ho Chi Minh, achieved the preeminence to make such a proclamation that would ultimately lead to two major conflicts in Southeast Asia.

The Gathering Storm

In many ways, North Vietnam was the creation of one man, Ho Chi Minh. After going to sea in 1911 and visiting the United States, Great Britain and Germany, he settled in France. He soon became active in left-wing politics and joined the French Socialist Party. As a fervent Communist he helped found the French Communist Party in 1920.[5] Later on in the 1920s Ho attended Communist Party schools in Moscow. Upon completing his indoctrination, Ho went to China where he organized Vietnamese emigrants and went on to serve as a roving agent in Southeast Asia for the Comintern (Communist International). While working to set up party cells in Vietnam, he was arrested by British authorities.[6]

Stories vary on what happened to Ho Chi Minh following his imprisonment in Hong Kong. One story has it that he escaped;[7] whereas, another source purports that he remained in prison until 1933 when he was released by the British due to poor health.[8] There is agreement that following his departure from prison, he spent the next decade as an underground agitator. During that period he was said to be in charge of the external arm of the Indochinese Communist Party with his reach extending to Canton, Hong Kong and Yunnan province.[9] He was also seen in such places as Berlin, Moscow and Shanghai where he worked in the shadows as an organizer for the party. He emerged in 1941 as the leader of the Viet-Minh, a "national front" formed by Ho Chi Minh and his Communist followers. Ho returned to Vietnam secretly two years later to prepare to seize power when Japan was defeated at the end of World War II. Some historians contend that while working in China and Southeast Asia during the 1930s and 1940s Ho was under direct command of Moscow.[10]

Ho Chi Minh was quick to move into the power vacuum created by Japan's surrender in 1945. Posing as liberators the Viet-Minh moved into Hanoi in the north and Saigon in the south and occupied many of the smaller cities and villages.[11] Their goal was to seize control before the French administration could be reestablished. When the French were reinstated to their pre-war colonial rule, they immediately proposed the establishment of a federation of autonomous Indochinese states within a French Union. However, the Viet-Minh insisted on complete independence. Negotiations were terminated and the Viet-Minh launched a campaign of widespread unrest while carrying out a program to consolidate their position. Political opponents were eliminated and control of the news media was placed in the hands of the newly created Viet-Minh Ministry of Propaganda.[12]

In the southern part of the country, the French were rapidly regaining control, and by the spring of 1946 the Viet-Minh had been driven underground in that part of the country. In the north where the Nationalist Chinese had been assigned the role under the Potsdam Agreement to occupy Vietnam above the 16th Parallel until French administration could be reestablished, the Viet-Minh were constrained. The Chinese were not eager to relinquish control to the French and were unwilling to allow the Communists to seize power.[13] To ease the pressure the Viet-Minh leaders decided to cooperate with the French and reached a provisional agreement with the French in which France recognized Vietnam as an autonomous state within an Indochinese federation within a French Union. This was a ploy by the Communists to buy time until the Chinese departed and the Viet-Minh could consolidate their position. By the summer of 1946 the negotiations between the Viet-Minh and the French had reached an impasse over the details of the provisional agreement. Meanwhile, the Viet-Minh were secretly preparing for the future armed struggle that they anticipated. Preparations included formation of People's Committees in every province. Guerrilla forces were formed and trained in military tactics and intensive political indoctrination in Marxism-Leninism.[14]

With the failure of the negotiations on the provisional agreement, Ho Chi Minh accepted a compromise agreement with the French that bound both sides to cease all hostilities and acts of violence beginning October 10, 1946. However, relations between the two parties quickly deteriorated, and by the end of November armed clashes took place in several cities. On the night of December 19, 1946 the Viet-Minh launched a surprise attack on the French in Hanoi at which many French civilians were massacred. The first Vietnam War was underway. Ho Chi Minh's goal was to drive out all the remnants of colonialism and impose Communist control over all of Indochina.[15]

Ho Chi Minh was assisted in his quest for power by two very able men who followed him to top leadership positions in North Vietnam and the Lao Dong Communist Party. Pham Van Dong began his association with Ho in 1925 in Canton, China. He was trained as an agitator and returned to Vietnam in 1926 where he was arrested and held by the French until 1932. After his release, he spent the next four years in school in Moscow. From 1936 to 1943 he did party work in Vietnam and China. In 1943 he organized the first North Vietnamese guerrilla force which became the vanguard of the Liberation Army. Dong served as North Vietnam's Minister of Foreign Affairs from 1954 to 1961. Dong later became Prime Minister and Premier of North Vietnam.[16]

The other key figure who became an important part of Ho's regime was General Vo Nguyen Giap. As World War II came to a close, Giap returned to Vietnam after military training under the Chinese Communists. He became the commander of all guerrilla activities in North Vietnam. Giap was also an active revolutionary at an early age and was arrested by the French in 1930. After his release, he attended the University of Hanoi from 1933 to 1939 and received a doctorate in history. When the Communist movement was outlawed by the French in 1939, Giap took refuge in the hills of North Vietnam where he gained experience in military operations. Giap became the commander of North Vietnam's armed forces and led the Vietnamese Communists in their fight against the French.[17] Giap was later elevated to the position of Defense Minister of North Vietnam.

In the aftermath of the attack on the French in Hanoi in December 1946, Ho Chi Minh's forces withdrew to prepared hideouts in the jungle and engaged the French in hit and run guerrilla warfare for the next eight years. Under the command of General Giap, the methods used by the Viet-Minh were identical to the guerrilla warfare principles of Mao Tse-tung. These same tactics would be seen later in South Vietnam and Laos. The victory of the Chinese Communists over Chiang Kai-shek's Nationalists in 1949 heralded a turning point for Ho Chi Minh's struggle with the French. Soon Chinese and Soviet military advisers and military supplies began flowing into North Vietnam for the Viet-Minh fighters. By 1954, the revitalized Viet-Minh were well equipped with Soviet light artillery, antiaircraft guns, Katyusha rocket launchers, and Molotova trucks. The buildup gave the Viet-Minh the strength to defeat the French in the final showdown battle of Dien Bien Phu.[18]

The defeat at Dien Bien Phu broke the will of the French. The loss of will along with the opposition to the war at home, forced France to concede independence to Indochina at the Geneva settlement of 1954. With the exception of Dien Bien Phu, the French were not defeated militarily in Vietnam. They lost the war on the home front in France, not unlike what was to happen to the United States twenty years later.[19]

The Geneva Accords

The Geneva agreements divided the Vietnamese portion of Indochina at the 17th parallel, creating the Communist regime led by Ho Chi Minh in the north and a non-communist state in the south. Cambodia and Laos were also designated as independent kingdoms. This ended the French colonial era in Indochina. The Geneva conference included representatives of Cambodia, the Democratic Republic of North Vietnam, France, Laos, Communist China, South Vietnam, the Soviet Union, Great Britain and the United States. The conference resulted in four documents: three agreements on the cessation of hostilities in Cambodia, Laos and Vietnam and one overall unsigned declaration of the conference. In addition, two declarations were issued. These two declarations, one by South Vietnam and the other by the United States, weighed heavily on the decisions to come.[20] Therefore, pertinent passages are quoted below.

> Declaration by South Vietnam:
> The representative of the State of [South]Vietnam stated his government's unwillingness to be bound by any agreement between the other parties concerning the political future of the people of South Vietnam... the statesman then representing the State of [South] Vietnam, protested that the others had arrogated to themselves "the right without prior agreement from the delegation of the State of Vietnam, to fix the date of the future elections despite the clearly political character of such a provision"...The Vietnamese delegation... protests solemnly against the hasty conclusion of the armistice agreement by the French and Viet Minh (Communist) High Command alone,...and above all in view of the fact that several clauses of this agreement are of a nature to compromise gravely the political future of the Vietnamese people...Consequently, the Government of the State of Vietnam demands that it should be put on record that it protests solemnly against the way in which the armistice was concluded and against the conditions of this armistice, which takes no account of the profound aspirations of the Vietnamese people, and that it reserves complete freedom of action for safeguarding the sacred right of the Vietnamese people to territorial unity, independence, and freedom.[21]

> United States' Declaration:
> The United States through its representative, Under Secretary Walter Bedell Smith, declared the United States unwillingness to join in the declaration of the conference. He repeated the U.S. position on free elections, saying, "In the case of nations now divided against their will, we shall continue to seek to achieve unity through free elections supervised by the United Nations to insure that they are conducted fairly...." With

respect to the statement made by the State of Vietnam, the United States reiterates its traditional position that people are entitled to determine their own future and that it will not join in an arrangement which would hinder this....

The reason for the protest of the United States and the State of Vietnam was simple: Unless the proposed elections were held under U.N. supervision with full freedom of opposition, secret ballots, and impartial counting of the ballots, the people of South Vietnam, whatever their feelings might be, would be totally at the mercy of Communist government in the North. For in North Vietnam, the Communists held under absolute control slightly more that half the Vietnamese population...As for the agreements reached between the other parties, Under Secretary Smith stated that the policy of the United States would be to refrain from force or the threat of force to disturb those agreements, and that the United States would view any renewal of aggression in violation of the agreements with grave concern and as seriously threatening international peace and security.[22]

As a result of the forgoing objections, neither the United States nor the Republic of (South) Vietnam signed the final declaration.[23] Critics at home and abroad ignored this fact in their haste to condemn the United States and South Vietnam for violating the Geneva Accords. Neither the United States nor South Vietnam agreed to hold elections in 1956 as stipulated in the Geneva Accords for a number of reasons. The Communist delegations at Geneva had refused to have the elections supervised by the United Nations to insure that they were conducted freely. North Vietnam was a dictatorship where conditions were not conducive to free voting; its population was greater than in the South which would tip the election to the Communists; and the "fair" elections in North Vietnam had always given Ho Chi Minh 99.9 percent of the votes. Moreover, the North Vietnamese had violated the Geneva Accords in a number of ways, including greatly increasing the size of its army. Conditions for fair elections became more improbable as time went on.[24]

United States policy toward Indochina began to change as the Geneva Conference closed. This revision was spurred by the belief that Geneva had been a major setback for the Free World's security interests in the Far East, giving the Communists a new foothold in Southeast Asia and enhancing Peking's (Beijing's) prestige, while restricting the movements of the Free World.[25]

Southeast Asia Treaty Organization (SEATO)

In order to give support to the nations of Southeast Asia, the United States took the lead in the creation of an alliance embodied in a treaty and reinforced by a collective security system known as SEATO--the Southeast Asia Treaty Organization. In this alliance the United States joined with Great Britain, France, Australia, New Zealand, Thailand, Pakistan, and the Philippines to guarantee the security not only of the member nations but also to come to the aid of certain protocol states and territories if they so requested. South Vietnam was included in this protocol.[26]

In joining the SEATO alliance the United States took on an obligation with far-reaching implications. It was to have a major influence on policy decisions for the United States' involvement in Vietnam. The provisions of the alliance under Article IV obligated each party to act to meet the common danger in accordance with its constitutional processes, if an armed attack occurred on any members of the alliance, including protocol states. The treaty did not require a collective finding or decision of members to take actions to meet a common danger. If one member determined that there was an attack on any nation under the protection of the alliance, it was obligated to act to meet the common danger, the views or actions of other members notwithstanding.[27]

The United States Senate gave its consent to the ratification of the SEATO Treaty by a vote of 82 to 1. The provisions of Article IV were to be invoked by more than one president of the United States to assist the Republic of South Vietnam in meeting aggression and preserving its independence. North Vietnam attempted to confuse the relevance of the treaty by trying to make their aggression appear to be an internal, indigenous uprising. This subterfuge did not fool those who were familiar with the Communist use of "wars of national liberation."[28]

This smoke screen will be exposed in the next chapter, but it is useful to acknowledge here that there were critics at home and abroad who, throughout the war, proclaimed the authenticity of this myth, and there are still people today who espouse this theory. Tell that to the people of South Vietnam who were overrun by the 20 divisions of the North Vietnamese army in 1975 and have been living in subjugation and an oppressive Communist regime ever since.

The Mounting Threat

As part of the Geneva Accords, elements of the Communist guerrilla forces were to be withdrawn to North Vietnam; however, highly trained party members and guerrilla forces were left south of the partition line, along with cashes of weapons and ammunition. While most of the units loyal to Ho Chi Minh moved to North Vietnam, some of the best trained guerrilla units hid out in remote areas in the South, particularly in the mountainous areas along the Cambodian and Laotian borders and in the jungle regions in the Mekong delta. These units and cells were instructed to lead normal lives and wait for orders from the party in the North. The stage was thus set for Hanoi's plan for the conquest of South Vietnam. The stay-behind guerrillas would soon join infiltrating forces from the north to mount a campaign of subversion and terror across the countryside.[29]

The Cold War was in full bloom by the time world attention turned to Vietnam. The end of World War II was followed by the Soviet Union's ambitions in Europe. Almost immediately after the war's end, all of Eastern Europe was brought under Moscow's domination and the leaders in the Kremlin were eyeing Western Europe. They supported the Communist insurrection in Greece and tried to intimidate Turkey and other nations in the Eastern Mediterranean. In 1948 the Soviet Union blockaded Berlin, and in violation of the allied four party agreements, began integrating the zone they occupied in Germany into a political entity of the Soviet Union. In 1949 the non-communist world was shaken by the news that the Communist Chinese had defeated Chiang Kai-shek's Nationalist forces and had taken control of mainland China. Soon after the fall of China, North Korea, with the backing of the Soviet Union, attacked across the 38th parallel in a massive invasion of South Korea. The Korean War was barely over when the French gave up the struggle against the Communists in Vietnam and began withdrawing from that part of the world. Laos and Cambodia were already under pressure from the Communists, and in the next several years, Communist insurrections began to boil in Malaya, the Philippines, Burma, Thailand and Indonesia. Cuba became a Soviet client state, and Communist revolutions were being fomented in several Central and South American nations. The leaders of the non-communist nations of the world were faced with difficult decisions: stand up to the aggression as we and allied forces did in Korea, or stand back and watch as the Communists extended their domination over the weaker nations.[30]

The Communist menace was clearly in evidence by the pronouncements of the leaders of Soviet Union and China in their own words. In response to a question put to the Secretary of Defense, Robert McNamara, concerning Vietnam, he answered:

> It is a war that is being fought to counter the strategy of the Communists, a strategy which [Soviet] Premier Khrushchev laid out very clearly in the famous speech which he made on January 6, 1961...he divided all wars into three categories. He spoke of world wars, meaning nuclear wars; he spoke of local wars, by which he meant large-scale conventional wars; and he spoke of what he called "wars of national liberation." He ruled out world wars as being too dangerous to the existence of the Communist states. He ruled out local wars because he said they could very easily escalate into nuclear wars....But he strongly endorsed "wars of liberation" and made it perfectly clear that it would be through application of that strategy that the Communists would seek to subvert independent nations throughout the world, seek to extend their domination, their political domination, of other nations.[31]

Secretary of Defense Robert S. McNamara, in an address on March 26, 1963 at the Forrestall Memorial Awards Dinner, had this to say about the threat of insurgency: "Communist interest in insurgency techniques did not begin with Khrushchev or for that matter with Stalin. Lenin's works are full of tactical instructions, which were adapted very successfully by Mao Tse-tung, whose many writings on guerrilla warfare have become classic references. Indeed, Mao claims to be the true heir of Lenin's original prescription for the worldwide victory of

Communism. The North Vietnamese have taken a leaf or two from Mao's book—as well as Moscow's—and added some of their own."[32]

General Maxwell Taylor, a close advisor to President Kennedy, believed that we were facing serious difficulties in dealing with the lower level threats of wars of national liberation. He warned, "The techniques of the so-called War of National Liberation were designed by our Communist adversaries to avoid the risks of overt warfare [where they would have to confront our full military arsenal] and to substitute subversion and the exploitation of internal weaknesses as an indirect means of conquest."[33]

In January 1961, Khrushchev had this to say about wars of liberation: "The Communists fully support such just wars and march in the front rank with peoples waging liberation struggles."[34] General Giap, the Commander in-Chief of the North Vietnamese forces, made the following comments about wars of liberation: "South Vietnam is the model of the national liberation movement of our time. If the special warfare that the United States imperialists are testing in South Vietnam is overcome, then it can be defeated anywhere in the world."[35]

In 1953, Chou En-lai, the Prime Minister of the Peoples Republic of China, told the Soviet Union of Mao Tse-tung's strategy for world conquest: "The United States must be isolated by all possible means.... After Southeast Asia has been 'liberated', 20 million well trained troops should be available to force the capitalist countries to keep on increasing defense expenditures until economic collapse overtakes them....After the 'liberation' of Vietnam, Burma and Thailand would capitulate, and Indonesia would fall to the Communist camp like ripe fruit and the Malay peninsula would be encircled."[36]

In June 1965 Marshal Lin Piao, the Defense Minister of Communist China, stated, "In the final analysis the whole cause of world revolution hinges on the revolutionary struggles of the Asian, African and Latin American peoples...."[37] In September 1965 Lin Piao announced that Mao Tse-tung planned to utilize "wars of liberation" to expand Communism in Latin America, Africa and Asia.[38] The Chinese Communists voiced their position on the use of violence to overthrow the non-communist countries in a letter to the Soviet Union in June 1965. "Two-thirds of the world's population need to make revolution... Violent revolution is a universal law of proletarian revolution. To realize the transition to socialism, the proletariat must wage armed struggle, smash the old state machine, and establish the dictatorship of the proletariat."[39]

Six Presidents Speak

President Truman. Each of the American presidents from Truman forward had the ominous task of deciding on the best way to respond to the threats of wars of national liberation and Communist expansionism. President Truman was the first of our presidents to face the challenge of a Communist insurgency. Following World War II, Greece was besieged by armed Communist guerrillas aided and supported covertly by the Soviet Union. At the same time Turkey was under pressure by the Soviets to share control of the Dardanelles Straits.[40] Truman foresaw that if Greece were to fall to the Communists, Turkey would be more vulnerable, and Communist influence could even spread to the Middle East. This led to what came to be known as the Truman Doctrine, which states in-part, "I believe that it must be the policy of the United States to support free peoples who are resisting attempted subjugation by armed minorities or by outside pressures. I believe that we must assist free peoples to work out their own destinies in their own way. I believe that our help should be primarily through economic stability and orderly political process….Should we fail to aid Greece and Turkey in this fateful hour, the effect will be far reaching to the West as well as the East."[41]

The Truman Doctrine resulted in the United States providing economic and military aid to Greece and Turkey. There followed an effort by the Truman Administration in 1948 to develop a policy for defense against Soviet expansionism. A National Security Council study, NSC 68, dated March 30, 1948 emphasized the global dimensions of the Soviet challenge. It stated, "The ultimate objective of Soviet-directed world Communism is the domination of the world…." NSC 68 comprised the final and most elaborate attempt by the Truman leadership to define a national security policy….It warned, "The issues that face us are momentous, involving the fulfillment or destruction not only of this Republic but of civilization itself."[42] From that point forward global containment of Communist adventures became a fundamental doctrine of United States policy.[43]

The fall of China to the Communists in 1949 caused the Truman administration to designate Vietnam as the focus for containment of Soviet expansionism in Asia. A National Security Council report in the summer of 1949 concluded that Southeast Asia was the target of a coordinated offensive by Moscow.[44] In May 1950 the United States began providing economic aid and military equipment to South Vietnam, Cambodia, Laos and France to help them in their efforts to maintain the peace and develop democratic institutions. A U.S. Military Assistance Advisory Group (MAAG) was established in Saigon to coordinate the military aid.[45] The invasion of South Korea by Communist North Korea raised the stakes in Asia to a new height. Chinese intervention with thousands of "volunteers" on the side of North Korea signaled a new boldness by the Communists and raised concerns for the possibility that China might have its sights on other territorial conquests in Asia and beyond. These events made Southeast Asia into a new battleground against Communism.[46]

President Eisenhower. When President Eisenhower took office in January 1953 he continued to support the French army fighting Ho Chi Minh as a necessary defense against the expansion of Communist power. At the same time he was in the midst of negotiations for the settlement of the Korean War. Later, with the French faltering in Indochina, President Eisenhower expressed his fear if South Vietnam were to fall: "South Vietnam's capture by the Communists would… set in motion a crumbling process that could, as it progressed, have grave consequences for us and for freedom."[47] At a presidential press conference on April 7, 1954, President Eisenhower commented on the strategic importance of Indochina to the free world:

> You have, of course, both the specific and the general when you talk about such things [importance of Indochina].
>
> First of all, you have the specific value of a locality in its production of materials that the world needs.
>
> Then you have the possibility that many human beings pass under a dictatorship that is inimical to the free world.
>
> Finally, you have broader considerations that might follow what you would call the "falling domino"

principle. You have a row of dominos set up, you mow over the first one, and what will happen to the last one is the certainty that it will go over quickly. So you could have a beginning of a disintegration that would have the most profound influence.

But when we come to the possible sequence of events, the loss of Indochina, of Burma, of Thailand, of the Peninsula, and Indonesia following, now you begin to talk about areas that not only multiply the disadvantages that you would suffer through loss of materials, sources of materials, but now you are talking about millions and millions of people.

Finally, the geographical position achieved thereby does many things. It turns the so-called island defensive chain of Japan, Formosa [Taiwan], of the Philippines to the southward; it moves in to threaten Australia and New Zealand.

It takes away, in its economic aspects, that region that Japan must have as a trading area, or Japan, in turn, will have only one place in the world to go—that is, toward the Communist areas in order to live.

So, the possible consequences of the loss are just incalculable to the free world.[48]

The domino theory was discredited by some during and after the war. That controversy will be addressed later; however, for now it is enough to say that the people in Laos, Cambodia and the former South Vietnam who came under the brutal oppression of the Communists would not deny the correctness of the theory. The two million Cambodians whose lives were ended in the "killing fields" are further evidence that President Eisenhower was justified in his concern over the efforts of the Communists to spread their influence over Southeast Asia.

President Eisenhower saw that the French were faltering in their fight against Communist forces in Vietnam. He addressed his concerns in a letter to Prime Minister Winston Churchill in April 1954:

> If they [the French] do not see it through and Indochina passes into the hands of the Communists the ultimate effect on our and your global strategic position with the consequent shift in the power rations throughout Asia and the Pacific could be disastrous and, I know, unacceptable to you and me....This has led us to the hard conclusion that the situation in Southeast Asia requires us urgently to take serious and far-reaching decisions....
>
> The preliminary lines of our thinking were sketched out by Foster [Dulles] in his speech last Monday night when he said that under the conditions of today the imposition on Southeast Asia of the political system of Communist Russia and its Chinese Communist ally, by whatever means, would be a grave threat to the whole free community, and that in our view this possibility should now be met by united action and not passively accepted....
>
> If I may refer again to history; we failed to halt Hirohito, Mussolini and Hitler by not acting in unity and in time. That marked the beginning of many years of stark tragedy and desperate peril. May it not be that our nations have learned something from that lesson?[49]

Unfortunately, Churchill chose not to join the United States in its efforts to stem the tide of Communism in Indochina.

After the Geneva Accords the U. S. Military Assistance Advisory Group (MAAG) became the only outside source of military aid for the South Vietnamese armed forces. In the fall of 1954 President Diem of South Vietnam appealed to the United States for assistance. Nearly one million Vietnamese had fled from the Communist North to South Vietnam, which was temporarily permitted under the Geneva Accords. In a reply to Diem in October 1954, President Eisenhower assured Diem that the United States would assist in this humanitarian problem. He explained the policy behind our assistance: "The purpose of this offer is to assist the Government of Vietnam in developing and maintaining a strong, viable state, capable of resisting attempted subversion or aggression through military means."[50]

In a speech at Gettysburg College on April 4, 1959, President Eisenhower explained that South Vietnam was faced with two great tasks: "self-defense and economic expansion." He did not believe that South Vietnam could meet the dual threat of aggression from outside and within, unassisted. In justifying aid for South Vietnam he emphasized, "We reach the inescapable conclusion that our own national interests demand some help from us in sustaining in Vietnam the morale, the economic progress and the military strength necessary to its [South Vietnam's] continued existence in freedom."[51]

On October 26, 1960 President Eisenhower sent President Diem a letter of good wishes on the fifth anniversary of the birth of the Republic of Vietnam. He praised Diem and the citizens of the Republic for their success in building the country's economy and democratic institutions, while at the same time being faced with a growing threat to their independence by the Communist insurgents. He stressed, "Vietnam's very success as well as its potential wealth and its strategic location have led the Communists of Hanoi, goaded by the bitterness of their failure to enslave all Vietnam, to use increasing violence in their attempts to destroy your country's freedom....Although the main responsibility for guarding that independence will always, as it has in the past, belong to the Vietnamese people and their government, I want to assure you that for so long as our strength can be useful, the United States will continue to assist Vietnam in the difficult yet hopeful struggle ahead."[52]

President Kennedy. Although President Kennedy was hesitant about committing United States' combat troops to defend South Vietnam, he was consistent and determined in his objective to prevent Communist domination of South Vietnam.[53] His firm position on Vietnam as far back as when he was a United States Senator is illustrated in a speech he presented at a symposium on America's Stake in Vietnam in September 1956:

First, Vietnam represents the cornerstone of the Free World in Southeast Asia, the keystone to the arch, the finger in the dike. Burma, Thailand, India, Japan and the Philippines and obviously Laos and Cambodia are among those whose security would be threatened if the red tide of Communism overflowed into Vietnam... Moreover, the independence of the Free World is crucial to the free world in fields other than the military. Her economy is essential to the economy of all of Southeast Asia; and her political liberty is an inspiration to those seeking to obtain or maintain their liberty in all parts of Asia—and indeed the world.

Secondly, Vietnam represents a proving ground of democracy in Asia...If this democratic experiment fails, if some one million refugees have fled the totalitarian [regime] of the North only to find neither freedom nor security in the South, then weakness, not strength, will characterize the meaning of democracy in the minds of still more Asians.

Third and in somewhat similar fashion, Vietnam represents a test of American responsibly and determination in Asia...And if it [South Vietnam] falls victim to any of the perils that threaten its existence—Communism, political anarchy, poverty and the rest—then the United States, with some justification, will be held responsible; and our prestige in Asia will sink to a new low.

Fourth and finally, America's stake in Vietnam, in her strength and in her security, is a very selfish one—for it can be measured, in the last analysis, in terms of American lives and American dollars...And the key position of Vietnam in Southeast Asia, as already discussed, makes inevitable the involvement of this nation's security in any new outbreak of trouble.[54]

When President Kennedy took office, the situation in Laos had become critical; North Vietnamese and Pathet Lao forces, supported by a Soviet airlift of weapons and supplies, were close to victory over government forces. At that time President Kennedy decided that the place to make a stand was in Vietnam not in Laos. His reasoning was that the South Vietnamese seemed more willing to defend themselves, access by sea for supply lines was better, and U.S. air and naval power could be brought to bear more easily. Kennedy never questioned whether Southeast Asia was vital to American security. His only question was where we should draw the line and fight.[55]

President Kennedy resisted urging by General Taylor and other national security staff to send combat troops to Vietnam. His first major policy decision was issued in NATIONAL SECURITY ACTION MEMORANDUM NO. 52 dated May 11, 1961 (NSAM 52) (see Appendix A). This NSAM stated the United States' purpose in Vietnam: "The U.S. objective is to prevent Communist domination of SVN [South Vietnam] and to create in that country a viable and increasingly democratic society." NSAM 52 directed an increase in aid including 400 Special Forces troops to train Vietnamese Special Forces, an increase in personnel assigned to the Military Assistance Advisory Group (MAAG), a Combat Development Test Center, fourteen Americans to increase public works projects, and a small contingent to help border surveillance.[56]

Six months later, as conditions worsened in Vietnam, President Kennedy approved NSAM 111 (see Appendix B) which stated that "the U.S. Government is prepared to join the Vietnam Government in a sharply increased joint effort to avoid a further deterioration in the situation in South Vietnam." NSAM 111 pledged that the U.S. would immediately undertake a number of actions in support of South Vietnam. Among many other elements of support actions NSAM 111 included:

> (1) Provide increased air lift to the GVN [Government of South Vietnam] forces, including helicopters, light aviation, and transport aircraft, manned to the extent necessary by United States uniformed personnel....
>
> (2) Provide such additional equipment and United States uniformed personnel as may be necessary for

air reconnaissance, photography, instruction in and execution of air-ground support techniques, and for special intelligence.

(3) Provide the GVN with small craft, including such United States uniformed advisers and operating personnel as may be necessary for operations in effecting surveillance and control over coastal waters and inland waterways.

(4) Provide expedited training and equipping of the civil guard and the self-defense corps with the objective of relieving the regular Army of static missions and freeing it for mobile offensive operations.[57]

In a letter to South Vietnam's President Diem in December 1961, President Kennedy assured Diem of America's commitment. He said, "In accordance with the declaration [Geneva Accords], and in response to your request, we are prepared to help the Republic of Vietnam to protect its people and to preserve its independence. We shall promptly increase our assistance to your defense effort as well as help relieve the destruction of the floods which you describe. I have already given the orders to get these programs underway."[58]

Dean Rusk, the Secretary of State during Kennedy's brief presidency, explained some of the thinking that he felt paralleled President Kennedy's:

For me, the issue at stake in Vietnam was collective security. In 1961 the United States had a treaty commitment to South Vietnam and forty-two other allies. The integrity of the American commitment to collective security involves the life and death of our nation. When an American president makes a commitment, what he says must be believed. If those opposing us think that the word of the United States is not worth very much, then those treaties lose their deterrent effect and the structure of peace dissolves rapidly. If the president cannot be believed, we will face dangers we've never dreamed of....

What might have happened had Nikita Khrushchev not believed John Kennedy during the Berlin crisis of 1961-62 or the Cuban missile crisis of October 1962? There could easily have been general war...The credibility of an American president at a time of crisis and the fidelity of the United States to its security treaties are not just empty matters of face and prestige. They are pillars of peace in a dangerous world.[59]

At a news conference in September 1963, just two months before his assassination, President Kennedy stated what he termed "a very simple policy" of the United States in Vietnam: "We want the war to be won, the Communists to be contained and the Americans to go home. That is our policy. I am sure it is the policy of the people of Vietnam. We are not there to see a war lost."[60]

President Johnson. President Johnson moved quickly to make it known that he was determined to uphold the policies of his two predecessors to block the spread of communism. On November 26, 1963, just days after President Kennedy's death, President Johnson approved NATIONAL SECURITY MEMORANDUM NO. 273 (see Appendix C) which clearly spelled out his policies and programs to provide economic and military assistance to South Vietnam. The basic policy was stated as, "It remains the central objective of the United States in South Vietnam to assist the people and Government of that country to win their contest against the externally directed and supported Communist conspiracy."[61]

In his news conference on June 2, 1964, President Johnson outlined four basic themes that governed United States' policy in Southeast Asia:

First, America keeps its word.

Second, the issue is the future of Southeast Asia as a whole.

Third, our purpose is peace.

Fourth, this is not just a jungle war, but a struggle for freedom on every front of human activity.

On the point that America keeps her word, we are steadfast in a policy which has been followed for 10 years in three Administrations. That was begun by General Eisenhower, in a letter of October 25, 1954.

Like a number of other nations, we are bound by solemn commitments to help defend this area against Communist encroachment. We will keep this commitment.

We have one single central purpose in all that we do in Southeast Asia, and that is to help build a stable peace. It is others and not we who have brought terror to small countries and peaceful peasants.

We are determined to support the freedom and the independence of South Vietnam...the United States seeks no wider war...if others would keep the solemn agreements already sighed at a conference table, there would be no problem in South Vietnam.[62]

The most comprehensive and important address to the nation by President Johnson was delivered at Johns Hopkins University on April 7, 1965 (see Appendix D). A brief summary of this speech is presented below.

The Nature of the Conflict:
The first reality is that North Vietnam has attacked the independent nation of South Vietnam. Its object is total conquest...trained men and supplies, orders and arms, flow in a constant stream from north to south....

This support is the heartbeat of the war....

And it is a war of unparalleled brutality. Simple farmers are the targets of assassination and kidnapping. Women and children are strangled in the night because their men are loyal to the government. Small and helpless villages are ravaged by sneak attacks. Large-scale raids are conducted on towns, and terror strikes in the heart of cities....

Why Are We in Vietnam?
We are there because we have a promise to keep. Since 1954 every American President has offered support to the people of South Vietnam. We have helped to build, and we have helped to defend. Thus, over many years, we have made a national pledge to help South Vietnam defend its independence.

I intend to keep our promise.

To dishonor that pledge, to abandon this small and brave nation to its enemy, and to the terror that must follow, would be an unforgivable wrong.

We are also there to strengthen world order. Around the globe, from Berlin to Thailand, are people whose well-being rests, in part, on the belief they can count on us if they are attacked. To leave Vietnam to its fate would shake the confidence of all their people in the value of an American commitment and in the value of America's word. The result would be increased unrest and instability, and even wider war.

We are also there because there are great stakes in the balance. Let no one think that retreat from Vietnam would bring an end to conflict. The battle would be renewed in one country and then another. The central lesson of our time is that the appetite of aggression is never satisfied. To withdraw from one battlefield means only to prepare for the next.

Our Objective in Vietnam:

Our objective is the independence of South Vietnam, and its freedom from attack. We want nothing for ourselves – only that the people of South Vietnam be allowed to guide their own country in their own way....

In recent months, attacks on South Vietnam were stepped up. Thus, it became necessary to increase our response and make attacks by air. This is not a change of purpose. It is a change in what we believe that purpose requires.

We do this in order to slow down aggression.

We do this to increase the confidence of the brave people of South Vietnam who have bravely borne this brutal battle for so many years and with so many casualties. And we do this to convince the leaders of North Vietnam – and all who seek to share their conquest – of a simple fact: We will not be defeated. We will not grow tired. We will not withdraw, either openly or under the cloak of a meaningless agreement.

We know that air attacks alone will not accomplish all these purposes. But it is our best and prayerful judgment that they are a necessary part of the surest road to peace...

We hope that peace will come swiftly. But that is in the hands of others besides ourselves. And we must be prepared for a long continued conflict. It will require patience as well as bravery – the will to endure as well as the will to resist....[63]

The events in the Tonkin Gulf on August 2, 1964 and August 4, 1964 represented a major turning point in the war in Southeast Asia. On August 2 the USS Maddox was attacked in the Tonkin Gulf in international waters by North Vietnamese torpedo boats. On August 4 a second attack occurred, this time on the USS Maddox and the USS Turner Joy. President Johnson has been criticized relentlessly about the authenticity of these attacks which were used, along with other reasons of equal importance, to justify obtaining the Tonkin Gulf Congressional Resolution which gave him broad authority to carry out military operations in Vietnam. There is an abundance of evidence that the attack on August 2 took place, although there are some who question whether the second attack on August 4 actually happened. On the day of the first attack, intercepts of North Vietnamese communications indicated that the North Vietnamese were preparing for military operations. Later that day, another message was intercepted which directed the enemy boats to attack. The attack on the Maddox occurred soon thereafter. A skirmish took place in which the Maddox was assisted by fighter aircraft from the carrier Ticonderoga.[64]

In his book, *Following Ho Chi Minh,* the former North Vietnamese Colonel Bui Tin described the incident in this way: "But Le Duan, on being informed of the situation [the Maddox patrolling about 20 nautical miles offshore], immediately instructed the Chief of General Staff, General Van Tien Dung, to attack...General Dung complied straight away by passing it on to the Commander of the Navy, Admiral Giap Van Cuong, and our ships opened fire."[65]

The debate over the second attack on August 4 went on for several years. Secretary of Defense, Robert McNamara, testifying before the Senate Foreign Relations Committee in 1968, divulged that "he had 'unimpeachable' proof: four intercepted radio messages revealing Communist intentions to attack the U.S. destroyers on the night of August 4. He refused to disclose the text of the messages, arguing that making them public might compromise clandestine intelligence methods."[66] This is certainly not unusual when it comes to revealing methods and sources of information gathered by electronic intercepts. I can attest to this from my personal experience during 28 years in the Air Force.

The argument about the second attack is essentially irrelevant because it is clear that President Johnson made his decision on information that had been verified beyond a doubt before he took action. Secretary McNamara went to extraordinary measures to have the second incident investigated from the top down before he was satisfied that the incident had in fact taken place as originally reported. McNamara spoke directly with the Commander in Chief of the Pacific (CINCPAC). He emphasized that "we obviously don't want to carry out the retaliatory strike unless we are damned sure what happened."[67]

After further investigation, Admiral Sharp, CINCPAC, reported back to McNamara that "he was fully assured the attack took place."[68] A complete chronology of events related to the Tonkin incident is included in Appendix E.

Even if the second attack had not taken place, the first one was enough to signal the aggressive intent of the North Vietnamese. Moreover, President Johnson cited other equally important reasons why he felt it was time to seek congressional approval to carry on with our support of South Vietnam. Nevertheless, the antiwar critics, including several congressmen, would use this incident to hammer the president and accuse him of lying to get approval to expand the war. The president's message to Congress on August 5, 1964 in which he justified his request for the Southeast Asia (Tonkin) Resolution is quoted in part below. This is a primary source document for the United States' involvement in the war; therefore, the full text of this address is included in Appendix F. Key excerpts from this address follow:

> These latest actions of the North Vietnamese regime have given a new and grave turn to the already serious situation in Southeast Asia. Our commitments in that area are well known to the Congress. They were first made in 1954 by President Eisenhower. They were further defined in the Southeast Asia Collective Defense Treaty approved by the Senate in February 1955 [by 82 to 1 votes].
>
> The treaty with its accompanying protocol obligates the United States and other members to act in accordance with their constitutional processes to meet communist aggression against any of the parties or protocol states....
>
> The threat to the free nations of Southeast Asia has long been clear. The North Vietnamese regime has constantly sought to take over South Vietnam and Laos. This communist regime has violated the Geneva accords for Vietnam. It has systematically conducted a campaign of subversion, which includes the direction, training, and supply of personnel and arms for the

conduct of guerrilla warfare in South Vietnam territory. In Laos, the North Vietnamese regime has maintained military forces, used Laotian territory for infiltration into South Vietnam, and most recently carried out combat operations – all in direct violation of the Geneva agreements of 1962.

In recent months, the actions of the North Vietnamese regime have become steadily more threatening. In May, following new acts of communist aggression in Laos, the United States undertook reconnaissance flights over Laotian territory, at the request of the Government of Laos. These flights had the essential mission of determining the situation in territory where Communist forces were preventing inspection by the International Control Commission. When the Communists attacked these aircraft, I responded by furnishing escort fighters with instructions to fire when fired upon. Thus, these latest North Vietnamese attacks on our naval vessels are not the first direct attack on armed forces of the United States.

As President of the United States I have concluded that I should now ask the Congress, on its part, to join in affirming the national determination that all such attacks will be met, and that the United States will continue in its basic policy of assisting the free nations of the area to defend their freedom.[69]

The Gulf of Tonkin Resolution, officially known as the Southeast Asia Resolution of August 10, 1964, had such a profound impact on the involvement of the United States in Southeast Asia from that date forward that a copy of this document is included as Appendix G.
In February 1966 President Johnson and South Vietnamese leaders met in Honolulu to discuss progress in Vietnam. The two governments issued a joint communiqué which expressed their agreement on purpose and policy in what became known as the "Declaration of Honolulu." NSAM 343, dated March 28, 1966, provided

the president's guidance for implementing this declaration: "In the Declaration of Honolulu I renewed our pledge of common commitment with the Government of the Republic of Vietnam to defend against aggression, to the work of social revolution, to the goal of free self-government, to the attack on hunger, ignorance and disease, and to the unending quest for peace." He stressed that "the war on human misery and want is as fundamental to the successful resolution of the Vietnam conflict as are our military operations to ward off aggression."[70]

In his State of the Union Address on January 10, 1967, President Johnson was steadfast in his conviction that the United States must stand by its commitment to defend South Vietnam. He reasserted his policy on Vietnam:

> We are in Vietnam because the United States of America and our allies are committed by the SEATO Treaty to "act to meet the common danger" of aggression in Southeast Asia.
>
> We are in Vietnam because an international agreement signed by the United States, North Vietnam, and others is being systematically violated by the Communists. That violation threatens the independence of all the small nations in Southeast Asia and threatens the peace of the entire region and perhaps the world.
>
> We are there because the people of South Vietnam have as much right to remain non-Communist—if that is what they choose—as North Vietnam has to remain Communist.
>
> We are there because the Congress has pledged by solemn vote to take all necessary measures to prevent further aggression....
>
> We have chosen to fight a limited war in Vietnam in an attempt to prevent a larger war—a war almost certain to follow, I believe, if the Communists succeed in overrunning and taking over South Vietnam by aggression and by force. I believe, and I am supported

by some authority, that if they are not checked now the world can expect to pay a greater price to check them later.[71]

The most historic speech by President Johnson took place on March 31, 1968 in which he announced steps to limit the war in Vietnam and his decision not to seek reelection for the office of the presidency. He renewed his offer of August 1967 to stop the bombing of North Vietnam on the condition that talks would begin promptly. He explained that he was unilaterally reducing the level of hostilities by suspending all attacks on North Vietnam except in the area north of the demilitarized zone where the continuing enemy buildup directly threatened allied forward positions. He then talked about our purpose in Vietnam:

> Our objective in South Vietnam has never been the annihilation of the enemy. It has been to bring about a recognition in Hanoi that its objective—taking over the South by force—could not be achieved.
>
> We think that peace can be based on the Geneva Accords of 1954—under political conditions that permit the South Vietnamese—all the South Vietnamese—to chart their course free of any outside domination or interference, from us or from anyone else....
>
> Throughout this entire, long period, I have been sustained by a single principle: that what we are doing now, in Vietnam, is vital not only to the security of Southeast Asia, but it is vital to the security of every American....
>
> And the larger purpose of our involvement has always been to help the nations of Southeast Asia become independent and stand alone, self-sustaining, as members of a great world community—at peace with themselves, and at peace with all others....

Finally, my fellow Americans, let me say this: ...I believe that now, no less than when the decade began, this generation of Americans is willing to *"pay any price, bear any burden, meet any hardship, support any friend, oppose any foe to assure the survival and the success of liberty"* [emphasis added]. Since those words were spoken by John F. Kennedy, the people of America have kept that compact with mankind's noblest cause. And we shall continue to keep it.[72]

The irony of the unilateral bombing halt announced in the forgoing speech is that it was not enough for the doves and antiwar critics. Soon after the bombing halt north of latitude 20 degrees (almost 90 percent of North Vietnam), our air forces made a heavy attack on facilities near Thanh Hoa which was an important communications and transportation center just south of 20 degrees latitude. This was an important strike to stop the flow of war-making supplies into the south. When the antiwar critics found out about the strike through the press, they claimed that President Johnson had lied about the bombing halt. The clamor from the antiwar critics caused further restrictions of the authorized target area, this time limiting the attacks to below 19 degrees. This made a large part of the Communist buildup area free of any interdiction, including the important center at Thanh Hoa, and increased the risks to all allied forces south of the demilitarized zone. A case can be made that the antiwar critics aided the enemy and very likely caused additional casualties of American and allied forces.[73]

In announcing his decision not to run for another term in office, President Johnson made it clear that he would not allow partisan politics, the antiwar critics included, to get in the way of his management of the war effort. He shook the nation when he announced, "With America's sons in the fields far away, with America's future under challenge right here at home, with our hopes and the world's hopes for peace in the balance every day, I do not believe that I should devote an hour or a day of my time to any personal partisan causes or to any duties other than the awesome duties of this office—the Presidency of your country."[74]

Thus, the Vietnam War and the disunity at home were instrumental in ending President Johnson's presidency. These same factors were also to have a major influence on the next wartime president, Richard M. Nixon.

President Nixon. President Nixon had a concise answer to those who opposed the war. On this question, he wrote, "Of all the questions asked during those years, none had an answer more simple and apparent. The United States intervened in the Vietnam War to prevent North Vietnam from imposing its totalitarian government on South Vietnam through military conquest, both because a Communist victory would lead to massive human suffering for the people of Vietnam and because it would damage American strategic interests and pose a threat to our allies and friends in other non-Communist nations."[75]

On May 14, 1969 President Nixon addressed the nation on Vietnam. The President stressed that he wanted to end the war, but was not willing to abandon the South Vietnamese people, which he thought would risk a massacre and jeopardize our long term hopes for peace in the world. If we were to withdraw unilaterally as some critics in Congress and elsewhere had proposed, he felt that "the cause of peace might not survive the damage that would be done to other nation's confidence in our reliability." He went on to explain why we had to stay the course in Vietnam:

> If Hanoi were to succeed in taking over South Vietnam by force—even after the power of the United States had been engaged—is would greatly strengthen those leaders who scorn negotiations, who advocate aggression, who minimize the risks of confrontation with the United States. It would bring peace now but it would enormously increase the danger of a bigger war later.
>
> If we are to move successfully from an era of confrontation to an era of negotiation, then we have to demonstrate—at the point at which confrontation is being tested—that confrontation with the United States is costly and unrewarding.
>
> Almost without exception, the leaders of non-Communist Asia have told me that they would consider a one-sided American withdrawal from Vietnam to be a threat to the security of their own nations.

> In determining what choices would be acceptable, we have to understand our essential objective in Vietnam: What we want is very little, but very fundamental. We seek the opportunity for the South Vietnamese people to determine their own political future with out outside interference.
>
> Let me put it plainly: What the United States wants for South Vietnam is not the important thing. What North Vietnam wants for South Vietnam is not the important thing. What is important is what the people of South Vietnam want for South Vietnam.[76]

In a lengthy speech to the nation on November 3, 1969, President Nixon summed up his efforts to end the war, a pledge he made during his presidential campaign. This became known as the "silent majority" speech. In it he appealed to the people: "And so tonight--to you, the great silent majority of my fellow Americans--I ask for your support." He also explained the principles he would use as guidelines for future American policy for Asia.

> First, the United States will keep all of its treaty commitments.
>
> Second, we shall provide a shield if a nuclear power threatens the freedom of a nation allied with us or of a nation whose survival we consider vital to our security.
>
> Third, in cases involving other types of aggression, we shall furnish military and economic assistance when requested in accordance with our treaty commitments. But we shall look to the nation directly threatened to assume the primary responsibility of providing the manpower for its defense.[77]

These principles formed the basis for President Nixon's Vietnamization policy, which was his plan to disengage America from the war in Vietnam. He answered his critics who espoused the "get out now" theme, with strong admonition, "For the future of peace, precipitous withdrawal would thus be a disaster of immense magnitude." He emphasized that:

> A nation cannot remain great if it betrays its allies and lets down its friends.
>
> Our defeat and humiliation in South Vietnam without question would promote recklessness in the councils of those great powers who have not yet abandoned their goals of world conquest.
>
> This would spark violence wherever our commitments help maintain the peace in the Middle East, in Berlin, eventually even in the Western Hemisphere. Ultimately, this would cost more lives. It would not bring peace; it would bring more war.[78]

President Nixon was still in office on January 23, 1973 to announce the conclusion of the Paris Agreement which was to end the war and restore peace in Vietnam. In announcing the agreement he stated, "The people of South Vietnam have been guaranteed the right to determine their own future, without outside interference...We shall continue to aid South Vietnam within the terms of the agreement and shall support efforts by the people of South Vietnam to settle their problems peacefully among themselves..."[79] These pledges would prove hard to keep.

In July 1973, Congress passed a bill setting August 15, 1973 as the cutoff date for the use of any appropriated funds to support directly or indirectly combat operations in or over Cambodia, Laos, North Vietnam and South Vietnam or off the shores of these countries by United States forces. This bill cut off the means for the president to enforce the Paris Peace Agreement against Hanoi's violations. This bill, along with the War Powers Act passed in November 1973, prevented President Nixon and his successor, President Ford, from responding to open and deliberate aggression. South Vietnam was left to fight on without U.S. air support or urgently needed supplies.[80]

President Ford. President Nixon's resignation on August 9, 1973 left President Ford to deal with the problems in South Vietnam with his hands tied. Nonetheless, in an address to a joint session of Congress, he pledged to continue support for our allies and friends in Asia: "I pledge continuity in our support for their security, independence, and economic development. In Indochina, we are determined to see the observance of the Paris Agreement on Vietnam and the cease-fire and negotiated settlement in Laos. We hope to see an early compromise settlement in Cambodia."[81]

During 1974, Congress continued to cut funds for support of South Vietnam. President Ford pleaded with Congress to restore some of the aid, but Congress was unwilling to respond to his requests even though it was evident that the cuts in funds had resulted in a significant decline in South Vietnam's ability to resist the flagrant violations of the agreement. By January of 1975, the North Vietnamese had infiltrated over 170,000 troops into South Vietnam, building up their army to 300,000. They had increased their armor in the South by 400 new tanks and armored personnel carriers, and had significantly increased their artillery and antiaircraft guns. By March 1975, South Vietnam's military had critical shortages in fuel, ammunition, equipment and supplies. With tons of supplies flowing to North Vietnam from China and the Soviet Union, South Vietnam had little chance of survival. Congress was still unwilling to honor President Ford's requests for additional aid.[82]

At a joint session of Congress on April 10, 1975, President Ford made an impassioned plea for aid for South Vietnam. His comments, a last ditch appeal to save South Vietnam, are worthy of repeating:

> A vast human tragedy has befallen our friends in Vietnam and Cambodia. Tonight I shall not talk only of obligations arising from legal documents. Who can forget the enormous sacrifices of blood, dedication, and treasure that we made in Vietnam?
>
> Under five Presidents and 12 Congresses, the United States was engaged in Indochina. Millions of Americans served, thousands died, and many more were wounded, imprisoned, or lost. Over $150 billion have been appropriated for that war by the Congress of the United

States. And after years of effort, we negotiated, under the most difficult circumstances, a settlement which made it possible for us to remove our military forces and bring home with pride our American prisoners. This settlement, if its terms had been adhered to would have permitted our South Vietnamese ally, with our material and moral support, to maintain its security and rebuild after two decades of war.

The chances for an enduring peace after the last American fighting man left Vietnam in 1973 rested on two publicly stated premises: first, that if necessary, the United States would help sustain the terms of the Paris Accords it signed two years ago, and second, that the United States would provide adequate economic and military assistance to South Vietnam.

The universal consensus in the United States at that time, late 1972, was that if we could end our own involvement and obtain the release of our prisoners, we would provide adequate material support to South Vietnam. The North Vietnamese, from the moment they signed the Paris Accords, systematically violated the cease-fire and other provisions of that agreement. Flagrantly disregarding the ban on the infiltration of troops, the North Vietnamese illegally introduced over 350,000 men into the South. In direct violation of the agreement, they sent in the most modern equipment in massive amounts. Meanwhile, they continued to receive large quantities of supplies and arms from their friends.

In the face of this situation, the United States—torn as it was by the emotions of a decade of war—was unable to respond. We deprived ourselves by law of the ability to enforce the agreement, thus giving North Vietnam assurance that it could violate that agreement with impunity...Encouraged by these developments, The North Vietnamese, in recent months, began sending even their reserve divisions into South Vietnam. Some 20 divisions, virtually their entire army, are now in South Vietnam.[83]

President Ford went on to describe some of our options, ranging from doing nothing, in which South Vietnam would be left to save itself, or to live up to our obligations and provide the military and humanitarian assistance urgently needed for South Vietnam to have a chance to survive. He continued:

> I am also mindful of our posture toward the rest of the world and, particularly, of our future relations with the free nations of Asia. These nations must not think for a minute that the United States is pulling out on them or intends to abandon them to aggression. I have therefore concluded that the national interests of the United States and the cause of world stability require that we continue to give both military and humanitarian assistance to the South Vietnamese.
>
> Assistance to South Vietnam at this stage must be swift and adequate…Half-hearted action would be worse than none. We must act together and act decisively. I am therefore asking the Congress to appropriate without delay $722 million for emergency military assistance and an initial sum of $250 million for economic and humanitarian aid for South Vietnam.[84]

President Ford also addressed what he referred to as the tragic situation in Cambodia. He pointed out that "with the military successes [of the Communists], steady external support, and their awareness of American legal restrictions, the Communist side has shown no interest in negotiations, compromise, or a political solution. And yet, for the past 3 months, the beleaguered people of Phnom Penh have fought on, hoping against hope that the United States would not desert them, but instead provide the arms and ammunition they so badly needed…In January, I requested food and ammunition for the brave Cambodians, and I regret to say that as of this evening, it may be too late."[85]

President Ford closed with a final appeal, "Members of Congress, my fellow Americans, this moment of tragedy for Indochina is a time of trial for us. It is a time for national resolve…We cannot, in the meantime, abandon our friends while our adversaries support and encourage theirs. We cannot dismantle our defenses, our diplomacy, or our intelligence capability while others increase and strengthen theirs…At this moment, the United States must present to the world a united front."[86]

The antiwar element, then in full control of Congress, ignored President Fords' pleas. No funds for South Vietnam or Cambodia were forthcoming.[87]

South Vietnam fell to the North Vietnamese Communists 20 days later. Cambodia and the killing fields were not far behind.

Chapter Three

Hanoi's Grand Facade

South Vietnam is the model of the national liberation movement in our time. If the special warfare that the United States imperialists are testing in South Vietnam is overcome, then it can be defeated anywhere in the world.

—General Vo Nguyen Giap

The North Vietnamese went to extraordinary measures to conceal their role in planning, controlling and directing the insurgency in South Vietnam. The fact that the Vietnamese Communist Lao Dong Party in Hanoi directed every aspect of the insurgency was evident from the outset to those who took the time to find out. Even after irrefutable proof was presented to the world, the antiwar critics at home and abroad continued to propagate the myth that it was a "civil war" brought about by internal unrest. Nothing could be further from the truth. The evidence to refute this myth is available in the form of captured enemy documents, interrogation of enemy defectors and prisoners, statements by officials of North Vietnam (now the Socialist Republic of Vietnam) and numerous pieces of hard evidence such as observation of thousands of North Vietnamese troops crossing into South Vietnam across the demilitarized zone and over various routes into the South via Laos and Cambodia. Captured plans and orders along with intercepted communications clearly disclosed that political, military and operational direction emanated from Hanoi.[1]

The absurdity of Hanoi's efforts to hide its involvement in the insurgency is revealed in the following passages:

> The so-called presence of forces of the Democratic Republic of [North] Vietnam [in the South] is but a myth fabricated by the U.S. imperialists by way of justification for their war of aggression in South Vietnam.
>
> >   Premier Pham Van Dong
> >   Hanoi Radio, 28 January 1966 [2]
>
> It is wrong to say that we cannot defeat the enemy, because at the present time, our troops are gaining many outstanding victories and many troops are being sent from North Vietnam to South Vietnam to deal with the limited war.
>
> >   General Nguyen Chi Than, member North Vietnam's Politburo and National Defense Council and Commander-in-Chief of the Viet Cong Army, captured January 1967 [3]

North Vietnam still denied its involvement in the insurgency in the South while thousands of its troops poured across the demilitarized zone with tanks and artillery in a full scale conventional invasion in 1972. They showed complete disdain for the truth and the ability of the free world to see through their thinly veiled façade. As we shall see, the evidence of the Hanoi's direct control of the insurgency in South Vietnam and other countries in the region is overwhelming and irrefutable.

State Department White Paper on Vietnam, *Aggression from the North,* February 27, 1965, provides a summary of the massive evidence of North Vietnamese aggression against South Vietnam. This is a key position paper on Vietnam produced by the Johnson administration; accordingly, it has been included in its entirety in Appendix H. A few excerpts from this document are cited below:

> South Vietnam is fighting for its life against a brutal campaign of terror and armed attack inspired, directed,

supplied, and controlled by the Communist regime in Hanoi. This flagrant aggression has been going on for years, but recently the pace has quickened and the threat has now become acute.

The war in Vietnam is a new kind of war, a fact as yet poorly understood in most parts of the world. Much of the confusion that prevails in the thinking of many people, and even governments, stems from this basic misunderstanding. For in Vietnam a totally new brand of aggression has been loosed against an independent people who want to make their way in peace and freedom....

Above all, the war in Vietnam is not a spontaneous and local rebellion against the established government.... In Vietnam a Communist government has set out deliberately to conquer a sovereign people in a neighboring state. And to achieve its end, it has used every resource of its own government to carry out its carefully planned program of concealed aggression. North Vietnam's commitment to seize control of the South is no less total than was the commitment of the regime in North Korea in 1950. But knowing the consequences of the latter's undisguised attack, the planners in Hanoi have tried desperately to conceal their hand. They have failed and their aggression is as real as that of an invading army.[4]

One of the most powerful and comprehensive policy statements concerning the United States' involvement in Vietnam was presented to the Senate Foreign Relations Committee by, then, Secretary of Defense, Robert S. McNamara, on March 3, 1966. In this address, McNamara gives us extensive insight into the nature of the conflict in South Vietnam and Hanoi's strategy to conquer the South. A copy of this key address is included in Appendix I. Concerning the nature of the conflict, McNamara had this to say:

Some...have inferred that the war is a civil war, an "internal affair," in which the United States therefore should not be involved. Any such conclusion is wholly unwarranted.

Indeed, it is belied by all we know and have learned about the nature of the war – its origins, its development and its conduct – over the years down to the present. Of course, many Viet Cong troops – especially low-ranking troops and irregulars – are from South Vietnam. But that fact reveals only one scrap of a much larger and quite different story. The controlling fact – from which all else flows – is that the North Vietnamese regime has, almost from the time the Geneva Accords of 1954 were signed, undertaken to do all that would be necessary to achieve a single aim: to overthrow the government of South Vietnam....

When it became clear in the late 1950's however, that South Vietnam could and would develop as a viable political and economic entity – indeed, that South Vietnam was outpacing North Vietnam is economic improvements and in advances in health and education – Hanoi directed its agents in the South [thousands left behind when the 1954 accords were implemented] to begin a program of terror and sabotage designed to destroy the developing allegiance of the people of South Vietnam to their government. Hanoi's "War of National Liberation" began.[5]

The State Department White Paper along with McNamara's address to the Senate and an address by Douglas MacArthur II, Assistant Secretary of State for Congressional Relations, on June 30 1965, set the stage for what is to follow in dispelling the civil war myth. Assistant Secretary MacArthur made a strong case against the contention that the fighting in South Vietnam was a civil war:

Let there be no mistake about this point. What is happening in Vietnam is not a civil war. It is not an insurrection. It is not a popular uprising, nor is it, in the terms Hanoi and Peiping [Beijing] prefer to use, "a war of national liberation." It is aggression, pure and simple.

Aggression does not lose its character because efforts are made to conceal its naked character or because the time schedule is drawn out—or because trained men and weapons of war are introduced by stealth across frontiers and then unleashed in a savage assault on free peoples—or because the aggressor's troops speak the same language as the victims.

This is what has been happening and is happening today in Vietnam. We are, in short, confronted with aggression by the Communist regime in Hanoi, spurred on by Peiping, against the Government and people of South Vietnam.[6]

MacArthur was also convinced that the struggle in Vietnam was only the beginning of Communist expansionism in Southeast Asia if it were allowed to go unchecked. Mao Tse-tung left no doubt in the correctness of this conclusion. As far back as 1953, Mao proffered, "Once foreign intervention is out of the picture [in Southeast Asia], vigorous propaganda, infiltration, the forming of united fronts with progressive elements in and outside the reactionary regimes will accelerate the process of liberation. A firm stroke of force will complete the task. After the 'liberation' of Vietnam, Burma and Thailand would capitulate, and Indonesia would fall to the Communist camp like ripe fruit and the Malay Peninsula would be encircled."[7]

Mao left no doubt in what he had in mind for the future of Southeast Asia. Neither did Ho Chi Minh. As far back as 1927, Ho spoke adamantly about his plans: "I intend to form an Indochinese national revolutionary movement whose leaders will bring its members step by step to orthodox communism."[8] Since the formation of the Communist Party by Ho Chi Minh in 1930, its ultimate aim was extension of its control over all of Indochina, including Vietnam, Laos, Cambodia and even Thailand.[9] Senator John McCain III has first hand knowledge of the ambitions that Hanoi had toward its neighbors:

The Communists left no doubt in my mind that it was not a question of South Vietnam alone. Two North Vietnamese generals said to me at separate times [while he was a POW in Hanoi], "After we liberate South Vietnam, we're going to liberate Cambodia. And after Cambodia we're going to liberate Laos and after we liberate Laos we're going to liberate Thailand and after we liberate Thailand we're going to liberate Malaysia and then Burma. We're going to liberate all of Southeast Asia. That is what Communism is all about – armed struggle to overthrow the capitalist countries."[10]

For a number of years the original Vietnamese Communist Party remained somewhat obscure while taking advantage of nationalism to build a coalition and establish control of the provisional government of Vietnam. In 1951, the party re-emerged as the Lao Dong Workers Party. The aims of the party as spelled out below portend the direction that the party was destined to take:

The Lao Dong is the party of the Viet Nam working classes and laboring people. It accepts the doctrines of Marx, Engels, Lenin, Stalin and the ideology of Mao Tse-tung, and combines them with the characteristics of the Viet Nam Revolution to serve as an "ideological base and magnetic needle" for every action of the party. The major tasks of the Viet Nam Revolution are to drive out the imperialist invaders, remove feudal and semi-feudal traces [personal property and wealth], and develop the people's economy, political understanding and democratic culture so as to ensure conditions for promoting the construction of a Socialist regime....To achieve the above tasks, the Lao Dong must strengthen the National United Front....and strengthen and develop the People's Army. The party recognizes that the Viet Nam Revolution is an integral part of the world revolution led by the Soviet Union.[11]

Ho and his followers spoke of the war in Indochina as having wider international significance in a Marxist-Leninist perspective. They characterized Hanoi's role as "the 'vanguard' of a great world front for 'peace and democracy,' and especially as the leader of the effort to expel 'U.S. imperialism' from all Southeast Asia."[12] China and the Soviet Union each had their own stakes in the war. Communist China was eager to see United States' influence removed from Southeast Asia to end competition for dominance of that region. Although the Soviet Union did not favor seeing China in control of Southeast Asia, they relished the idea of seeing the leader of the capitalist world drained of its resources in a fight where there were no risks for them.[13] South Vietnam, with an economy and political system that had been devastated by WW II and the Viet Minh war with the French, faced a Communist insurgency from the North that was supported by Communist China, the Soviet Union, Cuba, North Korea, and the Soviet dominated countries in Eastern Europe. Standing alone, South Vietnam did not have a chance of survival.

The Geneva Accords were to have ended the hostilities in Indochina in 1954. However, even as the accords were being negotiated the Communists in the North were making plans to take over all of Vietnam. With the completion of the truce agreement "the communists moved an estimated 80,000 to 100,000 hard core Viet Minh soldiers and political cadre, some with families, to the North."[14] While most southern Communists went north, certain key Communist leaders and several thousand cadres were left behind to form the nucleus for the renewal of the struggle. For a time they remained relatively inactive while maintaining their secret organization and communications network and regularly receiving orders from Hanoi.[15]

Ho Chi Minh's regime in the North (the Democratic Republic of Vietnam, DRV) was convinced that the elections scheduled in the Geneva Accords for 1956 would give them control of all of Vietnam. In preparation for this eventuality, the Communists focused on political action and promoting discontent in South Vietnam in an effort to turn the populace against the Saigon government. When the elections did not materialize, the Communists stepped up their agitation.[16] Late in 1956, Le Duan, a party official in Hanoi, proposed to the North Vietnamese Politburo that they launch a war of liberation in the South. Le Duan, who had previously lived in the South, was given the job of organizing the insurgency. He traveled secretly to the South where he set about planning and organizing the insurrection using the stay-behind cadres to form the nucleus of the insurgent forces.[17] The use of terror and subversive means increased sharply as the Communists sought to undermine and destroy the government in South Vietnam. They carried out a campaign of assassinations, kidnappings, and bombings aimed at decapitating the countries leadership from the top down. Police, teachers, government officials, village chiefs, and anyone who was thought to have even the slightest potential for assuming a leadership role were all targets.[18]

The leave-behinds were valuable in preparing the infrastructure for the southerners who had regrouped in the North in 1954. After 1956 the North Vietnamese set up special camps in the North to provide political and military training for the regrouped soldiers in preparation for infiltration to the South. These troops were a valuable asset because many were originally from the South and spoke the local dialect that would not attract attention as being an outsider. A great number of these "regroupees" as they were known were infiltrated into South Vietnam in the next several years. There was clear evidence that "some were sent as political agents after 1956 to help expand the Viet Cong apparatus; some went to staff the intricate courier/communications system and to select and establish secure routes for future infiltration. Specialists in guerrilla techniques went south, prior to 1960, to organize Viet Cong training programs; others were the cadres and technicians who, between 1956 and 1959, helped prepare the Viet Cong combat units."[19] The full extent of infiltration from the North will be covered later in this chapter.

The Decision for Armed Insurgency

In 1959, the Communist regime in the North realized that its subversion in the South was being successfully countered by the government of South Vietnam. Le Duan was recalled from his mission in the South, and the Politburo gathered to consider a new strategy. A crucial decision with far reaching implications came out of this meeting. "The Central Committee decided in January 1959 to launch an armed insurrection in South Vietnam. In May 1959 the Fifteenth Plenum of the Central Committee formally adopted the policy and sent orders to that effect to South Vietnam...In July of that year the vanguard of some 4,000 trained regroupees began infiltrating into South Vietnam."[20] On May 13, 1959, the Lao Dong Party Central Committee declared, "The time has come to struggle heroically and perseveringly to smash the South Vietnamese Government."[21]

North Vietnam's decision to prosecute an insurrection in the South was explained by Ho Chi Minh in an interview with the Italian Communist newspaper *L'Unita*, published on July 1, 1959:

> We [Vietnamese Communists] are building Socialism in Vietnam, but we are building it in half of the country, while in the other half we still have to complete the democratic-bourgeois and anti-imperialist revolution. Briefly, our party today has to make two different revolutions at once, in the North and in the South. This is one of the more characteristic traits of our struggle.[22]

In late 1960 a Viet Cong district headquarters was captured. The Viet Cong district chief was killed and a notebook with the outline for a Viet Cong training course was recovered. It read:

> Our purpose: To incite the people to rise against the US-Diem clique in order to achieve the objective of the revolutionary liberation of the South...Whether we should resort to the use of arms or not depends on the actual situation at the moment. This should not occur too early or too late, and it is only up to the Central Committee [Communist Party in the North] to determine when the time is appropriate and reach a decision. The revolution in the South at the present time has two possibilities:
> —a general uprising to seize power.
> —a long-term armed struggle.
> But our final objective is a general uprising to seize power.[23]

The Communist Front

If there were any doubts about Hanoi's intentions, they were put to rest by Le Duan, the First Secretary of the Lao Dong Party, during the Third Congress of the Party held on September 5 to 10, 1960. He stated:

"The immediate task of the revolution in the South is to overthrow the dictatorial clique now in power in South Vietnam and to set up a democratic government of national coalition in South Vietnam."

In the execution of this program, the "Front for the Liberation of the South" was created. Its subordination to the Lao Dong Party and its allegiance to the Communist authorities of North Vietnam are undeniable by anyone. In order to reach the above quoted goal, the Hanoi regime furnished all the necessary means, men and material to this Front.

This participation was manifested by the following forms:
1. Infiltration of the military forces to South Vietnam;
2. Introduction into South Vietnam of various arms, munitions and equipment derived from the aid finished to North Vietnam by countries in the communist bloc.[24]

The forgoing statement by Le Duan is very telling, for it clearly indicates beyond any doubt that the Front for the Liberation of the South was under the direction of the Lao Dong Communist Party in North Vietnam. From the time of the Fronts formation, all the way to the conclusion of negotiations in 1973, North Vietnam denied this fact. The origin of the National Liberation Front can be traced to Le Duan's call for a united national front in the South at the Party's Third Congress in September 1960:

> At present our party is facing momentous tasks: to promote socialist construction in the North and to consolidate the North into an ever more solid base for the struggle for national reunification; to strive to complete the national people's democratic revolution throughout the country to liberate the South....
>
> In order to assure the complete victory of the revolutionary struggle in South Vietnam, the South

Vietnam people, under the leadership of the Marxist-Leninist Party and the working class, should endeavor to build a worker-peasant army coalition bloc, and set up a broad national united front against the United States-Diem clique on the basis of the worker-peasant alliance."[25]

In September 1960 the Central Committee of the Lao Dong Party in Hanoi responded to Le Duan's call for the formation of the Front. It announced, "The common task of the Vietnamese revolution at present is to accelerate the socialist revolution in North Vietnam while at the same time stepping up the National People's Democratic Revolution in South Vietnam."[26] The party called for the creation of a front organization to undertake the subversion of South Vietnam. Three months later, on December 20, 1960, the National Front for the Liberation of the South (NFLSVN), known as the National Liberation Front, (NLF) was established.[27] Le Duan proclaimed that the Front would "rally 'all patriotic forces' to overthrow the Diem Government [in the South] and thus ensure 'conditions for the peaceful reunification of the Fatherland'"[28]

The Front was declared to be a movement comprising people of all political persuasions, all religions, all races, and all social classes in South Vietnam. It was a total fraud concocted by Hanoi to give legitimacy to the insurgency in the South.[29] This ruse became a major hurdle in the peace negotiations that went on from 1968 until the settlement in 1973, for the North Vietnamese insisted, without the slightest humiliation, that the NLF was the sole legitimate representative of South Vietnam. As ridiculous as it might seem, they stuck with this claim to the end, and the NLF with its political front, the Provisional Revolutionary Government (PRG), was eventually accepted by the United States as a party to the negotiations.[30] The most disturbing aspect of this issue is that the antiwar critics in the United States recognized the legitimacy of the NLF from the outset and supported Hanoi's contention that the NLF was the sole representative of South Vietnam. Once again, they took Hanoi's word over that of their own government.[31]

A letter recovered from Communist sources, Number 4660 dated October 24, 1961, provides additional insight into the formation and policies of the Front: "In the execution of the resolution of the [Third] Party Congress, the Party Central Committee has organized the National Front for the Liberation of the South with a view to unifying all the forces in the revolutionary struggle to overthrow the American-Diemist Administration and set up a people's democratic Government of Union, in view of a consultative conference for national reunification."[32]

Another excerpt from this same letter illustrates the contradiction in Communist thinking: "In the reports read at the Third Congress of the Party, our comrades Le Duan and Le Duc Tho have made it clear that although the youths, students, intellectuals and bourgeois in the urban centers as well as the wealthy and middle class peasants in the countryside have all a very keen consciousness, they, however, are easily disconcerted and agitated and unfavorable to a socialist revolution, to Marxism and Leninism. They, moreover, are selfish and averse to danger and discomfort." The letter went on to explain that in the face of the present situation, different classes should be included in the Front, but this did not mean that the party was not remaining faithful to the policy of class struggle. The inference was that the party intended to make use of the bourgeois and intellectuals during the revolutionary struggle in the South. After victory, the struggle between the "working" class and the bourgeois would resume.[33]

In 1961 another element of Hanoi's façade was formed. Known as the People's Revolutionary Party (PRP), it was created by the Communists to give the impression that there was a separate Marxist-Leninist party associated with the NLF, independent of the party in North Vietnam. A party circular dated December 7, 1961, explained, "The People's Revolutionary Party has only the appearance of an independent existence; actually our party is nothing but the Lao Dong Party of Vietnam, unified from North to South under the direction of the Central Executive Committee of the party, the chief of which is President Ho...."[34] Further proof of the PRPs relationship to Hanoi was found in captured Viet Cong documents which clearly stated that the People's Revolutionary Party, the controlling element of the Front and Viet Cong, was the Lao Dong Party's apparatus in South Vietnam.[35] Simply put, the People's Revolutionary Party was the southern branch of the Lao Dong Communist Party in North Vietnam.

The structure for direction of the insurrection in South Vietnam was a complex integration of political and military entities (See Figure 1, end of chapter). The Lao Dong Central Committee in Hanoi exercised control of the insurgency through the Central

Office for South Vietnam (COSVN). COSVN served as the bridge between the Communist leadership in Hanoi and the party in South Vietnam. COSVN functioned as the Central Committee for the PRP. It exercised control over the PRP, the Liberation Army and the NLF. The PRP provided political direction and control. The NLF served as a propaganda unit. Its purpose was to organize the South Vietnamese populace for the fight against the government of South Vietnam and represent the revolution to the outside world. The People's Liberation Army (PLA) conducted terror and military operations. All significant political and military positions down to platoon leaders and district NLF cadre were occupied by PRP members to provide tight control from the top down. There were indications that the northern half of South Vietnam was primarily under the direct control of the Lao Dong Party and the Army High Command in the North.[36]

The COSVN was essentially the field office of the Lao Dong Party. Although its exact location was obscure, COSVN was known to be north of Saigon near the South Vietnamese border in Cambodia. According to a North Vietnamese officer, Colonel Le Xuan Chuyen, who defected in 1966, the COSVN was staffed by senior North Vietnamese Communist officials. They included "General Nguyen Chi Thanh, known personally to Colonel Chuyen, who was commander of the Viet Cong....He was a four-star North Vietnamese general second only to North Vietnamese Defense Minister, General Giap, and ranked No. 8 in the Lao Dong Politburo."[37] Three other North Vietnamese generals were also named by the defector as serving in South Vietnam. They were "Generals Tran Do and Tran Van Tra, senior officers in the North Vietnamese Army and members of the Lao Dong Party Central Committee. They were also deputy commanders of the Viet Cong. General Tran Do was identified as General Thanh's Political Deputy in COSVN and General Tran Van Tra as Thanh's Military Deputy.... A third officer, General Le Trong Tan, Deputy Chief of the North Vietnamese General Staff....was identified by Major Huynh Cu [Viet Cong defector] as military operations staff officer in COSVN."[38]

Following General Thanh's death in July 1967, Pham Hung took command of COSVN. He was one of North Vietnam's five Vice Premiers and a member of the Central Committee and Secretariat of the Lao Dong Party. He was considered the fifth most powerful man in North Vietnam. According to Colonel Tran Van Dac, a defector and former political officer of the COSVN, Pham Hung held all the top positions in the South, including Chief of the COSVN, Secretary of the PRP and commander and chief political officer of the Liberation Army.[39]

The staffing of COSVN with prominent senior officers from North Vietnam clearly reflects Hanoi's control of the insurgency in the South.

Infiltration

Infiltration of military personnel, armaments and supplies from North Vietnam into the South began in earnest in 1960. According to the official history of the People's Army of (North) Vietnam (PAVN), their troop strength in the South, after losses, went from 15,000 soldiers by the end of 1960 to 70,000 by the end of 1963.[40] However, this was only the beginning. Many thousands more were to follow, but to facilitate the increase in resources necessary to expand the war in the South, a much larger pipeline was needed. Along with the decision to "liberate" South Vietnam, Ho Chi Minh directed a major effort to expand and extend the infiltration route from the North into South Vietnam. "In May 1959, the 559th Transportation Group was organized in North Vietnam to begin the arduous and critical process of establishing a communications and transportation link to the South. Its first activities were to establish the way stations and paths through the Laotian side of the Annamite Mountains, which in later years became the highways and pipelines of the Ho Chi Minh Trail."[41] In the early stages of development, the way stations were built about a day's march apart. Food, shelter and medical facilities were provided. Guides assisted the infiltrators.[42] (See Early Infiltration Routes, Figure 2 at end of chapter.)

In 1961 infiltration of military personnel, sometimes in organized units, had reached major proportions. Initially, the majority of the infiltrated personnel were drawn from the Communist units that moved North when the Geneva Accords went into effect. In late 1964 North Vietnam began sending regular North Vietnamese Army units into the South. All the cadres selected for infiltration had to undergo, without exception, a military, political and propaganda training course at the special camp at Xuan-Mai in Ha-Dong province of North Vietnam. Specialty camps operated at Son-Tay for political training of civilian cadre; at a site near Hanoi for Montagnard cadre; at Lo-Duc Street in Hanoi for military intelligence training; at other camps for special training in ordinance, medical, signal; and two centers for training of infiltrators.[43]

After training, a typical infiltration in the early 1960s began with the unit being moved to Vinh on the east coast of North Vietnam. The journey went like this:

> From there, they [would] go by truck to the vicinity of the North Vietnam-Laos border...At the North Vietnam-Laos border crossing point, the infiltrators were re-equipped. Their North Vietnamese Army uniforms had to be turned in. They were instructed to give up all personal papers, letters, notebooks, and photographs that might be incriminating... [Hanoi was still trying to conceal its hand in the war.] For the journey through Laos, infiltration groups were usually issued a set of black civilian pajama-like clothes, rubber sandals, a sweater, a hammock, mosquito netting, and waterproof sheeting. They [would] carry a three to five-day supply of food. A packet of medicines and bandages was usually provided.
>
> After several days of rest, infiltrators [would] then move southward through Laos. Some groups moved along the Laos-South Vietnam border, but many groups moved fairly deep into Laotian territory to the vicinity of Tchepone. After a time, the infiltration groups turned eastward, entering South Vietnam in Quang Nam or Kontum or another of the border provinces.[44]

By early 1965 complete units of the North Vietnamese Army were operating within the borders of South Vietnam. These units were "the 95th, 32nd and 101st Regiments of the 325th Division...The initial regiments were merely the precursors of a continuing military invasion that steadily increased in size and scope....In 1965, besides the initial three regiments, Hanoi sent eight additional regiments to infiltrate into South Vietnam (12th, 22nd, 33rd, 66th, 250th, 21st, 95B and 18B Regiments) for a total of over 25,000 men, not including those infiltrators sent as replacements. As of 1 April 1967 there was a total of 21 confirmed North Vietnamese Army Regiments and six NVA Divisions in South

Vietnam."⁴⁵ A North Vietnamese Division was made up of 8,000 to 10.000 troops.

In his memoirs, Colonel Bui Tin reflects that when he made his first trip to the South in 1961 by way of the trail, "he had to hack and crawl his way through the jungle." By early 1964 he recalls that "the trail was still narrow and only passable by bicycle...."⁴⁶ According to Bui Tin, a heated debate ensued within the North Vietnamese Army General Staff in 1964 on the need to further expand the Ho Chi Minh Trail in order to pursue the war. The decision was made to expand the trails to between six and eight meters wide to accommodate Chinese and Russian trucks. This required strengthening bridges, setting up a network of repair facilities and fuel depots along the trails. It also required the placement of antiaircraft guns along the trail to protect against enemy interdiction. By 1973 the Ho Chi Minh Trail had been widened and modernized.⁴⁷ General Davidson, former Chief of Intelligence at MACV, described the expanded trail in this way: "A new all weather road was pushed from Khe Sanh down the east side of the Annamite [mountain] Chain to link up to Highway 14 down to An Loc. Altogether the NVA [North Vietnamese Army] added 12,000 miles of roads. A fuel pipeline was built from North Vietnam deep into South Vietnam, and a modern radio net linked NVA forces throughout South Vietnam."⁴⁸

Progress on the improvements of the trail correlates to some degree with the number of troops infiltrated from North Vietnam over the years. In 1960 approximately 2,700 were introduced into South Vietnam. By 1966 the rate for that year was up to 73,000.⁴⁹ In 1968, the Military Assistance Command Vietnam (MACV) placed the number of infiltrators from the North at 229,000 for that year alone.⁵⁰ To further illustrate the extent of developments of the trail, General Davidson describes what took place within two weeks after the signing of the Paris Peace Agreement in early 1973:

> Included among these violations [of the Paris Agreement] was the movement on 6 February of a 175-truck convoy through the DMZ and the march of 223 tanks from Laos and Cambodia into South Vietnam. By mid-April, some 7,000 NVA truck crossings of the DMZ were reported. Hugh convoys rolled down the expanded and hardened Ho Chi Minh Trail system. During 1973,

Hanoi infiltrated over 75,000 troops, increased its tank strength from 100 to 500, and almost doubled its heavy artillery strength...By the end of April, thirteen *new* AA (antiaircraft) regiments had taken up positions in South Vietnam, and the 263rd Surface-to-Air Missile (SAM) Regiment had established itself at Khe Sanh.[51]

To refer to the Ho Chi Minh Trail as if it were one trail to South Vietnam is misleading. In fact, it was made up of numerous trails, some were main roads and others were mere paths. Some infiltration routes were by land and some by sea. There was a dense network cutting across the DMZ into a number of welcome centers in the South. There was the corridor into the South via lower Laos. There was an extensive network along the Vietnamese-Laos frontier. There was also a land route through Cambodia which consisted of seven different corridors to infiltrate into the South. For years, supplies and troops were brought into the Cambodian port of Sihanoukville and transported over land to near the border with South Vietnam. War materials of all types along with spies and special agents were introduced into the South by sea along the long coastal shore.[52] A captured NVA sergeant revealed that war supplies for the NVA/Viet Cong were being flown directly from China to the Cambodian airport at Phnom Penh and were then transported by truck to storage areas near the South Vietnam border.[53] As previously mentioned, supplies and equipment were airlifted into Tchepone airport in northern Laos just 20 miles from the South Vietnam border by Soviet aircraft. In 1973, thirteen new airfields were built on South Vietnamese territory. The North Vietnamese did not have tourist travel in mind. In violation of the Paris Agreement, they were getting ready for the final conquest.[54]

The Communists in Hanoi were just as adamant about denying their presence in Laos as they were for their insurgency in South Vietnam. Intelligence reports and interrogation of captured North Vietnamese troops told a different story. As early as 1959 North Vietnam advisors began training and supporting Pathet Lao guerrillas. The support of the Pathet Lao insurgency in Laos was motivated by North Vietnam's interest in gaining control of the southern panhandle of Laos to use as an infiltration route into South Vietnam.[55] In an article in the PAVN's official newspaper in February 3, 1959, Communist Party First Secretary, Le Duan, told a group of infiltrators about to depart in 1959, "If we can open a road to Nam Bo [southern part of South Vietnam], the revolution in South Vietnam will be 50 percent won, because only if we have a road to Nam Bo will out great rear area in North Vietnam be able to send personnel and supplies to the south. If you, the members of the first military group to go to Nam Bo, make it your destination, a great army will follow you."[56]

While denying their presence in Laos, the PAVN official history shows that "by the first half of 1961 a total of 12,000 PAVN troops, including regular infantry, artillery and engineer battalions from the PAVN 325th Division, the 316th and 335th brigades and 271st Regiment, were fighting in Laos alongside their Pathet Lao [Communist] allies... Their main objective was to seize control of a large area of the Laotian panhandle to provide a new route on the western side of the Annamite Mountains and enable completion of the infiltration route to the southern part of South Vietnam."[57] This action would prove to be a major factor in the infiltration into South Vietnam as well as giving Pathet Lao and North Vietnam control of half of the territory of Laos. The Geneva Agreement of 1962 which required withdrawal of all foreign troops from Laos had little effect on North Vietnam's involvement in that country. After the agreement was signed, North Vietnam continued its operations in Laos, and soon had 40,000 regular armed forces in Laos. Approximately 25,000 were there to protect the infiltration routes into South Vietnam, and 15,000 supported Pathet Lao operations.[58]

The CIA concluded that "roads completed or under construction in the Laotian panhandle during 1965 will facilitate the movement of men and supplies to South Vietnam and will increase the ability of the Communists to deploy and support forces in Southern Laos. These roads in Laos are oriented to the east and south toward South Vietnam. Men and supplies can now be moved from the panhandle by a combination of truck and river transportation across the border of South Vietnam into an area 100 miles farther south than was possible prior to late 1964 or early 1965."[59] Le Duan had his wish for the new infiltration route to Nam Bo.

It would be incorrect to give the impression that only troops infiltrated into the South were involved in the war. Besides the Viet-Minh troops that were left behind by Ho Chi Minh after the Geneva Accords, the Communist cadres who remained in the South along with those who infiltrated from the North had an extensive recruitment campaign to enlist South Vietnamese to their cause. Their recruiting techniques were often quite effective. Some joined to prevent their families from being harmed, some were kidnapped and for some their very lives were threatened. A young Vietnamese who was captured in action in South Vietnam was interviewed by an American correspondent. The reporter asked the 17 year old "volunteer" why he had joined the Communists. He answered, "Because they took my father away for 10 days and tried to force him to join their organization. But my father refused. Then they took me and forced me to cooperate. They threatened to kill my father if I refused..."[60] According to American authorities, similar situations were reported by hundreds of young Vietnamese men.[61]

International Control Commission (ICC)

The International Commission for Supervision and Control in Vietnam was established under the Geneva Accords of 1954 to supervise the cease-fire and investigate violations of the agreement. The commission was made up of representatives from India, Canada and Poland. South Vietnam presented volumes of evidence to the commission proving that North Vietnam was committing aggression and violating several articles of the agreement, including the following:

> Article 10 of the agreement called for "the complete cessation of all hostilities in Vietnam."
> Article 19 required both sides to insure their zones "were not used for the resumption of hostilities or to further aggressive policy."
> Article 24 required each side to respect the territory of the other, and "to commit no act and undertake no operation against the other party."
> Article 27 specified that the agreement applied to all elements of the military command. This included regular, irregular, and guerrilla forces.[62]

In the face of objections and dissention by the commission member from Poland (then a Communist bloc country) the commission report in June 1962 left no doubt about aggression from North Vietnam:

> Having examined the complaints and the supporting material sent by South Vietnam Mission, The

Committee [commission] has come to the conclusion that in specific instances there is evidence to show that armed and unarmed personnel, arms, munitions and other supplies have been sent from the Zone in the North to the Zone in the South with the object of supporting, organizing and carrying out hostile activities, including armed attacks, directed against the Armed Forces and Administration of the Zone in the South. These acts are in violation of Articles 10, 19, 24, and 27 of the Agreement on the Cessation of Hostilities in Vietnam.

In examining the complaints and the supporting material, in particular documentary material sent by the South Vietnamese Mission, the Committee has come to the further conclusion that there is evidence to show that the PAVN (Army of North Vietnam) has allowed the Zone in the North to be used for inciting, encouraging and supporting hostile activities in the Zone in the South, aimed at the overthrow of the Administration in the South. The use of the Zone in the North for such activities is in violation of Articles 19, 24, and 27 of the Agreement on the Cessation of Hostilities in Vietnam.[63]

In response to the ICC's inquires about subversive activities in South Vietnam, the People's Army of North Vietnam issued this statement: "The PAV High Command will resolutely reject all decisions taken by the International Commission relating to the so-called subversive activities in South Vietnam, a question which has no relevance to the Geneva Agreement...Henceforth the Mission [Commission] would find itself constrained to resolutely reject all possible requests for comments of this kind...."[64]

The ICC was powerless to enforce the Geneva Agreement. North Vietnam ignored the ICC and proceeded to escalate its aggression with regular North Vietnamese forces. Unsurprisingly, Hanoi continued to deny its involvement in the "national liberation movement" in the South:

North Vietnam's refusal to accept the return of 40 prisoners – reported by the South Vietnamese Government to the International Control Commission on December 2, 1968 – is one of the latest examples of Hanoi's continued unwillingness to admit publicly that its armed forces are fighting in the South.

A previous attempt to return the prisoners captured in the Tet offensive earlier in 1968 was rejected by the North Vietnamese as "a cunning move" which could "deceive nobody." ([North] Vietnam News Agency, August 11). These men, the agency added, must either have been "illegally" arrested on board North Vietnamese cargo or fishing vessels, or they were of South Vietnamese origin.[65]

The ICC issued another report on February 13, 1965 which shreds North Vietnam's denial of aggression in the South:

> The Legal Committee [of the ICC] concludes.... that it is the aim of the Vietnam Lao Dong Party (the ruling Party in the Zone in the North) to bring about the overthrow of the Administration in the South. In September 1960, the Third Congress of the Vietnam Lao Dong Party held in Hanoi (in the Zone in the North) passed a resolution calling for the organization of a "Front" under the leadership of the Vietnam Lao Dong Party. They are present and functioning in the Zone in the South branches of the Vietnam Lao Dong Party and the Front for the Liberation of the South along with its armed branches, namely, the "forces for Liberation of the South" and the "People's Self-Defense Armed Forces." The Vietnam Lao Dong Party and the Front for Liberation of the South have the identical aim of overthrowing the Administration in the South....[66]

The Legal Committee further concluded:

(1) The Vietnam Lao Dong Party in the Zone in the North, the various branches of the Vietnam Lao Dong Party in the Zone in the South, the Front for Liberation of the South, and the People's Self-Defense Armed Forces have incited various sections of the people residing in the Zone in the South, to overthrow it by violent means and have indicated to them various means of doing so.

(2) Those who ignored their exhortation and continued to support the Administration in the South have been threatened with punishment and in certain cases such punishment has been effected by carrying out of death sentences.

(3) The aim and function of the Front for Liberation of the South, the Forces for Liberation of the South and the People's Self-Defense Armed Forces are to organize and to carry out under the leadership of the Vietnam Lao Dong Party, hostile activities against the Armed Forces and the Administration of the South by violent means aimed at the overthrow of the Administration of the South.[67]

The ICC report included an extensive list of the arms and munitions seized in the South from June 1962 to the end of March 1968. The primary suppliers were Communist China, the Soviet Union, East Germany, and Czechoslovakia.[68]

Communist Bloc Support

North Vietnam did not have the economic, financial, technical or military resources to carry out the war against South Vietnam and its allies. Without the support of the Communist bloc countries, Hanoi's aggression in the South would have dried up and South Vietnam would be a free and independent nation today.[69] For those who have espoused the theory that the conflict in South Vietnam was an internal insurgency against the Government in Saigon, ponder this: Twelve Communist countries provided extensive aid to North Vietnam in its aggression against South Vietnam. This included the Soviet Union, Communist China, Bulgaria, Poland, Hungary, Romania, East Germany, Albania,

Czechoslovakia, North Korea and Cuba. Add to this the Communist Pathet Lao in Laos and the Khmer guerrillas and government of Cambodia. On the other side, countries supporting South Vietnam included the United States, Australia, New Zealand, South Korea, Thailand and the Phillipines.[70] It is a very long stretch to claim this was a "civil war."

The Soviet Union was outspoken in its support for Hanoi's war effort. At the meeting held in the Kremlin on November 3, 1967, on the 50th anniversary of the October Socialist Revolution, Leonid Brezhnev, the General Secretary of the Communist Party of the Soviet Union, was reported by the Vietnam News Agency to have said:

> The Soviet Union is fully resolved to give maximum aid and support to the Fraternal Vietnamese people in their struggle for a just cause. This aid will continue until the U.S. imperialists cease their criminal and dishonoring adventure and get out of Viet Nam.[71]

Moscow Tass International Service on November 29, 1970 reported Brezhnev as saying at a speech in Soviet Armenia:

> With the support of the Soviet Union and other socialist countries the fighting people of Vietnam have thwarted the plans and calculations of the American military... The right cause of the people of embattled Vietnam will undoubtedly triumph. The [North] Vietnamese people may further rely fully on Soviet assistance and support. One more concrete piece of evidence of this are the agreements on Soviet economic and military assistance to the Democratic Republic of Vietnam, signed recently in Moscow. In its comments on these agreements the Party press of the Democratic Republic of Vietnam described them as a new expression of the vigorous support and tremendous and all-round assistance given by a fraternal Communist Party, government and people.[72]

A CIA report in March 1968 cites the Soviet Union as being in the lead in providing aid to North Vietnam. Excerpts of this report are quoted below. The complete report is included in Appendix J:

> The USSR continues to provide the overwhelming share of the increasing amounts of military aid being provided to North Vietnam and is willing to sustain this commitment at present or even higher levels....
>
> Soviet military aid has concentrated on air defense equipment including surface-to-air missiles, antiaircraft guns, radar, and fighter aircraft including MIG-21s. Chinese military aid has concentrated on the build-up of North Vietnamese ground forces and sustaining the military effort in radar of increasing sophistication and has supplied large quantities of Mig-17s in 1967--most of them being delivered in response to heavy losses in the latter part of the year.[73] Soviet and Chinese weapons deliveries from 1965 to 1967 are listed in Tables 1 and 2 in Appendix J.

In addition to providing economic and material support, the Soviet Union and the Communist bloc countries provided advisors in North Vietnam as well as training in the Soviet Union and other Eastern European Communist countries. North Vietnam's fighter pilots were trained in the Soviet Union's air force academy from the time North Vietnam began building an air force. Some 3,000 Soviet specialists were stationed in North Vietnam to provide training on the weapons the Soviets provided.[74] According to a report by the Hanoi correspondent of *Neues Deutchland* in January 1967, there were more than 12,000 Communist bloc specialists of all kinds in North Vietnam assisting with the war effort.[75] A North Vietnamese defector reported that from 1965 to December 1967, there were nine Soviet air defense missile battalions operating in North Vietnam. By the middle of 1967, North Vietnamese troops had taken over the operation of the Soviet missile batteries, but 500 or 600 Soviet missile battalion advisors remained.[76] The Soviet systems, along with Chinese missile batteries and crews, enabled North Vietnam to develop one of the most sophisticated and formidable air defense systems in the world. It accounted for the loss of thousands of U.S. aircraft and crews.

Leading up to the bold frontal attack by North Vietnam across the Demilitarized Zone (DMZ) in multidivisional strength on March 30, 1972, the Soviets stepped up their support, providing Hanoi with some of the most modern weapons systems. This included the rugged and deadly Russian T-54 tanks, the lighter T-34 tanks, and PT-76 amphibious tanks. By the start of the invasion on March 30, North Vietnam's tank strength was approximately 1000. A total of 575 of the Soviet–made tanks were sighted and engaged in battle in the March 30 invasion across the DMZ. The Soviets also beefed up Hanoi's artillery strength by providing their powerful 130mm gun and 122mm rockets. North Vietnam moved some of its surface-to-air-missile batteries south to support their invasion, including the shoulder fired SA-7 which was so deadly to helicopters and other low flying aircraft. By this time, North Vietnam had 250 MIG fighter planes, some from the latest models of the Soviet inventory.[77]

The support from Communist China was by no means less formidable than the Soviet Union's. A revealing conversation took place in Beijing on April 8, 1965, between Liu Shaoqi, Chairman and Head of State of the People's Republic of (Communist) China, and Le Duan, General Secretary of North Vietnam's Lao Dong Party:

> Le Duan: We want some volunteer pilots, volunteer soldiers…and other volunteers, including road and bridge engineering units.
> Liu Shaoqi: It is our policy that we will do our best to support you. We will offer whatever you are in need of and we are in a position to offer…
> Le Duan: We want the Chinese volunteer pilots to play a role in four respects: (1) to restrict American bombing to areas south of the 20th or 19th parallels; (2) to defend the safety of Hanoi; (3) to defend several main transportation lines; and (4) to raise the morale of the Vietnamese people.[78]

In December 1971, Mao Tse-tung, Chairman of the Central Committee of the Communist Party of China, Tung Pi-wu, Vice Chairman of the People's Republic of China, and Chou En-lai, Premier of the State Council of the People's Republic of China, sent a message to the leadership of the National Liberation Front. In addition to expressing congratulations for the 11th anniversary of the National Liberation Front, the message also pledged support for the war against the United States:

> The Chinese people always regard the struggle of the Vietnamese and the other Indochinese peoples as their own struggle and take it as their bounden internationalist duty to support and assist the Vietnamese and the other Indochinese peoples in the war against U.S. aggression and for national salvation. So long as U.S. imperialism does not stop its aggression and so long as the national aspirations of the Vietnamese and the other Indochinese peoples are not realized, the Chinese people will continue to give all-out support and assistance to your struggle till complete victory.[79]

In addition to over $600 million in economic aid in the years immediately following the Geneva Accords, China provided extensive military aid to North Vietnam. The Chinese military aid consisted of construction of a strategic transportation network. They constructed eleven highways which connected North Vietnam with China and two railway lines from key provinces in China deep into North Vietnam. The Chinese provided extensive training of North Vietnamese, Laotian and other Communist troops at three main training centers in China. The troops were trained in such disciplines as guerrilla tactics, military infiltration, political organization, erosion of the party and political cadres of the enemy, radio communications and languages. From 1955 to 1963 the Chinese trained over 200,000 enemy forces. Military supplies provided by China consisted of arms, ammunition, mortars, trucks, cars, tanks, aircraft, air defense antiaircraft guns and SAM missile systems, gasoline, food, clothing and more.[80]

In 1963 alone, China provided North Vietnam over 50 aircraft of various types. In August of 1964, nine separate groups of the Chinese Air Force, 9th Division, with 36 MIG fighter planes were assigned to a newly constructed airfield near Hanoi and assumed an air defense role. In addition, Chinese MIG fighters from Nanning, China and Hainan Island performed patrol duty over North Vietnam. The fighter planes of the 9th Division were turned over to North Vietnam in 1965. Also in 1964, China began training North Vietnamese pilots at two training centers in China. In early 1965 a battalion of the Chinese Air Force was sent to North Vietnam to augment North Vietnam's air defense. A few months later, a Chinese antiaircraft artillery (AAA) division was sent to North Vietnam. Antiaircraft units were stationed at three locations around Hanoi. In addition to AAA, the air defense network was equipped with radar systems for ground control, interception and fire control. This was the early phase of a formidable air defense system that was to be developed in coordination with the Soviets.[81]

The exact number of Chinese soldiers providing aid to North Vietnam is in contention. In the summer of 1966 the number was estimated at 40,000. Near the end of that year, U.S. authorities in Saigon believed that the number of Chinese soldiers in the North had risen to 100,000. Some estimates have gone as high as 250,000. Although the exact number is uncertain the fact that they were there helping the North Vietnamese in their effort to take over South Vietnam by force is not. There are numerous direct observations and detailed reports from agents, defectors, interrogation of captured enemy troops and statements by Communist officials that leave no doubt about China's assistance to the regime in Hanoi.[82] The Communist military and economic aid to North Vietnam from 1970 to 1974 was estimated by the CIA to be $5.6 Billion.[83] While antiwar protesters marched in the streets of America, the General Staff and the General Political Department of the Chinese People's Liberation Army (PLA) called a meeting in June 1967 to celebrate the great victory of the army and people in North Vietnam in downing 2,000 U.S. aircraft. The Deputy Director of the PLA General Political Department addressed the group: "The great victories won by the Vietnamese people provide eloquent proof that people's war is the most effective weapon for putting an end to US imperialism…Personally indicated and led by our great leader, Chairman Mao, the unprecedented, great proletarian cultural revolution in China has already scored great victories. The Chinese people and the Chinese PLA who are armed with Mao Tse-tung's thought always give firm and strong backing to the Vietnamese people."[84]

Fidel Castro's Communist regime in Cuba also provided aid to the Communists in North Vietnam. In July 1967, Castro pledged support to North Vietnam:

Cuban Premier Fidel Castro said today [July 26, 1967] that the Vietnamese Communists could win the war against American imperialists if they called on the Socialist countries for volunteers. He said Cuba would send "whole combat units with their equipment" if Hanoi asked....The day Vietnam asks for such help will mean the burial of imperialist aggression...Castro denounced President Johnson as "an ignoramus from Texas...."[85]

An article carried in the Vietnam Courier in November 1967 expressed North Vietnam's appreciation for the aid from Cuba:

Standing in the forefront of the struggle against U.S. imperialism in Southeast Asia and the Western Hemisphere, the South Vietnamese [Communist] people and the Cuban people, although separated by a long distance have become comrades for life.... For long, the Cuban people, the Communist Party of Cuba and the Cuban Revolutionary Government led by beloved Premier Fidel Castro Ruz have been sparing no effort in assisting the South Vietnamese [Communists] people, morally, politically as well as materially.[86]

In that same year Cuba gave recognition to the National Liberation Front as the sole representative of South Vietnam and a permanent mission of the National Liberation Front was established in Cuba. The "affection" of the Cuban people for the South Vietnamese [Communist] people was expressed by Fidel Castro: "For Vietnam we are ready to give even our blood."[87]

One way that Cuba aided Hanoi was by providing Cuban officers to interrogate and exploit U.S. POWs held by North Vietnam. Retuning POWs reported being victims of some of the most brutal, ruthless interrogation by Cuban officers.[88] While Cuban officers were busy torturing our POWs, hundreds of America's "enlightened" youths and intellectuals traveled to Cuba to ostensibly help with the sugar cane harvest and learn about the "glorious" Communist revolution in Cuba. In reality, they were there to be indoctrinated in Communist ideology and learn how to carry out the revolution back home. Some also received training in subversion and sabotage. Those who traveled to Cuba for the "harvest" were identified as the Venceremos Brigade. Much more will be discussed about this radical antiwar/anti-American group in a later chapter.[89]

From Ceasefire to Defeat

On 27 January 1973 the Paris Agreement to end the war in Vietnam was signed by the United States, South Vietnam, North Vietnam and the National Liberation Front. This "four-power" agreement represents several obtrusive but blatantly obvious contradictions. First of all, North Vietnam maintained the façade all along that the conflict in South Vietnam was an internal insurgency, fought solely by South Vietnamese people. If this were the case, why was North Vietnam a party to the agreement to end the war? Secondly, there was an abundance of evidence that the National Liberation Front was an arm of North Vietnam's Lao Dong Communist Party, yet the NLF was accepted as a representative of South Vietnam and was made a party to the agreement. How is it possible that the United States and South Vietnam could have accepted such a subterfuge in concluding the agreement to end the war? Were we that desperate to get out of Vietnam?

Further evidence of the United States' desperation to extricate itself from the conflict was the provision of the Paris Agreement that allowed North Vietnam to maintain thousands of forces in South Vietnam—forces that North Vietnam denied were in the South but known by all parties to be there. The South Vietnamese government officials vehemently opposed this provision, but were forced to accept it by the United States. This facet of the agreement gave North Vietnam the foothold it needed to continue the war and undermine South Vietnam.[90] As North Vietnam would later acknowledge, the Paris Agreement was designed to "get the Americans out and gain time to make preparations to overthrow the GVN [Government of South Vietnam], which had been forced to concede its heretofore 'basic requirement'—the withdrawal of North Vietnamese troops from South Vietnam."[91]

The Paris Agreement did little to slow the aggression from the North. By September of 1973, just eight months after the agreement was signed, North Vietnam had sent 140,000 tons of war supplies to the South and had infiltrated an additional 100,000 troops into the South. This included infantry divisions, artillery regiments, an antiaircraft artillery division, an armored regiment, an engineering regiment and other reinforcements. The United States did nothing to counter this buildup, for the Fulbright-Aiken amendment which became effective on August 15, 1973 provided that "no funds herein or heretofore appropriated may be obligated or expended to finance directly or indirectly combat activities by United States military forces in or over or from off the shores of North Vietnam, South Vietnam, Laos or Cambodia."[92] The buildup of North Vietnamese forces in the South continued into 1974 and 1975 with the infiltration of thousands of additional troops and tons of war supplies many times those of previous years.[93]

In October of 1973, just nine months after signing the Paris Agreement, North Vietnam's Communist Party Central Committee's 21st Plenum set forth the plan combining the political, military and diplomatic struggle to overthrow South Vietnam. An article titled the *Great Spring Victory* by Senior General Van Tien Dung, published in the Lao Dong Party newspaper, *Nhan Dan*, on April 1, 1976, outlines the 21st Plenum's resolution and concept for the final offensive in the South. The basic guidance was expressed in the following terms: "The path of the revolution in the south is the path of revolutionary violence. No matter what the situation, we must firmly grasp the opportunity and the strategic offensive line and effect flexible leadership to advance the southern revolution."[94]

General Dung's article describes a meeting of North Vietnam's senior military officials, the Central Military Party Committee, in March 1974 to study and implement the 21st Plenum resolution. The Committee concluded that "the southern revolution must firmly grasp the concept of strategic offensive. We must resolutely counterattack and attack the enemy, and we must firmly maintain and develop our active position in all respects." Following the Party Committee meeting, the General Staff set about formulating strategic combat and battlefield plans. Additional armies were organized and trained, and orders went out to the various battlefield units to "step up activities, conduct offensive and uprising waves, win victories and seize the initiative in order to change the battlefield situation and to facilitate large-scale offensives to be launched everywhere in 1975."[95]

According to General Dung, by late 1974 South Vietnam's combat capability had been weakened to the point where North Vietnam's capability was "altogether superior" and the balance of forces had shifted to their favor. He described South Vietnamese forces as being "passive and utterly weakened." He saw that the reduction of U.S. aid had made it impossible for the South Vietnamese to carry out their combat plan and build up their forces. Dung stated that South Vietnam was then "forced to fight a poor man's war." Dung described South Vietnam's combat capability in these terms: "Enemy firepower had decreased by nearly 60 percent because of bomb and ammunition shortages. Its mobility was also reduced by half due to the lack of aircraft, vehicles and fuel. Thus, the enemy had to shift from large-scale operations and helleborn deep-thrust and tank mounted attacks to small-scale blocking, nibbling and searching operations."[96]

In October 1974, the Political Bureau and Central Committee gathered in Hanoi to assess the situation in the South. They welcomed the assessment that South Vietnam had become militarily, politically and economically weakened, and correctly concluded that the United States was unable to come to the South's aid due to "the internal contradictions within the U.S. administration and among U.S. political parties..." The Political Bureau resolved to proceed with all determination to carry out the two-year strategic plan for 1975 and 1976 to liberate the South. Eying the weakened position in the South, the Political Bureau stressed the desire to launch the offensive earlier than originally planned.[97]

In early March 1975 the final offensive consisting of 20 army divisions was launched by North Vietnam. The South Vietnamese armed forces, weakened by the withdrawal of support by the United States, were no match for the overwhelming forces from the North which were fully equipped with the latest in military hardware from the Soviet Union and China. Saigon fell on April 30, 1975, less than two months after the offensive began and far short of the two year campaign anticipated by Hanoi.[98]

The Façade Exposed

Irrefutable evidence has been presented in this chapter showing that the armed insurgency in South Vietnam was planned, coordinated, supported and directed by North Vietnam; that the National Liberation Front was an arm of the Lao Dong Party in Hanoi; that the main military forces were infiltrated from the North; that the International Control Commission confirmed that the aggression was from the North; that the Soviet Union, China and Communist bloc countries provided the war materials necessary for Hanoi to carry out its war in the South;

and that in the end, North Vietnam launched a massive, conventional invasion to finally defeat South Vietnam.

So much for Hanoi's "civil war" façade!

Charts of the Viet Cong Organization, North and South
(See section IV.)

Lines of control, political and military, from the Hanoi regime to the Viet Cong in South Viet-Nam.

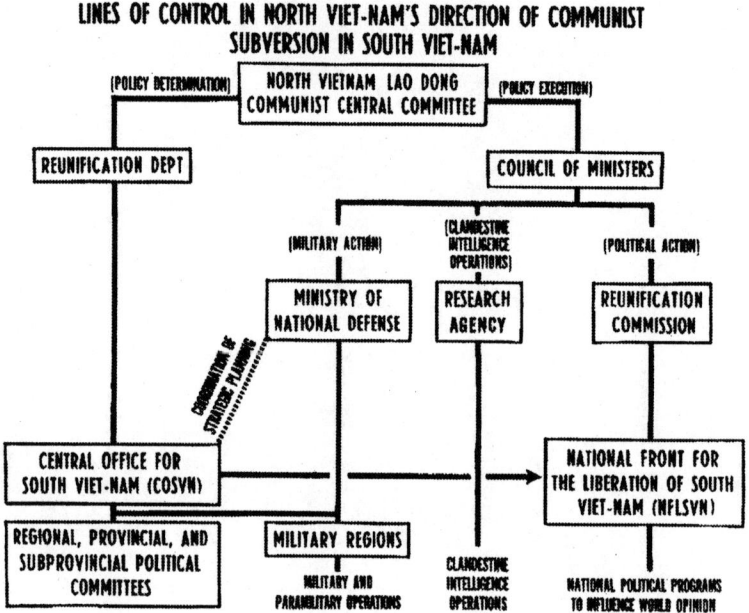

Figure 1. Department of State Pub. 7839, Feb. 1965

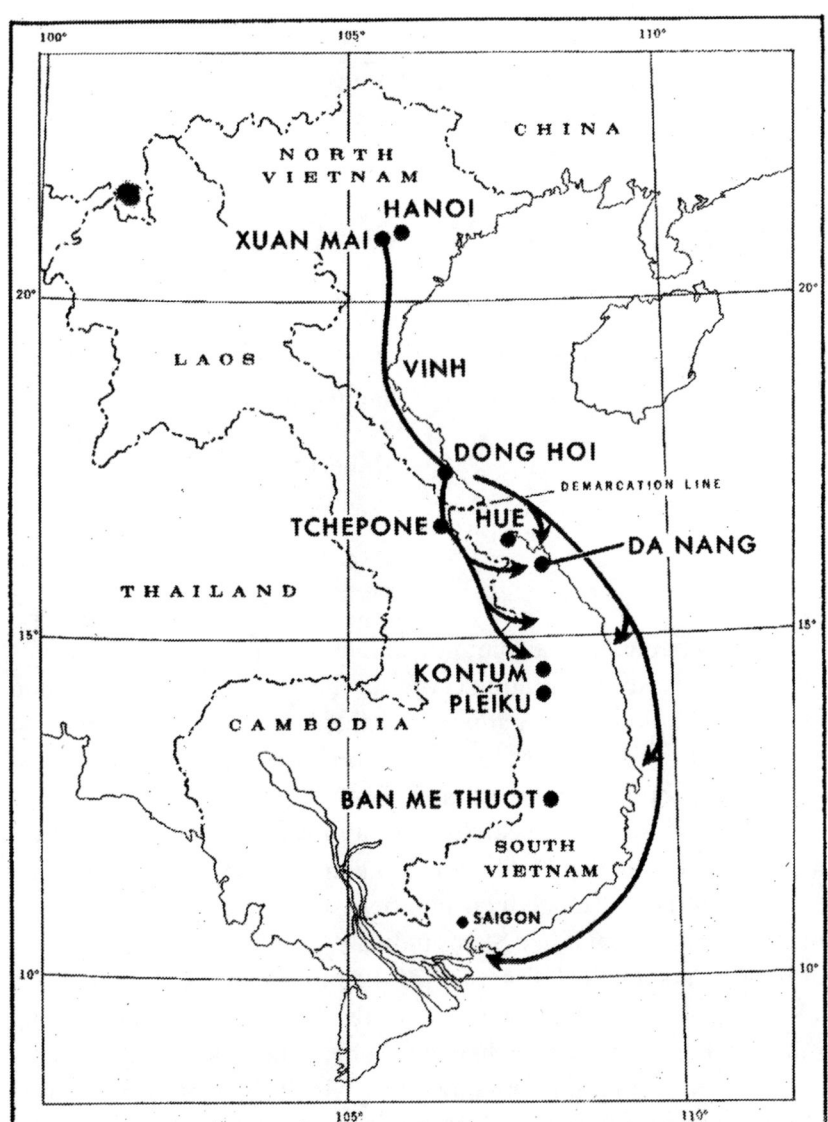

Figure 2. Early Infiltration Routes. Dept. of State Pub. Feb. 1965

Chapter Four

The Rise of the Second Front

A nation's deepest strength lies not in its military prowess but, rather, in the unity of its people

—Robert S. McNamara

This chapter is about the antiwar factions that formed the nucleus of the antiwar movement and served as the vanguard of the second front. It will explore the organizations, their leaders, their objectives, their political leanings and their international connections. The most incredible aspect of the antiwar movement is that so many could have been misled by so few. In researching the antiwar movement, it becomes evident almost at once that a handful of activists were able to attract a following that far exceeded their numbers. A 1967 CIA memorandum to the President of the United States indicates that "the responsibility for coordination and tactical direction [of the movement] is delegated to a small staff of key leaders. The names of these key coordinators turn up regularly, wherever the action happens to be." Many of the key activists were involved in multiple organizations which facilitated interaction and coordination between the various antiwar groups. The 1967 CIA memo reflects that the political leanings of the activists ranged from left of center to the far left. The memo outlined the Communist connection in these terms: "Many are Marxist-oriented, but the Marxists come in all colors. Take the Communists: the 'orthodox' Moscow-oriented Communists, the Peking-influenced 'Marxist-Leninists,' and the self-oriented Trotskyites are all energetically active in the Vietnam protest activity. It would be surprising if they were not since the objectives of the movement are consistent with the national interests of the USSR and

Communist China....Both the individual peace [antiwar] groups and the coordinating organizations, are well infiltrated with Communists of one stripe or another."[1]

In testimony before a United States Senate Subcommittee in 1969, Max Friedman, who had infiltrated the antiwar movement, summed up Communist infiltration and domination of the U.S. peace movement in this way:

> 1. The Communist Party-USA [CPUSA] has maintained overall leadership of the peace movement by its use of cover party members who have gotten into key leadership positions of the various regional and specialized peace groups.
>
> 2. The Socialist Workers Party – Young Socialist Alliance [SWP-YSA] has made an open attempt to manipulate the peace movement at the Cleveland Conference by attempting to stack the meeting in its favor.
>
> 3. While there is a definite doctrinal split between the two major communist parties, CPUSA and SWP, there is however a unity in their efforts to weaken the will of the United States in resisting Communist aggression against the Republic of South Vietnam.
>
> 4. Many legitimate peace groups in the U.S. are now being manipulated or duped by the Communists to further communist goals, i.e. defeating the U.S. and Allies in their efforts to resist communist aggression in the Republic of South Vietnam, an overall weakening of the U.S. defense posture in world affairs, and helping to set up the groundwork for an overall Communist military and political victory in all of Southeast Asia.
>
> 5. The SWP-YSA has made great inroads into capturing leadership of the student protest movement in the U.S. and has made significant progress in recruiting students into the anti-Vietnam war movement....[2]

When the true nature and purpose of the antiwar activists are understood, it is difficult to comprehend how they were able to incite such a large and diverse following. In almost every case, the leaders and their organizational hierarchy sided with the enemy; some openly wanted the other side to win; they supported the negotiation points offered by the Communists; they wanted unilateral withdrawal by the United States; they were ready to sell out our allies in Southeast Asia; they felt that South Vietnam would be better off under the totalitarian rule of the Communist North; they were willing to have us sign a peace agreement which left our POWs unaccounted for and still in the hands of our enemies; their role models were Mao, Marx, Lenin, Castro, and Che Guevara; they believed that the road to peace was the Marxist-Leninist road of revolution against imperialism; and their objective in the United States was a revolution to tear down the existing government and evil capitalist system, and replace it with some form of a socialist (communist) system. One of many illustrations of this thinking comes from a conference of antiwar groups from throughout the nation held in Cleveland in April 1967. A member of the steering committee, Professor Douglas Dowd, summed up the objectives of the forthcoming demonstration:

> The short-run aim of the Washington demonstration will be to end the war in Vietnam, but not to end the movement. A second longer range goal of the demonstration would be to change the system, to end the imperialist system which produced the war, racism, and poverty, and he referred to "this insane society," referring to the American society. He added that the time had come not to resist, but to fight.[3]

The question that begs an answer is how any American could buy into such a distorted view of their own country and the war, especially when many of the leaders and proponents were intellectuals and academics from our most prestigious universities and institutions. James Webb, a Marine platoon leader and company commander in Vietnam and a former Secretary of the Navy, was also perplexed by this question. In *Sleeping with the Enemy*, he wrote:

It is difficult to explain to my children that in my teens and early twenties the most frequently heard voices of my peers were trying to destroy the foundation of American society, so that it might be rebuilt according to their own narcissistic notions. In retrospect, it's hard even for some of us who went through those times to understand how highly educated people—most of them spawned from the comforts of the upper-middle class—could have seriously advanced the destructive ideas that were in the air during the late '60s and early '70s. Even Congress was influenced by the virus.[4]

Before delving into the various antiwar groups, it is worthwhile to see how Hanoi felt about the antiwar movement in the United States. In a reply to a message from two of America's leaders of the peace/antiwar movement, Dr. Benjamin Spock and Professor Stuart Hughes, Ho Chi Minh had this to say:

> Thank you for your message dated October 26, [1965]....I take this opportunity to warmly hail the American people's struggle for the immediate ending of the U.S. Government's criminal war of aggression in Vietnam, the cessation of the air attacks on the territory of the D.R.V., the withdrawal of the U.S. troops, and for democratic liberties against racial discrimination.[5]
>
> Sincerely,
> Ho Chi Minh

The antiwar movement spawned a wide variety of organizations on the local, regional and national scene. There are far too many to fit into the space of a single book or even several books. Therefore, only a few of the major organizations that had influence on a national scale will be addressed here.

Teach-ins

The early activities of the antiwar movement were characterized by teach-ins led by professors at many of the colleges and universities across the nation. The teach-in movement is said to have had its beginning at the University of Michigan, where it was launched in March 1965 by Eric J. Wolf, professor of anthropology; William A. Gamson, assistant professor of sociology; and Arnold S. Kaufman, associate professor of philosophy. The teach-ins were promoted by members of the academic community as a new tool in the education process designed to freely explore all aspects of the war in Vietnam. They were to be a critical analysis and unbiased discussion of government policies by "scholars" in the academic community.[6] An investigation by the Internal Security Subcommittee of the Senate Committee on the Judiciary found something quite different:

> In reality, the great majority of the teach-ins (there were a few notable exceptions to this rule) have had absolutely nothing in common with the procedures of fair debate or the process of education. In practice they were a combination of an indoctrination session, a political protest demonstration, an endurance contest, and a variety show.
>
> At most of the teach-ins the administration's [White House] point of view was given only token representation. The great majority of the speakers, by deliberate design, were critics of the administration....
>
> Communist propaganda films were frequently shown. Communist literature was frequently distributed. People of known Communist background were frequently involved.
>
> And at virtually every teach-in, the anti-administration speakers vied with each other in their extremist denunciations of administration policy.[7]

A study in 1965 by the American Security Council, a former think tank on international politics and national security, resulted in the following findings:

It may be argued that one of these new forms [of propaganda and subversion] is the "teach-in" which is being used to persuade Americans that victory over the Viet Cong is impossible. The term is misleading, of course, for the aim of the "teach-ins" is not to teach, but to indoctrinate the public in defeatism and to subject the U.S. government to moral condemnations.

In many instances the supporters as well as those who condemn the Administration's policy in Vietnam have been allowed to speak. However, all too frequently the "teach-in" had less resemblance to a debate or a course of university lectures than to the kind of public "trial" often used by Communist states to destroy individuals and ideas inimical to their revolutionary societies.

The root source of the entire Vietnam protest campaign is the "New Left," a coalition of Communists, Maoists, and militant Marxists of various shades....

Among the left-wing organizations taking part in the psychological warfare campaign, in addition to the regular Communist parry channels, are the Socialist Workers Party, the Young Socialist Alliance, Workers World Party, Youth Against War and Fascism, Progressive Labor Movement and the May 2 Movement [all with Communist affiliations]. In a space of months, a vast network of new front groups has been created. Manipulated by a core group of veteran signers of front petitions, many hundreds of university professors have attached their names to statements aimed at taking pressure off the Viet Cong.[8]

It is obvious from the foregoing investigations that for the most part, teach-ins were used as a tool to turn the minds of our youths on college campuses, as well as anyone else who could be reached, into antiwar and anti-administration zealots. They were a powerful instrument of psychological warfare, and were successful in stirring up opposition to the government and support for the antiwar movement.

The American Security Council concluded that "the aim of the 'teach-ins' seems to have been—and, in the future, will be—not so much to promote learning as to disorient the student and faculty participants. And not these alone but beyond them the American people. The ultimate aim seems to be to disorient the American public and make the American people lose faith in their government and in the correctness of our policy in Southeast Asia and Latin America."[9]

As early as mid-1965, the Senate Internal Security Subcommittee investigating the anti-Vietnam agitation and the teach-in movement uncovered the extremist nature of the antiwar and teach-in movement. The subcommittee reached the following conclusions:

> The control of the anti-Vietnam movement has clearly passed from the hands of the moderate elements who may have controlled it at one time, into the hands of Communists and extremist elements who are openly sympathetic to the Viet Cong and openly hostile to the United States, and who call for massive civil disobedience, including the burning of draft cards and the stopping of troop trains....
>
> The evidence is overwhelming that the world Communist apparatus—in the United States, in Moscow, in Peking [Beijing], in Hanoi, in Havana, and elsewhere—has been able to exploit the anti-Vietnam agitation and the teach-in movement for the purpose of confusing their own people, for the purpose of fostering the impression that the majority of the American people are opposed to the administration's policy in Vietnam, and for the purpose of attacking the morale of American servicemen in Vietnam.[10]

The question that was raised earlier about why American intellectuals and academics would be drawn into such destructive and even disloyal activities still begs for an answer. Stewart Alsop, a noted columnist for the *Saturday Evening Post*, was also perplexed by this behavior. In May of 1965 he wrote, "It is mysterious that so many American intellectuals look forward with complacency—even positive relish—to Communist victory in Asia, which they regard as inevitable."[11]

With the growth of the antiwar movement, teach-ins declined and emphasis shifted to large demonstrations promoted by a proliferation of antiwar groups and coordinating committees.

May 2nd Movement (M2M)

The May 2nd Movement was one of the early antiwar movements to be established on campuses. The name was derived from the date, May 2, 1964, when it was founded by college students. According to the FBI, "It was founded and was directed largely by members of the pro-Peking Communist organization in the U.S., the Progressive Labor Movement (PLM). It was extremely well-financed, in large measure through the generosity of a Harvard student who was a millionaire. Headquarters were in Cambridge, Mass., where some ten to twenty full-time staff were employed."[12] The May 2nd Movement focused its efforts on opposing the war in Vietnam, and FBI reports suggest that it was supported by Moscow Communists and other splinter groups. This movement was highly successful during the first year, but declined as other more powerful groups sprang up.[13]

The Inter-University Committee for Debate on Foreign Policy

This was a national organization formed after the first teach-in at the University of Michigan. Most of the founders were from that University, but the membership was expanded to include a number of other colleges. An FBI report in 1965 described this group and its activities:

> The group spurred scores of teach-ins on other campuses during the spring of 1965 and ultimately produced the national teach-in in Washington, D.C. on May 15. Its latest undertaking [in 1965] was an international seminar, following the pattern set by the teach-ins, at Ann Arbor on September 15-16. As in the past, only known opponents of U.S. policy were included as participants. The professors involved on the policy-making committee included pacifists, left-liberals,

socialists and communists, with a smattering of Asian experts. The group was responsible, in large measure, for the outburst of newspaper ads, particularly in the New York Times, last spring from various groupings of university professors. Much of the financing comes from one of the Michigan professors. In addition, it is believed that funds come also from such sympathizers of the Communist cause as Cyrus Eaton, the millionaire industrialist, and Corliss Lemont, of the financial family.

The cost of a single page of advertising in the N.Y. Times [in 1965] exceeds $6,000. We estimate that the cost of the Times ads placed by the opposition amounted to $60,000 to $100,000 during 1965's first eight months. Similarly, the group paid for all plane and travel expenses of the conference participants at Ann Arbor in September. Such an ambitious undertaking involving participants from many parts of the world could not have been carried out for less than $50,000.[14]

Students for a Democratic Society

The Students for a Democratic Society (SDS) was the largest and most influential organization of the 1960's. At its peak, membership reached approximately 40,000 with 170 chapters located mainly on college campuses throughout the United States. Its national headquarters was located in Chicago, Illinois.[15]

The House of Representatives conducted an extensive investigation of the Students for a Democratic Society in 1970. The resulting report, *Anatomy of a Revolutionary Movement*, describes how a self-proclaimed anarchistic group was bent on ending our present form of government. The report is much too lengthy for inclusion here except for a few excerpts:

> SDS began, in seemingly relative innocence, as a peacefully inclined, anti-communist but left-leaning organization of students anxious to right the wrongs and correct the abuses, real and imagined, which they

felt most strongly made their America's democratic society imperfect in the extreme.

In its founding days (1959-62), SDS languished. As it became more activist, later increased its militancy, and turned toward more radical leaders, methods, tactics, and objectives, it achieved a growing following. In the mid-1960's its doors were opened to extremists bearing the banners of communism, anarchism, and nihilism....

By the late 1960's the voice of SDS became more strident. No longer did it seek reform, rather—revolution. Dissent was not enough. It sought destruction of the entire free enterprise, democratic system under which this Republic had grown and prospered.

SDS leaders began describing themselves as revolutionary communists, studied Marx, Lenin, and the "thoughts" of Mao Tse-tung, and hero-worshipped the Latin American communist guerilla fighter, Che Guevara. But FBI Director J. Edgar Hoover wisely warned the Congress in 1968, in comparing the New Left—of which SDS was then a "primary spokesman"— with the Old Left:

> The new left should not be arbitrarily equated with the traditional old-line left. Although they become prey to the superior organizational ability and talents of the old-line subversive organizations, such as the Communist Party-U.S.A., the Socialist Workers Party, and the like, to simply identity them as Moscow or Peking Communists would be missing the point. To put it bluntly, they are a new type of subversive and their danger is great.[16]

In hearings on the Students for a Democratic Society by the House Committee on Internal Security in 1969, additional facts about SDS were brought to light:

The Port Huron Statement [the manifesto of SDS]—drafted by Tom Hayden and adopted with some revision at a national convention of SDS at Port Huron, Michigan in June 1962—introduced the aim of achieving "participatory democracy," described in the statement as social changes which would increase individual participation in [the] decision-making process in the political and economic life of America. The convention decided that the "profit system" is "a fundamental thing to be moved aside so that the country can move ahead," Tom Hayden stated during testimony before the House Committee on the Un-American Activities....

The policy-making National Council of SDS, in December 1968, adopted a resolution stating that SDS must reach out beyond campuses to recruit "working class youth" for the purpose of building SDS into a "revolutionary youth movement," which in turn would build a "full revolutionary working class movement." Another National Council resolution, adopted in March 1969, stated: "We become a vanguard force when we educate the people that fulfillment of their demands requires a socialist revolution." The same resolution declared that the American educational system cannot really be changed to "serve the people" until "the power of the whole capitalist class is challenged and destroyed."[17]

Testifying before the House Committee on Internal Security in September 1968, J Edgar Hoover said:

In recent months, student disturbances have exploded on college and university campuses throughout the United States, initiated by student activists, many of whom are affiliated with the SDS or campus-based black extremist groups.

> The protest activity of the new left and the SDS, under the guise of legitimate expressions of dissent, has created an insurrectionary climate which has conditioned a number of young Americans—especially college students—to resort to civil disobedience and violence....[18]

An FBI report released in 1968 summarizes the political leanings and objectives of the Students for a Democratic Society:

> The Students for a Democratic Society advocates what many of its leaders and members call revolutionary communism. Along this line, at the organization's 1968 national convention, two of the newly elected national officers publicly identified themselves as communists, "with a small c," as many New Left adherents do to signify that while they are communists they are a brand apart from the old-line communist movement.

> While the distinction may seem important to them, it is irrelevant to the rest of America because the basic objective of both New Left and the old-line communists and their adherents in our society is to completely destroy our form of government.[19]

Irrespective of the brand of communism associated with SDS and the New Left, their stand on Vietnam leaves no doubt about where their allegiance resided. Walt Rostow, former National Security Advisor to Presidents Kennedy and Johnson, made the following observation about the New Left's position on Vietnam:

> Finally there was the New Left position: that authentic American security interests in Asia, as elsewhere, are nonexistent, but are simply fabricated by the economic and other vested interests of the private and public bureaucracies that control American life. Therefore, the defeat of the United States in Southeast Asia is required to destroy the grip of these institutions so that

American society can move forward, restructured, on a more humanistic basis.[20]

Statements by national leaders of SDS and former leaders give us additional insight into the true nature of SDS. As you read these statements, consider that these are the people who were on our campuses extolling the youths of American to follow them in tearing down everything that was good about this country.

<u>Mark Rudd</u>, an SDS leader in riots at Columbia University, in a letter to president of the university dated April 12, 1968, prior to the seizure of campus buildings:
> "You are quite right in fearing that the situation is potentially dangerous. If we win, we will take control of your world, your corporations, your university and attempt to mold a world in which we and other people can live as human beings. We will have to destroy at times, even violently, in order to end your power and your system—but that is a far cry from nihilism."

<u>Greg Calvert</u>, an SDS spokesman who traveled in the Midwest to speak before various SDS chapters, was quoted as describing SDS motives and goals in society as follows:
> "We are trying to build a guerrilla force in an urban environment; we are actively organizing sedition."

<u>Michael Klonsky</u>, SDS national secretary, speech at a rally at the University of Florida, April 11, 1969:
> He said that it was time for revolution and for students and the oppressed minority to kick out the present system and form a "truly communistic society that would work for the poor and the oppressed."

<u>Carl Davidson</u>, an SDS spokesman, speaking at the University of Illinois in 1967:

Davidson stated that students could not free their universities without freeing all of society and that anything destroying the "United States system" would be beneficial. He told the student listeners that one weapon was to shut down "this place."

Thomas Hayden, drafter of Port Huron Statement of principles of SDS and president of SDS 1962-1963, testified December 3, 1968 before the House Committee on Un-American Activities:

> "But I do advocate action that could bring a university to a halt, as the actions of the students and faculty at San Fran [Francisco] State have brought that university to a halt, to try to straighten the university out."[21]

In another investigation, the Senate Subcommittee on the Extent of Subversion in Campus Disorders documented the following testimony concerning SDS by Ernesto E. Blanco, Associate Professor, Tufts University:

> The Marxist students are classified here as Students for a Democratic Society which is a loose and unstable confederacy of Marxist students. The composition of SDS, as I explained before, consists of the Progressive Labor Party, (Maoists); W.E.B. DuBois, the youths arm of the American Communist Party; the Communist Party (USSR); the Young Socialist Alliance (Trotskyites); Castroite followers; and black radicals, plus other dissident elements....You may wonder how they align themselves, because they actually are bitter enemies. The reason is that they all hope to control the eventual outcome of the revolution so they are aligning themselves to destroy American society, the common enemy, and then they will struggle among themselves.[22]

In justifying the actions of SDS activists in disrupting the Democratic national convention in Chicago in 1968, Thomas Hayden, one of the conspiracy defendants, shows contempt for the democratic institutions of the United States and allegiance with our enemies in his book, *Trial*. He wrote:

> First of all, we were internationalists....Not only were we against the war in Vietnam; we aligned ourselves with the Vietnamese people....The world we see is one in which a decadent and super-rich American empire, with principles of racial superiority, private property, and armed might, is falling apart. We want to join with the new humanity, not a dying empire.[23]

One of the most disturbing aspects of the movement and activists like Tom Hayden was their desire for the defeat of their own country. As Hayden states in the previous quote, they aligned themselves with the [North] Vietnamese people. Hayden writes in *Trail* that the movement was effective in several ways, one of which was that "it gave encouragement to the Vietnamese revolutionaries [Viet Cong and North Vietnamese] while demoralizing the American military and the puppets they supported." He also writes with obvious glee that "in the year 1968 we [antiwar activists] achieved the first clear setback in the American escalation strategy. It was the year of military defeat [the Tet offensive] and political catastrophe."[24] As one who lived through the 1968 Tet offensive, I find that anyone who was pleased with our "setback" and the major loss of American lives during that offensive is guilty of treason and does not deserve to avail themselves of the opportunities offered by living in a free, democratic society.

Although the mounting turmoil on the nation's college and university campuses in 1968 and 1969 was attributed to SDS, factionalism erupted at the June 1969 SDS convention which resulted in a breakup of SDS into three disparate groups. According to the FBI, SDS split into three organizations in June 1969. They were the Weathermen faction; the Worker Student Alliance (WSA); and the Revolutionary Youth Movement (RYM). In 1970 factionalism within SDS/WSA led to the complete takeover of that organization by the Progressive Labor Party (PLP), a Marxist-Leninist organization that advocated the violent overthrow of the government.[25] The Weathermen faction of SDS became one of the most virulent practitioners of violence in the nation.

Weathermen (AKA Weatherman)

The Weathermen group, which became known as the Weather Underground (WUO), rose out of the ashes of SDS in June 1969. The basic ideology of this group was stated as "Marxist-Leninist in content but with strong advocacy that action, not theory, would bring about revolution in the United States." In mid-February 1970, members of the Weathermen entered underground status with an intended program of "strategic sabotage" with police and military installations as primary targets.[26]

A more ominous mission statement appeared in a book titled, *Prairie Fire,* prepared by the Weather Underground. It advocated "the violent overthrow of the bourgeoisie, the establishment of the dictatorship of the proletariat, and the eradication of the social system based on profit."[27] The expression of this ideology is of no surprise in that, according to the FBI, the Cuban revolution became the model for the student revolutionary movement in the United States. Meetings between antiwar activists and representatives of North Vietnam in Czechoslovakia and Havana from 1967 to 1969 led to a pronounced increase in the influence of Vietnamese Communists on SDS leadership. Likewise, frequent trips to Havana by Weather Underground members gave them first hand knowledge on how to create a revolution. In July 1969, Bernadine Dohrn, Eleanor Ruskin, Dianne Donghi, Peter Clapp, David Millstone and Diana Oughton, all representing WUO, traveled to Cuba to meet with representatives of North Vietnamese and Cuban governments. According to the FBI, Cuba had an enormous influence on the developing WUO.[28] That influence is clearly evident in the following statement of WUO's goals and strategy:

> The goal is the destruction of US imperialism and the achievement of a classless world: world communism. Winning state power in the US will occur as a result of the military forces of the US overextending themselves around the world and being defeated piecemeal; struggle within the US will be a vital part of this process, but when the revolution triumphs in the US it will have been made by the people of the whole world. For socialism to be defined in national terms within so extreme and historical an oppressor nation as this is

only imperialist national chauvinism on the part of the "movement"....

Our final goal is the destruction of imperialism, the seizure of power, and the creation of socialism.

The strategy...is what Che called "creating two, three, many Vietnams" to mobilize the struggle so sharply in so many places that the imperialists cannot possibly deal with it all. Since it is essential to their interests, they will try to deal with it all, and will be defeated and destroyed in the process...[29]

From its formation in June 1969, the Weather Underground left a trail of bombings, riots and violent protests. The FBI attributed numerous bombings to the WUO. Police, educational institutions and large corporations seemed to be the favorite targets. Some of the bombings attributable to WUO by the FBI or which WUO claimed to have done are listed below:

October 26, 1969: The WUO kicked off the National Action protest with the bombing of the Haymarket police station in Chicago.
February 16, 1970: A bomb detonated at the Golden Gate Park Branch of the San Francisco police department, killing one officer and injuring a number of other policemen.
May 10, 1970: The National Guard Association building in Washington D.C. was bombed.
June 9, 1970: The WUO bombed the headquarters building of the New York City police department. The same day they bombed the Bank of America building in New York City.
October 8, 1970: The WUO bombed the hall of Justice, Marin County, CA. On the same day they bombed the National Guard facility in Santa Barbara, CA.
October 10, 1970: The Long Island City, New York Court House was bombed by WUO.

<u>March 1, 1971:</u> The United States Capitol in Washington D.C. was bombed by WUO.
<u>May 19, 1972:</u> The Pentagon in Washington D.C. was bombed.
<u>January 28, 1975:</u> The U.S. State Department in Washington D.C. was bombed by WUO.[30]

These incidents are just a sampling of several dozen bombings by the WUO between 1969 and 1975. During an 18 month period, 20 police officers were killed and 100 were wounded in unprovoked, politically motivated attacks and bombings. A number of the WUO members were indicted by a Federal Grand Jury for these attacks. Many became Federal fugitives, and some fled the country, finding refuge in Cuba and elsewhere.[30]

The influence of Castro's Cuba, the Weather Underground and other New Left revolutionaries is evidenced not only in ideology, but in a pattern of actions. For instance, Mark Rudd, leader of America's violent left, visited Cuba in February and March of 1968 with 20 other activists. Two months later, with Rudd in the lead, Columbia University was the scene of one of the most devastating uprisings ever to occur on a college campus.[31]

Similarly, as described in an FBI report, "Bernadine Dohrn, the mini-skirted Weatherwoman and 30 fellow activists met with Vietnamese Communists in Havana in July, 1969. Three months later, with the fiery Bernadine in command, a shocked Chicago watched as several hundred ultra-radical Weathermen staged a wild, window-smashing rampage which they called 'Four Days of Rage' in protest against the Vietnam War."[32]

A note left behind by those who bombed the University of Wisconsin Army Math Center clearly linked the incident to the Cuban Revolution. The note indicated that "the destruction of the Math Center was not an act of a lunatic. Rather, the note stated it was a 'conscious action taken in solidarity with the Viet Cong, the Tupamaros and the Cuban people and all other heroic fighter against U.S. imperialism.'"[33]

The FBI concluded, "Beyond any doubt, Cuba has shaped, supplied technical training to, given political indoctrination for and, perhaps most important of all, served as the inspiration for the American radical movement in its avowed aim to bring down the American system that it so fiercely despises." What had become clear was that the contacts between Communists and American radicals had reached a stage of hard core indoctrination and even collaboration. By 1965 Havana became filled with North Vietnamese delegations, and Cuba opened an embassy for the Viet Cong. Soon, thereafter, "U.S. radicals were meeting with the North Vietnamese in Havana, and even getting suggestions on antiwar activities in the United States."[34]

The FBI estimated that approximately 4,000 American left and radicals of various shades visited Cuba during the 60's.[35] Many of them were there as part of what was known as the Venceremos Brigade.

Venceremos Brigade

"Venceremos" is Spanish for "We shall win." The pro-Castro Venceremos Brigade was a creation of SDS leadership, primarily Weathermen, to help Cuba with the annual harvest of sugar cane. According to the FBI, Julie Nichamin, who was a key person in setting up these trips, "spent January through April 1969 in Cuba obtaining her revolutionary experience and being influenced directly by the Cubans and North Vietnamese. Her statements on the international aspects of revolution go to the heart of the future Weather Underground rationale for committing armed struggle within the United States."[36]

A CIA report in December 1969 described the first contingent of the Brigade which departed for Cuba in November 1969:

> These [Brigade members] were predominantly Black Panthers and members of Students for a Democratic Society, plus other radicalized American youth, all sharing pro-Castro sentiments and opposing what they term U.S. imperialism.
>
> The Brigade "campamento" (tent camp) was located near Aquacate, about a two-hour bus ride from Havana. Its Director was Javier Ardizones, international relations coordinator for the Young Communist League, who told the volunteers their presence helped to destroy the U.S. attempts to "blockade Cuba from the rest of the world." His listeners cheered when they learned the Cuban harvest was dedicated to the people of Vietnam.

Brigade members will work for 6 weeks. The final two weeks of the two-month visit are reserved for recreation including a tour of Cuba....Havana [radio] Prensa Latina carried taped messages...from Brigade members....Three Bostonians...told their friends in the U.S. how Cuba's struggle against U.S. imperialism...is "the same struggle that we will fight when we get back to the United States."[37]

Beginning in November 1969, there were dozens of Venceremos contingents traveling to Cuba, some with as many as 500 in one group. It is important for the survival of our form of government to understand the nature of the ideology these individuals brought back to the United States and there purpose in doing so. The most enlightening expression of this purpose was presented in the June 18, 1969 issue of *New Left Notes*, the official publication of SDS. It is captioned, "A Proposal on the Cuban Revolution," and has ominous overtones even today, for there are a number of graduates of the Venceremos Brigade scattered throughout the country and the Venceremos organization is still in existence today. Excerpts from the proposal are provided below.

As Participants in an anti-capitalist, anti-imperialist movement, we fully support the Cuban revolution on the basis of the following:

1. The Cuban socialist revolution has brought about a redistribution of wealth and created an economic policy aimed at creating the economic basis (abundance) for a communist society.

2. Cuba is among the vanguard of an effort to revitalize socialism and create a new socialist man, having clearly learned a great deal from the shortcomings of socialism as practiced in the Soviet Union and Eastern Europe. The gradual elimination of money, the use of moral incentives, mass participation in the military and political process, the building of mass consciousness, authentic measures to destroy class differences and to prevent the emergence of a new bureaucratic class—all

are part of Cuba's experiment in the creation of a new socialism.

3. Cuba has developed a new concept of internationalism…"the duty of every revolutionary is to make the revolution." Che's call for "two, three, many Vietnams" is a strategy for the defeat of imperialism, and the guiding concept for a new international center in the Third World and linked to the black liberation struggle as well as struggles in all advanced capitalist countries.

4. Since Cuba is the first liberated territory in the Americas, it is under constant attack by the US government. As North Americans dedicated to the destruction of imperialism, it is our obligation to oppose our government's policies in the most effective and concrete way possible.[38]

Excerpts from an interview in Havana with Julie Nichamin reported in the December 10, 1969 issue of *GRANMA*, the official organ of the Central Committee of the Communist Party of Cuba, provide some answers to the reasons for the existence of the Venceremos Brigade:

QUESTION: How did you get the idea for the Brigade? And why do you call it Venceremos?

NICHAMIN: We had the idea of forming a brigade to be sent to Cuba to fight beside the Cubans in the battle of the ten million tons [sugar cane harvest]. We want people to understand that the battle of the Cuban people, like the battle of the Vietnamese people is the same battle to which we are committed, a battle against American imperialism. We thought that by coming here we could demonstrate things….

QUESTION: Who made up this brigade?

NICHAMIN: The National Committee of the Brigade was responsible for organizing in the United States. They set up regional committees in 15 cities. These committees were made up of people who wanted to help the Brigade and support Cuban Revolution.

QUESTION: What benefit have you gained from your experience here in Cuba, working with the Cuban people?

NICHAMIN: One of the most important things we have learned and are learning is a revolutionary conscience.

QUESTION: How do you feel in Cuba?

NICHAMIN: Now I can understand better the nature of the battle and how the Cubans can be so sure of the advance of the battle in the United States and the rest of the world. I think it is the most important thing I learned here to believe in our power to change things, believe in the power of the people to conquer and destroy imperialism.

Between questions, Nichamin stated that "The way for us to attack American imperialism is by fighting on many fronts."[39]

The Brigade members from America had their own idea of what their visits to Cuba were about, but the Cuban government had its own reasons for promoting the Brigade, most having nothing to do with harvesting sugar cane. Cuban leaders were naturally pleased with their brand of revolution and communism being spread to the United States by the Brigade; they were eager to foster anything that would undermine the United States; and they were very interested in recruiting converts who could help them gather intelligence on the United States. Many of the Brigade members were approached by agents of Castro's General Directorate for Intelligence (DGI). A Top Secret FBI Report (now declassified) on Cuban interest in Brigade members reveals DGI's objectives:

The DGI's interest in the VB is an extension of its overall policy relating to the collection of intelligence on the U.S., its primary target. The DGI considers recruitment of the VB [Venceremos Brigade] members, selected after detailed assessment, as one of the primary means through which intelligence can be collected on the U.S.

The DGI believes that it is to their advantage to establish and maintain contact with organizations, groups and individuals who are sympathetic to the Cuban revolution and who are disenchanted with present conditions in the U.S., and it sees the VB as such a group.

The ultimate objective in the DGI's participation with the VB is the recruitment of individuals who are politically oriented and who someday may obtain a position, elective or appointive, somewhere in the U.S. Government, which would provide the Cuban government with access to political, economic and military intelligence. In addition, the DGI attempts to select individuals who can legitimately apply for membership to various political or student-type organizations to report on the activities, personalities and political orientation of each group. The DGI also seeks individuals among the VB who can fulfill an operational support role; that is who wittingly or unwittingly would serve as an accommodation address or serve in some other intelligence support capacity. [There are rumors that two Venceremos graduates are now serving in elected positions high up in our government.]

The DGI has provided various forms of special training to a few persons from each VB contingent. The fact that the DGI has provided training to an individual, including training in clandestine intelligence tradecraft, does not necessarily mean that he is a recruited agent.

The Cubans view training as a service to revolutionaries rather than as part of a formal recruitment process. A very limited number of VB members have been trained in guerrilla warfare techniques, including use of arms and explosives. This type of training is given only to individuals who specifically request it and only then to persons whom the Cubans feel sure are not penetration agents of American intelligence.[40]

The success of the Cuban hosts in indoctrinating Brigade members is illustrated by the comments of several Venceremos graduates: A young New Yorker was asked if he would fight for Cubans against his countrymen. His response was, "Sure I'd pick up a gun and fight with the Cubans if they'd let me. We're all here to fight for the Cuban revolutions."[41] One of the leaders of the WUO and an instructor at Drew University, Madison, New Jersey, told a Rutgers University teach-in audience that "he was a Marxist and Socialist and would welcome a Viet Cong victory."[42]

The Venceremos Brigade was not the only organization that had such sentiments about the war and an ideology that ran counter to our form of government. One whose actions were particularly despicable was the Women Strike for Peace.

Women Strike for Peace

According to the FBI, "Women Strike for Peace (WSP) is a heavily Communist- infiltrated mass organization of 'housewives' run by a few trained and capable leaders, who are self-appointed. They generally oppose U.S. foreign policy, whatever it may be. In July [1965], a ten-woman delegation met with women representatives of Hanoi and the Viet Cong in Jakarta 'to explore possibilities of negotiations.' The meeting ended with a joint denunciation of the U.S. in Vietnam."[43]

An article in the *Washington Post* in October 1967, gives us a clear understanding of the nature of the Women Strike for Peace:

> Dagmar Wilson, leader of the Women Strike for Peace, described antiwar activity in the U.S. as a *"second front"* [Emphasis added] in what she called Vietnam's fight against "American aggression." "The Vietnamese are resisting violence on their side," she said, "and we

resist in our way here. We are a second front in the same war. We need each other's support."

Mrs. Wilson continued...It is an aggressive war and the aggressor is the U.S....The National Liberation Front does not regard it as a civil war, but resisting an outside invader.[44]

Once again, the statements by Mrs. Wilson are another example of an American siding with the enemy, even in the face of overwhelming evidence that the aggression was from the North. In Chapter Three, solid evidence was presented proving that the National Liberation Front was a subsidiary of the Lao Dong Party in the North; thousands of troops were being infiltrated from the North; and the war was being directed, supplied and supported by Hanoi. It is astounding that any American could say the things attributed to Mrs. Wilson. Unfortunately, she was speaking for the full membership of the Women Strike for Peace.

Cora Weiss, another leader of WSP, was one of the founders of the Committee of Liaison, which arranged to be the instrument of North Vietnam for exchanging mail and information about American POWs held by Hanoi. The wives of American POWs were essentially held hostage by the WSP activists and forced to accept outrageous propaganda as a price for getting mail from their husbands. A spokesman for the Defense Department explained that the Liaison Committee "is in a position, if it sees fit, to blacklist and punish them [wives] by withholding mail from their husbands." One of the POW wives expressing her anger and frustration to the Pentagon wrote this:

> We feel...that we have been put in a compromising position in having to deal with this class of people. We don't agree with their views and we have made that quite clear. But any information about our husbands is so precious that if dealing with these so-called peace groups will open up communications with Hanoi – even if the North Vietnamese are using us for propaganda, and they are – we have to play their game.[45]

The use of POW mail and information about prisoners for propaganda was an insidious play on the emotions of POW wives, and illustrates how low the antiwar activists would go in achieving their goals. Testimony of some of the POW wives before Congress regarding the Committee of Liaison will be presented in a subsequent chapter.

Spring Mobilization to End the War in Vietnam

In September of 1966, a new antiwar group was formed with the 82 year old peace activist, A. J. Muste as the chairman. Four other well known activists were "appointed" as vice chairman. They were David Dellinger, editor of *Liberation;* Ed Keating, publisher of *Ramparts;* Sidney Peck, a professor at Western Reserve University; and Robert Greenblatt, professor at Cornel who headed the previously mentioned Inter-University Committee. This was an attempt to bring together a broad coalition of antiwar groups. As it turned out, it was very successful, and brought together groups from every major political affiliation. Representing this coalition, in December 1966 more than 250 members of leftist organizations gathered in Chicago to consider the proposal for a nation-wide student strike against the war. The makeup of the organizations at this meeting is not surprising. It included representatives from the Communist Party, the Progressive Labor Party, the Socialist Workers Party, and Youth Against War and Fascism.[46]

Bettina Aptheker, the initiator of the idea of the nationwide student-faculty strike to protest and undermine America's efforts to prevent a Communist takeover of South Vietnam, was an admitted member of the Communist Party of the United States. A reporter for the *Newspaper Enterprise Association* who interviewed Aptheker in 1966 had this to say about his conversation with her:

> This school year, for example, she has it in mind to spearhead a student revolution which will hopefully lead to what she calls the "erosion of the democratic form of government" and eventual establishment of a Kremlin like leadership in the United States. "It's coming," she insists. "The nation is disgusted. One day the people will go to the polls and throw both the Democrats and Republicans out of office."
> And elect whom? [The reporter asked.]
> "Communists! Who else?"[47]

Aptheker's proposal for a student strike was rejected by the conferees. In its place, the Chicago conference decided to support the "Vietnam Week."

> A "Call to Vietnam Week" was adopted. The call included many of the words and phrases which have characterized Communist propaganda on the war in Vietnam. It claimed that, in Vietnam, the United States was waging a "war of aggression." It said the war in Vietnam waged by the United States "is a racist war, a murderous war against a colored people, an illegal war [and] but one symptom of a diseased society." The call attacked the draft claiming that it "perpetuates a system of racism in the United States, penalizes the poor" and is used by the government to crush the aspirations of "racial minorities."
>
> It proposed that Vietnam Week demonstrations be focused on the following issues:
>
> (1) Bring the GI's home now;
>
> (2) Opposing the Draft, and supporting the right of individuals to refuse to cooperate with the military system; and
>
> (3) Ending campus complicity with the war effort.
>
> The call ended with the statement that the United States was denying the people of Vietnam "the right to self-determination."[48]

The House Un-American Activities Committee conducted extensive hearings on the Communist Origin and Manipulation of Vietnam Week in 1967. The Committee found that "the decision to stage Vietnam Week (April 8-15) was made, instigated and dominated by the Communist Party, U.S.A., and the W.E.B. Dubois Clubs of America. The W.E.B. Dubois Clubs were, according to the FBI, a Marxist-oriented youth organization established by the Communist Party. The

House Committee also established that "the immediate objective of Vietnam Week and the April 15 demonstration is to reverse the U.S. policy of resisting Communism in Vietnam."[49]

The House committee came to the following conclusions about the consequences of Vietnam Week:

> The Communist propaganda apparatus throughout the world will capitalize, in every way possible, on the Vietnam Week and April 15 demonstrations. The global publicity given to them by the Communist propaganda machine will have the following effects:
>
> (a) It will give aid and comfort to Communists everywhere, particularly in Vietnam.
>
> (b) Among non-Communists, it will tend to create the false impression that a truly large segment of the U.S. population is vehemently opposed to this country's policy in Vietnam.
>
> (c) U.S. leaders will be faced with greater difficulties in convincing our allies of the correctness of this country's policy in Vietnam.[50]

A wide variety of mobilization committees arose during the Vietnam War. In some cases they overlapped in time and purpose, but seldom did they differ on their objective of organizing and promoting protests against the war. The Spring Mobilization Committee which was just discussed was a descendant of the November 8 Mobilization Committee. The Spring Mobe morphed into the National Mobilization Committee to End the War in Vietnam. The National Mobe is known for the march on the Pentagon in October 1967 and the violent demonstrations in Chicago during the Democratic National Convention in August 1968. In July 1969, the New Mobilization Committee to End the War in Vietnam came into being, superseding he National Mobilization Committee. This was a significant development in the antiwar movement; therefore, the New Mobilization Committee (New Mobe) will be examined in some detail.

New Mobilization Committee to End the War in Vietnam

In 1970, the House Committee on Internal Security conducted extensive hearings on the subversive involvement in the origin, leadership and activities of the New Mobilization Committee to End the War in Vietnam (New Mobe). The hearings revealed how "the New Mobe operated from its inception with significant domestic and international Communist support, and...the basic pattern of Communist participation has remained a characteristic of all Mobe activity."[51]

The New Mobe was formed at a national antiwar conference held in Cleveland, Ohio, in July 1969. The conference was attended by several hundred delegates from around the United States. According to the Committee on Internal Security, "A large percentage of the delegates were members of the Communist Party, U.S.A.; the Trotskyite communist Socialist Workers Party (SWP); the Young Socialist Alliance (YSA), the youth and training section of the SWP; and the Student Mobilization Committee to End the War in Vietnam, an organization controlled by the YSA."[52]

The Internal Security Committee report gives us an appreciation for what the leaders of the New Mobe had in store for America:

> The New Mobilization Committee to End the War in Vietnam is, in its own words, "a broad coalition of organizations and individuals whose purpose is to gain an immediate end to the war in Vietnam through immediate and total withdrawal of American men and materiel." The Mobe regards all United States proposals for peace in Vietnam as fraudulent, thinly veiled demands for the absolute surrender of Hanoi and the Provisional Revolutionary Government to the "fascist" forces supported by the United States in South Vietnam.
>
> A study of the official Mobe pronouncements discloses that the official stance of the coalition's leadership is militantly pro-Hanoi and anti-United States. The Mobilization's program calls for a "unilateral decision for withdrawal" by the United States, to be followed by

"reparations to the Vietnamese people for the damage the United States has done to their country."[53]

One of the most telling and disturbing aspects of the antiwar movement was the pronouncements of some of the leaders which placed them squarely in the enemy's camp; yet, not one of them was ever prosecuted for treason. The following statements by leaders of the New Mobe illustrate this point:

> Professor Sidney M. Peck, a national co-chairman of the New Mobe and former member of the Wisconsin State Committee of the Communist Party, U.S.A., stated: We want an end to the war – a war that is a war of intervention and aggression – and we want the complete and total withdrawal of American forces from Vietnam. *If that results in a victory of the National Liberation Front, we are pleased with that result because that would in effect be the wishes of the Vietnamese people.* [Emphasis added]
>
> Another New Mobe co-chairman, Professor Douglas Dowd, declared: One of the tensions that we've had to work out within the New Mobilization Committee is that the people who do the organizing for this kind of thing, almost all of them, really feel that not only the war should end but that if there had to be a side in that war I think most of us feel we would be on the other side.[54]

The New Mobe served as the focal point for groups around the nation in organizing antiwar activities which culminated in mass demonstrations in Washington and San Francisco on November 15, 1969. The New Mobe was assisted by the Student Mobe, Young Socialist Alliance and Socialist workers Party in staging the November offensive. The House Internal Security Committee also found that "the New Mobe operated from inception with significant international Communist support." The House Committee uncovered evidence that New Mobe members participated in the Stockholm Conference on Vietnam and the World Peace Assembly, both of which were projects of the Soviet-controlled World Peace Council. The Committee found evidence of New Mobe contacts with international Communist front organizations and conferences, including meetings with representatives of North Vietnam and/or National Liberation Front. Twelve New Mobe steering committee members attended the Hemispheric Conference to End the Vietnam War in Montreal, Canada; several of the steering committee members attended the Quebec meeting with representatives of North Vietnam, NLF, and various peace groups, the World Peace Assembly in (then) East Berlin, the Stockholm Conference on Vietnam, the Canadian Voice of Women meeting with representatives of North Vietnam and the National Liberation Front in Canada, and other similar anti-American, antiwar conclaves.[55]

The Stockholm Conference called for exploitation of antiwar sentiments in America. The conference's program of action stated:

> The issues of the war in Vietnam and in particular of the unconditional withdrawal of US troops and the ten-point programme of the NLF should be raised as widely as possible in all conferences, national and international....

> Increase international support for resistance in American and by Americans abroad in refusing the draft, in defecting from the US armed forces, for carrying on propaganda within the army and for militant action against the Selective Service System.[56]

The World Peace Assembly was held in Communist East Germany in June 1969. Eighteen representatives of the American left and antiwar groups, including the New Mobe, attended. They heard from the head of the Soviet delegation, E. K. Federov, as well as Leonid Brezhnev, general secretary of the Soviet Communist Party, and Alexei Kosygin, chairmen of the Council of Ministers of the Soviet Union. Federov denounced the United States policies and stressed the need for international coordination of the peace movement:

> We Soviet followers of the peace movement consider that a lasting peace is completely possible. The basis of this conviction is [that] the powerful social and

political force which confronts imperialism at the moment is against war and favors broad, international co-operation. <u>Joint actions</u> of the peace-loving forces are a very important factor. The Soviet followers of the peace movement consider it absolutely necessary to explore all avenues to find a road to common, coordinated action of all movements and organizations without exception, whose aims and activities serve the cause of peace.[57]

Brezhnev's and Kosygin's comments presented in printed text also hailed the conference:

In our times the solution to the problems of war and peace depends to a great extent on the people and their active, *joint struggle*. The *mass* actions of peace supporters and participants of various anti-war movements have achieved concrete and significant results in the struggle to thwart the aggressive plans of the imperialist circles.[58]

The American delegation's statement before the World Peace Assembly, with representatives of 60 other nations present, was the most shameful, anti-American speech that one would ever expect to come from the mouth of an American. The official text demanded:

That the American government begins the unconditional and total withdrawal of U.S. military forces from Vietnam....The statement further alleged that the U.S. has demonstrated since its founding days a systematic policy of exploitation, imperialism and genocide. We are consistently threatened by increasing repression of the voices of dissent. Since foreign policy is the mirrored image of domestic policy, a nation which employs racism, violence and repression on the domestic scene will resort in kind to racism, violence and repression in its international affairs. The war in Vietnam, above all else, is a racist war. The horrible crimes committed against the Vietnamese people reflect the arrogance, yet deadly sickness of a racist society which has not yet dared to inflict such inhumanity on a white nation.

The forces for peace in the U.S. must mobilize and exert pressure to end the war in Vietnam and make new initiatives involving power confrontations against both the political and military-industrial establishments of the nation.

We cannot close without paying deep tribute to the courage and remarkable heroism of our [North] Vietnamese friends who in this day, through incalculable sacrifices, are manning humanity's front line in the defense, first, of their own country and, second, of the cause of human freedom. Vietnam's example should lead us all to make, in this hall, a covenant that no sacrifice is too great - even the threat to life itself - to deter man in his quest to be free....The peace forces of the U.S. and the world, through our sacrifices, can become a beacon light....[59]

Irving Sarnoff, a member of the New Mobe steering committee, addressed the World Peace Assembly with unbelievable vehemence and condemnation of the United Status. His lengthy denunciation and indictment of the United States could not have been more disparaging if it had come from our worst enemy. The fact that it came from an American, speaking before an audience of several hundred people from 60 nations was very damaging to his country, and it was evident that his intention was just that. Here again, it is incredulous that any American could do such a thing unless he was bent on destroying the country. Sarnoff's speech is so lengthy that only excerpts can be presented here:

It is with shame and honour that I speak as a member of the American delegation. *Shame because it is my country that is responsible for so much of the evil being perpetrated in the world today.* I speak with the knowledge of the reality that for years the people of my country have permitted the warmakers to use the most modern, horrendous weapons of war to kill and repress the people of Vietnam as they struggle to determine their own destiny. I speak with a broken heart – as a father and a worker – when I think of the thousands of lives of children and workers we have destroyed *so that the rich in America can rob and plunder the lands belonging to other peoples in Vietnam and throughout the world.*

This policy is rooted in our history as a racist society, whose system places profit and material wealth as the major national priority, above the respect for the lives and dignity of people. Our history is that of a nation that has destroyed the lives and dignity of millions of Indians and blacks, and today keeps millions in economic and political slavery throughout the world....These policies are in essence the same ones that oppress and brutalize our own people....

As if this were not enough, the rulers of America have used all the modern means of psychological warfare to destroy the conscience and humanity of our people, to condition our people to be insensitive to the needs of other people, and through racism to justify the robbing and killing in our own country and throughout the world....

From one end of America to the other Black Panthers, fighting against white supremacy at home and in Vietnam, are being killed, jailed and harassed. New forms of repression are now being prepared to investigate and jail those that would oppose the policies of war, racism and poverty....On Army bases across America, G.I.'s are organizing and speaking out against the war – the stockades are full, but this historic movement continues to grow....

We know that the heroic [North] Vietnamese people, who have defeated ...over one-half million American troops, will not be fooled as the neo-colonialists now try to force Vietnamese to fight Vietnamese...[Refers to Nixon's Vietnamization program which was intended to have South Vietnamese fight for their own country.]

Our task, more evident than ever before, is to broaden and unify the anti-war movement in America so that it becomes impossible for Nixon to continue his neo-colonialist, aggressive aims. Our task is to bring to our people an understanding that the nature of the neo-colonialist policy is not only to exploit and oppress the rest of the world, but to exploit and oppress the American people.

Long live the heroic Vietnamese people as they struggle for their national independence and sovereignty,

Long live the unity of the exploited and oppressed in America and throughout the world as we struggle against a common enemy.

Power to the People! [60]

Conflict between two factions within the New Mobe led to a split in mid-1970 which resulted in the formation of two new groups.

National Peace Action Coalition (NPAC) and Peoples Coalition for Peace and Justice (PCPJ)

As mentioned earlier, the New Mobe was a coalition of a number of antiwar groups and was dominated by two Communist factions, the Communist Party, U.S.A., and the Trotskyite Socialist Workers Party. According to the House Internal Security Committee, "both advocated the overthrow of the United States by force and violence." The investigation by the Internal Security Committee in the spring of 1971 found that friction within the New Mobe between the Communist Party and the Socialist Workers Party led to a split in mid-1970. The breakup of the New Mobe resulted in the founding of the National Peace Action Coalition (NPAC) and the National Coalition

Against War, Racism and Repression, which subsequently changed to the Peoples Coalition for Peace and Justice (PCPJ).⁶¹

The NPAC was organized around the Trotskyite Socialist Workers Party and its youth affiliate, the Young Socialist Alliance, along with the Student Mobilization Committee. The NPAC adhered to the one-issue-at-a-time strategy demanding immediate withdrawal of America from the war. The PCPJ was formed from a loose coalition of numerous free-wheeling radicals and unaligned groups. The PCPJ strategy consisted of a variety of demands as opposed to a single issue. The PCPJ strategy was designed to elicit support across a broad spectrum of discontent in America. They demanded:

> (1) That the U.S. set a date now for complete withdrawal of U.S. military air, land and sea forces from Vietnam.
>
> (2) That the U.S. set a date for guaranteed annual income for a family of four of $5,500 and
>
> (3) That the U.S. set a date for freeing political prisoners.

The NPAC and PCPJ jointly and separately were responsible for organizing large crowds of demonstrators in Washington in April 1971. As plans were being developed for the next round of protests, PCPJ leaders postulated that "direct action and civil disobedience which advance beyond marches and rallies are now the only viable forms of mass action to bring about an end to the Indochinese war."⁶³

Richard H. Ichord, Chairman of the House Committee on Internal Security, expressed concern for the lack of understanding of the significant Communist presence in the NPAC and PCPJ. He was particularly distressed by the fact that many prominent members of Congress were endorsing the demonstrations sponsored by these two groups. Ichord was surprised to learn that most members of Congress were not aware of the true variety of communists that were leading these groups. He was referring to the violent, revolutionary objectives of the Trotskyite Socialist Workers Party. He stressed that those in the principle leadership role were "not interested necessarily in obtaining peace in Vietnam except on the terms of the enemy. They are more interested in seeing the humiliation of America...."⁶⁴

NPAC and PCPJ were successful in staging large demonstrations that drew the attention of the Communist Party leadership in Vietnam. A captured enemy document, Circular on Antiwar Movements in the U.S., 16 July 1971, reveals how they viewed the antiwar movement in the United States. The document is too lengthy to include here in its entirety. Pertinent excerpts are quoted below.

> The antiwar movements in the US...have been widely developed from Washington DC and New York to other states. At the beginning, only a small number of people of the middle class, intellectuals, students, writers, artists, and religious people joined these movements, but now they have rallied a large number of people, including members of the Senate and House of Representatives, former ministers and ambassadors, ex-service men, and a portion of the working class. The majority of US workers were not politically aware because the US labor unions (supporting the government) only motivated them to struggle for their own interests.
>
> The spontaneous antiwar movements in the US have received assistance and guidance from the friendly delegations at the Paris Peace Talks. Of the US antiwar movements, the two most important ones are: The People's Committee for Peace and Justice and the National Peace Action Committee. These two movements have gathered much strength and staged many demonstrations. The PCPJ is the most important. It has made progress in its newly-adopted policy lines with the following strategic alteration:
>
> 1. To gain success in struggles, it is necessary to strengthen internal unity, contact other associations, other social classes, and influential personalities and take part in US congressional elections (instead of boycotting them); to eliminate reactionary candidates and plant progressive people in the Senate and House of Representatives.

2. Closely combine struggles of the people with those of the opposing faction in the Congress.

3. Step up the motivation of US soldiers and coordinate with them in the struggles.

4. Motivate US labor unions, especially those concerned with defense and communication and transportation work, to participate in antiwar movements.

5. In conjunction with slogans demanding the end of the war in VN [Vietnam], adopt other slogans demanding improvement of the US society. This is a further step because generally speaking, the US people are proud of their scientific and technical advancements and the prosperity of their country. The people have deep prejudices against the Communists. Most Americans do what they think they will be successful. They like patriotic propaganda and unusual enterprise.[65]

The captured document described at length the demonstrations organized by NPAC and PCPJ in the spring of 1971. It extolled the great success of the demonstrations on April 24, 1971 which produced 500,000 people in Washington DC and 30,000 in San Francisco. The document revealed extensive inside knowledge of the movement in the United States. Lessons learned from the demonstrations are cited in the document for the benefit of American activists;

1. The antiwar movements in April and May 71 were the people's greatest political struggle movements in the US. Although the people were terrorized, they were not demoralized.

2. The PCPJ realized that the slogan, "If the government does not end the war, the people will end the government" was not appropriate because the people would misunderstand this slogan and President Nixon would suppress demonstrations.

3. The application of the slogan, "Workers must disobey the government's orders" was not successful. Instead of encircling the White House and the Pentagon, the demonstrations blocked road intersections thus impeding the people's traffic. This caused the people to be discontented and gave President Nixon reasons to suppress demonstrations.[66]

The captured document exalted the antiwar movement and praised the revelation of the "secret documents of the Pentagon" [Pentagon Papers] which it said would enable the antiwar organizations in the U.S. to motivate the people. The document lauded the forthcoming protests in the U.S. on November 6, 1971, and the slogan demanding withdrawal of U.S. troops from Vietnam. Finally, it encouraged the coordination of the antiwar movements in the U.S. with those in South Vietnam timed for the forthcoming elections in that country.[67]

In mid-May 1971 the World Peace Assembly met again, this time in Budapest, Hungary. The conference was sponsored by the World Peace Council (WPC) which was dominated by the Soviet Union. The assembly delegates highly praised the antiwar efforts in the United States. A CIA report describes some of the events at the conference:

> The WPC secretary general, Romesh Chandra, a member of the Central Executive Committee of the Communist party of India, praised the 25 United States delegates for their antiwar efforts. Chandra advised the meeting that the WPC was urging massive demonstrations on 4 July at the United States embassies around the world with the central slogan "Set the '71 Date." This new slogan has been urged on the American antiwar movement by Communists abroad (including the chief Viet Cong negotiator at Paris) because the Communist feeling is that it is the most popular slogan in recent action....[68]

Soon after the conference in Budapest, John Rankin Davis addressed a gathering of the PCPJ and May Day Collective. He reported that he had just returned from Europe where he met with North Vietnamese and Viet Cong delegates in Paris. Davis indicated that he had visited Budapest, and a CIA report suggests that he had probably attended the WPC in Budapest. The CIA report stated, "According to Jack Davis, the North Vietnamese delegates in Paris made the following suggestions (reportedly in the form of 'instructions') for prosecuting the antiwar drive in the United States":

> (1). The creation of a new slogan for the peace movement, "Set the Date by December '71" [similar to the slogan noted before],
>
> (2). Concentrate the major antiwar efforts in an attempt to lobby members of Congress,
>
> (3). Support the proposals of Sen. George McGovern and Rep. Bella Abzug, and
>
> (4). Change the name of the May Day Collective and form a political party similar to SDS and establish chapters across the country.[69]

Both President Johnson and Nixon believed that the antiwar movement in the United States was being influenced by foreign agents. The previous CIA report and the one that follows leave little doubt in the validity of their convictions:

> Antiwar leaders met with Mme. Nguyen Thi Binh, the chief Viet Cong Paris negotiator, immediately following activities in early May [1971], and she reportedly both criticized and praised antiwar activists for their May efforts. Additionally, she indicated several desirable changes in American antiwar tactics that have since indeed been adopted by the American organizations. One area in which Mme. Binh criticized the American antiwar movement was their constant bickering which served to affect adversely the unity of the movement.... The PCPJ leaders, following the suggestion of Mme. Binh, have changed their slogan to "set the date." The Trotskyite controlled NPAC has recently adopted the slogan "out now." Both groups dropped the reference to "stopping the government." [As suggested by

Mme.Binh] Yet to be accomplished was the Mme. Binh guidance that antiwar activists in America form a political party that could eventually exercise ballot box strength.[70]

Additional evidence will be provided in forthcoming chapters to show the foreign connections to the antiwar movement. Before moving on to that topic, there is one more antiwar group that needs to be discussed.

Vietnam Veterans Against the War (VVAW)

The Vietnam Veterans Against the War (VVAW) was formed in 1967 in New York by six Vietnam veterans. Estimates of its membership ranged from 600 to 10,000 at its peak. Assuming that the membership reached 10,000, this group represented less than one-half of one percent of the American servicemen and women who served in Vietnam. The VVAW raised the ire of many of the veterans who served in Vietnam because the VVAW portrayed the veterans as a group of ragtag, drug/pot smoking misfits. Although the VVAW was in the beginning a legitimate antiwar protest organization, it soon became a militant and potentially violent organization that actually considered assassination of certain congressmen who supported the war. Ideologically, it leaned far to the left and was heavily infiltrated by Communist Party members and front organizations. It had the backing and funding of such antiwar activists as Jane Fonda. The VVAW led student strikes at major campuses across the country, merged with such leftist groups as the PCJP and NPAC in marches on Washington and other major cities, and joined in a coalition with many other leftist groups to promote disruptive activity at the Democratic and Republican national conventions in 1972.[71]

An FBI report in November 1971 provides a good understanding of what the VVAW was all about. The FBI report outlined the VVAW's objectives in detail:

> 1. To demand an immediate cessation of fighting and the withdrawal of all American troops from Indochina.
>
> 2. To demand Congress enact legislation for the immediate termination of all funds being utilized by

the United States government, its allies and the Central Intelligence Agency to support their illegal operations in Latin America, Africa, China, Europe, and the countries of Vietnam, Cambodia, Laos, and Thailand. [Note that they recognized only one Vietnam, no North or South Vietnam. This corresponds with Hanoi's position.].

3. To demonstrate that our military tactics dehumanize soldiers and civilians, and to make clear the United States government is prosecuting an illegal, unjust and immoral war in Indochina.

4. To show Americans that their society is structured by a racism which lets us view all non-whites as less than human....Thus, we send our minorities off to die in disproportionately high numbers while we kill Asians indiscriminately. We demand that the military recognize its complicity in America's domestic and international racism. [The record shows that 86 percent of those who died in Vietnam were white and 12.5 percent were black, close to the population distribution at the time.]

5. To make clear that the United States has never undertaken an extensive open investigation of American war crimes in Indochina....

6. To demand that all active duty servicemen and women be afforded the rights as citizens that are guaranteed by the United States Constitution and Bill of Rights that are presently denied them by the Uniform Code of Military Justice. [The UCMJ is based on the Constitution and the rights of servicemen are in fact protected.]

7. To support all military personnel refusing to serve in wars of aggression at home and abroad. We demand Congress enact legislation for the immediate repatriation with full amnesty to those brothers and sisters who

are in prison or in self-serving exile by reason of their refusal to serve in the military. We support all persons refusing to be drafted.

8. To demand immediate legislation to provide proper care and services of all veterans in V.A. hospitals; to make available job training and placement for every returning veteran; and to provide the funds and means necessary for their educational and vocational endeavors.

9. To affirm that the membership is not only concerned with ending this war, but changing the domestic social, political, and economic institutions that have caused and permitted the continuance of war.[72]

The most despicable act of the VVAW was their propaganda effort to smear American servicemen as murderous, drug-addicted psychotics. The VVAW organized several events which solidified this image in the minds of the public. One of these projects was the "Winter Soldier Investigation" organized by such celebrities as Jane Fonda, Dick Gregory and Mark Lane. This meeting, held in Detroit in early 1971, heard from 150 veterans who "testified to the war crimes committed in Southeast Asia, not as isolated incidents but crimes committed on a day-to-day basis with the full awareness of officers at all levels of command." This was part of the opening statement by the former Navy Lieutenant, John F. Kerry, speaking before the Senate Foreign Relations Committee on April 22, 1971. Kerry related the following testimony before the committee:

> They told the stories at times they had personally raped, cut off ears, cut off heads, taped wires from portable telephones to human genitals and turned up the power, cut off limbs, blown up bodies, randomly shot at civilians, razed villages in fashion reminiscent of Genghis Khan, shot cattle and dogs for fun, poisoned food stocks, and generally ravaged the countryside of South Vietnam in addition to the normal ravages of war,

and the normal and very particular ravaging which is done by the applied bombing power of this country.[73]

Kerry claimed that the American people were saying that we should "get out of Vietnam now." [This was a prime slogan of the Communists at home and abroad] Kerry proceeded to accuse the United States of "taking umbrage in the Geneva Convention [maybe he meant Geneva Accords!] and using that as justification for continuation of the war, when we are more guilty than any other body of violations of the Geneva Conventions, in the use of free fire zones, harassment interdiction fire, search and destroy missions, the bombings, the torture of prisoners, the killing of prisoners, accepted policy by many units in South Vietnam" [74]

Could it be that Navy officer training failed to teach Kerry that interdiction fire, search and destroy, bombing and killing the enemy are fundamentals of war? His statement that torturing and killing prisoners was an accepted U.S. policy is totally false. The policy taught in the MACV Advisors Training Course, attended by the author, and the official policy in the MACV U.S. Forces Handbook went to extraordinary lengths to make it clear that enemy POWs were to be treated in accordance with the Geneva Prisoner of War Convention, and included detailed instructions for protection and humane treatment of POWs. A copy of the MACV policy for treatment of POWs in provided in Appendix K.

Still speaking before the Senate Committee, Kerry admitted that he had met with representatives of North Vietnam and the political leadership of the Viet Cong in Paris. Kerry supported the main provisions of Madam Binh's peace plan which included setting a date for withdrawal of American forces; unilateral withdrawal of our forces [but not the Communist forces from North Vietnam]; ending our support of the Thieu-Ky regime in South Vietnam; agreeing to a coalition government in South Vietnam with the Communists; and accepting the Communists word that the POW issue would be "settled" after our acceptance of the peace agreement. This was a clear prescription for capitulation with no real assurance for the return of American POWs.[75]

Senator Aiken, referring to the fate of South Vietnamese if the U.S. pulled out, asked Kerry, "What do you think would be the attitude, of the large, well-armed South Vietnamese army and the

South Vietnamese people? Would they be happy to have us withdraw or what?" Kerry responded, "Well, Senator, this obviously is the most difficult question of all, but I think that at this point the United States is not really in a position to consider the happiness of those people as pertains to the army in our withdrawal."[76] In other words, we could not be bothered with the fate of those we left behind in South Vietnam.

The Senate Committee continued questioning John Kerry for several hours, asking his opinion on every conceivable aspect of foreign policy and military strategy for Southeast Asia. It is astonishing and even disturbing that the Senate Committee would seek the input of such an inexperienced person on such broad national security matters. That was what the generals, Director of CIA and the Secretary of State were for. Accordingly, why would they choose to rely on a Navy Lieutenant who served only four months in a combat zone in Vietnam on a boat patrolling the coast and rivers? Surly this did not qualify him as a military or international relations expert. Furthermore, he represented only a very small minority of Vietnam veterans. He had admitted to carrying out some of the same atrocities that he accused the rest of the servicemen of doing. If the Senate Committee had bothered to check they would have learned that Kerry was involved with an organization that had far left leanings and had been infiltrated by Communists and front organizations, and if they had made even a minimum effort, they would have found out that the VVAW was under investigation by the FBI for subversive activities, including consideration of assassinating members of Congress.[77]

The only logical conclusion for the Senate Committee's interest in testimony by Kerry is that politics were at play. A Democratic controlled Senate with many members who opposed the war was eager to have open testimony from someone who could present information that was damaging to the Republican president and the war effort. By this time the war had become politicized, very much like it did with the war in Iraq.

One of the few positive outcomes of Kerry's appearance before the Senate Committee was the call by Senator Hatfield for the Commandant of the Marine Corps to investigate the war crimes alleged by Kerry. In a recent article, Mackubin Owens, a professor at the Naval War College and Marine platoon leader in Vietnam, describes some of the findings of the investigation:

When the Naval Investigative Service attempted to interview the so-called witnesses [Detroit/Winter Soldier meeting], most refused to cooperate, even after assurances that they would not be questioned about atrocities they may have committed personally. Those that did cooperate never provided details of actual crimes to investigators. The NIS also discovered that some of the most grisly testimony was given by fake witnesses who had appropriated the names of real Vietnam veterans.[78]

Guenter Lewy, in researching his book, *America in Vietnam*, found similar disparities. He confirmed that many of the veterans refused to be interviewed, and they claimed that VVAW leadership had directed them not to cooperate with military authorities. He cites several specific cases of falsified testimony:

> A black marine who agreed to be interviewed was unable to provide details of the outrages he had described at the hearing....He admitted that the question of atrocities had not occurred to him while he was in Vietnam, and that he had been assisted in the preparation of his testimony by a member of the Nation of Islam. But the most damaging finding consisted of the sworn statements of several veterans, corroborated by witnesses, that they had in fact not attended the hearing in Detroit. One of them had never been to Detroit in all his life.[79]

More disparities have been revealed about certain high level members of the VVAW. For example, John Kerry and Al Hubbard appeared on NBC's *Meet the Press* on April 18, 1971 where they alleged widespread atrocities by U.S. soldiers in Vietnam. Al Hubbard, Executive Secretary of the VVAW, was presented as a former Captain in the US Air Force who had been wounded while serving as a pilot in Vietnam. The truth is that he was actually a staff sergeant who had never served in Vietnam.[80]

After extensive research for his book, *Stolen Valor*, H.G. Burkett found that the negative, stereotyped depiction of the Vietnam veteran as a whining, suicidal, drug crazed, homeless welfare case was a gross distortion of reality. Burkett makes the case that many of the stories portraying the Vietnam veterans as sadistic killers were "not only far-fetched, they were deliberate lies spread by political foes of the war, calculated to turn American public opinion against our intervention." Burkett's research revealed some other interesting truths:

> Most often I checked those I called the "image makers," the veterans used by reporters to illustrate stories on homelessness, PTSD [Posttraumatic Stress Disorder], Agent Orange illnesses, criminality, drug abuse, alcoholism, and war crimes....Often the records revealed that the veteran I investigated was bogus—had never been there [Vietnam]. Or if he had, he wasn't the hero he claimed to be. Those claiming to be involved in covert operations or members of elite military groups like the Navy SEALs or Green Berets were even more likely to be imposters.
>
> Burkett discovered that over the last decade, some 1700 individuals, including some of the most prominent examples of the Vietnam veteran as dysfunctional losers, had fabricated their war stories. Many had never even been in the service. Others, had been, but had never been in Vietnam.[81]

In October 1970, Al Hubbard and Jane Fonda went on a nationwide lecture tour covering over 50 college campuses to raise money for the VVAW and create new chapters. Fonda and Mark Lane appeared on the Dick Cavett show to promote the VVAW.[82]

In March 1971, Fonda, Mark Lane and VVAW member Michael Hunter went to Europe where they met with Madam Binh, political representative of the Viet Cong. From there they went to London where "Fonda alleged American atrocities that included applying electrodes to prisoner genitals, mass rape, slicing off of body parts, scalping, skinning alive, and leaving 'heat tablets' around which burned the insides of children who ate them."[83]

The activities of the VVAW and the other antiwar groups discussed in this chapter are just the tip of the iceberg of what these groups did to undermine our war efforts. The next several chapters will take up the many ways in which the antiwar activists gave aid and comfort to the enemy.

Chapter Five

From Hanoi with Love

With a people divided by contending factions, we may fail to obtain a satisfactory peace.

—Lyndon B. Johnson

The antiwar movement provided aid and comfort to North Vietnam in many ways. It gave encouragement to the leadership in Hanoi to fight on; it led them to believe they were winning the war in the United States and world arena; it greatly aided in the success of their global propaganda campaign; and it boosted the morale of the enemy troops and civilian populace. Hanoi made every possible effort to encourage the movement and heaped praise on the antiwar groups at every opportunity. The evidence is overwhelming that the leadership in Hanoi knew well that they could not win on the battlefield in Vietnam and were counting on the antiwar movement to win the war for them on the home front in America. Hanoi showed its appreciation in numerous ways. It is enlightening to look at some of their efforts to encourage and assist the antiwar activities in the United States.

In April 1967, the leaders of the Spring Mobilization Committee to End the War in Vietnam, Messrs. D. Dellinger, S. Lynd, and Mrs. B. Deming, sent a telegram to the Premier of North Vietnam, Pham Van Dong, advising him of the coming massive protest of the American people. Premier Pham Van Dong replied:

Dear Friends,
I sincerely thank you for your telegram. I am glad to learn that broad sections of the American people are organizing a "Spring Mobilization" to demand that the U.S. government stop its war of aggression against Vietnam and bring American troops home.

We Vietnamese people are very thankful to the American people for their positive efforts against the U.S. war of aggression in Vietnam. By so doing they are giving valuable support to the Vietnamese people's struggle for independence and freedom, and at the same time, fighting for their own interests....

With sincere wishes for full success to the "Spring Mobilization" drive.

Cordial greetings,
Pham Van Dong [1]

On December 23, 1966, Ho Chi Minh sent a message to the American people:

"On the occasion of the New Year, I would like to convey to the American people cordial wishes for peace and happiness....More and more Americans are valiantly standing up in a vigorous struggle, demanding that the American government respect the constitution and the honour of the United States, stop the war of aggression in Vietnam and bring home all U.S. troops. I warmly welcome your just struggle and thank you for your support to the Vietnamese people's patriotic fight...."[2]

Professor Ta Quang Buu, Minister of Education for North Vietnam, sent American professors and students a letter in March of 1966, praising the antiwar campaign in the United States. The letter reads in-part:

Dear Friends,
We are aware of the reasons which have led you to oppose resolutely the American rulers' policy of aggression and support actively the Vietnamese people's struggle for independence, freedom and peace....It is

precisely because you are heirs to those fine traditions, to the progressive thinking of Washington, Jefferson and Lincoln that you are now supporting us, following dictates of your conscience.

We wish to avail ourselves of the present opportunity to express our sincere gratitude to the American people and particularly to you friends, American intellectuals, teachers, students and youth who have given us your warm support. Your ever-growing struggle is a strong backing and a great source of encouragement for the people of our country, in their fight for independence and peace....

We must unite and fight to put an end to all those crimes perpetuated in the name of the American people.

We must unite and fight so that no more Vietnamese and American blood will be shed for the selfish interests of a small minority within the American ruling circles. We earnestly call on you to give a still greater impetus to your actions with a view to:

1. Making the American people and the people in the whole world clearly see that the war of aggression being waged by the Johnson ruling clique in Vietnam is a direct attack on the lives and democratic right of the American people, that it is an unjust, cruel, inhuman, illegal and immoral war, which tramples underfoot the right of the Vietnamese people to self-determination.

2. Compelling the present American rulers to respect the 1954 Geneva Agreements, put an end to their war of aggression in South Vietnam, stop their war of destruction against North Vietnam, withdraw all U.S, and satellite troops from South Vietnam, recognize the South Vietnam National Front for Liberation as the sole genuine representative of the people of South

Vietnam and let the Vietnamese people decide their own destiny.

We have recently been informed that the National Coordinating Committee to End the War in Vietnam will start a new wave of protests in the United States and the world over on March 25-26, 1966. We eagerly look forward to your active participation in it and wish you great success in your noble activity.[3]

An article by Seymour Topping, dateline Hong Kong, October 19, 1965, carries a message that is repeated in many statements and news reports emanating from North Vietnam:

Asian Communists say they are "profoundly thankful" for the series of demonstrations in the United States against the American military effort in Vietnam....The protest movement is cited as proof that the Johnson Administration will eventually be compelled to withdraw American forces from Vietnam....

Communist hopes for victory there now turn more on an American withdrawal through exhaustion or in response to the pressure of public opinion rather than on conventional military success....[4]

Christian Science Monitor correspondent, John Hughes, reported from Hong Kong on October 17, 1965, that North Vietnam was focused on the real battleground, the United States, "where it has sought to capture public opinion and with it batter the Nixon administration into submission." The article pointed out that Hanoi has been giving "extensive daily coverage to the American people's 'fall offensive' against the Nixon administration...." According to Hughes, the Communists often send open letters to the American public, usually targeting students and intellectuals. He cites one letter to American students which "urged them to consider themselves a 'shock force' in the protracted and hard revolutionary struggle...." The letter asked, "How can we tell you all our profound admiration for your courageous and persistent struggle in the past years against the criminal aggressive war of the American Government in Vietnam?..."5

Madame Nguyen Thai Binh, Minister of Foreign Affairs for the People's Revolutionary Government of South Vietnam (political arm of the Viet Cong), wrote from Paris a long letter to American friends participating in the spring campaign in April and May 1971, expressing her gratitude and support. Her comments, as broadcast by the Vietnam News Agency, are quoted in-part below:

> Dear American Friends.
> I would like to extend my warmest greeting to all American friends of various circles and political and religious tendencies who will participate in the spring campaign.
>
> Once again, you will gather in Washington, New York, San Francisco and in other big U.S. cities to strongly express the voice of the authentic United States, (words indistinct) (?freedom and justice,) and to demand that your government put an end to the Vietnam war.
>
> More than ever before, the end of the war has become an extremely pressing demand of our peoples so that the Vietnamese people may escape from sufferings and death, rebuild their ragged country, and heel the wounds in each person's feelings, and the American people may concentrate their resources and their strength on the pressing demands of life....[That would have been easy. All North Vietnam had to do was stop their attack on the South!]
>
> We demand that Mr. Nixon put forth a reasonable deadline for a total U.S. troop withdrawal so as to achieve a cease-fire between the liberation troops [North Vietnamese] and U.S. troops and to discuss the questions of insuring safety for the withdrawal of U.S. troops and the question of releasing (words indistinct) captured in the Vietnam war....

I wish you splendid victories in your spring activities movement and hope that the antiwar movement is the United States will further coordinate (its activities) so that it will be effective in demanding that the Nixon administration seriously negotiate a political settlement in order to end the war and restore genuine and lasting peace in Vietnam.[6]

In addition to the letter quoted above, Madam Binh made other attempts to influence the antiwar movement. In April 1972, she spoke directly via telephone to a large gathering of PCPJ demonstrators who were meeting in Harrisburg, PA. She said, "Let us unite to resolutely demand that the Nixon administration immediately stop the policy of Vietnamization of the war and really end the U.S. commitment in Vietnam. Let us demand that the Nixon administration continues to participate in the Paris conference as usual and seriously respond to the PRGRSV's [People's Revolutionary Government of the Republic of South Vietnam, a Communist front] correct proposals." Madam Binh also condemned the U.S. for trying seven antiwar people in Harrisburg; she denounced U.S. war crimes in Vietnam; and condemned the U.S. for "sabotaging" the peace conference in Paris. Madam Binh ended her conversation with the antiwar group with what was purported to be a quote from American POWs, but is highly suspect:

We, the U.S. POWs want to tell the United States that Vietnam does not belong to us so we do not care about gaining it or losing it. Let us advance for the sake of peace and may we wish you success. With our keen affection, we hope that you grow stronger.[7]

The importance that Hanoi placed on the antiwar movement in the United States became obvious when in the fall of 1967, a Vietnam Committee for Solidarity with the American People was formed by the Communist Party in North Vietnam. The stated purpose was to strengthen friendly ties and close solidarity with American people; however, the real reason was to strengthen the antiwar movement in the United States and coordinate activities to the greatest extent possible. The motivation for the establishment of this committee is made clear in the founding document prepared in Hanoi. The statement is quoted in-part below:

> In the past few years, reasonable, democratic and progressive Americans have one after another voiced their protest and struggled more and more strongly in various forms against the U.S. government's policy in Vietnam.
>
> The Vietnamese people, together with the world people, highly value the American people's valiant acts of resistance against the U.S. war in Vietnam. These acts constitute a just struggle to defend the finest traditions and honor of the United States and the legitimate rights of the American people.
>
> The Vietnamese people consider these acts as a valuable encouragement in their struggle for national liberation.
>
> Braving all obstacles and difficulties, many Americans have visited Vietnam in war time, thus creating favorable conditions for better mutual understanding between the peoples of the two countries. Representatives of various strata of the people in Vietnam and the United States have had opportunities to meet one another and sincerely exchange views on questions concerning the fate of the two peoples, and to create fine relations which can exist only between comrades-in-arms pursuing the same ideal and objective: peace and friendship among nations.
>
> In that spirit, the Vietnam Committee for Solidarity with American people has been founded to strengthen the existing relations of friendship between the Vietnamese and American peoples.
>
> On this occasion, the Vietnam Committee for Solidarity with American people conveys to its American friends

its warmest greetings and wishes that the organizations in the antiwar movement in the United States will attain greater achievements in the struggle for an end to the war being conducted in Vietnam by the U.S. government, for the withdrawal of the U.S. troops and for the right for the Vietnamese people to settle their own affairs....

The causes of militant solidarity between the Vietnamese and American peoples will certainly triumph.[8]

The Committee for Solidarity was staffed by key members of the Lao Dong Communist Party, and was actively engaged in communicating with antiwar groups in the United States. Excerpts from some of this correspondence reflect the encouragement that Hanoi lavished onto the antiwar movement:

SOLIDARITY COMMITTEE WRITES TO U.S. PEOPLE.
Hanoi Vietnam News Agency (VNA), in English 1556 GMT 20 Oct 1968:
(Text) Hanoi—South Vietnam [Communist front] People's Committee for Solidarity with the American People—CSAP—has sent a letter to the American people on the occasion of its first founding anniversary....

Dear American friends....the South Vietnamese [actually the Communist Party in the North] people have followed with warm sympathy and appreciation the strong developments of the antiwar movement in the United States, from the 21 October 1967 confrontation at the Pentagon, the confrontation on the opening day of the congress of the of the Jeannette Rankin Brigade, the numerous demonstrations and petitions of the academic and professional community in protest against Dr. Benjamin Spock's trial, to the recent seething and bloody antiwar demonstrations at the Democratic convention in Chicago....

The South Vietnamese [Communist front] people have also followed with great attention and sympathy antiwar acts developing among the GI's in South Vietnam and U.S....On this occasion, CSAP [Solidarity Committee] wishes to extend its affectionate regards and admiration to those GI's and American youths now in jail because they have deserted, refused induction, or refused to go to Vietnam, as well as to their families....

This last year also marked a new step in the strengthening of friendly ties and close solidarity between our two peoples in the common struggle for peace, justice, freedom, democracy, and civil rights and an end to the war in Vietnam, from the Bratislava conference gathering representatives from South and North Vietnam and the United States, to the meeting between women from South and North Vietnam and the United States in Paris, and between youth from South and North Vietnam and the United States in Stockholm, Sofia, Budapest...and so forth.[9]

SOUTH VIETNAM [COMMUIST FRONT] SOLIDARITY COMMITTEE WRITES PROGRESSIVE AMERICANS.

Hanoi Vietnam News Agency (VNA) September 14, 1968:

The South Vietnam People's Committee for Solidarity with the American People has sent a letter to the National Mobilization Committee to end the War in Vietnam thanking the progressive American people of all strata for their seething, resolute and courageous struggle conducted last month at the convention of the Democratic Party....The letter said:

Despite the huge barbarous machine of repression unleashed by Johnson, Humphrey and their ilk, you have come down into the streets for demonstrations and shouted slogans demanding an end to the U.S. war of aggression in Vietnam, cessation of the Bombing on the whole territory of the Democratic Republic of Vietnam [North Vietnam] and withdrawal of troops of the U.S. and of its allied countries in the Vietnam war.

We express to you our deep sympathy and ask you to convey to the American people our heartfelt thanks for their participation in or support of the recent action in Chicago. We also voice the high indignation of our people at the news that on orders from Johnson and Humphrey, masked policemen repelled the demonstration by using tear gas and truncheons and firing at them. The terror and repression by the U.S. government, however, cannot hamper your activities. On the contrary, they will cause the antiwar movement to spread to the length and breadth of the United States.

We wish you greater successes. The common struggle of our two peoples for freedom, peace and social progress will certainly carry the day. We ask you to convey our best wishes to our American friends who were wounded or arrested during the recent demonstrations.[10]

PEOPLE'S COMMITTEE FOR SOLIDARITY SENDS MESSAGE TO NATIONAL MOBILIZATION COMMITTEE.
Liberation Press Agency (Clandestine) 17 January 1969:
(Text) South Vietnam January 17 GPA--The South Vietnamese [Communist front] People's Committee for Solidarity with the American People has sent a message to the National Mobilization Committee to End the War in Vietnam, in connection with a campaign intended for January 19 and 20 in the United States. The message reads:

We warmly welcome your new initiative to organize large-scale demonstrations and meetings, on Nixon's assumption of the presidency, to demand the U.S.

Government to put an end to its aggressive war in Vietnam and bring U.S. and satellite troops home....

Your campaign will help forestall new criminal acts by the U.S. Government which has put to use even bombs of 4,500kg and lethal toxic chemicals to massacre the people, and destroy villages and crops here. It will also pressure the U. S. Government to hold serious talks in Paris to seek a solution to the Vietnam problem.

Your antiwar acts will stimulate us more strongly to our just struggle for the independence and freedom of our country, and for peace in Southeast Asia and the world.

We are following your activities with the warm feelings of close friends who are bound to you by the same aspirations and interests that bind our two peoples.... Good successes in your New Year activities.[11]

<u>HO THU ACCLAIMS U.S. ANTIWAR DEMONSTRATIONS.</u>
Liberation Radio (Clandestine) in Vietnamese 27 April 1971:
(Text) On 24 April Ho Thu, Chairman of the South Vietnamese People's Committee for Solidarity with the American People sent a cable to the National Peace Action Alliance and the People's Alliance for Peace and Justice in the United States to acclaim the U.S. people's spring offensive wave. The cable said:

We warmly acclaim the broad spring offensive wave of the current year in the United States, which was initiated by you, friends, and many other U.S. progressive organizations, with the aim of demanding that the U.S. Government immediately end the aggressive war in Vietnam and unconditionally and immediately bring all U.S. troops home. The South Vietnamese [Communist front] highly value your persevering struggle for unity, considering it a valuable contribution to the common understanding for peace, independence, democracy, and social progress. May your struggle, friends, be crowned with great success.[12]

MASS ORGANIZATIONS BACK U.S. ANTIWAR EFFORTS.

Liberation Press Agency (Clandestine) 1533 GMT 2 December 69:

(Text) South Vietnam December 2nd LPA—Mass organizations of South Vietnam [Communist front] have expressed their strong support to the various American organizations involved in the "fall offensive" against the U.S. war in Vietnam.

Mme. Ma Thi Chu of the People's Committee for Solidarity with the American People in a message to the New Mobilization Committee to End the War in Vietnam, the Moratorium Committee, and the American Committee for Solidarity with the Vietnamese people said: "We highly value your achievements in forming the anti-Vietnam war front in the United States. Despite the Nixon administration's anti-democratic measures and deceitful arguments, you have succeeded with the strength of your unity in bringing forth the American people's strong antiwar sentiments."[13]

ANTIWAR LETTERS SENT TO U.S. PEACE GROUPS.

Liberation Press Agency (Clandestine) 1511 GMT 8 October 1969:

(Text) South Vietnam October 8 GPA--The South Vietnam People's Committee for Solidarity with the American People on October 5 sent the following message to the American Committee for Solidarity with the Vietnamese People:

Dear friends, we are very elated to learn that you will launch a big fall campaign against the Nixon administration's war policy, urging it to put an end to the war in Vietnam and to bring all U.S. troops home immediately....

We warmly welcome your initiative and highly appreciate your great efforts to coordinate actions in the campaign and believe that, for the U.S. people's vital interests, your struggle will be sympathized [with] and supported widely by all sections of the U.S. population regardless of the colour of their skin and political tendencies....

Dear friends, we think that the freedom and peace-loving American people can no longer permit the warlike circles in the U.S. administration, in the name of the United States of America, to continue the criminal war against the Vietnamese people.

Lastly, we wish you great success in the fall campaign to urge the Nixon administration to end the war in Vietnam and to bring all U.S. troops home immediately without posing any conditions [tantamount to surrender].

We would like to convey to you our sincere thanks and best regards.[14]

<u>VIETNAM ORGANIZATIONS LAUD AMERICAN ANTIWAR CAMPAIGN.</u>
Hanoi VNA International Service 1621 GMT 21 April 1971:
(Text) Hanoi VNA April 21—The Vietnam Committee for Solidarity with the American People has sent a message to the various antiwar organizations in the United States voicing support to their spring campaigns. The message said in-part:

Your April 24 demonstrations, May 5th moratorium, and other spring activities challenge seriously Nixon's war policy. They express the urgent demand of the overwhelming majority of Americans that the slaughter in Vietnam be ended for the respect of Vietnam's independence and sovereignty and for the safeguard of the United States' honor and interest.

The Vietnamese people and the world public opinion highly appreciate the broad coalition of different American antiwar groups and reaffirm their support for your work....[15]

HOANG MINH GIAM SUPPORTS U.S. ANTIWAR ACTIVITIES.
Hanoi VNA International Service 1557 GMT 17 April 1971:
(Text) Hanoi VNA April 17—Prof. Hoang Minh Giam, Chairman of the Vietnam Committee for Solidarity with the American People, has sent a message to antiwar fighters in the United States to express warm sympathy with the new antiwar campaigns in the spring.

"The nation-wide action," the message said, "together with the previous ones, are the high crests of the rising waves of indignation among the American people. They constitute an ever-growing force checking the advance of the Nixon administration's adventurous and warlike policies.

"Through concrete actions, you voice the aspirations of the majority of the American people, genuine Americans who cherish freedom democracy, and justice. You also contribute to consolidating and developing the solidarity and mutual understanding between our two peoples....

"You have started to mobilize all the forces in ethnic groups, religious communities, and different social strata to build for antiwar activities around the nation this spring....Your diversified activities, either centralized or decentralized, if able to stimulate and involve peace forces, all contribute to checking the war policies of the U.S. administration while preserving the interests of the American people and the honor of the United States. At the same time they are a strong encouragement to the Vietnamese people in their fight for independence and freedom."[16]

PEOPLE'S LIBERATION ARMED FORCES DEPUTY COMMANDER REPLIES TO BLACK PANTHER TROOP OFFER.

Liberation Press Agency (Clandestine) in English to East Europe and the Far East, 1610 GMT 14 Nov 70 and Hanoi VNA International service in English 0546 GMT 29)ct 70:

The South Vietnam National Liberation Front for the Liberation and the Provisional Revolutionary Government of the Republic of South Vietnam [Both Communist fronts for North Vietnam] recently received a letter from Mr. Huey Newton, Defense Minister of the Black Panther Party, informing them that the party is ready to send volunteers to fight shoulder to shoulder with the South Vietnamese [Viet Cong/NVA] people against the U.S. imperialist aggressors....

After extending fraternal greetings to the South Vietnamese liberation fighters [VC/NVA] the letter said: "In the spirit of international revolutionary solidarity, the Black Panther Party hereby offers to the National Liberation Front for the Liberation and Provisional Revolutionary Government of South Vietnam an undetermined number of troops to assist you in your fight against American imperialism. It is appropriate for the Black Panther Party to take this action at this time in recognition of the fact that your struggle is also our struggle, for we recognize that our common enemy is U.S. imperialism which is the leader of international bourgeois domination. There is no fascist or reactionary government in the world today that could stand without the support of United States imperialism. Therefore our problem is international, and we offer these troops in recognition of the necessity for international alliance to deal with the problem....Such alliance will advance the struggle toward the final act of dealing with American imperialism..."

In her letter of reply to Mr. Huey Newton, Mrs. Nguyen Thi Dinh, Deputy Commander of the South Vietnam People's Liberation Armed Forces [VC/NVA], said:

"On behalf of the cadres and fighters of the SVN PLAF, I welcome your noble deed and convey to you our sincere thanks for your warm support against U.S. aggression, for national salvation. We consider it as a great contribution from your side, and an important event of the peace and democratic movement in the United States giving us active support, a friendly gesture voicing your determination to fight side by side with the Vietnamese [Communist] people for the victory of the common cause of revolution....

"With profound gratitude, we take note of your enthusiastic proposal. When necessary, we will call for your volunteers to assist us.

"We are firmly confident that your just cause will enjoy sympathy, warm and strong support from the people art home and abroad, and will win complete victory, that our ever closer coordinated struggle will surely stop the bloody hands of the U.S. imperialists and contribute to winning independence, freedom, democracy and genuine peace.

"Best greetings for 'unity, militancy, and victory' from the South Vietnam People's Liberation Fighters."[17]

AMERICANS ATTEND HANOI SOLIDARITY MEETING.

Hanoi VNA International Service 1633 GMT 26 April 1971:

A meeting was held here [Hanoi] this evening under the sponsorship of the Committee for Solidarity with the American People to welcome the 1971 spring offensive of the American people demanding immediate and total withdrawal of U.S. troops from Vietnam and an end to the U.S. war of aggression in Indochina.

The meeting was attended by representatives of Solidarity and Hanoi public offices and mass organizations and representatives of the Hanoi population of various strata.

Vice Chairman of Solidarity, Dang Thai Mai, spoke of consolidating the solidarity of the Vietnamese people with the American people in the common struggle against Nixon's war of aggression. We especially welcome the presence at this meeting of two American scientists, Arthur Galston [Professor of Yale University] and Ethan Singer [or Singner, Professor of Boston University], the genuine representatives of those American intellectuals. We are meeting here today in the inspiring atmosphere of the victories won by the peoples of Vietnam, Laos and Cambodia on all the Indochina fronts. We warmly hail the antiwar movement of the American people which is surging up forcefully. We welcome the American working people, youths, students, intellectuals, mothers and women, religious believers, public figures, statesman, and servicemen who are valiantly confronting the most bellicose and barbarous administration ever seen in the history of America. The struggle of the American people against war, for the interests of the American people, for the interests and honour of the United States, also constitutes a great encouragement to the fight of the Vietnamese people for independence, sovereignty, reunification and territorial integrity.[18]

OUR WISHES FOR YOUR VICTORY IN THE 1971 FALL OFFENSIVE.

Letter 10/18/1971 from Mr. Ho Thu, National Liberation Front Central Committee and Chairman of Committee for Solidarity with American People, to American People:

The South Vietnamese [Communist front] people are overjoyed at the growth of the anti-Vietnam War movement in the United States. They highly appreciate the last Spring Offensive of various strata of the American people, including war vets and active servicemen. In the last months of summer, in defiance of fascist repression, the movement for peace, democracy and the right to live in the United States took stronger actions, demanding that the Nixon administration seriously respond to the 7-point peace initiative of the Provisional Revolutionary Government of the Republic of South Vietnam....

This fall, carrying forward your fine tradition of struggle, you are actively preparing for a new and nation-wide offensive for peace in Vietnam and for the fight to live [in] democracy in the United States. The South Vietnamese [Communist front] people fully support your initiative and activities to urge that the Nixon administration seriously respond to the RSVN PRG 7-point peace proposal, immediately end the war of aggression in Vietnam, Laos and Cambodia, bring all your sons and brothers home, and respect the right to self-determination of each Indochinese people.

We are convinced that your Fall Offensive this year will enjoy wide support from the world and will obtain many greater victories.[19]

As an adjunct to the Solidarity Committee, student organizations were formed in North Vietnam to interact with American students. One such group representing Hanoi University students sent a telegram to American students offering support for the November 1969 antiwar activities. The telegram read, in-part:

> Last night, 13 November, in Hanoi, the Vietnamese Students Federation organized a meeting to acclaim and support the struggle phase for 13, 14 and 15 November of American university students and the American people to demand the rapid and complete withdrawal of American troops out of South Vietnam. Over 1,000 representatives of students, teachers, and teaching cadres from Hanoi University participated.
>
> Secretary of the Vietnamese Students Federation, Le Tam, expressed warm acclaim and complete support for the just struggle of American university students and the people who are demanding an end to the war of aggression in Vietnam, and a rapid and complete withdrawal of American and American-faction foreign nation troops from South Vietnam....
>
> Dr. Nguy Nhu Kon Tum, president of the Hanoi University, speaking for the university teachers, and Miss Nguyen Thuy Van, student at the Polytechnic College, speaking for Hanoi university students, expressed the unity and support of the Vietnamese intellectuals and students for the new struggle phase of the American intellectuals, students and people.
>
> The meeting unanimously approved the resolution acclaiming and supporting the November struggle phase of American university students and the people who are demanding that the Nixon administration withdraw all American troops and the troops of the American satellite nations out of South Vietnam....[20]

The Communists clearly understood the role that American women could play in opposing the war. They formed several front organizations whose sole purpose was to appeal to American women, including mothers and wives of servicemen, students, and any other women who could be persuaded to join in the antiwar effort. To this end, several front organizations were formed by the Communists, such as the Vietnam Women's Union Standing Committee, the South Vietnam Liberation Women's Union, and the National Liberation Front Women's Union. Following are but a few of the appeals sent to American women from these Communist fronts:

WOMEN SUPPORT U.S. STRIKE FOR PEACE.
Hanoi VNA 1428 GMT 20 March 1962:
(Text) Hanoi, 20 March —"All Vietnamese women wholeheartedly support the 'Women Strike for Peace' launched by the women of Washington with the participation of women from many other towns in America," said the Vietnam Women's Union Standing Committee in its letter to Mrs. Ruth Gage Colby of New York. The letter proclaimed:

From the radio, the newspapers, and the message of the Women's International Democratic Federation we are very elated to learn that American women are engaged in a campaign to safeguard world peace and to end the danger of nuclear war. With the same aspiration for peace—and to protect women's interests and children's happiness—Vietnam women always side with American women, the letter states.

Vietnamese women harbor no hatred toward women and other people in America. They all have the same goal: peace, friendship, and happiness. That is why we support each other.[21]

WOMEN, YOUTH SEND LETTERS TO GROUPS IN U.S.
VNA International Service 1608 GMT 11 February 1968, Hanoi:

(Text) Hanoi—The South Vietnam Liberation women and youth unions sent letters to American women and youth on the occasion of the current concerted struggle of the South Vietnamese [Communist front] people against U.S. aggressors and the Thieu-Ky administration according to Liberation Press Agency.

The letter signed by Nguyen Thi Thanh, secretary general of the South Vietnam Liberation Women's Union [Communist front], and addressed to American women, said [in-part]:

The South Vietnamese women and other people are well aware that the American women do not approve of the unjust war conducted by the U.S. Government against the South Vietnamese people because it not only brings sufferings to the South Vietnamese people, but also causes many Americans the loss of their husbands and sons.

To protect their families' interests, to defend the United States' fine tradition of freedom and democracy, more and more American women have risen up valiantly against the U.S. war in Vietnam.

In the face of the present situation, we earnestly call on you to raise your voice strongly, and take more positive actions to demand an early end to this dirty war and the sufferings of our two peoples and to demand the repatriation of your husbands and sons who have been forced to go to Vietnam. No more American youths [should] be sent to Vietnam as American youth have no enmity for the Vietnamese people. There is no reason to let them kill South Vietnamese women and children, and then die uselessly and shamefully....[22]

NFL WOMEN'S UNION CONDEMNS TREATMENT OF ANGELA DAVIS.
Liberation Press Agency (Clandestine) 1613 23 December 1970:
The South Vietnam Liberation Women's Union on December 22 [1970] issued a statement condemning the U.S. administration for detaining Miss Angela Davis, an active peace-fighter in the United States....

The South Vietnam Liberation Women's Union sternly condemns this reactionary and brutal policy and firmly demands the Nixon administration to abolish the charges against Miss Angela Davis, Bobby Seale and other detained democratic, progressive, peace-loving Americans, white as well as coloured people, and release them immediately.

The statement called on progressive women and people all over the world to take strong actions in support of the struggle of the American people against the U.S. war in Vietnam, Cambodia, and Laos and against terror, repression and racial discrimination in the U.S.A.[23]

LETTER TO U.S. SENATE FOREIGN RELATIONS COMMITTEE.
Liberation Press (Clandestine) 1512 GMT 17 May 1971:
(Text) South Vietnam May 17 LPA—In a letter to the Foreign Relations Committee of the U.S. Senate made public on May 15 in Saigon, Mme. Ngo Ba Thanh, Chairman of the movement of Women's Actions for the Right to Live, pointed out: "We once again demand the total withdrawal of U.S. troops from Vietnam before the end of 1971." The letter said that "the restoration of peace is closely linked to the withdrawal of U.S. troops and troops of other countries (U.S. satellite countries— LPA ED) from Vietnam and the formation of a government really representing the South Vietnamese people's aspirations...."

> ....The letter also pointed out that the U.S. war of aggression "has resulted in 200,000 political prisoners, widespread robbery, social depravation, drinking, opium smoking, prostitution, contempt for the dignity of the Vietnamese people, and particularly the Vietnamese women."[24]

As presented earlier, Madam Binh, one of the leaders of the National Liberation Front and member of the Communist delegation to the Paris peace negotiations, was very active in promoting the antiwar movement in the United States and elsewhere. In April 1972, she took her efforts to a new level and addressed a letter to the United States Congress in a lengthy epistle about the evils of the Nixon war machine and his deceitful Vietnamization program. Her comments from Paris VNA to the VNA Hanoi at 0940, 26 April 1972, are quoted here, in-part:

> I can assure you that, no matter to what level Mr. Nixon escalates the war, he cannot retrieve his "Vietnamization" policy from bankruptcy, nor can he prevent the South Vietnamese people from achieving their genuine independence, freedom and self-determination. The only thing Mr. Nixon can do is to pile up crimes that are unbearable to any person of conscience throughout the world and that further smear the honor of the United States.
>
> According to the U.S. Constitution, the Congress has the power to decide on the question of war and peace. Therefore, I urge you to stop President Nixon in taking an adventurous path fraught with unpredictable consequences. What do I want?...The American Government should withdraw all its forces within a determined period. We are prepared to ensure full safety for such a withdrawal....We advocate an independent, peaceful and neutral South Vietnam.[25]

The Peoples' Republic of China was also active in encouraging and supporting the antiwar movement in the United States and around the world. An article from the *Peking People's Daily*, appearing in the *Washington Star* on March 28, 1966, is representative of China's attitude toward the antiwar movement. In this article the Chinese describe and glorify the recent round of protests in the United States. Liao Cheng-chih, vice chairman of the China Peace Committee, is quoted as saying, "The Chinese admire and firmly support the antiwar movement in the United States." The article continued, "This once again demonstrates that on the Viet Nam question the American people stand on the side of the Vietnamese people and not on the side of the U.S. government. That the broad masses of the American people have arisen against the imperialism of their own country is something unprecedented in the United States history...."[26]

The signing of the four-power Peace Agreement in Paris on January 27, 1973, did not end the efforts of the Committee for Solidarity to influence the American People. On February 8, 1973, Professor Hoang Minh Giam, Chairman of the Solidarity Committee, sent another letter to the American people. The letter was full of praise for the assistance of the antiwar movement in bringing about peace and victory for the Hanoi regime. It was also aimed at keeping the movement active to prevent the United States from providing further aid to South Vietnam as that country continued the fight on against the incursion from the North. Hanoi had no intention of ending its conquest of the South, but it wanted to be sure that their continued incursion did not cause the United States to take any action to interfere with their plans. In recognition of the signing of the "peace" agreement and to encourage continued pressure on the Nixon administration, the chairman of the Solidarity Committee sent the following message to American activists:

> The Vietnamese people jubilantly welcome this historic victory of their struggle full of hardships and sacrifices for independence and freedom. Peace-loving people all over the world and the American people also rejoice before this initial result of their persistent struggle for peace.

Over the last ten years, braving many big sacrifices, you have struggled perseveringly against the dirty war in Vietnam. You have held high the American people's tradition of peace, freedom and justice to safeguard the interests and honor of the United States. The Vietnamese people want to express their heartfelt thanks to you, to different anti-war organizations, circles and groups throughout the United States....

The Paris Agreement on ending the war and restoring peace in Vietnam has set a historic landmark in the relations between our two countries. However, the reactionary forces have not yet given up their plot to sabotage the agreement, undermine peace and stifle liberty and democracy, obstructing the path to independence and national concord of the Vietnamese people....[27]

The forgoing messages and statements by Communist officials are only a small sample of their continuous efforts to encourage and promote the antiwar movement. It is not possible to present all of these documents here, for they would occupy all of the pages of this book and more. Since space has only allowed inclusion of excerpts from some of these documents in this chapter, several complete documents have been included in Appendix L.

Almost all of the excerpts presented above referred to the "South Vietnam" National Liberation Front (NLF), the "South Vietnam" Solidarity Committee, the "South Vietnam" Provisional Revolutionary Government (PRG), and etc. All of these entities were a creation of the Lao Dong Communist Party in North Vietnam. They did not exist except as tools and front organizations for Hanoi. The continuous reference to South Vietnam in this way was a fundamental aspect of the Communist propaganda effort to make people in the United States and other countries believe that such organizations existed in South Vietnam and represented popular support for the Communists in the South.

The People's Revolutionary Government was a shadow organization created to "provide North Vietnam with a quasi-legal cover for their continuous presence and military build-up in the South, but it was also the primary instrument of an ongoing North Vietnamese 'diplomatic offensive' which was aimed at destroying public confidence in the GVN [South Vietnam government], most particularly within the U.S."[28]

As presented in Chapter Three, the National Liberation Front was also a creation of the Lao Dong Party. This was confirmed by North Vietnamese Army Colonel Bui Tin when asked in an interview for the Wall Street Journal if the NLF was an independent political movement of South Vietnamese. He responded, "No. It was set up by our Communist Party to implement a decision of the Third Party Congress of September 1960. We always said there was only one party, only one army in the war to liberate the South and unify the nation. At all times there was only one party commissar in command of the South."[29]

In forthcoming chapters the leaders of these front organizations will be seen meeting with antiwar activists from the United States and elsewhere and will incredulously be given a seat at the Paris peace negotiations.

Chapter Six

The Collaborators

America will never be destroyed from the outside. If we falter or lose our freedom, it will be because we destroyed ourselves.

—Abraham Lincoln

The spectacle of mass antiwar demonstrations in the streets of America gave the North Vietnamese great encouragement and comfort, but the visits to Hanoi and other world capitals by the antiwar leaders were viewed with special appreciation by the Communist leadership. The former North Vietnamese Army Colonel, Bui Tin, provided evidence of this point in his interview for the Wall Street Journal in August of 1985. He stated, "Visits to Hanoi by people like Jane Fonda and former Attorney General Ramsey Clark and ministers gave us confidence that we should hold on in the face of battlefield reverses. We were elated when Jane Fonda, wearing a red Vietnamese dress, said at a press conference that she was ashamed of American actions in the war and that she would struggle along with us...."[1] Colonel Bui Tin confirmed this view in a conversation with the author in 2003.

The exact number of Americans who traveled to Hanoi to meet with North Vietnamese officials is not known for certain but is estimated to be in excess of 200. Visits to North Vietnam by American citizens violated United States restraints on travel to hostile areas. For that reason most of those who traveled to North Vietnam took circuitous routes via various European countries, Moscow, Cuba, Cambodia, etc. Some made more than one trip. Consequently, it was difficult to keep track of how many traveled to Hanoi. In addition to travels to Hanoi, there were many meetings between American antiwar activists and North Vietnamese and other Communist officials in other parts of the world. They all had the same effect—to undermine the United States war effort in Vietnam, to give impetus to the Communist propaganda effort, and to give encouragement to the enemy. The House Committee on Internal Security conducted hearings in 1972 on American citizens' travel to countries or areas engaged in armed conflict with the United States. Excerpts from the House Committee report show how the majority of the members of the committee felt about Americans traveling to Hanoi and other hostile areas:

> This and other committees of the Congress have developed a vast body of information which reveals that a substantial number of United States citizens have traveled abroad to hostile areas and have there engaged in a variety of activities which necessarily give aid and encouragement to the enemy and have in a variety of ways caused direct injury to our fighting men, including the torturing of prisoners of war....
>
> The recent travel of Jane Fonda to Hanoi, which prompted the initiation of this committee's inquiries in the last Congress, was only one of a series of similar events which must be a matter of concern to the Congress. Such activities—as her broadcasts from the enemy's territory to our forces in the field—have an obvious tendency to encourage the enemy and to undermine the morale of our forces to whom she owed primary allegiance. As described to us by several experts in psychological warfare, they can have no other result than to advance the enemy's interest at the expense of our own....[2]

As mentioned in the Committee on Internal Security's report, some of the American citizens who traveled abroad caused grave physical and psychological harm to our servicemen held prisoner (POWs) by the Communists. The impact of these visits on our POWs is so compelling that a complete chapter will be devoted to this topic. For now, it is important to see who these "travelers" were and the ways in which they gave aid and comfort to the enemy. The number of travelers is too great to present details of all the visits with representatives of North Vietnam; therefore, only a few representative trips can be covered here. We begin with the most notorious of the fellow travelers.

Jane Fonda

Probably the most well known traveler to Hanoi is Jane Fonda. Her most famous visit to North Vietnam was from July 8 through July 22, 1972. During that visit, she made 21 broadcasts from Hanoi, many of which were aimed at U.S. servicemen fighting in Vietnam.[3] On July 22, 1972, a report by United Press International, carried in the *Japan Times*, stated that Jane Fonda had accused President Nixon of "betraying everything the American people have at heart." The same article cited by the Vietnam News Agency quoted Fonda as saying, "She was returning from a visit to Hanoi 'more convinced than ever of the victory of the Vietnamese in their fight to safeguard their independence and freedom.'" Fonda continued lashing out at President Nixon and insisted that the United States accept North Vietnam's seven-point peace plan, which included unilateral withdrawal of U.S. troops, setting a date for withdrawal, and ending U.S. support of the Thieu government in the South.[4] These were the usual Communist terms for surrender.

Although Fonda's broadcasts from Hanoi are well known, it is worthwhile to review the theme analysis of her broadcasts produced by the staff of the House Committee on Internal Security and included in the report of hearings. The analysis focuses on a specific set of broadcasts aimed at U.S. servicemen:

> 1. "Hanoi VNA International Service in English, 0246 GMT 14 July 72." Fonda statement preceded by Vietnamese broadcaster noting that the message was addressed to "all the U.S. servicemen involved in the bombing of North Vietnam." Fonda's own statement included a description of alleged U.S. bombing of dikes in the vicinity of NAM SACH (60 km. E of Hanoi) on the Red River on July 12 just before her visit to that area. After a quasi-humanitarian appeal on how that district was strictly an agricultural area and devoid of military targets, she accused the U.S. of "terrorist tactics" because of the bombing raids of July 12. In

making her appeal to U.S. servicemen, she asserted: I (? implore) you, I beg you to consider what you are doing. In the area I went yesterday it was easy to see that there are no military targets,...no important highway,....no communication network,....(and) no heavy industry.... All of you in the cockpits of your planes, on the aircraft carriers, those who are loading the bombs, those who are repairing the planes....please think what you are doing.

2. "Hanoi in English to American Servicemen Involved in the Indo-China War, 1300 GMT 17 July 71." Fonda Statement begins: This is Jane Fonda speaking from Hanoi, and I'm speaking particularly to U.S. servicemen who are stationed on the aircraft carriers in the Gulf of Tonkin, in the 7th Fleet, in the Anglico Corps in the south of Vietnam. [Anglico – a little known term for Air-Naval Gunfire Liaison Company, a fire coordination team for Marine and Naval air and artillery strikes by Navy ships. Not a term that you would expect Fonda to know on her own.]

After a rather pointed diatribe about U.S. producers of military weapons, Ms. Fonda then accused the American military leadership of employing "illegal" weapons, such as "toxic chemicals," guava/spider/pineapple bombs and combinations of napalm, phosphorous and thermite. She concludes: "And the use of these bombs or condoning the use of these bombs makes one a war criminal."

Endorsing the current Democratic Party nominee as "an example of the overwhelming, [repeat] overwhelming feeling in the United States among people to end the war," who also "represents all that is good to these people, end to the war, or end to the bombing," Fonda asserted that it was not "the interests" of U.S. troops to attack North Vietnam.

Fonda then described the alleged bombing of the BACH MAI hospital which she visited earlier that day. After claiming that a bomb had hit the center of the hospital, "obviously dropped there on purpose," she added: "With the kind of bombs, the kind of techniques that have been developed now, you know, particularly you pilots know that accidents like that don't happen.... Why do you do this? Why do you follow orders telling you to destroy a hospital or bomb the schools?

Obviously begging the question by compounding a false supposition with another, Fonda goes on to relate the use of "plastic pellets" (which, in her expert knowledge of medical technology, "doesn't show up on X-rays") which preclude extraction, and "chemical bombs," which causes pregnant women to produce "deformed babies."

In essence, this message employs quasi-humanitarian "scare" tactics and hyper-legal rhetoric which, while not openly advocating U.S. servicemen to disobey orders, certainly distorts the actual nature and purpose of U.S. air operations to a degree that if a servicemen believed all of her a priori arguments, then he could have only one logical alternative, i.e., to refuse to participate in the bombing raids. The message, therefore, represents a highly subliminal appeal to servicemen to disobey orders, etc., evidently prepared by professional propagandists.

3. "Hanoi in English to Europe, Africa and the Middle East, 2000 GMT 19 Jul 72." This is a North Vietnamese news broadcast with excerpts of another Fonda "address to American servicemen" describing her visit to the textile center of Nam Dinh on July 18, which did not appear in FBIS [Foreign Broadcast Information Service] for some reason. Fonda then described the ruins of the hospital, schools, churches, recreation centers and the textile factory in Nam Dinh, all of

which were allegedly targeted by U.S. fliers, in spite of the fact that "no military targets" exist in that city. In addition, she alleged that the nearby dike system had "large fissures" from several bombing raids. Following this, she then appealed to U.S. troops:

> What are your commanders telling you? How are they justifying this to you? Have you any idea what your bombs are doing when you pull the levers and push the buttons.

4. "Hanoi in English to Southeast Asia, 1000 GMT 21 Jul 72." Introduced as a "recorded message...to U.S. pilots involved in the Vietnam War," this broadcast generally denounced the U.S. employment of antipersonnel bombs which "were outlawed by the Hague Convention of 1907." She also reiterated the "plastic pellet" story. More importantly, Fonda asked U.S. fliers:

> How does it feel to be used as pawns? You may be shot down...even killed, but for what, and for whom?....We are afraid of what, what must be happening to you as human beings. For isn't it possible to destroy, to receive salary for pushing buttons and pulling levers that are dropping illegal bombs on innocent people without having that damage your own souls?

Carrying this subliminal, quasi-humanitarian appeal further, Fonda continued:

> Tonight when you are alone, ask yourselves: What are you doing? Accept no ready answers fed to you by rote from basic training on up, but as men, as human beings, can you justify

what you are doing? Do you know why you are flying these missions, collecting extra combat pay on Sunday?...I know that if you saw and if you knew the Vietnamese under peaceful conditions, you would hate the men who are sending you on bombing missions."

5. "Hanoi in English to American Servicemen Involved in the Indochina War, 1300 GNT 22 Jul 72." In this broadcast, Fonda appealed to everyone involved in the bombing raids over North Vietnam, including specifically naming six U.S. aircraft carriers, "the Anglico Corps" and USAF B-52 and F4 "Phantom" crews. She then accuses President Nixon of lying to the American people about Vietnam and to American servicemen about the real purpose of the raids on North Vietnam. [Sound familiar? Change the names to Bush and Iraq!] Switching her appeal to U.S. troops, she again became rhetorical and asked:

All of you...know the lies. You know the cheating on the body counts, the falsified battle reports, and the number of planes that are shot down and what your targets really are. Knowing who was doing the lying, should you then allow these same people and the same liars to define for you who your enemy is. Shouldn't we then, shouldn't we all examine the reasons that have been given to us to justify the murder that you are being paid to commit? If they told you the truth, you wouldn't fight, you wouldn't kill....You have been told lies so that it would be possible for you to kill.[5]

Anyone interested in reading the full text of Jane Fonda's broadcasts can find them at the Texas Tech University Vietnam Archive, call number 2185011009. Before leaving Jane Fonda behind, it is insightful to see some of the statements she made prior to her trip to Hanoi. "On November 22, 1969, she made a speech at Michigan State University at East Lansing, Michigan as part of a 32 stop tour to raise funds for the Defense of GIs in Trouble with the Army, the Vietnam Veterans Against the War (VVAW) and the Black Panther Party." According to the *Detroit Free Press* reporter who covered the speech she stated:

> I would think that if you understood what communism was, you would hope, you would pray on your knees that we would someday become communists.
>
> The peace proposal of the Viet Cong is the only honorable, just, possible way to achieve peace in Vietnam.
>
> Black Panther leader Huey P. Newton is the only man I've ever met that I would trust as the leader of this country.
>
> (While discussing U.S. soldiers) They're a new kind of soldier. They're not John Wayne freaks over there. No order goes unchallenged.
>
> When they're sent out on patrol they just go out a little ways. They lie down on a little knoll and blow grass and star gaze.
>
> They're good soldiers. We should be proud of them. They're not only doing what they're not supposed to do, but they're not even performing the basic functions of soldiers.

During the speech she indicated that there was work to be done on behalf of the Vietcong and referred to the VC in the following fashion:

Vietcong are "driven by the same spirit that drove Washington and Jefferson."

Vietcong are "the conscience of the world."

I think that the majority of the students are scared of the word "socialism." It's a good message (socialism), and the more people give it the better.[6]

Fonda's accusations that Americans had bombed dikes riled the pilots who flew missions over North Vietnam. The *Stars and Stripes* carried an article in August 1972 which quoted several U.S. Air Force pilots. Colonel George Rutter, Commander of the 366th Fighter Wing, firmly denied targeting or hitting any dams or dikes. Major Gary Alden, an F4 Phantom pilot, echoed Rutter's sentiments, "I'm very irritated about the dike charges because it's far from true. I've never seen a dike targeted and I've never seen one hit." He continued, "There's enough water around there at the moment without bombing the dikes." Major Stephen Levine, a B52 pilot, nailed the pilots' case with this comment, "If we deliberately set out to bomb the dikes there wouldn't be any left."[7]

John McLaughlin, a speech writer for the White House, in another article appearing in the *Stars and Stripes* in October 1972, made it unequivocally clear that only sites of military value were ever targeted by U.S. aircraft. He stressed that "no armed force in history has gone to greater efforts to avoid endangering civilians than the U.S. military. Our personnel have sustained casualties themselves rather than take certain legitimate military actions because such actions might also inflict casualties on innocent civilians." It was also made clear that North Vietnamese leaders could end the bombing overnight if they stopped their aggression against their neighbors.[8]

Ramsey Clark

Another well known traveler was the former Attorney General Ramsey Clark. Hanoi Vietnam News Agency International Service in English 0726 GMT 6 Aug 72 gave this report on his visit to North Vietnam:

The bombing should be stopped immediately, should have never been done in the first place and should never be done again, declared Ramsey Clark...during a visit Thursday to the village of Phu Vang in Thai Binh Province (North Vietnam) bombed by U.S. war planes on July 21.

Ramsey Clark, together with the other members of a visiting team of the International Commission for Inquires into U.S. War Crimes in Indochina, was also shown the damage caused to the Lan sluice near the seafront in the same area, as a result of several U.S. raids at the end of last month....[Clark has denied that he was a member of the War Crimes Commission.]

Reporting on Ramsey Clark's visit to DRV continued with this broadcast by Hanoi Radio in Mandarin to Southeast Asia 0530 GMT 16 Aug 72:

Listeners, please listen to remarks made by Ramsey Clark, formerly attorney general of the United States and member of the third team of the International Commission for Inquiries into U.S. War Crimes in Indochina, to this station's reporter. Lawyer Clark visited North Vietnam during the period from 29 July to 12 August. He said: After visiting North Vietnam and seeing with my own eyes what is happening here, I am more impressed by North Vietnam itself than by what I have read from books and newspapers, seen in pictures, or heard from people who had visited Vietnam. Everyone will be deeply impressed by the people of the Democratic Republic of Vietnam....

I have come to understand that the determination and strength of the Vietnamese people stem from their (? conviction) that their government is one that serves the country and the people. Here is justice and equality. [Since when did a Communist country serve the people? Under communism, the people serve the state.]

> My personal experience here has enabled me to see that this country is pursuing a revolutionary cause of international significance, that is, an aspiration for equality. In this country, one sees no internal conflicts, but sees a people closely united. I feel that in Saigon and other cities of South Vietnam I cannot travel from place to place as safely as in North Vietnam, because in South Vietnam, (?an upheaval) is taking place, the society is in chaos, and the people lack (? faith)....[10]

Clark's comments about not feeling safe are unbelievable! Didn't Clark know that the South was being pummeled by North Vietnam? Where was he in March through July 1972 when six divisions of the North Vietnamese regular army troops were attacking South Vietnam in the Easter offensive? [11] Clark had more to say in Bangkok, Thailand on August 13 on his way home. He told newsmen that "at least at three points on the dikes he was able to see the result of U.S. bombings." "I have seen dikes bombed and shelled in different ways," he said. "I have seen many houses, villages and dikes destroyed. I know that humanely, the bombing I have seen is unjustifiable, irregardless the cause and purpose." Clark continued, saying that he had a talk with captured U.S. pilots. He also remarked, "The pilots have been well treated and [are] healthy."[12] The chapter on POWs will prove otherwise.

Hanoi Radio broadcasting in English to American servicemen on 15 August 1972 included some of the comments made by Clark in Bangkok:

> Former U.S. Attorney General Ramsey Clark...declared August 13 in Bangkok that the U.S. bombing of North Vietnam was on purpose. On his first leg in Thailand while on his way home...Clark said he would publish evidence on U.S. bombings of dikes and other civilian targets in North Vietnam he had gathered during his stay there, once he is back in the United States. He also said he had a clear-cut opinion of all what has happened on U.S. bombings of dikes in North Vietnam. Anyway, this bombing is on purpose, he added.[13]

Clark continued espousing North Vietnamese propaganda after he reached the United States. At a news conference at San Francisco airport that was broadcast by Hanoi on August 15 Clark said, "American war prisoners in North Vietnam will be released as soon as the U.S. ends the war and gets out of Vietnam. It is known that U.S. military men detained in Vietnam are in good health and they are given human treatment."[14]

The Vietnam News Agency (VNA) monitored in Tokyo quoted Clark as saying two things about American bombing of North Vietnam. Clark said:

> First, that there has been massive inhuman bombing on cities, villages, churches, schools, hospitals, dykes, sluices, canals and the wide water system that supports the culture and the life of the country. Whatever the cause and the purpose of that bombing there can be no possible justification in the eyes of common morality.
>
> Secondly, the people of this country (North Vietnam) believe their cause is just. Every person I have seen has shown by his acts and his word his total commitment.... The lesson is the hope of the future of mankind...we must learn that a people who believe their cause is just, however poor or few, can never be conquered.[15]

Secretary of State William Rogers was shocked by Clark's statements while in Hanoi. Rogers called Clarks actions contemptible. The North Vietnamese broadcast quoted Clark "as having begged villagers of a bombed area to 'forgive the criminal actions of the American people.'" Referring to Clark's actions, Rogers said, "Imagine going to a nation that we are at war with, taking their version of everything that is said and then going on their radio and broadcasting back to the U.S. and around the world, at a time when American men are fighting over there and losing their lives."[17]

Representative Fletcher Thompson (R-GA.) also weighed in on Clark's actions. He accused Clark of lending support to enemy propaganda attacks on the United States and questioned whether Clark's activities constituted sedition or treason. He remarked, "It is too bad that a former Attorney General of the United States would lend himself to support propaganda activities of the enemy and not condemn the thousands of murders and atrocities they have committed."[18] We will hear more about Clark in forthcoming chapters.

Vietnam Veterans Against the War (VVAW)

Members of the Vietnam Veterans Against the War traveled to Hanoi and Paris to meet with representatives of North Vietnam and Communist front organizations such as the NLF and PRG. A CIA report in July 1972 stated that "16 members of the VVAW left for Paris for a 3-day meeting with veterans of the South Vietnamese Liberation Front [NLF], North Vietnamese Army, the [Communist] Pathet Lao and the Cambodian Liberation Government." According to the CIA report, "This meeting was arranged by a group of left-wing French activists in an attempt to bring former enemies together to seek a mutual understanding about what can be done to end the war."[19]

Hanoi VNA International Service in English at 1501 GMT 27 March 1972 reported on the visit of U.S. antiwar veterans:

> Vice Premier Nguyen Duy Trinh recently met and had a cordial talk with Al Hubbard, national coordinator of the Vietnam Veterans Against the War, who had come here for a visit at the invitation of the Vietnam Committee for Solidarity with the American People.
>
> Al Hubbard condemned the schemes and crimes of the American authorities in carrying out its "Vietnamization" policy to prolong the war, which had brought new difficulties to the United States. At the same time he denounced the tricks and moves the U.S. ruling circles had resorted to [to] fool the public and repress the movement for democracy and peace in the United States, especially the movement of the colored people.
>
> Al Hubbard expressed his admiration for the unity and militancy of the Vietnamese people, and promised to work still harder for the movement against the criminal war of aggression of the U.S. Government.

For his part, the DRV vice-premier highly praised the activities of the VVAW and other antiwar organizations in the United States....[20]

An FBI report shows that Al Hubbard flew to Paris in November 1971 where he met with North Vietnamese and Viet Cong representatives. Hubbard revealed to members of the VVAW at a meeting in Kansas City that his trip had been financed by the Communist Party, USA. At the same meeting, Joe Urgo, a VVAW official, reported on his trip to Hanoi in August 1971 where he met with North Vietnamese officials. He said, "The reason for the trip to Hanoi ties in with the international action of active duty people to demonstrate against the Vietnam War." Urgo made the following proposals to the North Vietnamese:

(1) Tapes would be sent from the United States to North Vietnam to broadcast over Radio Hanoi to get U.S. servicemen to stop fighting in Vietnam;

(2) To send a VVAW delegation to Hanoi in the near future to negotiate the release of American POWs.[21]

At the Kansas City meeting of the VVAW in November 1971 it was decided to send a five-man delegation of the VVAW to Hanoi in December 1972 in an effort to gain the release of American POWs. The purpose of obtaining the release of a few POWs was to demonstrate to the persons participating in the national actions that "VVAW had real power."[22]

Stokely Carmichael

"Stokely Carmichael...traveled to Cuba and North Vietnam to condemn U.S. aggression against North Vietnam and call for total revolution against the imperialist, capitalist, and racialist structure of the United States."[23] Hanoi VNA International Service reported on 31 August 1967 that Premier Pham Van Dong had received Stokely Carmichael, a leader of the Movement of Black People in the United States, who was on a friendship visit to Vietnam. The news release stated:

The reception took place in an atmosphere of warm solidarity and friendship. After hearing Carmichael speak about the movement of black people in the United States against brutal racial discrimination by the U.S. ruling circles, Premier Pham Van Dong said: "The Vietnamese people deeply sympathize with the sufferings of black people in the United States and regard black people in the United States as their brothers and close comrades in arms in the struggle against the common enemy, U.S. imperialism. The Vietnamese people sincerely thank black people in the United States for the warm support they give to the Vietnamese people's cause of resistance to the U.S. aggression and of national salvation, and rejoice to see that this valuable support is developing with every passing day among black servicemen in the U.S. Army...."[24]

American Peace Fighters

Hanoi VNA International Service reported North Vietnam's Premier Pham Van Dong's interview with three American "peace fighters" on January 28, 1966. The three Americans, Herbert Aptheker, head of the Institute for Marxist Studies, New York; Staughton Lynd, professor of history, Yale University; and Thomas Hayden, a founder of the American Students for a Democratic Society, arrived in Hanoi in early January as guests of the Vietnam Peace Committee [a Communist front]. Some of the questions and answers during the interview with Premier Dong are quoted below.

> Question: If the United States withdrew its troops, would the DRV [North Vietnam] withdraw its troops from South Vietnam?
>
> Answer: The so-called presence of forces of the DRV in South Vietnam is but a myth fabricated by the U.S. imperialist by way of justification for their war of aggression in South Vietnam.

Question: Exactly how would the creation of a national coalition government in South Vietnam and the eventual reunification of South with North Vietnam comes about?

Answer: The setting up of a national coalition government in South Vietnam is an internal affair of the people of South Vietnam. It is to be settled by the people of South Vietnam themselves in accordance with the program of the NFLSV.... The urgent demand of our people throughout the country is to reunify the fatherland by peaceful means.

Question: It is often said by the U.S. Government that the NFLSV is an agent of the DRV and that the DRV is controlled by the Chinese People's Republic [CPR]. What is your reply?

Answer: This is a vile fabrication designed to slander the Vietnamese people, the NFLSV, the DRV, and the CPR. The NFLSV is the sole genuine representative of the people of South Vietnam....[25] [Remember, Colonel Bui Tin said that the NLF/NFL was an organ of the Lao Dong Party in North Vietnam.].

Joan Baez

On December 22, 1972, in Hanoi, Japanese correspondent, Tsuyoshi Doki, interviewed singer Joan Baez. Baez and other antiwar activists arrived in Hanoi on December 16, where they reportedly observed bombing of Hanoi and Haiphong and attended a press conference of captured B-52 crew members...She was reported to have said, "I hate Nixon. He is insane...." She also said, "Nixon is nothing but a madman who is wielding a dagger of colossal power...." She concluded, "When I return home, I will do my utmost so that the antiwar movement can be unified and become more powerful."[26]

Sydney Peck

On November 18 and 26, 1970, Hanoi Radio broadcast, in two parts, an interview with American Professor of Sociology, Sydney Peck, co-chairman of the New Mobilization Committee, who talked about the antiwar movement during his recent visit to North Vietnam. Peck's response to questions leaves no doubt about his political orientation:

> Question: Professor Peck, you come from the antiwar movement in the United States. Would you like to tell our listeners something about the movement that really concerns them?
>
> Answer: (Male voice with American accent—Ed.): Well, the most important thing about the movement against the war in the United States [did he mean Vietnam?] is that it is truly a majority movement of the American people....Millions of people demonstrated in the streets during the fall of 1969. So vast was the number of people demonstrating that Nixon was compelled to initiate a program of withdrawal. He was also compelled to say that the silent majority was with him. But the truth of the matter is that the antiwar movement in the United States reflects a great majority of opinion and is based on a true mass movement of the American people [music to North Vietnam's ears]....
>
> Question: At the Paris Conference on Vietnam, Madame Binh of the Republic of South Vietnam Provisional Revolutionary Government made an important statement on September 17 [1970]. What do you think of Madame Binh's proposal? What is your opinion on this point?
>
> Answer: Well, the proposals which Madame Binh put forward...were very well received by the people of the United States and in general, were well received throughout the world [not true].... Why were they [the proposals] fair and reasonable? First of all, the first point is that they get to the heart of the question and that is there can be no true peace in Vietnam and Indochina so long as the military forces of the United States and the military hardware of the United States remain in

your country....So that first important thing is to set a time, to fix a date when those forces will be withdrawn; that's the central question.

Peck continued to praise the provisions of the Communist peace plan. He mentioned another important feature which essentially said that once the date was set, there would be no problem for the people of South Vietnam (after takeover by the Communists) if they truly wanted peace, independence and democratic rights. We know what happened to the democratic rights when the North Vietnamese invaded the South in 1975 and imposed Hanoi's version of communism. We know that thousands were placed in re-education and concentration camps when the Communists from the North conquered the South and took away the freedom of the South Vietnamese people. That was almost 30 years ago and the former South Vietnamese people still have not seen "freedom" or "democratic rights."

The third provision of the peace proposal that Peck supported was almost comical. It promised to allow American forces to withdraw without being attacked by Communist forces. How generous of them! Peck thought that this formula (proposal) for capitulation and abandonment of our allies in South Vietnam was fair and reasonable.[27] One wonders how Peck would have liked to have spent the rest of his life in South Vietnam after it was taken over by the Communist North. One also wonders why someone with his academic and intellectual standing did not say one critical word about the totalitarian regime in the North and the total absence of democratic rights in that country.

Quakers Sail to Haiphong

A news brief in the Peace Information Edition of *Fellowship* announced that Quakers were to begin a voyage to North Vietnam: "The famous sailing ship 'Phoenix,' laden with medical and other supplies for the bombed civilian population of North Vietnam will sail early February [1967] from Tokyo for Haiphong....Several of the crew are preparing to stay in Vietnam to undertake humanitarian aid, 'to stand beside our brothers who suffer.'"[28]

U.S. Peace Group in Paris

On March 6, 1971, 170 Americans representing U.S. peace organizations were greeted in Paris by Madame Nguyen Thi Binh,

Minister of the Provisional Revolutionary Government. Madame Binh welcomed the Americans "who are concerned about the situation in Vietnam and who have come to Paris to try to understand the practical situation as well as the standpoint of the RSVN PRG Government...."

Madam Binh also said, "She hoped that, more than ever, there exists a mutual understanding between the Vietnamese and American people so that they could coordinate their actions with a view to ending the war and reaching a correct political solution to the South Vietnamese problem...."[29]

Antiwar Seven

A delegation of seven antiwar activists arrived in Hanoi on November 4, 1972. The delegation was made up of Howard Zinn, professor of history at Boston University who had been an antiwar activist for many years; Tom Hayden, antiwar propagandist and founder of SDS; reverend David Hunter, permanent secretary of the National Council of Churches; Mrs. Susan Miller, member of he People's Coalition for Peace and Justice (PCPJ); Mrs. Jan Austin, former editor of Ramparts; Mrs. Carolyne Mugar, member of the Indochina Peace Campaign; and Mr. Fred Branfman, director of Project Air War, which was a program denouncing alleged U.S. crimes of bombing and strafing in Indochina.

The seven were received by North Vietnam Premier Pham Van Dong on November 12. They "promised that back in the States they would step up the struggle to demand that the U.S. Government sign immediately the agreement already reached with the DRV."[30] The agreement the antiwar seven referred to here was a draft set of principles agreed upon by Henry Kissinger and Le Duc Tho during secret negotiation in October 1972, but which was strongly opposed by the government of South Vietnam.[31]

The antiwar seven traveled to the northern region of North Vietnam while on the November visit. In conversations with North Vietnamese while on this trip, the Americans had some unusual things to say. At a cooperative where young Vietnamese were present, Fred Bronfman had this to say, "We hope that the war will end soon so that you can grow up and study in peace. However, if the war continues we hope you will grow up and become valiant combatants and will be able to down many U.S. planes."[32] What more does it take to be guilty of treason? Other statements by members of this group raise similar questions about the loyalties of those in this group. Howard Zinn speaking to teachers and students at a normal school said:

> We are Americans who have struggled against the aggressive war in Vietnam. We and you, friends, know that a number of Americans have bombed and destroyed your country, but we also want you to know that the American people are humiliated by these actions and demand that the U.S. Government end its bombings and end the war and withdraw all U.S.troops from Asia. We want you to know that we are your friends. We will return to our country and we will struggle and organize the American people in the struggle to demand that the Nixon administration sign the peace agreement.[33]

The group attended a play by the Vietnamese while on the tour of the northern region. After the play, Tom Hayden expressed views on behalf of the delegation:

> Your cooperative [Communist collective organization], friends, is an example of how new values and a new social order can be established....Tonight we have witnessed your culture blooming in this area. In the United States reactionary historians boast that people in caves are savage and backward. But we hold that it is those who bomb children who are the savages and that it is the people singing in caves who are creating the future's culture.

> We live in an era of deceit. Today is Election Day in the United States where democracy is assumed to survive. Nixon has presented himself as a peace candidate busy deescalating the war, while actually he is continuing to conduct terrorist bombing which the American people cannot witness. The climax of his deceit is the election swindle in which he stressed that peace was within reach but refused to sign the nine-point agreement which the DRV made public.

> By making public the text of this agreement so that the American people can be aware of it, the Vietnamese people have shed more truth and democracy of the U.S. election, something Nixon has never done. The Vietnamese cause relies on the truth, but the cause of imperialism relies on deceit. We pledge to do all that we can do to force Nixon to sign the nine-point agreement and fully implement it and to build fine relations between the peoples of our two countries.[34]

PCPJ and NPAC Delegation

The Premier of North Vietnam, Pham Van Dong, met with Americans representing the antiwar groups, the People's Coalition for Peace and Justice (PCPJ) and the National Peace Action Coalition (NPAC) in August 1971. Premier Dong "highly praised the antiwar activities of the American people over the recent past, especially in the 1971 spring offensive." The Americans then had their say:

> For their part, the American guests praised the Vietnamese people's unity, determination and creativeness in their patriotic fight and national construction. They also welcomed the seven-point peace initiative of the Provisional Revolutionary Government [PRG] of South Vietnam and promised to push on [with] their coordinated antiwar actions.[35]

Ann Froines

Ann Froines visited North Vietnam as a member of the delegation of Americans Against Imperialism. She is quoted in an article in the Lao Dong official news organ on 21 October 1970. She said in-part:

> During our visit to Vietnam we saw with extreme clarity the beastly criminal nature of U.S. aggression in Vietnam....Through contact with the representative of the Provisional Revolutionary Government...we learned of the widespread and formidable destruction caused by the U.S. spreading more than 100 million

pounds of chemical poisons on the land and people of South Vietnam. We also learned that victims of torture within U.S. puppet prisons had died or been disabled due to the awful scars on their bodies. The U.S. army, which is presently building many additional tiger cages at Cong Dao [actually Con Dao, a South Vietnamese island prison], must bear direct responsibility for the countless crimes occurring within the prisons of South Vietnam.

All of these crimes have been perpetrated by the U.S. government in the name of "freedom" and "U.S. security." The unbelievable lies and distortions of the U.S. government can in no way conceal these crimes.

We and the people of the world clearly realize that these crimes cannot weaken the determination of the Vietnamese people to fight bravely until final victory is gained in their just struggle for independence and freedom.[36]

It is noteworthy that Froines said she learned of the misdeeds of the United States from the PRG. Is it any wonder that she would hear tales of horror from a Communist front set up by North Vietnam? Is it any wonder that she did not mention the 158,000 brutal terrorist attacks on South Vietnamese people by Communist forces from 1961 to mid-1970, and approximately 30,000 assassinations and 42,000 kidnappings of South Vietnamese people by Communists forces during the same time period?[37] Apparently she preferred to listen to the enemy instead of her own country.

Bratislava Meeting

An FBI report describes the first major antiwar activist meeting with North Vietnamese officials in Bratislava, Czechoslovakia, in September 1967. Nine leading SDS members were present along with 32 representatives of other antiwar organizations from the United States. A total of 23 officials from the DRV (North Vietnam) and Communist front organizations from the South attended the meeting. The meeting was set up in order to "exchange views and standpoints on the war on

Vietnam and to intensify mutual understanding."[38] A summary of the discussions at the meeting follows:

> The representatives of the people of South Vietnam [National Liberation Front] and the DRV reported on the political, military and economic situation in the respective parts of t he country. The standpoint of the DRV as well as the political program of the National Liberation Front (NLF) of September 1, 1967, which were discussed in detail, are evidence of the Vietnamese people's confidence in the final victory of their struggle against United States aggression for independence and peace.
>
> Members of the U.S. group reported on the attitude of the various groups in the U.S. on the war, and discussed development of the antiwar movement—presenting an analysis of the whole spectrum of political views in the United States.[39]

Seven members of the U.S. delegation to the Bratislava meeting went on to visit Hanoi. A radio broadcast from Hanoi on October 6, 1967 reported the visit:

> Seven youth Americans on a ten day "see for ourselves" visit to North Vietnam today called for an end to the escalation of the war and moves for peace.
>
> The group, two of them girls, came to North Vietnam to "learn for ourselves," about the war the United States is waging against Vietnam and to testify to the losses American bombing is inflicting on the civilian population. The seven are from no specific organizations, and are mostly intellectuals from various widely differing professions....[40]

The FBI report lists the following individuals who comprised the seven visitors to Hanoi:

Tom Hayden, SDS President, 1962-1963
Robert Allen, National Guardian
Jack Brown, Clergyman, San Francisco
Rennie Davis, SDS Chicago
Norm Fruchter, Movie Writer
Carol McEldowney, Community Organizer, Cleveland
Vivian Rothstein, SDS Organizer, Chicago.[41]

Thinking back again to what Colonel Bui Tin said about the NLF as an organ of the Communist North, it is astounding to see the extent to which the Americans were duped by the Communist propaganda. Here is a little bit of what SDS representatives reported to their membership when they returned from the meeting in Bratislava:

> The NLF is the instrument of a society which has had to organize itself against more than one foreign aggressor and in which the base of the struggle has been widespread for a long time. As a political mechanism, the Front has created both local administration structure and a Central Committee of leaders of mass organizations and different social areas (such as military, education and health). As a military force, it is a system of interlocking forces—there is a guerrilla unit for each hamlet (the 'fighting village'), a district force (10 villages together), a provisional force and a zonal army....[This was the attempted structure of areas in the South taken over by the VC/NVA.]
>
> It is that total endeavor by a society in revolution that came across in the course of our conversations. Against a society demanding freedom and independence from an imperialist force, there is no weapon save destruction of every individual in revolt that will bring about any end other than victory for the liberation forces.[42]

Budapest, Hungary Meeting

On September 3, 1968, 28 American war protesters departed John F. Kennedy International Airport enroute to Budapest, Hungary for a meeting with representatives of North Vietnam and the National

Liberation Front. The gathering was advertised to be for the purpose of discussing strategy on United States campuses. The American delegation had this to say, in-part:

> The North Vietnamese were told of plans for a National GI week just before the November 3, 1968, elections, when ministers will be asked to preach antiwar sermons. [The American activists] were also to try to stir up GIs in coffee houses.[43]

Bernadine Dohrn, a national SDS figure, spoke to several radical student groups after she returned from the meeting in Budapest. She said that "after her group left Budapest, the five NLF members were flying to Moscow, Peking, Hanoi and thence to South Vietnam. [She neglected to say which infiltration route they were going to take into the South.] She said two of the five specialized in working with American GIs in Saigon is [are] attempting to obtain information.[44]

Naomi Esther Jaffe, AKA Naomi Safier

Naomi Jaffe was the main speaker at a workshop at the SDS National Convention held in June 1968 at Michigan State University. She had just returned from a trip to Hanoi. She boasted of her accomplishments while in North Vietnam:

> When she was in North Vietnam she had shot down an American fighter plane with an antiaircraft gun with the assistance of a native North Vietnamese woman. Jaffe further claimed to have later assisted in or observed the capture of an American pilot who may have been the pilot of the plane she had shot down. Upon returning to the U.S. Jaffe wore a small piece of fuselage on a chain around her neck that came from the plane that she claimed to have shot down.[45]

Lou Cole AKA Lewis Cole

Cole was one of the leaders of the SDS riot at Columbia University in 1968. In June 1968, the FBI learned that Lewis Cole had traveled to Frankfurt, Germany, the Netherlands, Spain and France and had met with student leaders in these countries. On June 14, 1968, the

New York Times carried a story that indicated that Cole had met with student leaders from ten European countries. A rally was to be held to show solidarity for the unification of student groups from all over the world.⁴⁶

Linda Sue Evans

In July 1969, Linda Evans was identified as one of the people going to North Vietnam to arrange for the release of POWs. At a press conference just before her departure for Paris, she read a statement indicating that "SDS supported oppressed people throughout the world and supports the National Liberation Front's fight for freedom." When she returned to the United States in August 1969, she held another press conference at Kennedy Airport. Speaking for the peace delegation and identified as an official of SDS, she stated, "SDS is on the side of North Vietnam and the National Liberation Front. She called the U.S. the aggressor, and equated North Vietnamese youths fighting the U.S. with American youths in this country fighting U.S. policies."⁴⁷

In August and September 1969, Evans wrote in underground newspapers about her trip to North Vietnam. Her statements are as close as one can get to sedition:

> So, there is one alternative left for Nixon, and that is total withdrawal....Immediate withdrawal is what the Vietnamese define as total victory. This is what we are demanding in the National Action that SDS has called on October 8-11 in Chicago. To show our complete support and solidarity with the NLF, the PRG, and with the Vietnamese people, to demand the total and immediate withdrawal of all occupation forces not only from Vietnam, but from the black and brown colonies within the U.S., from all foreign countries, from the schools....We are expressing support and solidarity with the Conspiracy 8, and support of GI rebellions, all over the country, and especially in Vietnam....
>
> We're directly responsible for letting this war continue. And it is our responsibility to join the struggle of the Vietnamese people to help them in their fight by

opening another battle front here. We should bring the war home.[48]

During the SDS National Conference held in Cleveland, Ohio, August 29-September 1, 1969, Linda Evans gave a speech concerning her recent trip to Hanoi and Vietnam. Evans told about one of her experiences while she was in Vietnam. Evans explained that "she was shown an antiaircraft gun used by Viet Cong women, and she cradled it in her arms and wished an American plane would fly over." She ended her speech with an emotional exhortation about the glory of being a communist.[49]

Theodore Gold

Theodore Gold was one of the SDS leaders and one of the founders of the Weather Underground (WHO). He was killed on March 2, 1970, when a bomb factory in New York accidentally exploded. In November 1969, Gold spoke for three hours at Washington University in St. Louis. He talked about meeting with North Vietnamese representatives in Cuba. He made the statement that the WHO would use "Guerrilla Tactics" and the WHO wanted to form a "Red Army." At a speech at Gustavus Adolphus College in St. Peter, Minnesota, several weeks later, Gold espoused some of the most radical antiwar and anti-American views of the time:

> What we are about is becoming a part of a struggle that is going to defeat imperialism. The American ruling class is running the whole show and the war against it is being carried on all over the world.
>
> World communism is going to turn around the process that has existed for thousands of years. The reason Cuba is poor is because of 300 years of Spanish imperialism and 100 years of American imperialism to build up from. The same is true about China and Vietnam. Struggles are going on all over the world against U.S. imperialism....
>
> The biggest organizer of the Vietnam antiwar movement has been the Viet Cong. The Viet Cong organized the

Moratorium, has organized the mobilization and has organized us. The Viet Cong is winning and is in the highest level of struggle against imperialism that the world has ever seen. The U.S. is being "shellacked" worse than the French...The ruling class understands what Vietnam is about. It's about a Third World country that has to be free, and the U.S. is losing.[50]

Gold addressed a meeting of the University of Oregon SDS Chapter in December 1969, at which he stated, "The 'Weathermen' will now lead the revolution in America....[And] the WHO is headed towards a red-white army which will attack the U.S. from inside while the Viet Cong attacks from the outside."[51]

Other Travelers

There were many trips to Cuba, where North Vietnamese and Communist front organizations met with American antiwar activists. Likewise, there were many other trips by Americans to Hanoi and other countries, but there is insufficient room here to tell about all of them. They all had a similar purpose and outcome—to give encouragement to our enemies and undermine our war effort. Following the conclusion of the Paris Peace Agreement in January 1973, the visits by American activists continued. In November 1973, Cora Weiss, leading the American People's Delegation, visited "liberated" areas in South Vietnam. She was accompanied by Don Luce, a newsman, and Sam Noumoff, a history professor. The Hanoi news release stated that, "The delegation was received and entertained by Foreign Minister Nguyen Thai Binh and they carried on an intimate chat."[52]

Fidel Castro even got into the act after the Paris Agreement, leading a delegation of the Cuban Communist Party on a visit to the "liberated" areas of South Vietnam in September 1973.[53]

The antiwar movement in the United States had serious psychological effects on the U.S. POWs held by North Vietnam. Similarly, the Americans who traveled to Hanoi and met with our POWs caused unspeakable harm to those under North Vietnamese control. The antiwar activists have denied all allegations of this nature, but there is an abundance of proof to the contrary. The next chapter will reveal the truth.

Chapter Seven

Band of Traitors

Dying is Very Easy. Living is Difficult.

—Viet Cong Guard to POW
Michael Benge

The most despicable and cowardly acts of the antiwar/peace activists were their contributions to the hardship and suffering of our servicemen held as prisoners of war (POWs) in Vietnam. The harsh conditions under which these people struggled to survive were more than any human being should ever have to endure. Besides the isolation and torture, they were locked in stifling, filthy cells where they suffered from malnourishment, constant dysentery, fevers, respiratory diseases, skin infections and untreated wounds and broken bones. They spent years, in some cases six or seven years, under these conditions. Some did not survive. Yet, American citizens, some of them prominent figures, traveled to North Vietnam where they were cordially welcomed by officials of that government, and in many cases allowed to see American POWs. While in Hanoi some made speeches opposing their own government and our military forces fighting and dying in Vietnam. Without a doubt, this had the effect of undermining our troops and our war effort. Some openly sided with the enemy. Worst of all, they went home to the United States and praised the enemy for their humane treatment of our POWs.

One of these "peace" envoys, former U.S. Attorney General Ramsey Clark, reported upon his return from Hanoi that "they [American POWs] are in good health and their condition could not be better."[1] He described the POW camp he visited as "having windows in every bedroom (with no bars), a movie theater, bridge tournaments, a basketball court and paperback books." He said that the health of the POWs was better than his, and that he was particularly touched "by the hygienic conditions at the POW camp."[2] As you read testimony of former POWs later in this chapter, you will wonder what planet he was visiting!

Following one of her visits to Hanoi, Jane Fonda told the world press that "the U.S. prisoners of war are being well treated and not tortured." After the truth came out when the returning POWs told their story, Fonda called them "liars and hypocrites."[3]

At a news conference in Washington D.C. on January 27, 1970, Cora Weiss, leader of Women Strike for Peace and one of the founders of the Committee of Liaison, described the "excellent living conditions she observed in the North Vietnamese prison camp...the Hanoi Hilton." Testifying before a House Committee, she questioned the accuracy of statements of inhumane treatment by returning POWs Navy Lieutenant Robert Frishman and Seaman Douglas Hegdahl. Referring to an arm injury that Lt. Frishman had sustained, she said, "Since he was caught as a war criminal he was lucky to have an arm at all."[4]

In his book, *Return with Honor*, Colonel George Day, a former POW, argues that CBS appeared to be a willing partner of the antiwar activists. He states, "CBS reported, 'The Hanoi regime is treating POWs well.'" Colonel Day notes that this was reported nine times on that network, and air time was given to activists such as Ramsey Clark "who tried to tell us [that] POWs were happy and healthy."[5]

The American "peace" envoys caused untold suffering of the POWs who were often brutally coerced into meeting with them or were punished for not acting the way their captors wanted them to at the meetings. After hearing testimony from former POWs, the House Committee on Internal Security concluded that "the activities of many of our citizens who traveled to Hanoi without authority brought our men in the service only further deprivation, mistreatment, and torture, increased the confidence of the enemy and prolonged the war."[6]

The peace activists also caused grave harm to the POWs by deceiving the American people and the world at large with totally false reports of humane treatment, good medical care, nourishing food and the total absence of any abuse or torture by the North Vietnamese captors. The POWs were constantly bombarded with statements and broadcasts made by Americans activists while they were in Vietnam or when they returned to the United States. In addition, the statements of prominent figures in the United States, particularly by members of the Senate and House, were devastating to the morale of the POWs, as were the reports, usually exaggerated by camp officials, of massive demonstrations on the campuses and streets of the U.S.

In *Honor Bound,* Frederick Kiley and Stuart Rochester tell of prison loud speakers blaring for up to five hours a day with propaganda. Some of the most devastating forms of propaganda were statements by certain American antiwar politicians and broadcasts by well known personalities. This quote from *Honor Bound* shows the impact on the POWs:

> Taped appeals from prominent American peace advocates, many of them visitors to North Vietnam—personalities such as Jane Fonda, Joan Baez, Stokely Carmichael, and Ramsay Clark—at once incensed and demoralized the prisoners.[7]

Former POW Sam Johnson, now congressman from Texas, who spent nearly seven years in Hanoi's prison camps, saw the antiwar protesters as "propaganda tools in the hands of North Vietnamese Communists." In his book, *Captive Warriors,* he writes:

> The sit-ins, riots, and civil disobedience in America fueled the mental war the communists were waging against us, their captives. With every new report of American disenchantment over the war, the torture in Hanoi's prison camps intensified. We were like marionettes, dangling from the hands of indecisive, ambivalent politicians and peace activists, to tell the story our captors wanted told.[8]

This chapter will elaborate on the various ways the antiwar/peace activists made survival in the POW camps much more difficult for our servicemen and will reveal the cowardly attempts to turn the POW wives against the war. The testimony of the POWs who survived and made it home will expose many of the lies and distortions told by the activists.

POW Testimony and Statements

The House of Representatives Committee on Internal Security held hearings on restraints on travel to hostile areas on May 9 and 10, 1973. The purpose of the hearings was to determine what changes should be made to existing laws in order to prevent future travel of citizens like those who traveled to North Vietnam while hostilities were ongoing. The House Committee heard from a number of former POWs. Their testimony will give us a true picture of the harm those who traveled to North Vietnam caused American POWs. Their statements, in-part, follow:

Statement of Captain James a. Mulligan, U.S. Navy

Thank you, Mr. Ichord [Chairman]. I am James A. Mulligan, Captain in the United States Navy. I am presently attached to the Naval Hospital at Portsmouth. I reside in Virginia Beach. I have been in the U.S. Navy for 29 years.

I was shot down and captured 20 miles south of Vinh on March 20, 1966 in North Vietnam. And sitting next to me on my left is my wife, Louise.

Of course, I feel very strongly that there is a need to restrict certain travel by U.S. citizens to countries with whom we are engaged in armed conflict. This has been a major, major problem of the POWs.

Ever since I first became a POW, we had delegations coming into Hanoi in 1966, 1967, 1968, 1969, 1970, 1971, and 1972. Many Americans [POWs], including myself, were heavily pressured, heavily threatened. And some men were even physically forced and tortured to visit these delegations.

The appearance of American delegations in Hanoi, needless to say, did not contribute at all to our morale, except to lower it. The Vietnamese were able to exploit this as much as possible and tried to use the delegations to divide us. Fortunately, they weren't too effective in the areas that I was associated with.

I particularly think that the visits of American delegations to Hanoi aided the morale of the North Vietnamese. It was my opinion very, very early that the North Vietnamese felt that the war would be won in Washington, D.C., not in Vietnam.

They were on me, right at the start, about the antiwar movement. And they put great credence in the antiwar movement. And they actually felt, I think probably quite wrongly, that the antiwar movement was the major trend of thought in the United States. I think these delegations probably tended to substantiate this. The Vietnamese underestimated the position they were in. They thought that these delegations were truly representative of the American popular thought....[9]

Statement of Lt. Commander David W. Hoffman, U.S. Navy

My name is David Wesley Hoffman. I am a Lieutenant Commander in the U.S. Navy; I have been in the service for 11 years. I am currently assigned to the Naval Hospital in San Diego.

I was shot down on December 30, 1971, and was held for 15 months, which makes me the piker of this group by a long shot. My wife is with me. Her name is Mary.

I very strongly agree with what has been said already. I think there is a very definite need to restrict certain travel by U.S. citizens.

I had the unfortunate circumstances of being able to say that I was personally tortured in order to meet a delegation in February of 1972. The exact method used really isn't that important. It was a variation of the "rope treatment," that I am sure you have all heard described many times.

It was obviously detrimental to my health, as well as morale, but extremely detrimental to morale. I think this is one of the biggest factors for all of us. It was detrimental to morale to have to meet with or talk with these delegations.

In the first place, it is completely obvious—or should be completely obvious—that we were not at liberty to say what we wanted to when we had to talk with these people. It was a completely programmed thing. And if you made the wrong response, you stood a very definite chance of some severe consequences when you either returned to your camp or when the delegation departed the area. It did not pay to deviate from that script at all. There were a couple of instances I know of where people were punished, which is the word used rather than tortured, for deviating from the approved script.

One of the big problems was that it very definitely did have an effect on the Vietnamese themselves. These people were convinced that the delegations that came in there were representative of American public opinion. They were taking everything they said at face value. And it was very widely publicized in Vietnam.

After all, when you have a picture of an American sitting on an antiaircraft battery with a helmet on, as though shooting down an aircraft, that makes pretty good propaganda. It also made it much more difficult for us to continue to fight against the propaganda efforts that were being made, trying to use us for propaganda purposes, particularly where someone who, as far as the Vietnamese were concerned, was a very respected American, urged people to make continued written statements from Vietnam, so that people back home would get the word about how bad the war was and so forth, or words to that effect.

All in all, it created an untenable situation for us. I am sure that in many ways, it contributed—and this is purely personal opinion—to lengthening the war and contributed to their desire to keep going just that much longer before they would eventually capitulate....[10]

Statement of Commander Edwin A. Shuman III, U.S. Navy

My name is Commander Edwin A. Shuman III, of the U.S. Navy. I am presently assigned to the Portsmouth Naval Hospital. I live in Virginia Beach also. I have been in the Navy for 24 years.

I was captured on March 17, 1968, about 10 miles north of Hanoi. I was there just 2 days short of 5 years. I am here with my wife, Sue.

I feel, of course, that there is a need to restrict the travel of U.S. citizens to countries with which we are at war. Of course, I lived with a lot of people who had some severe problems. They were tortured and things like that to meet these people that came over there. I was not.

I will briefly cover what happened to me along those lines. They always wanted us to—the Vietnamese were wanting us to "work for the camp." "Work for the camp"—and that, of course, "crossing over to the people's side"—terms like that they used.

One of the ways you could "work for the camp" was to meet these visiting delegations. We did our best to resist these efforts. The only actual experience I had along these lines was September of 1969. I was tortured fairly badly. And at the end of this time, they wanted me to "work for the camp." One of the things they wanted me to do was to meet the visiting delegation. I did not know what this delegation was at the time.

At the end of this time, I told them—I lived with Lt. Comdr. Dale W. Doss—we both told them that we would not meet this delegation. And there were severe threats, such as back into the torture mill again, and all that. But at that time, the treatment got significantly better. And they never really forced us to go.

I feel that our morale was definitely lowered by Americans coming over there and saying the things that they did. It is my opinion that the only people they let into that country were either Communists or Communist sympathizers. And they almost without exception played ball with the Communists in the things they said.

All of their press conferences, appearances and stuff were broadcast to us on tape. We were doing the best we could to resist their efforts to influence our thinking on the war, et cetera. And it was very hard to do this, when we had people from our country spouting the same Communist line that they were.

As Captain Mulligan said, I think they took great hope from the U.S. antiwar movement. They even made statements like, "When you go home, the American people are going to beat you because you are reactionary." They would make comments like, "The U.S. ruling class is different from the people. The American people all want peace." And they got these ideas just from the antiwar movement and from the people that came over there to visit.

Of course, as Captain Mulligan said, they thought that the people would overthrow the Government over here. Dissention in the Government is something they are not really used to in their way of life....[11]

Statement of Lt. Commander Thomas Hall, Jr., U.S. Navy

My name is Thomas Hall, Jr. I am a Lieutenant Commander in the U.S. Navy. And I am presently attached to Balboa Naval Hospital in San Diego. I have been in the Navy for 9 ½ years.

I was shot down in June 1967, about 10 miles south of Hanoi. I was a prisoner for 5 years and 9 months. I feel that there is a need for restriction of travel by Americans to any country that we are engaged in conflict with.

They definitely had a demoralizing effect on us and also on our wives at home, my wife, anyway. Although I was not directly affected by any visiting delegations, I did live with people who were pressured, tortured to see delegations or in one case, tortured and punished, as they call it, for poor performance at the delegation visit.

One of the demoralizing factors up there was not so much what these delegations had to say to us, but the mere fact that they were in Hanoi, that they were Americans at large in Hanoi, while we were in conflict with that country and so many of us were in prison. And these people were allowed to come over at will and leave at will and make anti-U.S. statements.

I think they did increase the morale of the Vietnamese. I think the North Vietnamese were convinced—or at least they would have us believe they were convinced—that these people represented the majority consensus in the United States.

The delegations, of course, would spout the party line. And I think they did give a morale boost to the North Vietnamese, gave them something to hang onto. I know the lower class, the lower rankers, there in North

Vietnam were convinced that these people represented the U.S. people. They were convinced that the American people were totally against the war and that victory was just around the corner for them.

One other observation or point of interest up there, first of all, the delegations that concerned us mostly were the ones in the early stages, the first few years when Vietnamese were conducting intensive propaganda programs, pressuring POW's to extract propaganda from them. Most of these were very anti-U.S., antiwar, and pro-communist....[12]

Statement of Captain Larry Carrigan, U.S. Air Force

I am Captain Larry Carriagan, U.S. Air Force. I am on leave presently from March Air Force Base, Calif. I reside in Scottsdale, Arizona. I have been in the U.S. Air Force for 10 years and 10 months.

I was shot down on August 23, 1967 and captured 3 days later on August 26, 1967 and taken to Hanoi. I was a prisoner for just short of 5 years and 7 months.

As a military man, I felt, as did all the men in Hanoi that we had a responsibility to the United States. We had a responsibility, not only as fighting men, when we were in combat, flying an aircraft, but we also had a responsibility as prisoners of war to support the administration back home. And I feel that the men in Hanoi, to the best of their ability, did just that.

I also feel that the civilian community here in the United States has that same responsibility. Certainly, I agree that dissent is all right to a degree. But to carry that dissent to the capital of the country that we are in armed conflict with, I cannot agree with. And for that reason I am here today, to prevent just that, that is, to restrict certain travel by U.S. Citizens to countries with whom we are engaged in conflict.

As far as personal observations concerning travel by U.S. citizens to Hanoi, I was personally involved. And so, I will tell you a short story.

In September 1967 I had occasion to meet with women from an organization in the States, which I really didn't know much about, called Women Strike for Peace. These women had asked to speak to a prisoner of war who had been recently shot down. When I was shot down, I was in good health. And therefore, I qualified in the Vietnamese's eyes to meet a delegation, which I did.

When I went into the room and I saw these women, the first thing they asked me was if I had any questions. And I said yes. I asked them two questions. I asked them if they were Communists and they said no. I asked them if they had permission of the U.S. Government to travel to the capital of Communist North Vietnam. And they reluctantly said—they did answer the question and said no. They did not have permission. And of course, immediately I knew whom I was talking to.

What the Vietnamese wanted me to do was to say that in fact there were civilian targets bombed by the Air Force and the Navy, while in fact, civilian targets did not exist to the best of my knowledge. And I think all the men here could vouch for that same fact. They were hard military targets, each and every one of them.

I related that to these women. I told a story about an Air Force commander that was striking a particular target near Hanoi. The target was north of a road. South of the road was a hospital. The Force commander said there were going to be cameras on aircraft we were flying, 16 ships this particular day. And the No. 2 and No. 4

aircraft would carry cameras. He wanted to be certain that nobody let a bomb fall south of that highway. And he was very much adamant about the fact that no bombs would be near that hospital. They were to fall on the military target.

After the mission, the film was processed and all bombs were north of the road. Of course, he was very pleased.

At this point, the Vietnamese became a little bit upset. The women, I thought at the time, cheered this Air Force commander. They thought it was a gallant thing for him to do, to impress upon pilots to be certain the bombs were on target. And it was a good show on the part of the pilots. But the Vietnamese were somewhat disturbed about this.

When the evening was over, I went back to my cell. The next day, the Vietnamese pulled me out very early in the morning and took a photograph, a mug shot. That evening about 8 o'clock, the gong rang and we were to go to bed. And I did. About 1 ½ hours later, the Vietnamese came to my cell, opened up the door and told me to get dressed. I went to a quiz room, and an interrogation room. When I got there, one of the interrogators that I had been talking to prior to seeing this delegation asked me what a "wayward individual" meant, repeat a "wayward individual."

He did not know what this meant. I asked him to repeat it and he did. I proceeded to tell him what it was. It was willful, perverse, and disobedient. But he still didn't understand. So, he pulled out a dictionary. We went through the dictionary and finally, he understood what the word meant. He told me on several occasions—I am convinced that he did not know what this meant—he told me on several occasions that one of the women had told them, the Vietnamese, after I had gone back to my cell that I was a wayward individual.

After he was satisfied what "wayward individual" meant, they put me in a truck and took me to a camp called Hoala. You probably call it the Hanoi Hilton. He took me to an area of the camp called New Guy Village. And there they proceeded to pound on me. I hate to use the word "torture," because your definition and mine may not agree. But in any case, it was very bad for a few moments. During this session they did hurt my shoulders....After about 6 months, they appeared to be fairly normal. The only time it really hurt was when I put my hands over my head.

But this is the kind of thing that this committee and this bill perhaps can prevent....

For me personally, of course, these trips by the delegations—and I hate to use names. There have been several names that have been very well publicized in the press. But in a way, that is unfortunate, because there were many, many people, literally hundreds of civilians, that traveled to Hanoi. We are picking out one or two and are sort of putting the blame on them. In fact, what about the other hundreds? Are we just going to let them go and forget about things like that?

I personally know of several men who were either forced to go see a delegation or there were repercussions afterward. I will not go into those stories, because I do not know the full details. You can get the stories from those other individuals.

But from where I sat in the various camps, those delegations did absolutely nothing for the betterment of our camp life. It did not improve our living conditions because they came to Hanoi. In fact, it hurt us. And it hurt us badly.

These people, as the other gentlemen have stated today, gave aid and comfort to the Vietnamese. According to me, it prolonged the war. I think many, many of the POW'S would have to agree with that. The Communists in North Vietnam wanted the American people there during the war. They knew they couldn't beat us in the battlefield. But they hoped to beat us back in Washington....[13]

Statement by Former POW James H. Kasler, Colonel USAF [read into record by G.V. Montgomery, Representative from Mississippi].
It is difficult to describe the purge that hit our camp after an escape attempt in the spring of 1969. The escape generated an absolutely incredible amount of torture. The Vietnamese brutalized 45 to 50 men, one of which died in torture....

My worst session of torture began in late June 1968. The Vietnamese were attempting to force me to meet a delegation and appear before TV cameras on the occasion of the supposed downing of the 3000th American airplane over North Vietnam. I couldn't say the things they were trying to force me to say. I was tortured for 6 weeks. I went through the ropes and irons 10 times. I was denied sleep for 5 days and during 3 of these days was beaten every hour on the hour with a fan belt. During the entire period I was on a starvation diet. I was very sick during this period. I had contacted osteomyelitis in early 1967 and had a massive bone infection in my right leg.

They would wrap my leg before each torture session so I wouldn't get pus or blood all over the floor of the interrogation room. During this period they beat my face into a pulp. I couldn't get my teeth apart for 5 days. My ear drum was ruptured. One of my ribs broken and the pin in my right leg was broken loose and driven up into my hip. I lay in agony for 6 months until I was given an operation in January of 1969.

I surrendered a number of times during this torture session but when they tried to get me to do something I would refuse. By the time they finished with me I was in no condition to do anything.

During this torture session after they had broken me the first time, they gave me a few days before I went in for my briefing of what I had to say. I know what they were going to make me say, and I decided I would rather die. When I was called in, the political commissar whom we called the "Lump" gave me the list of answers and told me to memorize them, then we would rehearse. I told him he could torture me and put me before a delegation but when I got there I wasn't going to say a God-damn word. He then pulled out a stack of 8x10 prints showing antiwar groups marching in the States. The Vietnamese were trying to convince us that the antiwar group was going to end the war and we should get on the band wagon. Seventy-five percent of the propaganda we got on the camp radio concerned antiwar activities. As I was looking at one of the pictures, I saw in the background two elderly gentlemen with smiles on their faces and American Legion hats cocked on their heads. They were holding a sign which said: "Drop the Bomb." I knew I was in for it, but that picture gave me a renewed burst of courage for what I knew was coming.

Many delegations came to Hanoi, East Germans, Poles, Russians, Americans, and all wanted to see the POW's. So for each, American POW's were tortured to force them to give correct answers to the questions which the Vietnamese provided to the delegations. It made no difference where the delegations came from, the Vietnamese took no chances. They trust no one, not even their own allies.

The Americans who came to Hanoi could hardly wait to get on the Voice of Vietnam and echo the latest Communist propaganda. They would broadcast to our troops telling them to desert or refuse to fight. From the reports these groups brought back you probably thought that the city of Hanoi was lying in shambles when the fact is the city was barely touched as has been proven by unbiased photographers who visited there after our release. They distorted the truth about the bombing of civilian targets and the dikes in North Vietnam because they wanted the North Vietnamese to win and they were willing to betray their own country to attain that goal....

What I cannot understand is how any person could work actively for our enemy against their own country while we were engaged in war. Politicians and personalities who used their names to encourage our youth to burn their draft cards, to desert or flee this country to avoid the draft and those who came to Hanoi to work actively for the North Vietnamese. For these people I have nothing but contempt.

These people who came to Hanoi left little doubt as to where their loyalty lay when they broadcast the latest Communist propaganda on the Voice of Vietnam. Besides broadcasting to our troops and to the POW's they would spout the North Vietnamese complete surrender proposals, the phony dike propaganda and others. We were amazed at the speed that the Vietnamese propaganda campaigns were picked up by some of the politicians here in the States.

I cannot help but feel that the Vietnamese propaganda would have fallen short of its mark had it not been supported so actively by the antiwar groups here in the States....[14]

Responses to Committee Questions

Congressman Roger Zion of Indiana quoted the former Attorney General who had visited Hanoi as saying, "We're bombing the hell out of that poor land. You better believe we hit dikes and sluices and canals." This person visited ten POWs and said they were "humanely treated, unbrainwashed and healthy." The former Attorney General also repeated North Vietnamese claims that our pilots were "killing our children." Mr. Zion asked if any of the POWs then before the Committee had ever been asked to bomb such targets. All five former POWs gave a negative response.[15]

Congressman Zion asked if the POWs had an awareness of being considered war criminals rather than prisoners of war by people in the U.S. and in the eyes of the North Vietnamese. Captain Mulligan responded, "We were always considered, called, and treated as war criminals from the very first day I was in Vietnam."[16]

Congressman Preyer asked if the same pattern of conduct, when delegations would come, was present in all camps. Captain Mulligan answered, "They always wanted to get POW's to meet delegations. And they worked the various camps to get them. For example, during 1972, they attempted to get people from the Hilton, where most of the people were assigned at that time. They were unsuccessful. So they had a spinoff. They were working a new group of prisoners out at the Zoo. Actually, that was the show camp, where Mr. Clark went, and I suppose Miss Fonda went."[17]

Congressman Preyer asked Commander Hall if POWs were punished specifically because a delegation was visiting the camp and in order to get them to testify. Commander Hall responded:

> One individual I lived with continued to refuse to see this delegation. And the Vietnamese informed us that he had a very bad attitude. He was put into solitary confinement, where he remained for about a year and a half. During this period of time, he was constantly harassed. In a couple of instances, he was beaten as a form of harassment. They were continually after him to see a delegation. Finally, after about a year or so of this treatment, he finally consented to see a delegation. He saw a Cuban Delegation, I believe. It was a very

demoralizing experience for him and for the rest of his roommates, also.[18]

Chairman Ichord stated that all POWs testifying before the House Committee felt that the delegations had an adverse effect on their morale and a good effect on the morale of the North Vietnamese. Addressing Captain Mulligan, he said he understood that Mulligan had not met with any delegations. Captain Mulligan explained:

> That is right, Mr. Ichord. I refused. I was processed for three days in 1966 and twice....They had me manacled in stocks. I was in a semi-standing-kneeling position. I was kept in this position all day long from 5 in the morning until about 6 or 7 at night. I was taken into an interrogation room. And then they briefed me and told me what I was to say at his news conference I was going to have. They did this for about 3 days. I had not received any medical attention. I was in terrible physical condition. I had a broken shoulder, cracked ribs. And I was nearly out of my mind. After about 3 days, they made the mistake of taking me to the hospital. When I went to the hospital, fortunately, the doctor at the hospital got them to leave me alone. And I did not see that delegation.

> I would like to tell you a quick instance of what one delegation did to me. The delegation was in Hanoi to pick up three Americans last September. One of the female members of that delegation, on touring the war museum that the Vietnamese had [set up], made the comment that she thought that this was a very fine thing that every POW should see. So, the Vietnamese picked that comment up and decided that they would take us downtown to see the war museum....I was at that time living in the same general compound with General Flynn. There were General Flynn, General Winn, Captain Denton (Admiral Denton, now), Colonel Gaddis, Captain Rutledge, and myself.

> There were three other senior officers there. But the six of us were forcibly taken out on the 25th of September and dragged, beaten and put in a bus, handcuffed with rear handcuffs. I mean we were physically carried out of our rooms and physically dragged out of our prison and physically put on these buses; physically taken downtown, dragged through the war museum, forced to sit through a war propaganda movie, and then dragged back to Hoala prison. By the time it was all over with, we were in pretty bad shape. We had been physically beaten pretty badly. We were mocked and scorned. We weren't really injured. They used as much force as they had to, to get us through this thing.
>
> But the point I want to make is, this was all set off because some American woman in Hanoi decided that it was a good thing for us to see this....[19]

Chairman Ichord asked Commander Hoffman to explain the rope treatment which Hoffman had received when he refused to appear before a delegation. Commander Hoffman described a variation of the rope treatment:

> I was placed on a table and then on a chair, which was on top of the table. And there was a hook in the ceiling. I think the height of the ceiling was probably 20 feet or so. The rope was strung around my arms, up around the armpit. Then I was placed upon the chair on top of the table. And the table was kicked out from under me. I dropped the length of the rope, so that I would come to a couple of inches off the floor. They would put the table and chair back under me and stick me up there again and drop me again, until I eventually came very close to passing out....[20]

The rope treatment was also described in Craig Howes' book, *Voices of the Vietnam POWs*:

> In North Vietnam, a man's wrists and elbows were firmly bound behind his back with a log nylon rope that was then pulled upward until his arms were raised and his head was forced downward between his shackled legs. Binding the arms cut off circulation, and limbs turned blue, then black...Arms and legs [were] often dislocated, men felt like their rib cages were ripping open, and the nerve damage could last for months and years.[21]

The POWs appearing before the House Committee testified that they were continuously bombarded with tapes of antiwar and anti-American speeches by visiting delegations and antiwar activists in the United States. Mr. Zion asked the group of POWs who some of the Americans were who were quoted or in taped broadcasts. Commander Shuman stated that "a lot of them were Democrats. A lot of them were very liberal. Some were Republicans, but all were of the liberal element, the antiwar people who kind of opposed the war."[22]

Several House Committee members raised the question about the POWs being prepped for the appearance before delegations. Captain Carrigan explained that he was sure that the delegations had to give the Vietnamese a list of questions before they were allowed to meet with POWs. He added, "And at that time, the POW was subjected to sitting down with an interrogator and going over these questions...." Commander Hoffman interjected, "Just a little bit further on that. When the particular delegation that I was speaking of before presented a list of questions, I had to write the answers out and then memorize them and recite them until the interrogator was satisfied that I had word for word what was written on the piece of paper, with revisions that he made to my answer."[23]

Congressman Preyer continued the line of questioning about the "preparation" of POWs for meetings with delegations. Based on testimony he had heard about how the POWs were programmed for the meetings, he concluded that the delegations really had no opportunity for any true insight into what the conditions were for the POWs. He said, "Then, would you all say that the kind of reports that we got back in this country from the delegations misrepresented to the American people what the conditions were in the prison camps?"

Lieutenant Commander Hoffman answered, "Very grossly."

Captain Mulligan commented, "I would say not only the reports misrepresented the conditions in the camp, but the reports from those members of the U.S. press and television that got into Hanoi also misrepresented the conditions in Hanoi. When Mr. Salisbury was writing many articles out of Hanoi, many Americans were being tortured within a few blocks of where he was. And they were being tortured very badly. Some Americans probably died at the time."[24]

Statement of Colonel Norris Overly to House Committee on Foreign Affairs, March 23, 1971

Colonel Norris Overly, U.S. Air Force, was shot down over North Vietnam in September 1967 and released approximately a year later with nine other American POWs. Excerpts of his statement before the House Committee on Foreign Affairs provide more insight into the treatment of our POWs. Colonel Overly began by telling the committee about the subtle inhumanity and depravation of being locked in tiny cell without windows for years, some as long as almost seven years, and being fed a subsistence diet. He went on to explain in more detail:

> In addition to two radio broadcasts we had each day, the loudspeaker in the cell blared propaganda for 5 or 6 hours. The basis of this propaganda went something like this, and I heard it time and time again:
>
>> We are not going to defeat you in Vietnam. We are going to defeat you in your universities and on your streets by turning public opinion against the war, so that your administration will have to withdraw their troops, and when they are withdrawn to a sufficient level, we will launch an offensive and defeat you, just like we did the French at Dien Bien Phu.

The most frightening thing to me is that they believed it. In addition to that sort of propaganda for 5 hours a day, they showed us periodicals from this country, leading newspapers and magazines, showing only those articles carrying the dissidents of our country, things like My Lai, Kent State, the march on the Pentagon. The worst side of our society was portrayed to the prisoners day after day....

I am sure, I am positive they think that every student on every campus in this country is solidly against the administration, and that they solidly support the Hanoi regime. It gives them, the Vietnamese, the resolve necessary to carry on.

While I was there, I noted that medical treatment was given. However, I would like to qualify that statement. One of my cellmates was critically wounded. He received medical aid for his broken bones, which consisted of putting a cast on his bones for a specified time. When the time was up, they took the cast off, but they didn't check to see whether his bones had healed properly. In fact, his arms healed off center; his left shoulder healed in the broken position, and he can't lift his left arm.[25]

Congressman Burke asked Colonel Overly, "Would it be your opinion that our continued talk over here about withdrawing troops would indicate a weakness on our part, which would strengthen their own views about the outcome in holding prisoners?" Colonel Overly responded, "Well, of course, the danger about continual talk concerning withdrawal is that it is not conducive to the release of prisoners..."[26]

POWs as Pawns

"North Vietnam 'considers Allied war prisoners as a bargaining tool, as commodities to help them achieve their political objectives,'" according to Dr. Dang Tan, a defector and former medical officer for the Communists.[27] Based on the information presented thus far in this and previous chapters, there is little doubt that the travelers to Hanoi also had designs on using the POWs to further their own political/antiwar objectives. The very act of telling the people of America and the rest of the world that our servicemen held by North Vietnam were being treated humanely, which was a blatant distortion of the truth, is proof that the Americans who traveled to Hanoi had an objective that ran counter to the best interests of the United States and the POWs.

The torture and mistreatment of our servicemen was so pervasive and obvious that to say otherwise required a deliberate attempt to make the enemy look good. In this chapter only a small sample of the mistreatment has been presented. There are many, many additional reports of the torture and deprivation that our servicemen experienced at the hands of the North Vietnamese, as well as by enemy forces in Laos, Cambodia and South Vietnam. It would take many books to detail all that is known. To say that the POWs were mistreated is to make light of their experience. They were beaten, starved, drugged and tortured, sometimes until they were paralyzed or dead. Without mentioning names, here are a few brief examples of POW treatment as told by returning POWs:

- A Navy Captain was tortured at least ten times and kept in solitary confinement for four years. For three days he had no food or water and was kept seated on a stool and cuffed. He was forced to lie flat on his back while a ten-foot iron bar was placed across his chin and his captors stepped on the bar.[28]
- An Air Force Captain who was severely burned received only hot water twice a week as treatment. He had to use maggots to eat away the dead flesh. When the dead flesh was gone he had to urinate on the infected areas to wash off the maggots.[29]
- An Air Force Colonel spent three years in solitary confinement and was tortured with ropes, leg irons and handcuffs.[30]
- An Army doctor who was held prisoner for 5 ½ years had a bullet wound in the shoulder, a broken wrist and two fractured teeth. The bullet was removed without anesthesia. His treatment consisted of two aspirins.[31]
- A large group of POWs were paraded through the streets of Hanoi with thousands of angry Vietnamese civilians jabbing, hitting, and throwing stones at them. Many were injured.[32]

- A Navy Captain was tortured for seven days and six nights in a pitch black room. They beat him regularly and brutally while he was in irons with his hands cuffed behind his back.[33]
- An Air Force Major and six other prisoners received extreme torture for two weeks. They were beaten with a heavy rubber strip along with the ropes, cuffs and leg irons. They were kept blindfolded and without sleep for the entire time.[34]
- It is believed that an Air Force major was tortured to death following an attempted escape.[35]
- An American civilian was kept in solitary confinement for over four and a half years in a bamboo cage. He was buried up to his neck for a week for attempting to escape.[36]
- One man spent 27 months in solitary confinement, not in a jail cell, but in a box seven feet by three by three. He only got out to relieve himself.[37]
- One prisoner had a broken leg rebroken several times to get him to talk. Another one had his thumb sliced off in an effort to make him talk.[38]
- A Navy Lt. Commander was deprived of sleep, beaten, burned with cigarettes and had his fingernails torn off. He was dumped into solitary with untreated wounds.[39]
- A trial of American war criminals was held in a Hanoi stadium in which POWs were forced to get on their knees and confess. If they refused they were beaten until unconscious in front of the audience.[40]
- An Air Force Major was beaten with a large truck fan belt until his buttocks, back and legs hung in shreds of bloody raw meat.[41]
- A Navy Lt. Commander reported that he had been coerced into meeting with Jane Fonda and the former U.S. Attorney General Clark. He was hung by his broken arm and dropped at the end of a rope when a table was kicked out from under him.[42]

The Judas Travelers

One of the most treasonous acts by certain American travelers was exposing covert actions of our POW's. In his book, *Captive Warriors,* former POW Sam Johnson tells a story about a shortwave radio the POWs in his camp were secretly constructing from parts concealed in packages from the United States. They needed just one last missing part to complete the radio. The radio would have been a great morale factor, and they could have used it to coordinate pick-up points in an escape. The radio, which was completely assembled except for the final part, was discovered during a search by the North Vietnamese. Johnson leaned later from a congressman that a "peace envoy" from the United States had learned about the radio and informed the North Vietnamese. Imagine the enormous disappointment that this caused the POWs, and it ended their hopes of escaping since they had no way to coordinate a pickup point.[43]

In another case, an American Special Forces officer, the late Major Nick Rowe, was captured by the Viet Cong. He had deceived his captors into believing that he was an unimportant, low level person. His life hung by a thread when his true identity was exposed. According to a Central Committee official, the information about Rowe's identity came from "friends" of the National Liberation Front in America. American antiwar activists had frequent contact with NLF representatives in Paris, Cuba and elsewhere.[44]

Where was the Outrage?

It was well known at least by 1968 that our POWs held by North Vietnam and the Viet Cong were being brutally treated in complete disregard of the Geneva Convention. Where was the International Red Cross? Where was Amnesty International? Where was the United Nations Human Rights Commission? Where was the outrage from the U.S. Senate and House of Representatives? The answer is that there was outrage, but it was mostly against the war and their own government by the antiwar doves like Senator George McGovern, Senator Ernest Gruening, Senator Wayne Morse, Senator Eugene McCarthy, and Representative Allard Lowenstein, all liberal Democrats. These and other members of Congress called for unilateral withdrawal of our forces from Vietnam and acceptance of the peace plans offered by North Vietnam and the NLF, all of which amounted to surrender and left the fate of the POWs to be settled after the truce was signed.[45]

If the treatment of the American POWs in Vietnam had received even a fraction of the attention by the media, human rights organizations and Congress as the alleged mistreatment of Iraqi prisoners have had, the treatment of our POWs in Vietnam would have been much better and many who did not return might have survived. Forcing an Iraqi prisoner to take off his clothes and be blindfolded pales in the face of the brutal torture our servicemen received in Vietnam. Yet, today we hear the liberals, Congressmen, human rights organizations and the media screeching about the relatively mild treatment of a few Iraqi prisoners. There are several reliable reports that the North Vietnamese had 1205 to 1500 of our servicemen in captivity.[46] Yet, when they were finally released, only 591 came home. Where was the outrage by the administration, Congress, the "peace" activists, and the media? Most importantly, what happened to the rest of them?

Terrorizing the POW Wives and Families

The wives and families of the POWs were not immune to the actions of the antiwar/peace activists. They also suffered but in different ways. There were intimidating phone calls, false casualty notifications, and the collaboration with the North Vietnamese to interpose an antiwar group between the POWs and their families. Put yourself in the place of these wives and families. They went for months and sometimes even years before learning the status of their loved ones, whether they were alive or dead, their health, their location, etc. On top of that, inject the harassment and intimidation from the antiwar/peace activists and you have added greatly to their grief and fears. What kind of people would do that to fellow countrymen and for what reason?

An example of one of the lowest kinds of harassment of some wives is provided by Robert F. Turner, Assistant Director, Center for National Security Law:

> It involves my late brother, who served his first tour in Vietnam as a Marine Sergeant at the height of the war in 1967-1968. Around March or April of 1968, Ed's wife in Texas received a call from someone alleging to be with Western Union. They asked Dottie whether she wanted them to read the "urgent" telegram or to deliver it later in the day, and fearing the worst she asked that it be read. The caller began: "The Secretary of the Navy regrets to inform you that your husband...was killed in action...." It was a total hoax! [47]

The United States Senate took up the incidents of wives and families being tormented by what they called "telephone terrorists." Some of the incidents raised by Senator Dodd are mentioned below.

> The widow of…a 28 year old Army captain killed in Vietnam received a number of anonymous calls and letters. The first caller said to her about her husband: "He didn't belong in Vietnam in the first place. Your husband got what he deserved. I am glad. It serves him right." [The widow fainted.]
>
> An Army Major reported that several persons called on his wife and tried to convince her that he was trapped in sin because of the "evil war in Vietnam."
>
> A number of servicemen…reported that their wives had obtained unlisted phone numbers because of the calls or threats to them.[48]

There was also an organized effort to coerce the wives of POWs to join the antiwar movement and oppose the war. This was in the form of the Committee of Liaison which was formed, in collaboration with North Vietnam, by leading members of the antiwar movement in the United States. The New Mobilization Committee and the Women Strike for Peace were closely tied in with the Committee of Liaison. Those involved in setting up this committee were William Kunstler, attorney for the Chicago Seven (originally eight), who were tried on conspiracy charges; Cora Weiss, one of the leaders of the Women Strike for Peace, David Dellinger, one of the Chicago Seven; Stewart Meacham; Rennie Davis; Professor Donald Kalish; Reverend Richard Fernandez; and a staff member, Trudi Young, who was also a coordinator for the New Mobe. The wife of one of the POWs was told by one of the American visitors to Hanoi that each one of the members of the Committee of Liaison had been hand-picked by Hanoi. In January 1970, Cora Weiss, who had recently returned from a meeting with Communist officials in Hanoi, held a news conference concerning the establishment of the Committee of Liaison:

> She opened the conference by expressing criticism of the United States for the massacres which she alleged had been committed by U.S. troops in Vietnam, and said the United States Commander in Chief should

be held responsible....She described her inspection of North Vietnamese prison camps in Hanoi and quoted North Vietnamese officials as stating that North Vietnam would not negotiate concerning the treatment of prisoners until the U.S. withdraws all troops completely and recognizes a coalition government of South Vietnam. She said the antiwar movement would handle communications between the prisoners of war and their families.

She went on to question the accuracy of the information furnished by Navy Lieutenant Robert Frishman and Seaman Douglas Hegdahl, [released POWs] both of whom described the inhumane treatment given to prisoners of war in North Vietnam in their testimony before the committee [House Committee on Internal Security] in December 1969....

She also discussed the excellent living conditions she observed in the North Vietnamese prison camp described as the "Hanoi Hilton," but refused to be drawn into a discussion as to whether this represented typical treatment of American prisoners of war in North Vietnam.[49]

Several courageous POW wives appeared before the House Committee on Internal Security while their husbands were still captives in North Vietnam. They were incensed by having their communication with their captive husbands controlled by the activists who were doing Hanoi's bidding—people whose beliefs were contrary to their own and opposed to the policies of their government. At the risk of severing all contact with their husband, some of the POW wives chose not to cooperate with the Committee of Liaison. One of those was Sue Allen Shuman, the wife of Commander Edwin A Shuman III, U.S. Navy. Mr. Romines, House Committee counsel, questioned Mrs. Shuman:

> Mr. Romines. Could you explain to the committee why you decided to not cooperate with the committee?

Mrs. Shuman. It was the climax of a long series of events. I guess I just finally came to a very strong conclusion. It was a very emotional decision; it was something I had to question myself about, the pros and cons, because in the beginning, after I came back from Paris after talking with the North Vietnamese and I learned that the North Vietnamese had summoned William Kunstler and that we were to be told that we would have to deal with these people, I was very resentful then. However, I didn't know what to do, and I did accept the one letter from them.

Mr. Romines. That would be the February letter?

Mrs. Shuman. Yes. I did accept that letter because I still had not come to my decision. But as time went on, after I heard Mrs. Cora Weiss speak in January, the things that she said about Lieutenant Frishman, for whom I have the highest regard, and I read the things that she said at their press conference against this country, of which they are also members—they are citizens of this country—something inside me just simply could not compromise any longer. I do feel that it is a compromise to accept mail from these people...if this issue, this war this conflict was important enough for my Government to send my husband into combat, to lay his life on the line, and with the knowledge that he might be captured, and if it is important enough for him to sit there and resist, which he must be doing, then it is important enough for me to stand up for what I believe in. Therefore, I made my decision.

Mr. Romines. What did they [the North Vietnamese] tell you about the release of the prisoners of war [when Mrs. Shuman met with them in Paris]?

Mrs. Shuman. They told us that the prisoners would never be released until the last American was off their soil, out of Vietnam.

Mr. Romines. Did they indicate to you at all what you could do to help your husband?

Mrs. Shuman. They certainly did, throughout the whole interview. They suggested if we wanted to get camps, not three little propped up rooms [referring to the show rooms that "peace" envoys were shown when they visited Hanoi Hilton]....

Mrs. Doss. I refuse to let my husband's letters be used by the Committee of Liaison. I will give you an example of how they are using them: I know a woman at Virginia Beach whose husband has been a prisoner of war, a known prisoner of war, for twice as long as my husband. Every time these lists come out with the names of prisoners—[lists released by the Committee of Liaison]. This woman has sat time after time after time waiting for mail. The committee says that all the prisoners are being allowed to write. They are not, because this woman's husband is not being allowed to write, and each time a packet of mail comes out and there is not one from her husband, it just pounds her further into the ground....

If this Committee of Liaison were truly humanitarian and were truly what they paint themselves to be, then, No.1, when they bring mail out they would not do it with maximum publicity. No.2, when they go in, they would be truly concerned about the POWs and they would do their best to check into it, not gloss over it. No.3, they would not hold press conferences, as Fernandez did....

Mr. Romines. How did Rennie Davis inform you that he had obtained that letter [the fourth letter] to you from your husband?

Mrs. Doss. I received a telegram from him giving the context of my husband's letter.

Mr. Romines. Did the telegram contain anything else?

Mrs. Doss. Yes, it did. It said that he had contacted friends at *TIME* magazine about the possibility of publishing my husband's letter, that my husband's letter showed the great courage of the men who remained in the camps, and therefore he felt I would like to share it with the world.

Mr. Romines. Had he consulted with you at this time?

our husbands out that we should come home and join all of those who are in sympathy with them and are against our administration and against the policies of our country. In other words, to join those who were demonstrating that day. It was Moratorium Day in the United States.

Mr. Romines. Did they actually tell you to go out and demonstrate?

Mrs. Shuman. Absolutely, and they told us to get as many other people to join us as we possibly could....

Mr. Romines. Mrs. Shuman, what, in your opinion, is the objective or are the objectives of the Committee of Liaison?

Mrs. Shuman. In my opinion, their primary objective is to use the prisoner of war situation, which is really a very emotional thing and to subvert as many people as possible in this country. They are trying to put a good face on it, in my opinion, and they are using the suffering of hundreds of men to paint themselves in a different light than they really are, in my opinion.[50]

Another POW's wife who had the courage to testify before the House Committee on Internal Security was Martha Shaw Doss, wife of Lieutenant Commander Dale Walter Doss, U.S. Navy. Her testimony was similar to that of Mrs. Shuman. She, too, chose not to cooperate with the Committee of Liaison. She described the mail that she did receive via the Committee of Liaison as being full of procommunist propaganda and that attempts to send her letters by the Committee of Liaison kept coming even though she had made it clear that she would not accept them. Mrs. Doss also responded to Mr. Romines questions:

Mr. Romines. Mrs. Doss, what, in your opinion, is or are the objectives of the Committee of Liaison?

Mrs. Doss. As Mrs. Shuman said, they are trying to paint a pretty face on a very ugly situation. They are using our husbands; they are hindering our husbands, because as long as they are in there functioning they are taking the place of a body that could really do some good, a body that could get in there and inspect the

Mrs. Doss. No, he had not. To be quite frank, I was in a state of panic....I sent a wire to *TIME* magazine asking them not to publish his letter.

Mr. Romines. Was that letter published in *TIME* magazine?

Mrs. Doss. No, it wasn't. Before *TIME* magazine received my telegram, they called me. The editor of *TIME* magazine called and asked if they could publish it, and I asked them please, please not to, that it was something very personal, written to me and not to Rennie Davis and not to the American public....[51]

Mrs. Sue Allen Shuman also testified before the House Committee on Internal Security, Hearings on Restraints on Travel to Hostile Areas, which was concerned with the travel of Americans citizens to countries where hostilities existed with the United States. Mrs. Shuman spoke in favor of legislation being considered by the House Committee:

> Right at the time when we, the wives, were engaged in the extremely desperate struggle to make the American people aware of the conditions under which our men were trying to survive, this Committee of Liaison was formed in the fall of 1969.
>
> It was so obvious to us that this was the answer the North Vietnamese had found to be an embarrassment that we were bringing to them, due to the fact that they weren't allowing mail....
>
> I was bitter then. And I became increasingly incensed over the insidious methods that this committee used. They would bring out lists. And the average American citizen, unaware of how many men Washington knew were alive, would read these lists and say that it was wonderful that this committee was operating, that they were helping the families; whereas, really, they were just trickling names out.

And those of us who had known all along that our husbands were alive naturally were happy to see that they were still alive. But our sympathies were with our sisters, who weren't hearing anything. And maybe there would be two or three names every few months. And this went on and on.

Their statements, particularly at Mrs. Weiss' news conference up here in this same building, when she insinuated in every manner that the released prisoners' testimony was totally false and that what she saw in Hanoi was true, that the men were getting good treatment—*this was terribly detrimental to the efforts that we were trying to make to procure better treatment for our men* [emphasis added].

And since my husband's return, the things that he has told me have just verified what I knew from his letters, and the reason I was so terrified at that time.

So I can never forget the hardship that these people caused. But be that as it may, I am greatly happy and encouraged by what you people are doing. I do hope and pray that this bill does pass....

As a result [of not cooperating with the Committee of Liaison], I did go 9 months without mail. Now, my husband has told me since his release that they came to him and to his navigator [Mrs. Doss' husband, Lt Commander Doss] and told them that since they had a bad attitude that they would no longer be allowed to write. They never told my husband why, because I am sure if they had, in a way it would have boosted his morale. He would have known that I was resisting and that I was trying to support his efforts....

But anyway, he wasn't allowed to write for 9 months. And finally, in the fall of 1970, I did receive a letter from the committee. And I had said that I would never open a letter from them. But I was alone in this. I felt that it was hopeless for one very unimportant woman to try to prevail against the American Communist Party, when I wasn't getting any help.

...evidently, we just didn't have enough public sentiment against these people to do anything about them. So, I called the Navy and asked them what they thought I should do. They said, "Well, you have done all you can. Now, you have got to find out what condition your husband is in." And so, I did start to accept his mail. And I did up until the time he was released....[52]

The antiwar activists also directed their propaganda efforts at our servicemen fighting in South Vietnam and those on the bases and posts in the United States and elsewhere. The impact of this effort will be addressed in the next chapter.

Chapter Eight

Assault on the Troops

If there is one path above all others to war, it is the path of weakness and disunity

—John F. Kennedy

Another key element of the second front was a deliberate, organized assault on the armed forces of the United States, including those engaged in combat in Southeast Asia and on the home front. The methods used to undermine our military services by the antiwar factions included broadcasts to our troops fighting in the combat zones; distribution of leaflets and antimilitary newspapers at military installations abroad and in the U,S. which encouraged servicemen to disobey orders and refuse to fight; establishment of coffeehouses near military installations where antimilitary and antiwar activities were promoted; presentations of antimilitary/antiwar shows by well known entertainers; establishment of legal counseling services where troops were assisted in fighting legal actions and in applying for conscientious objector status; and planning antiwar activities in the military services to undermine discipline, stir up discontent and encourage the servicemen to challenge authority.

The measures used by the antiwar factions to attack our troops had the effect of tearing down morale and weakening our war fighting capability. Those who have been in the military service, especially in combat, know that if just one person on the team does not do his or her part, it can place the whole unit in danger and cost the lives of other team members. Accordingly, when the antiwar activists succeeded in turning just one of the members of a unit against the team's efforts, the people in that unit and the mission were placed in jeopardy. That is just what the activists wanted, but they must stand up and accept the responsibility for the American servicemen who died because of their actions. So far, none have ever had the courage to do that.

Broadcasts

Many of us have heard about the broadcasts made over Hanoi Radio by Jane Fonda; however, what is not so well known is that there were many other American citizens who went to North Vietnam where they made antiwar and anti-American broadcasts. In fact, according to the House Committee on Internal Security, 43 American citizens who traveled to North Vietnam between 1965 and 1972 made broadcasts over Radio Hanoi (See Appendix M). Some made more than one broadcast which yielded an accumulation of 82 different broadcasts during that time period. Some of these broadcasts were repeated time and again, in different languages, and there is no way of knowing how many times they were actually broadcast. Many were broadcast over Liberation Radio, a clandestine radio station located somewhere in the South or on the border with Laos and Cambodia. A large percentage of the broadcasts were aimed at U.S. troops in Southeast Asia addressed to, "American GIs," "U.S. Servicemen," "U.S. Flyers and Airmen," "All of you in the cockpits of your planes...in the 7th Fleet," etc.[1]

The House Internal Security Committee found that there were three main categories of radio broadcasts from North Vietnam. They included those made by antiwar activists while visiting North Vietnam; those made elsewhere and then broadcast on Radio Hanoi; and those by captured U.S. servicemen. It is not appropriate to be critical of the latter category, since it is quite probable that they were made under duress. Excerpts from some of the other two categories will shed some light on what the antiwar factions in collaboration with Hanoi were attempting to accomplish.[2]

Broadcasts by Visitors to Hanoi. During Jane Fonda's visit to North Vietnam in 1972 she made 21 separate broadcasts, most of which were aimed at U.S. armed forces in Vietnam. Although some of them were cited in a previous chapter, several other statements merit repeating here:

Radio Hanoi, 2000 GMT 28 Jul 72. [Text] We now bring you a recorded message by American actress Jane Fonda to U.S. servicemen in South Vietnam....

This is Jane Fonda speaking from Hanoi....

I have seen the dikes bombed....Some of them [bombs] are causing earthquakes which make deep fissures into the dike system, so that later when the heavy rains come, the dikes will break and the area will be flooded.

There is only one way to stop Richard Nixon from committing mass genocide in the Democratic Republic of Vietnam [North Vietnam], and that is for a mass protest all around the world of all peace-loving people to expose his crimes, to prevent him from following the people of the world into thinking that if there are floods this year it would be a natural disaster.

Radio Hanoi 2000 GMT 30 Jul 72. [Text] We now bring you American actress Jane Fonda's address to American GI's in South Vietnam....

This is Jane Fonda speaking from Hanoi. A phenomenon has been taking place in the United States called the GI movement....

I've seen the movement grow from a movement of individuals taking courageous action as individuals, to thousands of soldiers taking collective action to voice their protest against the war—marching, demonstrating in uniform and holding up their ID cards, risking—going to jail if necessary, jumping ship, the petition campaigns which started on the Constellation in San Diego and spread to the Coral Sea, the Ticonderoga, the Enterprise, the Hancock, the Kitty Hawk....

And word about the resistance within the American Military has spread throughout the United States. There was a time when people in the peace movement thought that anyone in uniform, anyone who was coming over here to support the Thieu regime, must be the enemy. But we have realized that most of these young men were not fortunate enough to get draft deferments, were not privileged enough to have good lawyers or doctors [words indistinct]. These are the sons of the American working class. They're the sons of the hardhats. They're guys who came because they thought it was the thing to do, or because it was the only way they could get an education, or because it was the only way they could learn a skill. They believed in the army, but when they were here, when they discovered that their officers were incompetent, usually drunk, when they discovered that the Vietnamese people had a fight that they believed in, that the Vietnamese people were fighting for much the same reason that we fought in the beginning of our own country, they began to ask themselves questions.

Perhaps the soldiers who have been the first to recognize the nature of the war in Vietnam are those soldiers who have suffered the most in the United States—the black soldiers, the brown soldiers, and the red soldiers....

Recently on a tour of the U.S. bases on the Pacific rim—in Okinawa, Japan and the Philippines—I had the chance to talk to a great many of these guys and they all expressed their recognition of the fact that this is a white man's war, a white businessman's war, that they don't feel it's their place to kill other people of color when at home they themselves are oppressed and prevented from determining their own lives....

[Speaking of women in the military] I heard horrifying stories about the treatment of women in the U.S. military. So many women said to me that one of the first things that happens to them when they enter the service is that they are taken to see the company psychiatrist and they are given a little lecture which is made very clear to them that they are there to service the men.

<u>Radio Hanoi to American Servicemen Involved in the Indochina War 1300 GMT 22 Aug 72</u>. [Text] Here's Jane Fonda telling her impressions at the end of her visit to the Democratic Republic of Vietnam:

This is Jane Fonda....One thing I have learned beyond a doubt since I've been in this country [North Vietnam] is that Nixon will never be able to break the spirit of these people; he'll never be able to turn Vietnam, north or south, into a neocolony of the United States by bombing, by invading, by attacking in any way. One has only to go into the countryside and listen to the peasants describe the lives they led before the [Communist] revolution to understand why every bomb that is dropped only strengthens their determination to resist.

But now, despite the bombs, despite the crimes being created—being committed against them by Richard Nixon, these people own land, build their own schools— the children are learning, literacy—illiteracy is being wiped out, there is no more prostitution as there was during the time when this was a French colony. In other words, the people have taken power into their own hands, and they are controlling their own lives.[3]

Before moving on to other voices from Hanoi, the comments by Fonda in the last broadcast just cited clamors for comment. Fonda says she visited an agriculture co-op where people were happy and cheerful. She goes on to say that the people own their own land and control their own lives. Fonda's knowledge of history is obviously extremely lacking, for what she does not know or will not acknowledge is that between 10,000 and 100,000 Vietnamese peasants in the North were slaughtered and many more were imprisoned in the forced collectivization of agriculture in the early years of the Communist takeover in the North, and that the primary tenant of collectivization was the elimination of private ownership of the agricultural lands as well as the fruits of production.⁴ The co-op which she visited and thought was so great was a product of the collectivization program. As for controlling their own lives, being forced to give up their land and move to a cooperative where all the production is for the government is far from being empowered or free.

Fonda paid a final visit to Premier Nguyen Duy Trinh on July 22, 1972, the day of her departure from North Vietnam. According to a broadcast on Hanoi Radio, she told the premier of her impressions during her visit:

> She said she had witnessed U.S. crimes in the Hanoi capital, Hai Hung, Ha Tay and Nam Ha provinces and was deeply impressed by the Vietnamese people's solidarity and mutual sympathy and their determination to materialize President Ho Chi Minh's testament and bring the anti-U.S. aggression for national salvation to a complete victory....She said she was convinced that under the wise leadership of the Vietnam [Communist] Workers Party and the DRV Government the Vietnamese people will certainly win brilliant victory.⁵

There were many other activists besides Jane Fonda who traveled to North Vietnam and made statements which were used by Hanoi to undermine the U.S. military forces. Several of the other broadcasts cited by the House Internal Security Committee follow:

> <u>Radio Hanoi, August 29, 1970</u>. At a ceremony commemorating black solidarity with the Communist Vietnamese "struggle" in Indochina on August 27, 1970, Eldridge Cleaver stated:
>
> The rise of the struggle of black people inside the U.S. is a sure sign that the days of U.S. imperialism are numbered....The combination of the external revolutionary forces and the internal revolutionary forces is an unbeatable combination and together, we are going to crush U.S. imperialism and thus usher in a new and happy day for mankind.

<u>Radio Hanoi, Quoted in FBIS Daily Report, 4 August 1969.</u> James A. Johnson, then overtly representing the National Black Anti-war Anti-draft Union, was quoted as stating:

We consider it fitting that I, a black man and an ex-GI who spent 28 months in U.S. prisons for refusing to fight against the Vietnamese people, should read this statement. Thousands of American GI's now feel that their fight is not with the people of Vietnam. Their fight is with those who make the war in this country....

<u>Radio Hanoi, delayed-tape broadcast, September 20, 1970.</u> Addressing his statement to "my black brothers in the U.S. forces in Vietnam," Reverend Phillip Lawson declared:

For two weeks, I have been visiting with the people of [North] Vietnam. I have seen what you have been ordered to do to these people. Very frankly, you know what you are doing is criminal, for the same action many persons were convicted of being war criminals. You must become men who will stand up and say no when you are given criminal orders....Black brothers, do not kill women and children. You can shoot over their heads, you can prevent the racist white soldiers from slaughtering these people. You can disobey all racist officers and their racist orders. Black brothers, the real war is being fought in the United States. What you do now in Vietnam will determine what you do back home. If you join the Vietnamese forces...your black brothers and sisters in the United States will welcome your return as a true black man, but if you continue to be used...your black brothers and sisters...will surely see you as members of the black police force returning to their black community.[6]

The Internal Security Committee report cites a number of other broadcasts by American citizens: "After Reverend Lawson's broadcast, a delegation from the National Student Association, which visited Hanoi to negotiate the 'People's Peace Treaty' in December 1970, made six separate broadcasts from Hanoi. Such antiwar activists as Noam Chomsky, Richard Fernandez, Robert Scheer, Sidney Peck and Ann Froines also made broadcasts during their respective 1970 visits to North Vietnam. In addition, 'Movement for a Democratic Military' leader Hideko 'Pat' Sumi, who traveled with the Cleaver Black Panther group to Hanoi, Peking, and Pyongyang [North Korea], was another individual identified as making GI broadcasts in September 1970." Harvard Professor and Nobel Prize winner, George Wald and folk-singer and identified Communist Party USA (CPUSA) member Pete Seeger also visited North Vietnam and made tapes for broadcast via Radio Hanoi.[7]

Broadcasts Originating Elsewhere. The second category of broadcasts includes those taped elsewhere and sent to North Vietnam for transmission over Radio Hanoi. Several of the earliest broadcasts of this type were taped in Peking by black militant Robert Williams and a black Korean War defector, Clarence Adams. The House Internal Security Committee described these broadcasts in this way:

> Aimed primarily at blacks and other minorities, these messages called on American servicemen to desert or to demand their return to the U.S. where they were to aid in the "real struggle," i.e., in the ghettos of American cities. This divisive theme, as can be seen with the previously mentioned "live' broadcasts by Cleaver and Lawson, has been continued to the present [September 1972]. In 1967-1969, black militant activists such as Charles Cobb and Stokely Carmichael of SNCC (now SCC), Julius Lester and James A. Johnson made similar appeals to black and minority GI's. With respect to Williams and Adams, however, both men have been permitted re-entry into the United States after making such blatant propaganda.[8]

There were many other broadcasts that were originated in the U.S. and sent to Hanoi for replay. For instance, a Fourth of July message in 1966 by an unidentified female declared the war unjust and accused the U.S. of war crimes. A Christmas message in the same year by Ed Anderson focused on racial strife, hunger and disease in America and called the war in Vietnam hopeless. These broadcasts were somewhat overshadowed by broadcasts from "Radio Stateside" which taped programs in Los Angeles for broadcasts in Hanoi. The House Internal Security Committee gave the following description of this project:

> Two announcers, Steve Fisher and Joe Epstein, combined music with a highly slanted analysis of the news, especially on the Vietnam War. Sandwiched in between were appeals for desertion and conscientious objector applications. In particular, the pair asked GI's to contact the heavily Communist-infiltrated Vietnam Day Committee which was headquartered at Berkeley, and also the Central Committee for Conscientious Objectors, located in Philadelphia, PA. In toto, Radio Stateside made three known broadcasts (January 4, February 16, and August 17) in 1966, and then ceased operations. According to testimony given during HCIS [House Committee on Internal Security] military subversion hearings in October 1971, this technique was again employed in early 1971 with WPAX, Inc., the brainchild of Yippie leader and "Chicago 8" defendant Abby Hoffman....[9]

Broadcasts and Psychological Warfare. The House Internal Security Committee's summary of the broadcasts clearly makes the case that they undermined the morale of our troops and the war effort, and gave aid and encouragement to the enemy. The committee summed it up with the following comments:

> In summary, the Vietnamese Communist manipulation of these three major types of U.S. broadcasts has, since 1965, provided a steady stream of propaganda directed against American forces in Southeast Asia. In terms of the first category alone, U.S. visitors to North Vietnam

have made 82 identified broadcasts. By co-timing broadcasts from all three types, it is apparent that the Vietnamese Communists have attempted to gain credibility for their propaganda by means of a technique called theme reinforcement, whereby various speakers from different backgrounds reiterate the same basic theme time and time again somewhat akin to the Nazi propagandist Dr. Goebbels' dictum: "Truth is merely an oft-repeated lie."[10]

Such activities—as her [Fonda's] broadcasts from the enemy's territory to our forces in the field—have an obvious tendency to encourage the enemy and to undermine the morale of our forces to whom she owed primary allegiance. As described to us by several experts in psychological warfare, they can have no other result than to advance the enemy's interest at the expense of our own....[11]

We will never know with certainty the full impact of the broadcasts on our fighting forces in Southeast Asia, but it is not a far reach to conclude that encouraging them to desert, disobey orders or not fight had some detrimental effect on the troops. Where it caused any of our servicemen to fail to carry out their duties in a combat zone, there is a high probability that their failure placed some of their comrades at risk and possibly caused additional casualties. The credit for these additional casualties rests squarely on the activists who made the broadcasts. There were other tactics used by the antiwar factions to undermine the troops. These will be explored next.

Subverting the Troops

The GI Movement. The antiwar factions attempted to subvert the U.S. armed forces in a number of ways besides the broadcasts from Hanoi. Collectively, this effort became known as the GI movement. The House Committee on Internal Security conducted an extensive investigation in 1971 into the attempts to subvert the U.S. armed forces. The House Committee defined the GI Movement in the following terms:

> The GI Movement is the term used by the Communist press and the underground press and the antiwar movement people to describe that aspect of the antiwar movement directed against the military. It is the organized efforts by relatively small numbers of GIs and pseudo pacifist civilians to enlist and engage the participation by United States armed services personnel in the so-called peace movement.
>
> As it is used in this study, it is a combination of GIs and civilians in contact with GIs, whose antiwar efforts are directed toward organizing servicemen against the war and the military system itself and linking that struggle with the subsequent struggle for the takeover of political power in the United States.
>
> There are numerous organizations involved in the GI Movement—ranging from those originated and promoted by the old left, such as the GI's United—backed by the Trotskyite Communist Socialist Workers Party—SWP—and its youth arm, the Young Socialist Alliance—YSA—to those which appear to be simply against continued involvement in the Vietnam War, such as the Concerned Officers Movement....[12]

Preliminary committee findings indicated that the groups in the GI Movement which had revolutionary Marxists in leadership positions included GI's United, U.S. Servicemen's Fund (USSF), Movement for a Democratic Military (MDM), American Servicemen's Union (ASU), and the Socialist Workers Party which was the most active of those in the GI Movement.[13]

The House Committee's investigation also found the aims of the GI Movement to have the potential to significantly undermine the morale and effectiveness of our armed forces in fighting the war in Vietnam:

> The main propaganda theme of the GI Movement is that imperialist militarism has instigated and perpetuated an illegal war and in the process has stripped the unwilling

draftee of his constitutional rights. The GI Movement professes to have the objective of awakening the soldier to the realization that induction has deprived him of his rights—particularly the right to speak and write freely concerning real or imagined mistreatment. The more radical in the movement feel that the aroused GI perhaps can be then induced to refuse to participate—under the Nuremberg principle—in the allegedly "illegal" war. An obvious benefit to the revolutionary movement is that any radicalization of the GI may carry over into civilian life.[14]

The GI Movement used a litany of subversive tactics, including underground newspapers, leaflets, GI coffeehouses, counseling, infiltration, and celebrity shows. The coffeehouses were usually set up near a military post or base, and served as centers for radical organizing among the servicemen. In the three years leading up to mid-1971, military authorities identified approximately 100 coffeehouses and underground papers. Starting in 1969, the U.S. Servicemen's Fund (USSF) subsidized 50 of the coffeehouses and newspapers. As of 1970, USSF organized USO-type entertainment troupes and supported increases in the legal defense activities for servicemen in trouble with the military. According to the committee report, USSF obtained its financial support from "donations" by individuals and groups which supported its cause. It is also noteworthy that USSF had close ties as well as common interests with Cuba, the Venceremos Brigade, North Vietnam and the NLF.[15]

The typical coffeehouse consisted of a small storefront business near a military installation, licensed to serve coffee and sandwiches, and operated by one of the radical antiwar groups. The walls were often lined with posters of various antiwar groups. They usually had a large supply of antiwar and Communist Party literature along with underground newspapers, teachings of Mao, and press releases from Communist sources such as the Peoples Republic of China. Some of the underground newspapers went so far as to suggest disobeying orders or "fragging" (shooting or blowing up) officers who gave orders which the GIs did not want to follow. Weekend programs at the coffeehouses consisted of rock music; showing revolutionary films, usually from Hanoi and other Communist sources; guest speakers and entertainers;

and counseling service. At some locations week-long training sessions were held with guidance on court-martial procedures, legal aspects of desertion, how to file a complaint against a superior officer, instructions on types of discharges, how to obtain conscientious objector status, and subverting the Uniform Code of Military Justice.[16]

One of the main organizations providing legal assistance to servicemen was the Pacific Counseling Service which had offices throughout the west coast and at several overseas locations. The Pacific Counseling Service published a pamphlet for servicemen titled, *A GI's Guide to His Rights in the Army*. Pacific Counseling Service offered counseling to GIs both off the post through its legal office and on the post without permission....This service focused on GIs who were dissatisfied with the service, those who were having trouble getting out, those looking for legal alternatives to going to Vietnam, and those with questions about the military justice system.[17]

The Pacific Counseling Service in Japan and Southeast Asia was known as the Military Counseling Service. The long range goals of the Military Counseling Service were stated as "exacting a toll upon the military abilities to maintain large numbers of troops in Asia without experiencing large-scale discontent among the soldiers and establishment of the basis for similar erosion of any future indigenous or external military power in Asia." The Pacific Counseling Service was linked to the People's Army Defense Committee, the Military Law Project and the Movement for a Democratic Military (MDM). The MDM deserves an in-depth look.[18]

The Movement for a Democratic Military (MDM). The Movement for a Democratic Military had as its objective the destruction of the very foundation of the U.S. military services. A House Internal Security Committee witness described MDM in the following way:

> The general purpose of the MDM was to recruit soldiers, to propagandize them, to encourage them to file for conscientious objector status, to hold demonstrations enlisting their sympathy against the Army and the establishment, to conduct certain clandestine—by "clandestine" I mean certain operations aimed at distributing propaganda literature upon the military reservation illegally, and to disrupt in general and

neutralize the effectiveness of Fort Ord as a military training base.[19]

MDM was behind many of the radical activities to subvert the GIs, including the establishment of coffeehouses, making antiwar movies to be shown to U.S. POWs, organizing protests and demonstrations, circulating literature encouraging the troops to disrupt and destabilize activities on military installations, and creating tension and dissention within the military ranks. MDM's major effort to undermine the U.S. military services was its manifesto consisting of 12 nonnegotiable demands, demands which if implemented would have rendered the U.S. military totally ineffective as a fighting force. The 12 MDM demands were:

1. We demand the right to collective bargaining.
2. Extend all human and constitutional rights to military men and women.
3. Stop all military censorship—we demand the right to individual conscience—moral, political or religious. We demand the right to refuse all politically objectionable duty such as riot control and Vietnam duty. We demand that MPs be kept out of our civilian lives.
4. Abolish all mental and physical cruelty in military brigs, correctional custodies and basic training.
5. We demand the abolition of the present court martial system: trial by jury and court of one's peers by rank. No more physical custody prior to legal hearing and non-judicial punishment. All cases subject to review by an elected civilian review board.
6. We demand wages equal to the federal minimum wage for civilians.
7. We demand the abolition of the class structure of the military.
8. End all racism everywhere and bring to trial all officers and senior enlisted men who foment and exploit racial tensions.
9. Free all political prisoners including Eldridge Cleaver, Huey Newton, the Conspiracy 8 and our brother war resisters at home and abroad.
10. Stop the glorification of war now prevalent in all branches of the military.
11. Abolish the draft and all involuntary enlistment.

12. Pull out of Vietnam now.[20]

FTA Shows. The most prominent and publicized form of entertainment at the coffeehouses was what became known as FTA shows. FTA has been assigned several meanings, such as Free the Army or Free Theater Association; however the most common and intended definition was F - - K the Army. With the latter definition, the theme of the FTA shows becomes obvious. Jane Fonda was the spokeswoman and organizer of the FTA shows. She used the shows to promote her views on the war and the American economic and political system. Testimony before the Internal Security Committee reveals some of her thinking:

> She [Fonda] has given many, many public statements concerning the [FTA] troupe and her activities in the movement. She has indicated on occasion that she is in charge of fundraising for the group also. She has stated her views about revolution in the U.S. She feels that the United States system or she has stated the United States system of government is so corrupt that even if you had saints for elected officials the system would still be unworkable. She believes in some form of socialistic government.
>
> In regard to the soldiers and what they are doing in the military, she says it is not organized, but it is mutiny and they are entitled to it. She has also indicated and in public appearance stated that, "What is needed is victory for the Viet Cong...."
>
> In a speech at the University of Texas in December 1971, Fonda said: We've got to establish a socialistic economic structure that will limit private, profit-oriented business...Whether the transition is peaceful depends on the way our present governmental leaders react. We must commit our lives to this transition....[21]

The House Committee report indicates that the primary sponsors of the FTA shows were United States Servicemen's Fund, which was mentioned earlier as the source of funds for underground newspapers and coffeehouses, and the Entertainment Industry for Peace & Justice (EIPJ). The EIPJ is an organization of entertainers whose goals were to fight for an immediate end to the Vietnam War and immediate withdrawal of U.S. troops from Vietnam. Committee witnesses described the shows as "composed of political vaudeville, short satirical skits and blackouts concerning the U.S., the U.S. imperialists in the Vietnam War and racial problems in the U.S. military, antimilitarism, and common complaints shared by GIs about military life." The Department of Defense characterized the shows as "antimilitary, antiestablishment and racially agitational."[22]

A typical FTA show, starring Jane Fonda and Donald Sutherland along with others, took place in the Philippines in November 1971. There were three shows, two of which took place near Clark Air Base. The troupe included 32 people, 10 of whom were performers. The rest were support personnel. A news conference was held upon the troupe's arrival in Manila at which the cast pledged their support for the GI Movement and denounced the U.S. policies, U.S. imperialism and white racism. Following a few words of antiwar/anti-American propaganda, the show began with several songs by members of the cast:

> The titles of some of the songs were "Kiss My A - -"(anti-military); "Genocide" (racial); "I've Tried with You, I've Cried with You, but I Won't Die with You" (anti-establishment and anti-military); "Move on Over" (racial); "Insubordination" (anti-military); "Set the Date" (Get out of Vietnam); and several others dealing with the same subjects. There were also several skits included in the program. These also concerned U.S. imperialism, suppressing Blacks and Filipinos and the evils of U.S. militarism, especially in Vietnam.... Another of the skits depicted a football game between the 101st Airborne Division and a crack Vietcong Battalion. During the mock game, innocent bystanders are killed by U.S. napalm bombing....Another skit, starring Jane Fonda, concerned a young girl who becomes a WAF [Defunct term for Woman in the Air Force], is then disenchanted with the military, and how the military

takes advantage of her and suppresses her... [Women were not drafted.]

The last portion of the show consisted of Jane Fonda announcing a rap session to be held...the next day.

At the entrance to the Park [where the show was held] a booklet entitled, "F.T.U.C.M.J." [F- -K the Uniform Code of Military Justice] was distributed. The booklet was a small, 20 page, compilation of articles concerning the alleged injustices of the military justice system, articles of advice on what to do if disciplinary action is taken against an individual, an explanation of an individual's rights, how to use them and protect them, excerpts from pertinent U.S. Army and DoD Directives, and excerpts of pertinent portions of the U.S. Constitution and the UCMJ. The booklet was published by the Military Research Group, P.O. Box 24942, Los Angeles, California, 90024. It was edited by Kenneth Cloke.[23]

In December 1971, the FTA troupe led by Jane Fonda and Donald Southerland presented a show near the Yokota Air Base in Japan. An unidentified American serviceman sang several protest-type folk songs. An appeal was made for support of the Pacific Counseling Service house in Tokyo. The show's theme was primarily antimilitary and antiwar, and included skits and comments against President Nixon. The show was characterized in the following terms:

> The use of profanity in the show was frequent and many of the songs and skits were crude, apparently being aimed at the young, first term enlisted man. Revolution was stressed and a strong effort was made to glorify insubordination. One skit ridiculed the privileges of rank by portrayal of the Yokata Air Base Commander's wife demanding preferential treatment.[24]

Infiltration and Subversion. As unbelievable as it might seem today, while the Vietnam War was raging, some of the antiwar groups were sending their members to enlist in the services for the sole purpose of undermining the U.S. military from within. Moreover, activists who went into the service involuntarily (drafted) were given explicit instructions on what to do to disrupt the military. Hearings before the House Internal Security Committee reveals how some of the antiwar factions operated from within the services.

The Socialist Workers Party (SWP) GI program had as its overall objective to "win as many GIs as possible over into participating, not only in antiwar activities, but to get them to exert their 'civil rights' to have meetings and discuss the war on post." As previously mentioned, SWP was the second largest and the most active of the Marxist revolutionary organizations. The Young Socialist Alliance (YSA), the youth arm of the SWP, gave their members who were infiltrated into the military specific instructions:

> Their program for YSA'ers [who were] called upon to enter the service is that they should enter the service not to help build it, but, as any comrade called upon to serve on a bourgeoisie government, to destroy it from within....While they will not counsel anyone to desert [which is against the law], they will help them find transportation, food, clothing, and lodging, to leave the country, or the destination of their choice.[25]

The Revolutionary Union (RU), a radical stepchild of the Movement for a Democratic Military (MDM), had a significant part in the efforts to radicalize and disrupt the military. According to the Internal Security Committee, this organization had close ties with Red China and a delegation of members had met with the Chinese Premier, Chou En-lai. The goal of the RU was to violently overthrow the Government of the United States. Its members had to be proficient in firearms, explosives and sabotage. Stress was placed on the importance of getting members into the military and key defense industries and facilities. A committee witness who had infiltrated the RU reported:

> Toward the last part of the time I was in the organization, more and more emphasis was stressed on getting into the Army....The goal in the Army was to show that he is going—and especially over the Vietnam issue—that he

is going over and dying simply to fatten the imperialist' pockets, to make them rich, to increase their money. In other words, they were dying for a price and this system was not good....

This order to infiltrate the Armed Forces was not at a local level. This was at the highest level, passed down through the whole organization to every collective, that they were supposed to imitate this and make it a priority thing."[26]

There are many instances where the activists who had infiltrated the services attempted to demoralize the troops and undermine the unit. It is enlightening to see how efforts were made by activists to recruit a member of the U.S. Army to do their bidding. While a young soldier was in an Army hospital in the U.S. he was visited by two soldiers who talked to him about the Progressive Labor Party and brought him literature about the organization. The two visitors, members of the Progressive Labor Party, attempted to recruit the soldier who was of Hispanic heritage. Excerpts from the soldier's testimony before the Internal Security Committee are an excellent example of how the activists worked:

<u>Mr. Ferry [Committee Counsel]</u>. Do you recall any discussions while you were in the hospital concerning what the Progressive Labor Party was? Do you recall specifically whether Michael Balter or John Fink said what the Progressive Labor Party was?
<u>Soldier.</u> Yes, the first time, because I asked what was meant by certain terms such as "communism," "socialism," what the difference was between Marxist, Leninist, philosophy, ideology, and just plain old communism, and what the organization stood for, what it tried to achieve and how.
<u>Mr. Ferry. Do you recall how they characterized the Progressive Labor Party?</u>
<u>Soldier.</u> They described it as being the only Marxist-Leninist party in the United States recognized, or

actively recognized, by Red China as being a true communist party.

Mr. Ferry. Did they tell you anything about the Progressive Labor Party?

Soldier. The told me that they were trying to achieve a revolution of sorts in this country to allow the working class to establish a dictatorship of the proletariat.

Mr. Ferry. Were you asked specifically to do anything?

Soldier. Yes, I was. I was asked to—well, initially, I was asked to help in a matter of some trouble they were having at the stockade there at Fort Ord in writing up some papers, articles about exploitation of the GIs and the working class.

Mr. Ferry. Did they indicate what type of society they were attempting to achieve; what was their ultimate goal?

Soldier. Their ultimate goal was a Marxist-Leninist-oriented society which would be ruled by a dictatorship of the proletariat [classic communism], which is a catch phrase they use to mean that society or government as it is now would be toppled, destroyed, and a different or another government would be put in its place which would assure, supposedly, better government on behalf of the working class.

Mr. Ferry. Did they indicate the means by which this would be acquired?

Soldier. This initially would have to be done by nonviolent means, such as organizing the rank-and-file membership of the people, but in any actual overthrow of the Government, it would require in the end a violent overthrow because the status quo would not allow itself to be taken over just by word of mouth.

Mr. Ferry. How did they characterize the military?

Soldier. The military was an instrument of the ruling class to be used to keep the working-class peoples of the world subservient to big business, which was, i.e., ruling class.

236   *Divided We Fall*

Mr. Ferry. How would they characterize or view the officers or senior NCOs of the military?

Soldier. Officers and senior NCOs were seen as puppets, tools—one of the phrases they used was "lackeys of the ruling class"—to carry out the ruling class wishes.

Mr. Ferry. Do you recall any letters, what was stated in his letters? [referring to a PLP member who had gone to Vietnam]

Soldier. I can't recall exactly, but there was a lot. He felt pretty bad because he had decided to go on to Vietnam to try and do work for PLP in Vietnam, to try and turn people against the war, and apparently the outfit he got in was a real gung ho Americanized outfit and they would not have anything to do with him.

Mr. Ferry. What would happen if John [make believe GI] received orders to go to Vietnam? How was Vietnam used? Was it used?

Soldier. Vietnam was a classic example that PLP used to show the United States' imperialist aggression against the working class people of Southeast Asia and the world. But I did not—I can't say that I really saw them telling the people not to go to Vietnam. Instead, if you were going to Vietnam, they would try to get you to work within the existing framework to destroy it from within, try and turn people, GIs, against the war, try to get them to work against the war and for PLP.[27]

Espionage

Another aspect of the antiwar movement that borders on the unbelievable was the formation of a group called the Ad Hoc Military Buildup Committee formed in early April 1972. This group consisted of representatives of many antiwar organizations which existed for the sole purpose of collecting sensitive/classified information pertaining to U.S. military activities associated with the Vietnam War. The information that was gathered included such things as deployment of Army and Marine units and movement of ships and air units. Collection efforts focused on U.S. Army, Navy, Air Force and Marine bases located in the United States and overseas bases in the Pacific.

An overall summary dated April 15, 1972, distributed by the Ad Hoc group was obtained by the Internal Security Committee and is quoted below:

> The Ad Hoc Military Buildup Committee is a group of individuals from various anti-war organizations including G.I. organizing projects, the Vietnam Veterans Against the War, and the peace movement, which has been collecting information on the U.S. large-scale military buildup in Indochina since April 8, 1972. Information on the movement of men and material to the war zone and the placement of other men and material on alert for possible movement has been gathered through telephone contact with G.I. organizing projects (coffee houses, bookstores, and the like near military bases where active duty men and women, antiwar veterans, and civilians get together) around the United States and overseas. Contact was made with the staffs of these projects, who contacted active duty men on the bases near them for word of any alerts or movements, and then in turn reported these back to the ad hoc committee.[28]

The initial purpose of the collection effort was to determine the buildup of U.S. forces in response to the massive North Vietnamese Easter Offensive across the demilitarized zone on March 30, 1972. The establishment of the Ad Hoc Committee was geared to expose to the U.S. public and the world the renewed deployment of American forces. The U.S. response to the Easter Offensive, indicated by the level of redeployments to Southeast Asia, would be a good barometer of the American will to continue to support South Vietnam.

The intent of the Ad Hoc Committee was to release the information in advance of the deployment with the objective of preventing it. The North Vietnamese were, of course, delighted to learn about U.S. military plans and deployments, and if public sentiment had prevented it, Hanoi would very likely have pulled off a major military victory against the South.[29] Is there any doubt about where the allegiance of the antiwar groups resided?

The collection effort of the Ad Hoc Committee was quite astounding. In a few short weeks, this committee gathered a complete picture of the entire U.S. military buildup in Southeast Asia. For example, an overall summary revealed the following:

<u>Forces Departed for Southeast Asia:</u>
650 planes (390 carrier aircraft); 37 ships (including 5 aircraft carriers); 33,900 plus men.
<u>Forces on Alert, Standby or Freeze for Deployment to SEA:</u>
10 planes; 1 cruiser; 27,770 men.
<u>Transferred to/Arrived at Support Areas for SEA:</u>
138 planes; 1060 men.
<u>Grand Total of Military Buildup in SEA:</u>
793 planes; 37 ships, 62,730 men.

[Note accompanying summary] In short, the United States has dispatched a large-scale air and naval armada to Indochina. Furthermore, she has substantial numbers of ground troops, mainly marines, prepared to move if needed. There are also indications that the United States is making at least contingency preparations to possibly bomb very sensitive targets in North Vietnam, and possibly mine Haiphong harbor from the air....

This information was gathered from many sources including active duty servicemen belonging to or friendly with the antiwar activists, coffeehouses, Pacific Counseling Service, Liberated Barracks, and Vietnam Veterans who still had contacts in the service. An Internal Security Committee investigator cited 38 specific items of information in the Ad Hoc summary report, each attributed to a specific source.[30]

The information collected by the AD Hoc Committee was made public three to four weeks prior to the release of the information by the Defense Department. A few examples of the numerous reports on U.S. military movements reveal the potentially damaging information being collected:

Hickam AFB, Hawaii, 9:00 PM EST, April 14, 1972.
The "Liberation Barracks" reports highly unusual activities on Hickam Air Force Base, Hawaii, particularly concerning the 548th Reconnaissance Group, one of the major units which have been plotting the targets for bombing over North Vietnam throughout the war....

The unit has been working under great pressure since Thursday, April 6, drawing up extra large targeting charts for Hanoi and Haiphong and major military targets in North Vietnam. Targets have included factories, storage depots, and at least two schools, as well as normal military targets. Men report rush orders for immediate work from generals (the 548th Reconnaissance Group is directly under Headquarters, Pacific Air Forces, which is based at Hickam.) The targeting is unusual because the men have not been plotting those targets before. The unit has also been plotting charts for and planning the mining of Haiphong Harbor from the air, also not routine activity.

Units of cooks, medics, security police, transportation personnel, aircraft maintenance personnel, intelligence personnel, as well as 150 members of the 548th Reconnaissance Group are all on 10-minute standby alert for temporary duty....One active duty source says the men have been told that they will be leaving anytime after midnight, Friday 14, 1972.
SOURCE: "Liberated Barrack" [GI coffeehouse] 808-839-4855 Honolulu, Hawaii.

McConnell AFB, Kansas, Monday, April 10, 1970.
70 to 90 F-105 all weather fighter bombers are scheduled to leave for Vietnam in the next week. One squadron has left already. People on "mobility" are restricted to base.

SOURCE: "The Covered Wagon" [GI coffeehouse near Mountain Home AFB, Idaho] 208-587-7474.

El Toro Marine Air Station, Santa Ana, CA, April 11, 1972, 2:00 AM.

The Third Marine Air Wing has orders to Vietnam. This Air Wing has approximately 80 aircraft. One Squadron of photo reconnaissance left this morning (Monday, April 10); the remaining squadrons, all composed of fighter bombers, were due to leave Monday afternoon.
SOURCE: Kent Hudson, Center for Servicemen's Rights, San Diego, CA, 714-263-4141....

Ft. Bragg, NC, 82nd Airborne Division, April 10, 1972, 5:00 PM.

Through information obtained from an enlisted man at Ft. Bragg, 82nd Aviation Battalion, 82nd Airborne Division, it was learned that they had been called back to the base by 5:00 PM, Sunday, April 9th, to go to the field with Special Forces elements for field exercises.

This is unusual, due to the fact that they've recently returned from the field and weren't due to go back. During the maneuver exercises artillery elements went into heavy drills and all battlefield gear was thoroughly examined. It has been indicated that the men in this unit expect transfer to Southeast Asia.
SOURCE: Mike Buckley, 67 Winthrop St., Vietnam Veterans Against the War, Cambridge, Mass. 607 492-5570.

Alameda, CA.

The USS Midway (aircraft carrier) left Alameda California on Monday morning, April 10, 1972, for Vietnam, at least a month ahead of schedule. It carried 4,500 sailors, 75 planes (these were armed with nuclear weapons, as is standard on this ship), and 200 marines, some 50 to guard the bombs.

SOURCE: Kent Hudson, Center for Servicemen's Rights [a GI counseling service], San Diego; 714-233-4142.

<u>Subic Bay, Philippines.</u>
On Easter Sunday, the attack carrier "Kitty Hawk" cut short her normal port call at Subic Bay, Philippines in such haste that 300 men were left behind. The ship was supposed to stay in port at Subic Bay for three to four days, but received urgent orders to return to station off the Vietnam coast. Also at Subic Bay, the destroyer escort USS Roard (DE1053) was given emergency orders to leave for Vietnam, and left.
SOURCE: Kent Hudson, Center for Servicemen's Rights, San Diego and Dale, Angeles City, Pl.[31]

Additional examples of clandestine reporting of U.S. military movements are included in Appendix N. In other wars, such as WW II, the unauthorized disclosure of information about force disposition and movement of military units would have been considered unlawful, and more importantly, un-American, unpatriotic and even traitorous. The potential harm to our war effort and our servicemen fighting in Vietnam was as real as in other wars. Why was Vietnam different? Why were American citizens willing to take actions that put our forces in Vietnam at risk?

There were other activities by the antiwar factions that undermined our war efforts in Vietnam. These will be covered in the next chapter.

Chapter Nine

Sabotaging the War Effort

North Vietnam cannot defeat or humiliate the United States. Only Americans can do that.

—Richard M. Nixon

We have seen how the antiwar factions attempted to undermine our war fighting capability by promoting a breakdown of the morale and discipline of our armed forces. At the same time they were actively engaged in a widespread effort to sabotage the war effort by interfering with the draft, aiding young men to avoid the draft, encouraging servicemen to desert the military, impairing the movement of ships and war materials, obstructing the recruitment by the military services on campuses, disrupting and blocking the Reserve Officer Training Corps (ROTC) programs on campuses to reduce the number of new officers for the armed forces, and driving defense oriented research projects from campuses. All of these activities placed our servicemen fighting in Southeast Asia at greater risk and increased the chances of more casualties. Anything that hindered our war effort worked in favor of our enemy. There is no doubt that Hanoi was gleeful when they saw these things happening.

ROTC Under Attack

Unfortunately for our side, some of the efforts of the antiwar factions were quite successful. For example, antiwar actions to drive ROTC off of campuses coupled with deriding those who participated in the program had a significant effect on enrollment of officer candidates in the ROTC programs. Overall enrollment in ROTC dropped by more than two-thirds from the mid-1960s to the early 1970s. Enrollment in Army ROTC fell from 165,000 cadets before 1965 to 50,234 in 1971/72. Air Force enrollment took an even bigger decline during the same period, going from 80,000 cadets in 1965 to 23,000 in 1972. The shortage of officers was most certainly detrimental to our armed forces and caused greater hardship for those who served. Many were required to serve more than one combat tour in Vietnam to make up for the shortage.[1]

ROTC was a visible symbol of the U.S. military and the war and was, therefore, an obvious target of the anti-military sentiment on campuses, but it was not the only target on campus. General William C. Westmoreland, the former Commander of U.S. forces in Vietnam and later the Chief of Staff of the Army, was concerned about the impact of dissent on the effectiveness of the Army. In discussing the effect of campus unrest, he wrote in his *Report of the Chief of Staff of the United States Army*:

> Virtually all government-funded college programs on the campus came under attacks—particularly those involving the Department of Defense. Removal of all government influence from the campus appeared to be the objective [of the antiwar activists]. To that end, many students and faculty members protested against local defense research projects and, in a number of instances, forced college administrations at leading institutions to cancel or significantly modify defense research programs. Included in the objective of student attacks was the military services' recruiting program on campuses. Recruiters who attempted to discuss opportunities for military careers with college students were frequently harassed, their interviews were disrupted, their movements were hampered, and they were sometimes barred from the campus entirely.
>
> When their methods failed to change college policies in regard to defense projects and ROTC, demonstrators destroyed or seriously damaged by fire a number of ROTC facilities. In one case a bomb explosion at the

research facilities on a Midwest campus caused the death of a graduate student.[2]

The attack on ROTC and government facilities on campuses around the nation was initially instigated and orchestrated by the Students for a Democratic Society (SDS). Protests ranged from non-violent demonstrations to violent, destructive actions on campuses across the country. Non-violent sit-ins took place at Boston University and Fordham University. During May 1969, with ROTC as the target, SDS members led the takeover of a meeting room at Northwestern University, and SDS-led activists occupied an administration building at Dartmouth.[3]

Throughout 1970 campuses across the nation were hammered with protests. ROTC, recruiters and all other government activities on campus were targeted:

> Thousands marched on Berkeley's ROTC building, sparking a five hour battle with police; the university was declared to be 'in a state of emergency' and closed the following day. In January, members of the "Vanguard of the Revolution" commandeered an ROTC plane and dropped three homemade bombs on a U.S. Army ammunition plant outside Madison, Wisconsin. The bombs landed in a snow bank and failed to go off.[4]

> Maryland students launched a "hit-and-run attack' on their school's ROTC headquarters and skirmished with state police. At Princeton, students firebombed an armory. Students battled police for more than three hours at Kent State, inciting a dusk-to-dawn curfew. Shortly afterward, "a fire of undetermined origin" roared through the schools wooden ROTC building; firemen were impeded by students slicing fire hoses and throwing rocks....Students at Stanford went on a rampage, breaking into shops and smashing windows....[5]

President Nixon's decision to strike at the Communist sanctuaries in Cambodia created a firestorm among the antiwar activists. To any reasonable person, the necessity of attacking the Communist sanctuaries in Cambodia should have been obvious. As reported in previous chapters, the North Vietnamese were using Cambodia to funnel troops and supplies into South Vietnam. Attacks on our troops and those of South Vietnam were mounted from across the border, and the enemy troops would slip back across the border when the going got rough. The North Vietnamese Colonel Bui Tin was convinced that cutting the supply routes in the sanctuaries of Laos and Cambodia would have been the one way we could have defeated the Communist forces.[6] Nixon's justification for mounting the assault on the Cambodian sanctuary was sound and long overdue. It enabled the continuation of the withdrawal of U.S. forces as part of the Vietnamization program. Accordingly, the massive opposition to this military operation was completely unjustified and only served to aid the enemy and undermine our image around the world. Nevertheless, the Cambodian incursion and the shooting of students at Kent State fueled an explosion in protests at many of the nation's campuses. In *The War Within*, author Tom Wells described the situation this way:

> America's campuses exploded. Student protests swept like an out-of-control brush fire across the country. Within three days of the Kent State shootings, the student strike sparked by the invasion of Cambodia had spread to several hundred colleges and universities.... Besides strikes and shutdowns, there were teach-ins and workshops, rallies and marches, building blockades and sit-ins, flag-lowering and symbolic funerals. Thousands of students, professors, and administrators descended on Washington to meet with officials and members of Congress;...[7]

The debate to abolish ROTC took place on many campuses with the opposition led by SDS and a number of professors and administrators. The argument to abolish ROTC on campus was closely integrated with the antiwar objectives, and was included in a 19 page pamphlet distributed by SDS. These arguments are a clear indication of the activists' goal to sabotage the war effort. The pamphlet exhorted:

The central role of the American Military is to implement a policy of securing worldwide markets for American investment and trade. This aim means installing and supporting reactionary governments and suppressing popular revolts. The case for abolishing ROTC rests on evidence that ROTC is essential to the smooth functioning of the American military in its pursuit of these goals in Vietnam and elsewhere.

First of all, ROTC is the main source of officers. The function of ROTC is well known and there is no argument on this point. It has best been summed up by GU [Georgetown University] ROTC cadet Col. John Hoffman: "The object of the military science program is to train military officers." This is its sole purpose and goal....According to the N.Y. Times (Jan. 5, 1969) ROTC supplies 50% of the Army officers, 35% of the Navy and 30% of the Air Force. Even more important is the fact that in the Army, ROTC provides 65% of the first lieutenants and 85% of the second lieutenants.

Secondly, there is no present alternative to ROTC. This would mean that a successful attack on the ROTC program would have the desired result on crippling the present imperialist policies of the U.S. government. Even with a considerable effort to expand OCS [Officer Candidate School] and West Point, the immediate result of the abolition of ROTC would be to dry up the supply of officers for the military. Thus to abolish ROTC would make it more difficult to continue the Vietnam War or initiate similar wars.

Thus an attack on ROTC is an attack on the imperialist policy of the U.S. Government.[8]

As mentioned earlier in this chapter, many university professors and administrators joined the students in opposing ROTC programs on campus. A letter written by Professor James Greene, Philosophy

Department, Georgetown University, and included in an anti-ROTC pamphlet in 1969, gives us insight into the thinking of university faculty who supported the removal of ROTC from campuses: Professor Greene wrote, in-part:

> I have talked to a number of faculty members about abolishing ROTC. Very often they raise two objections: first that such an action would be a violation of academic freedom; second, that it would create a hardship for those students who desire ROTC training. I hope I can generate some discussion by replying to these objections.
>
> Not every act of speech is just that. Words are the means by which we perform all sorts of actions. Thus we use words to vote, make promises, and issues commands. Therefore, even if we concede, as I am not sure we should, that no speech should be suppressed because of the wickedness of the ideas expressed, we must acknowledge that suppression may be permissible and even necessary if the speech is a part of a morally objectionable action. My objection to the continuance of the ROTC is based upon this principle and upon the fact that ROTC lectures are not simply acts of speech but parts of an action, the training of military officers, which is as much a part of waging war as the manufacture of bombs and napalm.
>
> I do not want to defend the idea that all wars are immoral, or that all military training at universities is immoral. I object to Georgetown's ROTC program because it is directly related to the war in Vietnam, which I believe is very immoral. I realize, of course, that many, perhaps most of the faculty believe that we are following a wise policy in Vietnam, or at worst, are making a political but not a moral mistake. This is not the place to argue the merits of our Vietnam policy. My point is that the continuance of the ROTC program is not morally neutral; it presupposes that either the administration

sees no connection between the ROTC and Vietnam, which is unlikely, or that it approves of the war, which is a strong possibility, or that it believes that although the war is wrong, abolishing the ROTC would have either no effect or bad effect on our Vietnam policy.

While I regret the inconvenience that abolishment of the ROTC might cause some of our students, I think we ought to balance this inconvenience against the inconveniences born by the people in Vietnam, and the poor in this country, black and white, who are sent to Vietnam in disproportionate numbers because of the injustices of the Selective Service System....[9]

In another part of Professors Greene's letter, he states that those who went to Vietnam were "poor, instead of rich, black instead of white," essentially due to the injustices of the Selective Service System. It's time to expose some of these myths that Professor Greene bought into:

Myth No. 1: The war in Vietnam was fought largely by the poor and uneducated.
Truth: Of those who served during the Vietnam era between August 1964 and March 1973, 8,720,000 were volunteers and 2,215,000 were drafted, which is essentially a four to one ratio. Two-thirds of the men who actually served in Vietnam were volunteers, and 77 percent of those killed were volunteers. Those serving in Vietnam with higher education, some of whom were from more affluent families, had a 10 percent elevated risk of dying because they were more likely to be pilots and infantry officers who had a higher casualty rate.
Myth No. 2: A disproportionate number of blacks were killed in the Vietnam War.
Truth: Of those killed in Vietnam, 86 percent were Caucasians, 12.5 percent were black, and 1.2 percent were from other races. The number of blacks killed was proportional to the number of blacks in the U.S. population at the time.[10]

In addition to efforts to restrict the number of new officers for the armed forces and hinder the recruitment of volunteers on campuses, there were many instances of actual sabotage of military equipment and systems and interference with movement of troops and ships. By the end of 1971, the Navy reported 191 cases of sabotage, 135 cases of arson and 162 instances of deliberate destruction. A suspicious fire on the USS Forrestal damaged the radar control center, and the USS Ranger was damaged when two twelve-inch bolts were put into one of the ship's reduction gears.[11]

The House Internal Security Committee investigating attempts to subvert the United States armed forces heard testimony that revealed that a campaign was launched in early 1971 to protest and oppose the deployment of U.S. Navy aircraft carriers for duty in Southeast Asia. Actions were carried out against the USS Constellation in Bremerton, WA and San Diego, CA. by a coalition of dissident military and civilian activists. The protest activities included an attempt to induce the servicemen assigned to the carrier to take actions which would decrease the ability of the ship to deploy for its mission in Southeast Asia. Tactics included letters and leaflets to the ships crew; efforts to get the crew members to sign a petition voting against the deployment of the Constellation and its participation in the war; attempts to get servicemen not to report for duty aboard the ship; providing sanctuaries for the servicemen who chose not to sail with the ship; and holding demonstrations to interfere with traffic to the ship. Similar tactics were used against the USS Kitty Hawk and USS Coral Sea, and although a few servicemen took the offer of sanctuary instead of boarding their ship, all three carriers departed their births without delay. There are unconfirmed reports that some of the bombs loaded on the carrier's aircraft for missions in Vietnam were rendered harmless by dissident armament technicians who opposed the war. If true, missions were rendered ineffective, and aircrews risked and possible lost their lives for nothing. All of the activities to subvert and sabotage our military operations aided the enemy and caused more casualties of U.S. servicemen.[12]

Many other U.S. military installations were the target of protests and demonstrations opposing the war and encouraging servicemen not to follow orders from their superiors. In some instances there were attempts to interfere with the movement of troops and equipment.[13]

The American Friends Service Committee, an antiwar organization, established a "Peoples Blockade of Arms to Indochina" project for the purpose of organizing a nation-wide effort to block the movement of war materials for the war. The Peoples Blockade headquarters, located in Philadelphia, offered literature, posters, organizing manuals, etc. to help antiwar groups to blockade land and sea movements. The Peoples Blockade office also provided lists of possible targets such as sea terminals, air bases, army posts and railroads tracks. The Peoples Blockade boasted of accomplishments made early in its formation, including the following:

> Actions like this are already taking place. At the Naval Ammunition Depot in Leonardo, N.J., people have begun a sustained campaign to blockade munitions shipments leaving for Vietnam. On several occasions a flotilla of canoes, sailboats, and small motor boats attempted to blockade ships; and others were arrested while holding a worship service on the railroad tracks which carry the munitions to the pier. In Bangor, Washington, people have attempted similar sea blockades of ships loaded with bombs for B-52's. And in Norfolk, Va., a few weeks ago, people attempted a sea blockade of the 5000-man aircraft carrier, USS America, which was to join 7 other carriers and the huge naval armada off the coast of Vietnam.[14]

At this point it is difficult to weigh the impact of the various efforts to interfere with the shipment of war materials to Vietnam; however, the personal experience of the author gives us some indication. On the eve of the 1968 Tet offensive, he and the other officers in his unit were issued their 38 caliber side arms with a sum total of FIVE rounds of ammunition. Many of these men had quarters several miles from the main base and were cut off and surrounded by the enemy when the offensive struck early the next morning. The reason for only five rounds was a shortage of ammunition of that caliber. In conversations with aircrews while in Vietnam, the author learned that some armaments such as bombs and missiles had to be jury rigged to make them work on certain aircraft because the right munitions were not available. This caused increased risks for the aircrews and had the effect of reducing the combat effectiveness of the mission.

The Anti-Draft Movement

The Selective Service System also became a target of the antiwar movement. As early as 1965 SDS launched a campaign against the draft. The anti-draft movement became an important element of the antiwar movement. As with the efforts to reduce the production of officers in the ROTC program, the antiwar factions felt that by impairing or eliminating the draft, they would make it impossible for the United States to continue the war.[15] Protests took on such things as draft card burnings, sit-ins, picketing of draft boards and even damage to Selective Service facilities and draft records.

The main thrust of the anti-draft campaign was to encourage and assist draft age men to avoid the draft by any number of ways, including failure to register, failure to report for induction, applying for conscientious objector status, faking mental or physical disabilities, and fleeing to another country such as Canada. Counseling offices were set up in every corner of the country to advise those subject to the draft on how to avoid it, and underground organizations sprang up to help those seeking to escape to another country. An anti-draft program established by the SDS national leadership during the 1965-66 academic year included:

> 1. Publication and sale of some 15,000 copies of a handbook on conscientious objection to the draft.
> 2. A campaign to persuade college professors not to turn in class ranking used by Selective Service boards in reviewing student draft deferments.[16]

In December 1966 the SDS National Council passed a resolution that declared that SDS was moving from the tactics of protest to active resistance starting with the issue of the draft. This resolution, set forth in a pamphlet with the title of *SDS and the Draft, from Protest to Resistance,* spelled out SDS's plan to undermine the draft as summarized below:

> The resolution committed national SDS to the task of providing staff, finances, and supplies for the

organization of "unions of draft resisters." Youths from high schools, colleges, and communities were to be solicited to join these unions, which would engage in demonstrations during pre-induction physicals, inductions, at draft boards and recruiting stations, and also to do "educational" work against the draft or war among potential inductees and men already in the military. The SDS resolution called upon all young men to resist the draft, urged college youth to quit the campus to organize draft resistance in the community, and promised to publish literature to aid resistance to the war effort among men in the armed forces....[17]

For the leadership of SDS, the anti-draft movement was simply a vehicle to get to their larger objective of "revolution." Carl Davidson, the national vice president of SDS, wrote in the *New Left Notes* in February 1967, "SDS should concentrate on stimulating a 'radical or revolutionary consciousness' in other persons." SDS organizers, he said, "should be creating permanent local centers for radical opposition with the capacity for becoming the foundation of an American resistance movement."[18]

Davidson revealed his scheme of using the draft as the Trojan horse for the revolution he envisioned for America in his *Essays on Draft Resistance*:

> The prime purpose of draft resistance, he noted at the outset, was to reach young Americans of draft age with SDS complaints against the draft, the Vietnam War, U.S. foreign policy, and domestic policies. A secondary purpose was to encourage and assist young men to get out of the draft or the military by both legal and illegal methods, he asserted.
>
> In Davidson's view—which called for resistance in preparation for eventual revolution—draft resistance also had the virtue of putting men of draft age or those already in the military to soon begin to translate their personal anxieties about the war and the draft into political dissent and opposition.[19]

SDS national secretary Gregory Calvert also promoted the draft resistance as a way to involve people in actions which would help build "revolutionary cadres." Calvert publicly advocated, "At this period the development in others of a 'radical or revolutionary consciousness' [is needed] in order to build a revolutionary movement allegedly for freedom from a 'brutal' and 'dehumanizing' system known as American corporate capitalism and its corollary, aggressive imperialism."[20]

SDS president Nick Egleson, who supported the draft resistance movement, described SDS's major role in the movement as "that of a 'catalyst' for change in society as a whole." Dismissing national elections as irrelevant, Egleson reportedly told the University of Illinois chapter that "SDS hoped to create a genuine revolution in American society which would decentralize government and bring about viable popular control of the institutions of power—the economic institutions."[21]

At SDS's national convention in 1967 in Ann Arbor, Michigan, 300 participating delegates voted for civil disobedience and disruption of the Selective Service System and a harsher view of the U.S. and South Vietnamese Military efforts against the Vietnamese Communists. The attacks on the Selective Service System grew more violent as other antiwar factions took up the call by SDS. Here are just a few examples of the many attempts to disrupt Selective Service operations:

> In suburban Catonsville, Maryland, on May 17, 1968, seven men and two women [led by Daniel and Philip Berrigen, both Catholic priests] quietly entered Local Draft Board 33. They walked directly to the file cabinets, grabbed handfuls of draft files, and...rushed to the parking lot where they incinerated the heap with homemade "napalm."[22]

> A month after Catonsville, The Boston 2 poured black paint over draft files in Boston.[23] After Catonsville, imitative raids occurred in Silver Springs, Maryland; Providence, Rhode Island; Chicago; and New York—all led by members of the Catholic left.[24]

> Catonsville was not a first for Philip Berriagan. Six months before, on October 27, 1967, he entered

a Baltimore draft office...with three others and methodically poured a mixture of human and duck blood over records filed there.[25]

Then, in September 1968, the Milwaukee 14 napalmed ten thousand draft records in that city. In 1969....Nine separate actions, including the first raid conducted by women [in Manhattan] resulted in the destruction of hundreds of thousands of draft records.[26]

Counseling draft age youths to avoid the draft was another major aspect of the anti-draft movement. A nationwide network of local, regional and national committees were set up solely for the purpose of assisting draft age people in filing or appealing conscientious objector status. The *Handbook for Conscientious Objectors*, published and distributed by the Central Committee for Conscientious Objectors, provided detailed information on all the aspects and procedures for filing for conscientious exemption from military service, and provides information on how to obtain free advice. It refered to two national agencies that coordinated the counseling effort. They were: The Central Committee for Conscientious Objectors (CCCO) located in Philadelphia, and the National Service Board for Religious Objectors (NSBRO), with offices in Washington, D.C., New York, and the state of Washington.[27]

Those counseling people to become conscientious objectors or to take other actions to avoid the draft were careful not to violate Federal laws by openly encouraging young men to avoid the draft. Instead, they "innocently" provided information laced with a good amount of propaganda. For example one of them counseled:

> You must realize that the basic function of the military is to wage war, not to "build men." It's really quite a sad commentary on the wealthiest country in the world that many young men who want to better themselves feel forced to join an organization that destroys other young men who doubtless would also like to better themselves.

No matter what slogans you may have heard—and they are almost exactly the same in every country—armies are for killing! As you consider your decision about military service, the question you must ask yourself is what you think of war; its purposes, its methods, its results....[28]

When conscientious objection was not the answer, advice shifted to another way of avoiding service to their country—that of fleeing to another country. The War Resisters League was one of the leading organizations that provided guidance and assistance to those wishing to evade the draft by escaping to another country, and provided the same service to members in the armed forces who chose to desert their units. The War Resisters League made their pitch in this way:

> **WHAT ABOUT CANADA?** Canada is a magnificent country. It is filled with nice people. It would be a good place to settle down and raise a family. And going to Canada to escape the draft is a perfectly honorable thing to do. (If you really want to do it we'll tell you where you can get legal information on immigration.) Many of us in the U.S. have ancestors who fled Europe to escape conscription. We used to be proud that America had no conscription—proud to offer haven to those fleeing European militarism.[29]

Just exactly how many draft age men and GI deserters fled to other countries to avoid their service obligations is uncertain. Estimates range that from 70,000 to 125,000 draft evaders and deserters fled to Canada. A smaller number made their way to Sweden and France where they were granted refuge. What is known is that dozens of organizations sprang up to provide advice and assistance to those who wanted to escape to another country. Besides those operating in the United States, there were organizations in Sweden, Germany, Japan, France and Canada. In exiting the United States, deserters and draft evaders were assisted by groups such as the Students for a Democratic Society, The Black Panthers, The Revolutionary Union, The Resistance, American Friends Service Committee, War Resisters League, The Committee for Peace and Freedom, New York Resisters League, San Francisco

Resistance, Campus Christian Ministry and many local chapters of these and other organizations.[30]

In May 1969, the Canadian government announced a policy whereby deserters from the U.S. applying for landed immigration status would be treated as normal applicants and that having deserted would not be held against them.[31] This in-effect opened the door for all those wishing to flee to Canada. Several major organizations were created in Canada even before the change in immigration policy to aid draft evaders and deserters. Two of the principal groups set up for this purpose were the American Deserters Committee and the Toronto Anti-Draft Programme. The Toronto Programme claimed to be the largest group in Canada helping young American immigrants who refused to fight in Vietnam. The credo of this group, "Where the guys who said 'no!' come for help," signifies its purpose. Literature from this group gives the following description of its objectives:

> The Programme works closely with the Vancouver Committee to Aid American War Objectors in providing legal research and information to the other Canadian aid groups (there are 26) and is a contact with 2,200 draft counselors in the U.S., providing background information, reporting changes in immigration practice, and verifying or denying the ever-present rumors....
>
> Trained councilors are available seven days a week to advise people planning to immigrate, and this is our major function. But the Programme also helps immigrants once they arrive in Canada.
>
> We have two hostels to provide temporary lodging and nearly 200 Torontonians have offered to house draft resisters temporarily. Our American Immigrants Employment Service has a full-time counselor to help find job offers for applicants and jobs for landed immigrants. And there is a small load fund for immigrants who experience special difficulty and have no place else to turn. Several Toronto lawyers have offered to advise immigrants with special problems.

The Programme is assisted by dozens of volunteers, both new immigrants and Canadians. Church groups and the faculty of the University of Toronto have been especially valuable sources of assistance and support.[32]

The American Deserters Committee was the second largest group aiding deserters and draft evaders, with major operations in Montreal and Vancouver. A flyer describing the Vancouver American Deserters Committee's program reflects the strong antiwar sentiments of this group. It states, "Every GI must be helped to get into Canada, and to survive here as long as he needs to....Deserters are acting against the system in the interests of their class. They are struggling for the survival of the strongest, healthiest and most militant young men of the black and brown and the white working class of America." In brief, the flyer outlines the following plan of action:

> **AID ALL DESERTERS.** To aid all deserters to remain safely in Canada whether or not they qualify under the Immigration Act as long as they need to....We will build support among the Canadian and Quebec people for sanctuary for deserters, and will work to prevent the return of any GI to the States to face prison, stockade sentence, shipment to Vietnam, or further service in the U.S. Military.
>
> Specifically, this means that we must build strong cross-Canada ties between all who are aiding desertion, and create an organized network for housing, transportation, financial help and competent immigration counseling stretching from Halifax to Victoria.
>
> We see the development of active underground sanctuary in Canada as vital to the disintegration of the U.S. military machine and as part of the struggle of all those within and without he U.S. who are fighting against imperialism.

MAKE PROPAGANDA. Desertion is a forceful act of "propaganda of the deed." Further, we will tirelessly undertake propaganda of the word, spreading information about the war, about desertion and U.S. imperialism....At every opportunity—through the mails, in the underground press, hand-to-hand, whenever a U.S. ship visits a Canadian port, throughout the world—we will spread the word: resist, rebel, desert!

We cannot overemphasize the importance of this work to the U.S. movement, the Canadian movement, and the liberation struggles of the third world. We view desertion as only a part of resistance. We believe that all who are drafted should disrupt from within, rebel, and finally desert as an act to avoid demobilizing imprisonment, shipment outside the U.S., or death....

...Deserters are the most advanced sector of the working class. They have already acted, sometimes violently, against the ruling class. We must lend anti-capitalist content to their act so that as the struggle progresses to open conflict they will be in the forefront.

Specifically, this means the creation, wherever possible, and however, temporary, of deserter collectives and communities for internal education, internal discipline and communal counseling. This will give us the means of being together and acting together.

SUPPORT CANADIAN AND QUEBEC STRUGGELES. The organization and growth of a strong and militant opposition to capitalism and American imperialism in Canada and Quebec is crucial to a strategy for the international movement. U.S. exiles know that in terms of crucial resources Canada is the most important colonial or satellite possession of the U.S. Canada is the most thoroughly and successfully exploited part of the empire.

We lend our urgent support to the struggle of Canadian workers and students and native Indian peoples for self-determination and socialism....Above all, we affirm the duty of revolutionaries to fight wherever they find themselves.[33]

Showing their disdain for their own country and complete disregard for their own countrymen fighting and dying in Vietnam, the American Deserters Committee gave aid and encouragement to the enemy in a letter to North Vietnam's National Liberation Front. The letter reads in-part:

> Moscow, Vietnam News Agency (VNA) in Vietnamese and English to VNA Hanoi 1743 GMT 20 Dec 71. We warmly greet the anniversary of the founding of the NFL and salute the courage of the Vietnamese people in resisting U.S. aggression....
>
> The U.S. and its puppet [words indistinct] have been defeated in the battlefield. Its pacification and Vietnamization of the war have failed miserably, the criminality of the U.S. has been exposed before world opinion, and now the American people are loudly demanding: End the War! Bring the troops home!
>
> The American-Thieu dictatorship has lost control of all but a few still-occupied enclaves. The NFL/PRG has truly proven it is the only real representative of the people of South Vietnam. Nixon has failed to respond positively to the honorable and fair solution as proposed by Madame Binh in Paris, but his lies and excuses are bound to offer only larger defeats for U.S. imperialism. The U.S. must set the date now for a total withdrawal of all U.S. and allied foreign troops.
>
> We extend best wishes for your continued success. Full victory will most certainly be yours.[34]

Some of the comments attributed the American Deserters Committee reveal the total lack of knowledge of the United States' relationship with Canada. Canada was never a colonial or satellite possession of the United States. Moreover, Canada was never a part of the U.S. "empire," nor is there any truth to the statement that the United States exploited Canada. With such a total lack of knowledge about history it is no wonder that such individuals could be led to believe in Marxist-Leninist theories and class struggle. The United States has sent its armed forces to fight and die for the freedom of many other nations, but never has it used its power for territorial acquisition or colonization. If the anti-draft and antiwar activists had known anything of the meaning of imperialism and the history of the United States, they could not have used the word imperialism to describe this country.

Another attempt to sabotage the war in Vietnam was the illegal release of thousands of SECRET and TOP SECRET documents from the files of the Defense Department, State Department, Central Intelligence Agency, Joint Chiefs of Staff and the White House. These documents, collectively known as *The Pentagon Papers*, were illegally reproduced from classified government files and given to members of the press by the former Defense Department staffer working at the RAND Corporation, Daniel Ellsberg The documents, which were actually a study of the history of U.S. decision making involving Vietnam from 1945 through 1968, were published in 1971. Besides being extremely damaging to national security, the entire study was heretical because it covered events only through 1968, and it consisted of numerous staff inputs with analysis, proposals and estimates, many of which had no effect on policy making. Taken alone, each document had no absolute meaning. Moreover, most did not reach senior policy makers and did not directly influence presidential decisions about the war. Unfortunately, the press and some of the political opposition were able to pick the information that suited their cause and use it to distort and misinform the public.[35]

The real damage done by the release of these documents will never be known with certainty; however, the possibilities for damaging our national security and endangering our forces in Vietnam were immense. Former Secretary of State Henry Kissinger was appalled by the release of the documents. He was worried that "the hemorrhage of state secrets would cramp his delicate diplomatic endeavors—especially his [secret] covert talks with the North Vietnamese and his tentative early maneuvers toward China."³⁶ President Nixon felt that publication of the papers was a significant threat to our national security. Some of those concerns were:

> The National Security Agency feared that the more recent documents would provide code-breaking clues and contain information about our signal and electronic intelligence capabilities that would be spotted by the trained eyes of enemy experts. The State Department was alarmed because the study would reveal SEATO contingency war plans that were still in effect. The Central Intelligence Agency was worried that it would expose past or current informants and would contain specific references to the names and activities of agents still active in Southeast Asia. One secret contact dried up almost immediately, and other governments became reluctant to share their intelligence information with us.³⁷

Moscow, Hanoi and Peking must have had a field day examining some 7,000 U.S. SECRET AND TOP SECRET documents. The possibility that these documents made it possible for our adversaries to break our codes is very real. For instance, encoded messages intercepted and recorded by Soviet listening stations, when matched with some of the classified documents in the Pentagon Papers, made it possible to break our encryption schemes (coding) and enabled decoding thousands of documents that had been previously intercepted. Of course, the documents made public in the Pentagon Papers did not require any decoding. They revealed much to the enemy about our tactics, strategy, intentions and our planning and policy making process. Many of the documents also revealed to the enemy how much we knew about their plans, strategy, tactics, capabilities and order of battle. All of these revelations were to our detriment and the enemies benefit. Hence, leaking these documents was another way that our war effort was undermined, and our own citizens aided the enemy.

In many ways the antiwar, hate America hyperbole over the Iraq War is just as aberrant and harmful to the nation as it was during the Vietnam War. Not unexpectedly, some of the same critics have come out of the woodwork to lead the efforts to defame and deride the United States as an imperialist nation. Fallacious statements like, "blood for oil" and "imperialism" are being used to describe President Bush's reason for going to war. Yet, it is abundantly clear that the United States has no "imperialist" designs on Iraqi territory, nor has it taken advantage of any of the oil resources in Iraq.

The United States today is becoming as divided as it was during the Vietnam War, and the lessons of Vietnam which led to America's defeat appear to have been forgotten. Ironically, the activist who leaked the Pentagon Papers recently launched a call to "patriotic" Americans to reveal secrets that involve alleged government cover-ups and lies.[38] The problem with this is that the interpretation of what is a lie and what is a cover-up is in the eye of the beholder, and whistle-blowing can be used as an excuse to get even with superiors or to express disagreement with government policies. Furthermore, the disclosure of classified information can seriously damage our relations with other countries. This is especially true where intelligence and military matters are concerned. For these reasons it is irresponsible for anyone to encourage government personnel to leak classified information. The effect is to benefit our adversaries.

Chapter Ten

Peace Initiatives

The basic assumption is that socialism is at war with capitalism on every front and that "negotiations" or "peace" are merely tactical expedients employed by the Socialist society in its confrontation with temporary, or locally, more powerful enemies.

—John P. Roche
On Maoist Doctrine

George Orwell once said, "The quickest way of ending a war is to lose it."[1] As unbelievable as it might seem, there were Americans in the antiwar movement during the Vietnam era who actually supported the defeat of the United States as the most favored outcome of the war. James Webb, a Marine platoon leader and company commander in Vietnam and former Secretary of the Navy, writes in *Sleeping with the Enemy* that the defeat of South Vietnam by the Communist North "was treated by many [war critics] as a cause for actual rejoicing." In that same article, Secretary Webb discusses a conversation he had with former Senator George McGovern in 1995:

> After I had argued that the war was clearly winnable even toward the end if we had changed our strategy, the 1972 presidential candidate who had offered to go to Hanoi on his knees commented, "What you don't understand is that I didn't want us to win that war." Mr. McGovern was not alone. He was part of a small

but extremely influential minority who eventually had their way.[2]

Consider for just a moment how those Americans who served in Vietnam and the loved ones of those who died there in the service of their country feel when they hear that a former U.S. Senator and presidential candidate didn't want his own country to win the war in Vietnam! This is incredible! How is it possible for a Senator and Democratic Party presidential nominee to be eager for his own country to lose a war? Unfortunately, this attitude is an indication of how fervent the antiwar zealots were in their determination to end the war. This attitude was not lost on the Politburo in North Vietnam and our (then) cold war adversaries around the world. Loyalty and patriotism were obviously not in the vocabulary of those at home who wished for our defeat.

There were many ways in which the antiwar activists tried to force an end to the war. One of their efforts to drive the United States out of Vietnam was through demands for negotiations. This was manifested in several ways, all from within. An often used approach was to try to force the United States to make unilateral concessions and accept the Communist's "peace" proposals even when they amounted to little more than our surrender and abandonment of South Vietnam to the Communists. Another major assault on our war effort was fomented by the Senate and House antiwar doves who introduced numerous resolutions and legislation seeking to end support for the war. As we shall see, some of these efforts successfully undermined our efforts to negotiate an honorable end to U.S. involvement in the war; they delayed settlement by several years; and they resulted in an agreement that was tantamount to our surrender and the eventual enslavement of the people of South Vietnam by the Communist North.

Peace Initiatives 1965-1968

The Johnson Administration. The United States went to extraordinary lengths to persuade North Vietnam to engage in peace talks. There were repeated contacts with other governments and individuals, both communist and non-communist, to encourage peace negotiations. Between mid-1964 and early 1967 there were 31 peace initiatives by the U.S. government and third parties. The Johnson administration stepped up its efforts as the level of the conflict accelerated in early 1965. Every initiative was rejected by North Vietnam until the Paris peace talks finally began in May of 1968. An indication of how aggressive the search for peace was may be gathered from the following summary of initiatives that were rebuffed by North Vietnam:

<u>April 1965</u>: In a speech at Johns Hopkins University on April 7, 1965, President Johnson, under pressure from congressional doves, repeated his willingness to do anything and go anywhere in the search for peace. Speaking of the U.S. determination for a peace settlement that would guarantee an independent South Vietnam, free from outside interference, the president pledged one billion dollars in economic development aid for Southeast Asia, including North Vietnam, and stressed his willingness for unconditional negotiations. He spoke with conviction:

> We will never be second in the search for such a peaceful settlement in Vietnam.
>
> There may be many ways to this kind of peace: in discussion or negotiation with the governments concerned; in large groups or in small ones; in the reaffirmation of old agreements or their strengthening with new ones.
>
> We have stated this position over and over again 50 times – and more – to friend and foe alike. And we remain ready – with this purpose – for unconditional discussions.[3]

Hanoi's response to President Johnson's speech was, "U.S. talk of peace only conceals its warlike acts."[4]

<u>May 1965</u>: U.S. unilaterally implemented a bombing halt of North Vietnam in an effort to encourage North Vietnam to begin talks.[5]

<u>July 1965</u>: President Johnson sent a letter to UN Secretary General U Thant asking for continued UN efforts to promote peace. Hanoi's position was that the UN has no role in Vietnam.[6]

July 1965: U.S. Ambassador to the UN Goldberg sent a letter to the President of the UN Security Council stating that "the U.S. will continue to explore all avenues to peace," and "the U.S. is ready to work with the UN Security Council and its members in search for a formula for peace in Southeast Asia." Hanoi's response was that they saw no role for the UN.[7]

December 1965: The United States carried out a 37-day pause in bombing North Vietnam, from December 24, 1965 to January 30, 1966 in another unilateral attempt to encourage Hanoi to come to the conference table. Hanoi used the bombing halt to pour men and supplies into South Vietnam. On the 35th day Ho Chi Minh announced on Hanoi Radio that he would not respond to the bombing pause. The U.S. resumed bombing two days later.[8]

Early 1966: The United States sent special envoys to major capitals around the world in another attempt to inform Hanoi of the U.S.'s offer of unconditional negotiations. This was in conjunction with the bombing halt which lasted until January 30, 1966. There was no response from Hanoi.[9]

January 1966: The U. S. introduced a resolution at the UN Security Council that "urged arrangement of a conference of 'appropriate interested governments' to help insure application of 1954 and 1962 Geneva Agreements." There was no UN action because of Hanoi's opposition.[10]

September 1966: In a speech to the UN, Ambassador Goldberg stated, "The U.S. is ready to stop bombing when assured this step will be 'answered promptly by corresponding and appropriate de-escalation on the other side.'" The result: Hanoi would not admit any involvement in South Vietnam.[11]

December 1966. Ambassador Goldberg sent a letter to U Thant that "asked UN Secretary General to take steps necessary to bring about discussions which could lead to a ceasefire." No response.[12]

February 1967: The United States implemented another bombing halt to encourage North Vietnam to begin peace talks. The bombing halt which lasted six days was branded by Hanoi as another "trick."[13]

February 1967: President Johnson sent a letter to Ho Chi Minh which "offered to end bombing of NVN and augmentation of U.S. forces in the South if infiltration from NVN ended. [He] proposed extension of the Tet truce through negotiations between NVN and

SVN, suggested diplomatic talks in secret [and] asked for any NVN suggestions." Ho's reply "called for an end to bombing 'definitively and unconditionally,' demanded U.S. forces leave SVN and called for recognition of the Liberation Front [NLF]."[14]

February 1967: President Johnson sent a letter to Pope Paul in which he declared, "We are ready to talk unconditionally and we are ready to discuss 'balanced reduction in military activity.'" Ho Chi Minh's response to the Pope "repeated Hanoi's insistence on an end to the bombing of the North and on its Four-Point settlement."[15]

July 1967: President Johnson made another open appeal to North Vietnam at a press conference on July 18: "We are ready and anxious to go to the conference table and meet the other side half way at any time, but we have no indication at this time that they [the Communists] are ready to do that."[16]

July 1967: At a press conference on July 19 Secretary of State Dean Rusk made the point that "if Hanoi was prepared to abandon its efforts to seize South Vietnam by force 'there can be peace within hours.'" In response, the NFL, North Vietnam's Communist front in the South, repeated its demands:

> [The U.S. must] withdraw its troops, and those of its satellites from South Vietnam; dismantle the U.S. bases; end definitely and unconditionally the bombing and the other war acts against North Vietnam; recognize the [National] Liberation Front as the sole genuine representative of the South Vietnamese people; and let the latter settle themselves their internal affairs.[17]

July-October 1967: During this time period, Henry Kissinger served as an intermediary for the Johnson administration, with the task of trying to get negotiations started. He established a communications channel with Ho Chi Minh using two French intellectuals which he knew. Messages were conveyed back and forth for several months, but in the end this avenue was abandoned as being unproductive.[18]

September 1967: During a speech in San Antonio, Texas on September 29, 1967, President Johnson spelled out a formula for stopping the bombing. He stated, "It will cease when it will lead promptly to productive discussion, and North Vietnam will not take military advantage of the halt."[19]

March 1968: On March 31, 1968, President Johnson ordered an end to air strikes above the 20th parallel which exempted 90 percent of North Vietnam from attacks. This was another attempt to encourage Hanoi to agree to peace talks. It coincided with the president's announcement that he would not seek reelection for a second term. The bombing restriction was lowered to the 19th parallel in April in response to antiwar critics who falsely complained that strikes were being conducted above the 20th parallel.[20] This gave the North Vietnamese freedom to establish staging areas closer to South Vietnam.

Third Party Initiatives. Between August 1964 and August 1966 the UN made three concerted efforts to get North Vietnam to come to the peace table. Each one failed. In the first UN overture, Hanoi rejected a proposal to meet with South Vietnam to discuss the Vietnam problem. In another attempt, the UN Secretary General proposed to visit Hanoi and other capitals to discuss peace in Southeast Asia. Hanoi responded that UN intervention was "inappropriate." Peking said, "U Thant should spare himself the trouble." In the third UN effort to promote peace, U Thant offered a three-point plan to get talks started. This included "[an] end to the bombing of NVN; mutual reduction of hostilities; and negotiations." Hanoi welcomed the end of bombing, naturally, but rejected the other points as negative and unsatisfactory.[21] Obviously, Hanoi was not interested in peace talks.

In April 1965, 17 non-aligned nations appealed for peace and called for negotiations without preconditions. The United States welcomed the 17-nation appeal, but Hanoi's response was that the proposal was "inappropriate."[22]

In June 1965, the Commonwealth Prime Ministers proposed to send representatives to capitals of all countries involved in Vietnam to explore opening peace talks. Hanoi responded, "It would not receive the Wilson mission; [and] called the offer a swindle.[23]

In July 1965, Harold Davies, Minister of the British Government, traveled to Hanoi to urge consideration of the Commonwealth Minister's proposal. Hanoi officials refused to receive Mr. Davies.[24]

Between August 1965 and August 1966, India, Yugoslavia, the United Kingdom, Cambodia, Thailand, Malaysia, Canada, and the Philippines all made various proposals to bring about a peace conference on Vietnam. Hanoi's reaction ranged from no response to outright rejection, calling one proposal "a cheap farce." Hanoi called Pope Paul's appeal for a truce a U.S. maneuver to conceal aggression.[25]

In October 1966, Britain proposed a six-point peace plan which included a peace conference, and an end to the bombing and a cessation of introducing new forces and supplies into South Vietnam by all parties. Hanoi sternly rebuffed the proposal, and "called it a 'rehash' of U.S. proposals."[26]

U Thant's 3-point proposals in August 1966 and March 1967 were rejected by North Vietnam. A North Vietnamese government official stated that "his government rejects all intervention by the United Nations in the Vietnam affair."[27]

Bombing Pauses. In addition to all the diplomatic efforts to bring North Vietnam to the conference table, the Johnson administration carried out ten different bombing pauses in an effort to encourage North Vietnam to begin peace talks. Two have already been mentioned, but it is significant to look at the complete history in order to judge the United States' efforts to begin talks, even though none were successful in changing North Vietnam's willingness to meet. The pauses took place on the following dates:

1. May 13-May 18, 1965.
2. Dec. 24, 1965—Jan. 31, 1966
3. Dec. 24-Dec. 26, 1966.
4. Dec. 31, 1966—Jan. 2, 1967.
5. Feb. 8-Feb. 14, 1967.
6. May 23, 1967 (for 24 hours).
7. Dec. 24-Dec. 25, 1967.
8. Dec. 31, 1967-Jan. 2, 1968.
9. Jan. 29-Jan. 31, 1968 (Canceled 9:30 a.m. Jan. 30 due to massive enemy Tet offensive).[28]
10. Mar. 31, 1968-Apr. 1972 (At first there was a partial cessation above the 20th and in November 1968 a complete halt of all bombing in North Vietnam was implemented which lasted until the massive invasion by North Vietnam across the DMZ in the spring of 1972.)[29]

Talks Begin. For many months, Hanoi insisted that North Vietnam's four-point stand was the sole basis for a political solution to the Vietnam problem. Briefly, the four-point plan demanded the following:

> 1. The U.S. Government must withdraw from South Vietnam all U.S. troops, military personnel and weapons of all kinds, dismantle all U.S. military bases there, cancel its "military alliances" with South Vietnam. It must end its policy of intervention and aggression in South Vietnam....the U.S. Government must stop its acts of war against North Vietnam, completely cease all encroachments on the territory and sovereignty of the Democratic Republic of [North] Vietnam.
>
> 2. The military provision of the 1954 Geneva Agreements on Vietnam must be strictly respected; the two zones must refrain from joining any military alliance with foreign countries; [and] there must be no foreign military bases, troops and military personnel in their respective territory.
>
> 3. The internal affairs of South Vietnam must be settled by the South Vietnamese people themselves, in accordance with the programme of the National Front for the Liberation of South Vietnam [North Vietnam's Communist front], without any foreign interference [presumably excluding the thousands of North Vietnamese troops in the South].
>
> 4. The peaceful reunification of Vietnam is to be settled by the Vietnamese people in both zones, without any foreign interference.[30]

North Vietnam's refusal to talk peace was exemplified by Premier Pham Van Dong comments to an American reporter: "The U.S. must stop bombing North Vietnam unconditionally before peace talks can begin." He added, "There will be no reciprocity. There will be no bargaining. There will be no blackmail, and we will not pay ransom to pirates."[31]

The 1968 Tet offensive brought a shift in policies on all sides. President Johnson's announcement that he would not seek a second term, and the initiation of a new bombing halt, coupled with the increase in demands at home to end the war, signaled Hanoi of a shift in America's resolve. Former Secretary of State Dean Rusk recalls that "after Tet things changed. Even though American and South Vietnamese forces dealt the North Vietnamese a shattering military blow, the Tet offensive unleashed a tidal change in American public opinion....[It] was a severe military setback for the enemy. And yet what was a striking military defeat for Hanoi was turned into a brilliant political victory [for Hanoi] in the United States because of Tet's effect on the American people."[32]

This shift in the mood in America did not go unnoticed by Hanoi. Faced with the loss of over 32,000 of its forces during Tet and many months needed to rebuild its forces in the South, the North Vietnamese strategy changed to fight and talk.[33] On April 5, 1968, the Foreign Minister of North Vietnam informed a CBS correspondent in Hanoi that they were prepared to meet with the American delegation. The first meeting between American officials and representatives from Hanoi took place on May 10, 1968. The talks reached an impasse within weeks with the United States insisting on withdrawal of North Vietnamese forces from South Vietnam and North Vietnam demanding that the Viet Cong be included in the South Vietnamese government.[34]

It took over four years and numerous attempts by the Johnson administration to finally get the North Vietnamese to the conference table. It would be five more years before a peace agreement was reached. Why did it take so long to simply get the North Vietnamese to sit down at the conference table? There are several probable reasons. For one thing, the North Vietnamese would have had to admit their involvement in the conflict in the South. More likely, the leaders in Hanoi were well aware that the French lost the war as a result of the lost will at home. There were numerous signs of weakening of American resolve. Many antiwar demonstrations in the United States were undoubtedly encouraging to Hanoi. This did not dispel the antiwar critics, including those in Congress, from protesting the war. Secretary Rusk was unequivocal about the effect the antiwar movement had on getting Hanoi to negotiate. He stated:

> ...North Vietnam had little incentive to negotiate an end to the war....From a strictly military point of

view, our men in uniform achieved their objective [by 1966]...But in late 1966 and early 1967 Hanoi began to hear signals coming out of the United States. For example, if we heard of fifty thousand demonstrators in Hanoi calling for peace, we would have thought the war was over, and we probably would have been right. One of the problems was that they could see two hundred thousand people marching on the Pentagon. And it was difficult trying to set up negotiations with those who are quoting your own senators back to you.[35]

North Vietnamese General Giap's strategy was to prolong negotiations while killing as many American troops as possible with the objective of undermining American support for the war.[36] Hanoi considered negotiations merely an extension of the battlefield, and peace was possible only when Hanoi decided that settlement was in their best interest.[37] It stands to reason that unilateral concessions such as bombing halts and permitting sanctuaries for enemy forces in Laos and Cambodia were not conducive to persuading North Vietnam to negotiate in good faith. Nonetheless, the leading antiwar critics, George McGovern, Eugene McCarthy and Edward Kennedy, gave Hanoi even more encouragement when they pressed for concessions to North Vietnam as a plank in the 1968 Democratic Convention platform. Their proposed platform included the following:

- An unconditional halt to all bombing of North Vietnam;
- Negotiation of a phased, mutual withdrawal of United States and North Vietnamese forces from South Vietnam;
- Encouragement of South Vietnam "to negotiate a political reconciliation with the National Liberation Front looking toward a ...broadly representative" government for South Vietnam; and
- Reduction of US offensive operations in South Vietnam, "thus enabling an early withdrawal of a significant number of our troops."[38]

Fortunately, this platform proposal was defeated at the convention, but undoubtedly it was not missed by Hanoi where it was another signal that America's support for the war was waning. This move along with other pressures by antiwar critics for the administration to negotiate had the clear effect of undermining the United States' leverage at the peace negotiations.

As 1968 drew to a close without any significant progress in negotiations, the search for peace was left to the Nixon administration.

Peace Initiatives 1969-1973

Nixon Administration's Efforts. Serious talks with North Vietnam did not begin until procedural issues dealing with the shape of the conference table and the status of the National Liberation Front were vetted in January 1969 just as the Nixon administration took office.[39] Weekly meetings with the North Vietnamese began in Paris in January. The United States delegation, led by Ambassador Henry Cabot Lodge, laid out the U.S. program for peace. It consisted of "mutual withdrawal of all non-South Vietnamese forces, supervised cease-fire, free elections under international supervision, and the early release of prisoners of war on both sides."[40] On May 8, 1969, Ambassador Lodge presented the administration's plan for peace:

> We are not seeking military victory.
>
> We believe that peace should give the South Vietnamese people the opportunity to determine their own future without external interference.
>
> We are seeking a mutual withdrawal of external forces from South Vietnam which could begin simultaneously with US and North Vietnamese withdrawals. This would be tangible and visible evidence of the professed desire of both sides to negotiate a peace settlement.
>
> We are seeking restoration of the Demilitarized Zone.
>
> We propose the early release of prisoners of war.
>
> We will support the reunification of Vietnam in the future by the free decision of the people of the North and the South.

We support the principle of non-interference between the two Vietnams, pending reunification.

We support full compliance with the Laos Accords of 1962, and respect for the territorial and neutrality of Cambodia.

We envisage a cessation of hostilities as an essential element in an ultimate settlement.

And, finally, we believe that adequate international agreements to verify and supervise the carrying out of military agreements and insure respect for and continued adherence to the military and political elements of a settlement is vital, so that the peace that will be achieved may be enduring.[41]

On May 14, 1969, President Nixon, speaking from the White House, spoke to the nation in a televised report on the war in Vietnam. He mentioned that our diplomats had been talking with the other side in Paris for 12 months without achieving any progress toward a peaceful settlement of the war. The president addressed the peace initiatives taken since his inauguration, the progress of the war, our purpose and objectives, the progress of negotiations and his plan to bring the war to a close. It is significant to compare the conditions for settlement of the war set forth in this address with those in the final peace agreement signed in Paris in January of 1973. It will show that by that time the United States had lost all of its leverage for a negotiated settlement except unilateral withdrawal of U.S. forces and the return of American POWs. The North Vietnamese essentially dictated the terms. It was tantamount to surrender, with our ally, South Vietnam, left to fend for itself against a belligerent force backed by the entire Communist bloc. This almost unimaginable outcome after more that ten years of fighting and the loss of 58,000 American servicemen had one major cause—disunity at home which gave encouragement to the enemy to hold out until opposition to the war forced the United States to give up the fight—something this country had never before done in all its history. Some of the pertinent excerpts from the president's address follow:

> **ESSENTIAL PRNCIPLES:**
> We have ruled out attempting to impose a purely military solution on the battlefield.
>
> We have also ruled out either a one-sided withdrawal from Vietnam, or the acceptance in Paris of terms that would amount to a disguised defeat.
>
> When we assumed the burden of helping defend South Vietnam, millions of South Vietnamese men, women and children placed their trust in us. To abandon them now would risk a massacre that would shock and dismay everyone in the world who values human life.
>
> Abandoning the South Vietnamese people, however, would jeopardize more than lives in South Vietnam. It would threaten our longer term hopes for peace in the world. A great nation cannot renege on its pledges. A great nation must be worthy of trust....
>
> If we simply abandoned our effort in Vietnam, the cause of peace might not survive the damage that would be done to other nations' confidence in our reliability....
>
> On determining what choices would be acceptable, we have to understand our essential objective: We seek the opportunity for the South Vietnamese people to determine their own political future without outside interference.
>
> Let me put it plainly: What the United States wants for South Vietnam is not the important thing. What North Vietnam wants for South Vietnam is not the important thing. What is important is what the people of South Vietnam want for themselves....

In this spirit [asking nothing for ourselves], let me be explicit about several points:

—We seek no bases in Vietnam.
—We insist on no military ties.
—We are willing to agree to neutrality if that is what the South Vietnamese people freely choose.
—We believe there should be an opportunity for full participation in the political life of South Vietnam by all political elements that are prepared to do so without the use of force or intimidation.
—We are prepared to accept any government in South Vietnam that results from the free choice of the South Vietnamese people themselves.
—We have no intention of imposing any form of government upon the people of South Vietnam, nor will we be a party to such coercion.
—We have no objection to reunification, if that turns out to be what the people of South Vietnam and the people of North Vietnam want; we ask only that the decision reflect the free choice of the people concerned....

In pursuing our limited objective, we insist on no rigid diplomatic formula. Peace could be achieved by a formal negotiated settlement. Peace could be achieved by an informal understanding, provided that the understanding is clear, and that there were adequate assurances that it would be observed. Peace on paper is not as important as peace in fact.

THE NEGOTIATIONS:
This brings us, then, to the matter of negotiations. What kind of a settlement will permit the South Vietnamese people to determine freely their own political future? Such a settlement will require the withdrawal of all non-South Vietnamese forces from South Vietnam and procedures for political choice that give each significant group in South Vietnam a real opportunity to participate in the political life of the nation.

To implement these principles, I reaffirm now our willingness to withdraw our forces on a specified timetable. We ask only that North Vietnam withdraw its forces from South Vietnam, Cambodia and Laos into North Vietnam, also in accordance with a timetable.

We include Cambodia and Laos to ensure that these countries would not be used as bases for a renewed war. The Cambodian border is only 35 miles from Saigon; the Laotian border is only 25 miles from Hue.

Our offer provides for a simultaneous start on withdrawal by both sides; agreement on mutually acceptable timetable; and for the withdrawal to be accomplished quickly.

If North Vietnam wants to insist that it has no forces in South Vietnam [as they had done for a number of years], we will no longer debate the point—provided that its forces cease to be there, and that we have reliable assurances that they will not return....

Recent statements by President Thieu have gone far toward opening the way to a political settlement. He has publicly declared his government's willingness to discuss a political solution with the National Liberation Front and has offered free elections....The South Vietnamese Government has offered to talk without preconditions.

This, then, is the outline of the settlement that we seek to negotiate in Paris. Its terms are very simple: Mutual withdrawal of non-South Vietnamese forces from South Vietnam, and free choice for the people of South Vietnam. I believe that the long-term interests of peace require that we insist on no less, and that the realities of the situation require that we seek no more.

PROGRAMS AND ALTERNATIVES:

To make very concrete what I have said, I propose the following measures, which seem to me consistent with the principles of all parties:

—As soon as an agreement can be reached, all non-South Vietnamese forces would begin withdrawals from South Vietnam.

—Over a period of 12 months, by agreed upon stages, the major portions of all U.S., Allied and other non-South Vietnamese forces would be withdrawn. At the end of this 12-month period, the remaining U.S., Allied and other non-South Vietnamese forces would move into designated base areas and would not engage in combat.

—The remaining U.S. and Allied forces would move to complete their withdrawals as the remaining North Vietnam forces were withdrawn and returned to North Vietnam.

—An international supervisory body, acceptable to both sides, would be created for the purpose of verifying withdrawals, and for any other purposes agreed upon between the two sides.

—This international body would begin operating in accordance with an agreed timetable, and would participate in arranging supervised ceasefires.

—As soon as possible after the international body was functioning, elections would be held under agreed procedures and under the supervision of the international body.

—Arrangements would be made for the earliest possible release of prisoners of war on both sides.

—All parties would agree to observe the Geneva Accords of 1954 regarding Vietnam and Cambodia and the Laos Accords of 1962....

We are willing to talk about anybody's program—Hanoi's four points, the NLF's 10 points—provided it can be made consistent with the few basic principles I have set forth here....

I have set forth a peace program tonight which is generous in its terms. I have indicated our willingness to consider other proposals. No greater mistake could be made than to confuse flexibility with weakness or being reasonable with lack of resolution....

Reports from Hanoi indicate that the enemy has given up hope for a military victory in South Vietnam but is counting on a collapse of American will in the United States. They could make no greater error in judgment.

Let me be quite blunt. Our fighting men are not going to be worn down; our negotiators are not going to be talked down; our allies are not going to be let down.

Tonight, all I ask is that you consider these facts and, whatever our differences, that you support a program which can lead to a peace we can live with and a peace we can be proud of. Nothing could have a greater effect in convincing the enemy that he should negotiate in good faith than to see the American people united behind a generous and reasonable peace offer.[42]

The president's eight-point plan presented in his May 14 address offered several new concessions, including participation of the NLF as a party to the negotiations and a commitment to set a precise timetable for withdrawal of U.S. forces. In the formal negotiations after President Nixon's May 14 address, the North Vietnamese adamantly refused to discuss the eight-point proposal. They repeated their usual demands which were essentially an ultimatum on what the United States must do to end the war. These demands were, "Total, unconditional, and unilateral US withdrawal, abolition of the South Vietnamese government, and American reparations for the war damage."[43]

As of November 1969, U.S. efforts to get North Vietnam to negotiate in good faith still met with an unyielding intransigence by the North Vietnamese. They insisted that their four-point proposal was the only basis for discussion, and refused to negotiate with the Republic of (South) Vietnam on any basis.[44] North Vietnam essentially demanded our surrender as a condition for beginning negotiations. They called for:

- <u>Unilateral, unconditional withdrawal of U.S./allied forces.</u> The other side does not admit that North Vietnamese troops are in South Vietnam, despite massive evidence to the contrary. They refuse to entertain any discussions of "mutual" withdrawal. They have denounced President Nixon's withdrawal of 25,000 U.S. troops as a "fraud," and the more recent Presidential order for the withdrawal of an additional 35,000 or more men as "a perfidious trick."

- <u>The replacement of the legitimate, elected government of the Republic of [South] Vietnam</u> by an imposed "provisional coalition" of their [Communist's] own choosing. This "provisional coalition" would rule South Vietnam during the interim between the restoration of peace and the holding of general "elections." [Which the Communists would obviously control if carried out by a "coalition" of this nature].

- <u>General elections</u> for a constituent assembly which would write a new constitution and would be obliged to install a permanent "coalition" government.[45]

A top secret letter captured by U.S. Forces in South Vietnam in January 1967, addressed to the Central Office for South Vietnam from Le Duan, First Secretary of the Lao Dong Communist Party, sheds some light on the strategy of the Communists with respect to negotiations: Excerpts from this document follow:

> As far as general strategy is concerned, we are advocating that the revolution in South Vietnam has to pass through several transitional phases prior to advancing toward national reunification and socialism. With regard to struggle, we stand for joint political and armed struggle, that is to say, the armed struggle must be simultaneously conducted with the political one. Heavy emphasis is to be placed on the political struggle which includes the diplomatic struggle, which is of prime importance. As a consequence, the strategy on war and negotiation must be properly used to efficiently serve the political and military aims of our strategy on pitting the weak against the strong [nations].
>
> The problem of war and negotiation is not quite new in the history of our country. Nguyen Trai had once used such a strategy to defeat the feudalist elements of Ming's dynasty. Our comrades in China had also adopted the "fight-and-negotiation" policy in their struggle against U.S. and Chiang [Kai Shek]. The same strategy had been used in the Korean War.
>
> However, this problem is very complicated considering that, at present, when speaking of negotiations, the views are quite divergent. The U.S. views hold that negotiation is to be conducted from a strong position. Some countries which sincerely support our struggle but, in view of diplomatic reasons and their domestic administration and misunderstanding of the situation in our country want to see us at the conference table in order to forestall aimless sacrifices on our part....
>
> At present, the U.S. imperialists, on the one hand, are attempting to widen the war in a move to save them from the sad predicament and quagmire but, on the other hand, are trying to force us to the negotiation table for

some concessions. As for us, we must constantly take the initiative, our strategy on negotiations must serve in a practical manner our concrete political aims. For this reason, the Party Central Committee has unanimously entrusted the Politburo with the task of carrying out the above strategy in conformity with the policy of our Party and on the basis of the situation between us and the enemy whenever necessary.[46]

In early 1970, the Nixon administration saw the futility of open talks with the North Vietnamese and chose to pursue secret talks with the North Vietnamese. After several months of rebuffs from Hanoi, the North Vietnamese finally agreed to the first secret talks to be held on February 21, 1970. The talks were held in the strictest secrecy in Paris, with Le Duc Tho representing North Vietnam and Henry Kissinger leading the American team. During the first round of talks Le Duc Tho continued the harsh stand the Communists had insisted on in the past. According to Henry Kissinger, "He [Le Duc Tho] insisted that before any negotiations the United States would have to set a deadline for unilateral withdrawal. The negotiations would then concern the modalities of our retreat...North Vietnam's sole reciprocal obligation would be not to shoot our men as they boarded ships and aircraft to depart."[47]

The first series of secret talks ended in April 1970 without progress. Hanoi's position was inflexible and unyielding. They rejected a schedule for mutual withdrawal, de-escalation, or any other proposal made by the United States to work toward a peaceful settlement. One must ask why North Vietnam was so intransigent and unwilling to work toward a mutual agreement to end the war. North Vietnam's top negotiator, Le Duc Tho, gives us the obvious clue in his statements to Henry Kissinger during one of their meetings. At this meeting, Le Duc Tho revealed the importance Hanoi attached to public opinion in the United States. He cited a poll which showed that the number of Americans who wanted immediate withdrawal had risen from 21 to 35 percent. He also referred to statements he had heard by members of the Senate Foreign Relations Committee and the Democratic Party who had demanded the total withdrawal of American forces from Vietnam and the overthrow of the existing government in Saigon.[48]

In Henry Kissinger's view, the domestic and bureaucratic pressures at home to end the war gave Hanoi "even more incentive to persevere in its intransigence." As he saw it, the Nixon administration was "caught between the hammer of antiwar pressure and the anvil of Hanoi."[49] There is much to be gained at this point to look at why Hanoi believed it could refuse to negotiate for over four years, and following that, spend four more years at the conference table rejecting every proposal presented by the United States:

Antiwar Critics and Negotiations

Congress and the Media. In earlier chapters we saw the antiwar critics making demands for the United States to "set a date," "get out now," "stop the bombing," "negotiate," etc. Antiwar demonstrations, even though they represented less than one percent of the nation's population, influenced U.S. senators and representatives from every corner of the country. Many of these congressmen exerted their influence in such a way as to give Hanoi the incentive to hold out for domestic dissent to win the war for them. Some of the key congressional actions and the view from Hanoi will be presented below.

When Congress returned from summer recess in September 1969, the attacks on Nixon's conduct of the war reached a fever pitch. Senator Kennedy attacked Nixon's Vietnam policy along with Muskie. Cyrus Vance called for a standstill cease-fire. Senator Mansfield made the same proposal. Senator Goodell announced plans to introduce a resolution to withdraw all U.S. forces from Vietnam by the end of 1970. He also proposed cutting off funding for U.S. combat forces by that date. Eleven antiwar resolutions were introduced by Congress in September and October, with Senators Hatfield and Church calling for an immediate withdrawal of all U.S. forces and Javits and Pell calling for a resolution for withdrawal of combat forces by the end of 1970 and the revocation of the Tonkin Resolution.[50]

A firestorm erupted in Congress and the media in February 1970 when Nixon approved B-52 strikes on North Vietnamese forces which had launched a major offensive to take over most of Laos. This offensive would have greatly expanded the sanctuaries for the North Vietnamese to use in attacks on the U.S. and allied forces in South Vietnam and would have caused greater casualties of our forces. Yet, we had senators like McCarthy, Church, Mansfield, Gore, Cooper and a host of others launching a major political attack on the Nixon administration for "expanding" the war.[51]

Similar to the Laos conflagration, there was an enormous uproar among the antiwar critics in the U.S. when the president announced the attack on enemy sanctuaries in Cambodia. Here again, the North Vietnamese were close to overrunning all of Cambodia with the help of the Khmer Rouge. A major enemy headquarters for North Vietnamese operations in South Vietnam was located just across the border in Cambodia, and major areas along the border were stockpiled with enemy war materials. Further expansion of sanctuaries and control of Cambodia would have placed our forces and the Vietnamization program in grave danger. Yet, the eruption of the antiwar critics consumed the entire United States including many in Congress. The upheaval led to the shootings at Kent State and riots at many of the campuses in the U.S. Senators Church and Cooper proposed an amendment to the Foreign Military Sales Bill prohibiting U.S. military aid and activities in Cambodia after June 30, 1970. The Senate passed the amendment by a 58-37 vote. The measure was deadlocked in the House for the remainder of 1970. However, by this time the North Vietnamese had gotten the message from the Senate that Cambodia was not going to be defended by the United States. Cambodia was theirs for the taking, and they eventually did just that.[52]

In August 1970, the Senate took up the McGovern-Hatfield amendment which set December 31, 1971 as the deadline for withdrawal of all U.S. forces from Vietnam. The administration feared that once a final date was established by law, our leverage for negotiations, including the return of our POWs, would evaporate. Fortunately, the amendment was defeated in September 1970, but the 39 Senators who supported it did not give up. The amendment was brought back each month thereafter, with increasing support each time. Hanoi could not help but be encouraged by the Senate's action and the obvious erosion of support for the war. The obvious effect was to reduce Hanoi's incentive to negotiate. Even worse, it weakened our capability to bargain for our POWs.[53]

The Son Tay raid to recover some of our POWs held in North Vietnam was accompanied by a diversionary bombing raid. Here again there was an outrage in Congress and the media for resumption of bombing against the North. It is hard not to question the judgment and loyalty of the media and congressmen who raised questions about this operation.[54]

With the withdrawal of U.S. forces under the Vietnamization program well underway, there was consensus in the administration that the enemy had to be prevented from taking over Cambodia and Laos to give Vietnamization a chance to succeed. Further, success was also contingent on disrupting the enemy's dry-season logistics buildup. An operation was undertaken in January 1971 by South Vietnamese forces with U.S. air support, to attack sanctuaries in Cambodia. Soon afterwards, a major cross-border operation by South Vietnamese forces was launched to cut the Ho Chi Minh trail and disrupt supply bases in Laos. These operations had to be done without American advisors or forward air controllers because the Cooper-Church amendment barred such U.S. participation in Cambodia and Laos. This limitation sharply reduced the effectiveness of U.S. air support and had a dire effect on the success of the operation. The operation was barely underway in Cambodia when 64 members of the House of Representatives introduced a bill to ban the use of funds for U.S. air or sea-based combat support for any military operations in Cambodia. A week later, Senators McGovern and Hatfield reintroduced their Disengagement Act requiring withdrawal of U.S. forces from Vietnam by December 31, 1971. The cross-border operation into Laos began February 8.1971. The very next day Representative O'Neil and 37 cosponsors introduced legislation barring direct U.S. intervention in Laos as well as any American support for any military operations in Laos. Hanoi was no doubt overjoyed.[55]

Between the beginning and end of the Laos operation, Congress introduced five resolutions limiting the president in conducting military operations, prohibiting the use of funds for combat operations in Cambodia and Laos and demanding unconditional withdrawal. "On February 22 the Senate Democratic Policy Committee unanimously demanded the withdrawal of all American forces, including air and support troops, from Indochina by December 31, 1972." Between April 1, and July 1, 1971, there were 17 House and Senate votes to restrict President Nixon's authority to conduct the war. In June of 1971, the Senate adopted Senator Mansfield's resolution declaring, "It is the policy of the United States to terminate at the earliest practical date all military operations in Indochina and to provide for the prompt and early withdrawal of all U.S. forces not more than nine months after the bill's enactment subject to the release of American POWs." Henry Kissinger felt that these resolutions would "keep the administration from pursuing a coherent strategy."[56]

One of the most damaging congressional actions that cut into our ability to negotiate with the North Vietnamese took place in June 1971 when the Senate passed the Mansfield amendment which required withdrawal of American forces from Vietnam within nine months, "if Hanoi agreed to release our prisoners." This amendment was like many others—irresponsible and a disastrous blow to the administration's ongoing secret negotiations. It made superfluous five of the seven points in our latest offer. It said nothing of the preservation of the independence or neutrality of Cambodia and Laos, and most importantly, the wording of the amendment was such that Hanoi would be able to hold our POWs until we had withdrawn our forces. We would no longer have had any leverage to gain the freedom of our POWs![57]

In September 1971, Senator McGovern met with the North Vietnamese representative, Xuan Thuy, in Paris. The North Vietnamese played him like the amateur that he was in dealing with the Communists. He left the interview with the belief that he had achieved a breakthrough with a new peace offer consisting of a fixed date for U.S. withdrawal in exchange for the release of our POWs. This was meant for American public consumption to make the administration appear to be the road block to peace. At the formal Paris talks, the North Vietnamese refused to confirm their offer to McGovern, and in fact still insisted as they had for years, that release of our POWs was contingent on a political settlement. Moreover, they still stuck by their demands in their seven and nine point peace proposals, both of which included a demand for the overthrow of the Saigon government. McGovern was left out on a limb. Not to be unexpected, some of the U.S. media still touted the North Vietnamese façade that the administration had scuttled another chance for peace.[58]

The Senate approved another version of the Mansfield amendment in September 1971. The new version made it national policy to remove all U.S. forces from Vietnam in six months, contingent upon the return of our POWs. This amendment told Hanoi that domestic pressures at home would guarantee that we would be out soon, and all they had to do was bide their time and we would be gone. Saigon's ability to survive if we pulled out on a short deadline was not promising. It meant that South Vietnam would not be up to strength, and its survival would be in jeopardy. This did not seem to matter to those who backed the Mansfield amendment. Henry Kissinger feared that we were running out of options to even get our POWs out.[59]

Facing repeated resolutions by the Senate for unilateral withdrawal in return for POWs, President Nixon spoke to the American people on January 1972. He disclosed the 12 secret meetings with the North Vietnamese, and revealed the plan we had offered as far back as May 1971. This proposal included an offer to set a deadline for unilateral withdrawal of U.S. forces; provisions for a political settlement which included Communist involvement in elections in the South; President Thieu's willingness to step down; and the latest secret offer to reduce the withdrawal deadline from seven to six months. Nixon saw the proposal as providing everything except "to join our enemy to overthrow our ally, which the United States will never do." This announcement pacified the critics for about a week. Again, the failure to reach an agreement with the North Vietnamese was said to be the administration's fault. Quite absurdly, the overthrow of the Saigon government became the platform of the antiwar critics and the media. Senator Mansfield called for the U.S. to cut all aid to the Thieu government if it did not reach an accommodation with the Communists—in essence surrender.[60]

On March 30, 1972, the North Vietnamese launched a massive invasion with 120,000 North Vietnamese (NVA) regular army troops in division strength. In a coordinated attack, three divisions rolled across the Demilitarized Zone (DMZ) separating the North and South and penetrated the northern provinces of South Vietnam. Another force struck from Laos into the Central Highlands, and a third force of three divisions of regular NVA troops attacked above the Saigon area from across the sanctuary in Cambodia. If there were ever a question in anyone's mind about the war being an internal insurrection or civil war, this open aggression should have ended all doubts. The invasion was supported by several hundred Soviet made tanks, artillery, rockets and antiaircraft guns and missiles. This three-pronged attack occurred at a time when most of the U.S. ground forces had departed under the Vietnamaization program. The South Vietnamese forces were hard pressed to respond to this massive enemy offensive. It was a test of the Vietnamization program, but was also designed to influence American public support for the war and force a precipitous end of all support for South Vietnam. The stakes were high. If South Vietnam failed to stand up against the onslaught, the United States would have been driven out in a rout, while at the same time our credibility and foreign policy across the globe would have been shattered.[61]

Ending a four year bombing halt over the North, President Nixon responded to the North Vietnamese offensive with B-52 strikes on fuel depots in the Hanoi-Haiphong area along with bombardment by naval gunfire for the weekend of April 15-16. Failing to stop the North Vietnamese offensive with the two-day strike, the president authorized additional strikes including the mining of Haiphong harbor to interrupt the flow of war materials from the Communist bloc. Another round of congressional and media outrage ensued. The president's actions were called "reckless and wrong" by one Senator. Senator Mansfield claimed that the latest decision would cause a protracted war. McGovern called for congressional action to stop Nixon. Senator Church, true to form, condemned the action. The media echoed all these charges and called for Congress to cut off all funds for the war. Less than a week after resumption of bombing and the blockade of Haiphong, the North Vietnamese indicated a willingness to resume negotiations which had been suspended by Hanoi prior to the beginning of the March offensive. Kissinger's secret meetings in Moscow to elicit Soviet support for a settlement also appeared to be influential in encouraging Hanoi to return to the conference table.[62]

As illustrated in countless examples above, while the Nixon administration attempted to arrange an honorable settlement with North Vietnam through secret negotiations with Hanoi and 174 open sessions in Paris, the Congress, media and antiwar protesters undermined these efforts and gave untold encouragement to the North Vietnamese. The extensive undermining at home gave Le Duc Tho confidence that he had the upper hand in negotiations and could demand settlement on his terms. He quoted statements of American critics to support his arguments. Le Duc Tho told Kissinger, "I would like to quote a sentence from Senator Fulbright to show you what Americans themselves are saying....Senator Fulbright said on April 8 that the acts of the liberation forces [VC/NVA] in South Vietnam are in direct response to your sabotage of the Paris Conference." Kissinger cut him off, saying that he wouldn't listen to such statements about domestic affairs in America.[63]

Finally, in October 1972 secret negotiations led to a proposed accord to end the fighting in Vietnam that appeared to be acceptable to both sides. Henry Kissinger made his now infamous announcement to the press: "We believe peace is at hand," he declared. "We believe that an agreement is within sight."[64] However, the proposed accord was not acceptable to the Saigon government, and rightly so, for it allowed North Vietnam to keep in place all of its forces already in South Vietnam. Kissinger did not blame President Thieu for his reluctance to accept the proposed accord, but he felt that "we had simply come to the end of our road—largely as the result of our domestic divisions."[65] Unfortunately, the talks became deadlocked again in December and were suspended on December 13. Kissinger was convinced that Hanoi had calculated that delaying the agreement could improve its position. It was apparent that Hanoi believed that the U.S. was on the ropes. The divisions at home and the forthcoming return of a Congress in January, reinforced with newly elected doves, gave Hanoi the encouragement to hold out until Congress returned, at which time more favorable terms could be anticipated.[66]

President Nixon and his close advisers came to the conclusion that the only way to deal with Hanoi under the circumstances was to apply force. This led to Linebacker Two, an eleven day pounding of North Vietnam by B-52s, intended to once and for all get Hanoi to negotiate in good faith.[67] Once again Congress and the press mounted another campaign of rage and indignation, giving Hanoi a pass, and attacking the administration for its madness and barbaric, shameful and immoral acts. There were more calls to abandon Thieu and for Congress to legislate an end to the war. From our own side, there were accusations of indiscriminate "carpet bombing" with the slaughter and extermination of innocent civilians.[68] None of which was true as verified by Stanley Karnow who observed that civilian casualties were in fact very low. According to Karnow's first hand observation of the bombed areas and other research, the populations of Hanoi and Haiphong had been largely evacuated to the countryside; damage to the buildings in Hanoi and Haiphong was minimal; targeting of air strikes was planned and executed to spare civilians; and the bombing was done with extraordinary precision.[69]

The bombing campaign had the desired effect, and in early January, Hanoi signaled a willingness to resume talks. As anticipated, when Congress returned from recess in January the Democrats immediately began actions that undermined the U.S.'s negotiating position. The House Democratic caucus voted to cut off all funds for military operations in Indochina, contingent on the safe withdrawal of U.S. forces and the release of our POWs. Two days later the Senate passed a similar resolution. Faced with almost certain legislation to force an end to the war, the Nixon administration pressed for a quick settlement. President Thieu objected to some key provisions in the draft agreement, but was left with no alternative but to agree. President Nixon threatened to sign the agreement alone and assured Thieu that Congress would immediately terminate all economic and military aid if he persisted in blocking the agreement. Thieu reluctantly acquiesced, and the final agreement was signed on January 27, 1973, ostensibly bringing peace to Vietnam and the rest of Indochina.[70] The United States withdrew its forces and got back its POWs. Hanoi got most of what it wanted—an end to U.S. involvement in Indochina and the enormous advantage of being allowed to keep its forces in South Vietnam. South Vietnam was the big loser with its defeat and loss of freedom two years later when it was invaded by a large armed force from North Vietnam. The question that historians should ask is how much Congress, the media and antiwar protests influenced this outcome. One way to find the answer to this question is to look at how Hanoi viewed the antiwar activities in the United States, particularly the actions of Congress.

The View from Hanoi

There is an abundance of information indicating that the North Vietnamese closely monitored the events and activities in the United States, especially those involving public officials and Congress. They used this information to generate propaganda at home and around the world and as the basis for their own tactics and strategy for fighting and negotiating.[71] A representative sample of the many ways that Hanoi used the words of members of Congress, the media and antiwar critics is presented below:

> McGovern quoted on Hanoi Radio International Service in English, April 27, 1972:
> Senator George McGovern was right when he said that Nixon's announcement of further troop withdrawals from Vietnam and continued bombing of the North "is a piece of political trickery and calculated deception to save the President's face and General Thieu's job...the bombing of Vietnam is a cruel hoax that dooms our prisoners in Hanoi, kills innocent civilians, invites

further attacks on our remaining soldiers and picks the pockets of every American citizen and taxpayer."[72]

<u>Liberation Press Agency (Clandestine) in English to East Europe and the Far East 1545 GMT 15 Jul 70:</u> [Text] 100 American senators and house members recently sponsored a bipartisan "anti-war conference" in Washington urging rapid recall of all American troops from South Vietnam and a "definite withdrawal schedule," according to reports from the U.S.

At this conference, which was part of a 3-week anti-war campaign launched by anti-war U.S. senators, many came out against Nixon's "Vietnamization of the war" program and his efforts to keep the Saigon puppet junta in power and to drag out the U.S. war of aggression in Viet Nam.

In a radio news program on July 12, Senator George McGovern, Democrat, South Dakota, accused Nixon of trying to maintain the Thieu-Ky puppet administration in power and urged him to withdraw troops from Viet Nam at a "set date."[73]

<u>Hanoi Vietnam News Agency International Service in English 1552 GMT 12 June 1971:</u> Amid antiwar demonstrations by large numbers of Americans around the Capitol, a debate began in the U.S. Congress yesterday on the McGovern-Hatfield amendment providing for a stop to the financing of U.S. military operations in Indochina after December this year, a foreign source said.

28 Senators were reported standing for the amendment and harshly criticizing Nixon's policy of prolonging the war.

Senator Hatfield called upon American legislators to waken the "Conscience of America," pointing out that an exact date for U.S. troop's withdrawal was the only path to constructive negotiations on the Vietnam problem.

Senator Edward Kennedy charged that the Nixon Administration has "grossly misled" the American people [sound familiar re Iraq] on "the tempo of the war" and "disguised the continuing violence and widening character of the conflict" in Indochina. Beyond that, he said, the administration "consistently exploited the helpless plight of American prisoners, so as to beat the war drum in Southeast Asia."[74]

<u>Hanoi Domestic service in Vietnamese 1430 18 Oct 71:</u>
[Station Commentary: "The American People Warn the Nixon Administration."]
[Text] On 13 October, a national moratorium day took place again in the United States to open the 1971 3-week fall offensive....The steps of the capitol and the squares in Washington, New York, the city halls in Ann Arbor, Boston, Chicago, Philadelphia, San Francisco, Portland, Seattle, and so forth, once again became forums for the demonstrators attacking the Nixon administration's Vietnamizations policy, condemning the Vietnam war as immoral, and stressing that the present all-around difficulties in the United States are being caused by Nixon's obduracy in refusing to end the Vietnam war of aggression.

They [American protesters] pointed out that the way to end the war is the PRGRSV's [Communist] seven-point initiative: complete repatriation of American troops, abandonment of Thieu, and so forth....[This generous offer of surrender did not assure the return of U.S. POWs.]

Among the U.S. politicians, many have stated their approval of the 13 October moratorium day. A number of prominent figures such as congressmen Dellums and

Bella Abzug and New York Mayor Lindsay participated in the rallies and spoke. At a rally in New York, Mayor Lindsay urged the Nixon administration to lend an ear to the American people's desires to put an end to the Vietnam War, and bring all U.S. troops home.[75]

<u>Moscow Domestic Service in Russian 1400 GMT 22 November 1965:</u> Senator Jacob Javits has called for a thorough condemnation by the Senate of policy toward Vietnam. Speaking on New York television, he explained that his proposal is based on growing alarm felt by Americans and on widespread opposition to the Vietnam war.[76]

<u>Hanoi Domestic Service in Vietnamese 1430 GMT 17 May 71:</u> [Commentary: "The U.S. War of Aggression in Vietnam and the Deepening Internal Division in U.S. Political Circles."] [Text] In the recent fierce spring offensive in the United States, noteworthy was that not only did broad segments of the American population participate in the Vietnam antiwar movement on an unprecedented scale, reflecting the mood of the American people against the war, but also never in the U.S. Congress and in political circles has Nixon run into such opposition as he has encountered at the present stage of his rough-sailing political career.

Since his great setback in southern Laos, the weariness and the antiwar mood in the U.S. Congress have been spreading and the voices of criticism of Nixon have grown louder. Not only are these the voices of the familiar opponents, but there has also been new criticism from several senators and representatives who had previously remained silent, including some who were considered the most conservative of conservatives and who previously supported Nixon's war of aggression in Vietnam.

On one occasion, a U.S. senator took the Senate floor to demand a troop withdrawal, not in the following week or month but the following day. He was surprised when he received prolonged applause from members of a conservative audience who had been hawks previously.

Not only have the ranks of antiwar U.S. senators and representatives swelled, but also their criticism of Nixon has become more vigorous. Some have called for Nixon's defeat and for preventing his re-election for another term. Some have demanded his impeachment or urgently asked the court to order him to end the war in the shortest period of time....

Many congressmen have introduced bills and resolutions demanding that Nixon's powers be curbed and that he not continue to prolong and widen the war in Indochina; and the most popular of these bills demands that Nixon set a date for the total withdrawal of U.S. troops....

During the period when the great antiwar movement of the masses was shaking the United States, the number of U.S. congressmen of both the Democratic and Republican parties who went out on the streets to participate in the mass demonstrations and marches greatly increased compared with previous offensives.

The antiwar movement, which is broadly developing in the U.S. Congress at present, has real significance. It shows that the U.S. war of aggression in Indochina is not only a disaster for the U.S. youths, students, workers, servicemen, black people, all strata of the laboring people, and so forth, but also that it has become a burden which is heavily weighing upon all of U.S. society. The news on the anti-Nixon debates in the U.S. Congress reflects the nature of the attack by the opposition party against the party in power.

More than ever before, many personalities in U.S. political circles have clearly realized that letting Nixon pursue his war policy will only lead the United States to more telling defeats.[77]

The Other Viewpoints

President Nixon is reported to have said, "The present situation in Vietnam compares to the crisis facing the nation during the Cuban Missile crisis. The great difference is that, while Republicans gave full support to Democratic President John Kennedy in time of crisis, Democrats have failed to give their support to a president. They have put party above country."[78]

President Nixon and his advisors felt that the antiwar movement had a negative impact on negotiations. Joan Hoff, writing in *An American Dilemma* believed that he [Nixon] took the antiwar movement seriously for two reasons: "First, Nixon and Kissinger were convinced that protestors were harming their attempts to negotiate a settlement. They believed that antiwar demonstrations indicated to Hanoi that the United States wanted out of the war....Second, some of his advisers...were convinced that there was 'ironclad proof' that the student demonstrations in the United States...were being 'bankrolled' and coordinated by communist groups in China and Cuba."[79]

In April 1972, former Secretary of Defense Melvin Laird speaking before the Rotary Club of Brooklyn said he was "mystified by some congressmen who talk of restricting President Nixon's authority to protect the withdrawal of American forces from Vietnam." He was apparently referring to the congressional uproar over renewed bombing in response to the massive invasion by North Vietnam which began on March 30, 1972. He went on to say, "As one who has been elected to the Congress for nine terms, I find it impossible to understand how those who sought no limits in the years when we were going up...in the U.S. military strength in Vietnam today seek limits on protection of Americans as our troop levels go down...."[80]

A statement by the Honorable Louis Frey, Jr., U.S. Representatives from Florida, before the Senate Subcommittee investigating internal security, puts the discussion of congressional attempts to legislate the war in perspective. He stated:

I am of the opinion that one of the most important reasons for the intransigence of the North Vietnamese in the Paris negotiations is the blurred picture of the American electorate which has been painted by the fringe minority who have traveled to Hanoi in deliberate violation of the restrictions imposed on foreign policy activities.

A case in point is the recent trip of Ramsey Clark. Clark, while in Hanoi, stated that he expected a big McGovern victory and if McGovern were elected the war would end on the day he came into office. He also inferred that McGovern would accept Hanoi's "seven points," and Nixon would not.[81]

McGovern himself gave credence to Clark's comments. In July 1972 while sensitive negotiations were in progress, Senator McGovern, speaking to a reporter at the Democratic Convention, proclaimed, "He would go to North Vietnam and beg if it would result in the release of U.S. prisoners."[82] In October of that same year, McGovern announced that immediately after taking office he would immediately stop all bombing and acts of force, terminate any shipments of military supplies for the war, and begin withdrawal of all American forces in Southeast Asia. He also said he would "notify Hanoi that the United States had taken steps to end the hostilities and call on them to honor their offer to return all prisoners of war and account for all missing in action."[83] Is there any wonder that Hanoi chose to break off talks soon after that announcement, just weeks before the presidential elections? Hanoi would have gotten everything it wanted without anything in return had McGovern won, and the return of our POWs would have been left to Hanoi's "good will." How many of our POWs would we have gotten back if we no longer had any leverage, and we had to rely on Hanoi's honor to get them back?

The war in Southeast Asia came to an end for the United States on January 27, 1973, but it was far from over for South Vietnam. The next chapter will address how the antiwar movement continued to aid the North Vietnamese in their quest to take over their neighbor to the south along with the other nations of Indochina.

Chapter Eleven

Sellout

A bad peace is even worse than war.

—Tacitus

In the view of some prominent Americans, the Paris Peace Accords of 1973 sounded the death knell of the Republic of South Vietnam. Former Secretary of State, Dean Rusk, saw the Paris accords as an outright surrender. He stated that "any agreement that left North Vietnamese troops in South Vietnam meant the eventual takeover of South Vietnam."[1] The terms of the accords required complete withdrawal of American and allied foreign forces from Indochina, while allowing all of the North Vietnamese forces to remain inside South Vietnam. This gave the Communists an enormous strategic advantage. In arriving at this provision in the negotiations, South Vietnam was forced to concede its most fundamental condition for ending the war—the withdrawal of North Vietnamese forces from South Vietnam. This placed the South Vietnamese at a great disadvantage. For the United States, our forces were out of Vietnam within 60 days of the signing of the accords, and our POWs were released concurrently. The Vietnamese Communists championed the accords as a great victory. Hanoi Radio's broadcast of a recorded speech by Le Duc Tho, North Vietnam's negotiator at the Paris talks, presented at the International Conference on Vietnam in Stockholm, Sweden, shows how the North Vietnamese viewed the accords:

> Dear friends, during 18 years of continuous interference
> in and aggression against Vietnam, the United States has

waged an extremely cruel war against the Vietnamese people. For the independence and freedom of the fatherland, the staunch and indomitable Vietnamese people have fought valorously and foiled one after another all U.S. military plans, and finally compelled the United States to sign the Paris Agreement on Ending the War and Restoring Peace in Vietnam.

The Paris agreement embodies a great victory of historic and epoch-making significance in the Vietnamese people's resistance war against U.S. aggression, for national salvation. It is also a brilliant victory of the militant solidarity of the three Indochinese people, a victory of the forces of peace, national independence, democracy and socialism throughout the world. The Paris agreement meets our most fundamental national interest and conforms to the trend of the world today....[2]

Radio Liberation (clandestine Communist radio) broadcasting in Vietnamese to South Vietnam had this to say about the outcome of the accords:

Defeated, the U.S. imperialists and their satellites had to withdraw from South Vietnam. Some of these satellites have probably learned a lesson from the tragic error they committed in tailing after the U.S. imperialists....Despite the more than one million U.S., satellite and Saigon troops at their disposal and despite the hundreds of billions of dollars they spent, the U.S. imperialists suffered a tragic defeat in the Vietnam war which caused incalculably disastrous consequences for the United States.[3]

Noncompliance

The Paris Agreement consisted of 23 articles, many of which specified what the United States would do, much like the provisions of an unconditional surrender. For example, Article 2 stated, "At the same time [as the cease fire goes into effect on January 27, 1973], the

United States will stop all its military activities against the territory of the Democratic Republic of Vietnam by ground, air and naval forces, wherever they may be based, and end the mining of the territorial waters, ports, harbors, and waterways of the Democratic Republic of Vietnam...." Article 6 required the United States to withdraw all military and other personnel and all armaments, munitions and war materials from South Vietnam. Nowhere did the agreement specify that the aggressor, North Vietnam, would stop any of its military operations in the South or remove any of its troops or equipment from South Vietnam. The most astonishing aspect of the agreement is that throughout its provisions, it referred to the "two parties in South Vietnam." The "second party" was the North Vietnamese front organization, the Provisional Revolutionary Government of South Vietnam (PRG), which was made a signatory to the agreement along with North Vietnam, the United States and the Republic of South Vietnam.[4] In essence, North Vietnam was able to hide behind its front, the PRG. This is why nowhere in the agreement did it say that North Vietnam would remove its forces from the South or that it must cease its military operations in South Vietnam. North Vietnam was still able to continue the façade that it was not involved in the "insurrection" in the South, even though it had between 210,000 and 220,000 North Vietnamese regular army troops inside South Vietnam when the peace agreement was signed.[5]

  The Paris Agreement called for the cease-fire to be observed by all parties throughout South Vietnam, and required them to "undertake to maintain the cease-fire and ensure a lasting and stable peace." The agreement allowed the "two South Vietnamese parties" to replace worn out or damaged armaments and war materials on a piece-for-piece basis. However, it specified that the two parties "shall not accept the introduction of troops, military advisers, and military personnel including technical military personnel, armaments, munitions, and war material into South Vietnam."[6] Within days of the cease-fire, the Communists began systematically violating these and all other provisions of the agreement.

  In less than one month after the cease-fire, major violations were underway by the North Vietnamese. In February 1973, a convoy of 170 trucks crossed the DMZ into the South. By early spring, 7000 convoys had rolled into the South from North Vietnam. By the end of 1973 an additional 75,000 troops were infiltrated into the South;

tank strength was increased to 500; air defense capabilities in the South were built up to include 100 surface-to-air missile batteries and 1800 antiaircraft guns manned by 33,500 troops; and 13 new airfields were built in South Vietnam. The infiltration routes were greatly expanded and extended, including the construction of a fuel pipeline deep into South Vietnam.[7] These massive increases in Communist forces and activities in South Vietnam were not for defensive purposes. They clearly represented North Vietnam's plan to takeover the South.

Articles 9 and 10 of the accords stipulated the right of self-determination for South Vietnam, free from external interference and settlement of all matters through negotiations and the avoidance of armed conflict.[8] The Communists began attacks on South Vietnam only 48 hours after the agreement was signed. Dozens of provinces and military units came under attack by the Communists. By January 1974, Communist forces committed 32,558 military violations and 6,194 acts of terrorism, assassinations and reprisals. They fired over a million shells, killed 3,142 civilians, wounded 7,012 and kidnapped and imprisoned 3,901.[9] The Communists were not interested in settling issues by negotiations as required by the agreement and withdrew from talks in May 1974.[10]

Article 11 included provisions that Communist countries such as North Vietnam have never recognized. Under the domination of the Communist totalitarian system, the people of South Vietnam (and those in the North) have never been blessed with the opportunity to live under the freedom called for in this article. Article 11, among other provisions required that the parties *"ensure the democratic liberties of the people: personal freedom, freedom of speech, freedom of the press, freedom of meeting, freedom of organization, freedom of political activities, freedom of belief, freedom of movement, freedom of residence, freedom of work, right to property ownership, and right to free enterprise."*[11] [Emphasis added] None of these freedoms exist today in the Socialist Republic of Vietnam (North and South Vietnam combined under Communist rule). How many American antiwar activists who supported a Communist victory over the South would, themselves, want to live in such an oppressive society where no freedoms exist?

Hanoi showed little interest in Article 15 which dealt with reunification. They refused South Vietnam's proposals for talks. "More concretely, the North Vietnamese violated with impunity the

Demilitarized Zone and demarcation line, which all pledged to respect, in order to facilitate the build up in northern South Vietnam."[12]

Article 16-18 related to the control mechanisms to be exercised by the Four-Party Joint Military Commission. Tasks included ensuring joint actions by all parties to complete the troop withdrawal and return of captured military and civilian personnel. The Communists used the commission for propaganda and intelligence gathering and suspended all participation in June 1974. The International Commission for Control and Supervision (ICCS) was ineffective largely because its efforts were blocked by the Communists in Vietnam as well as commission members from (then) Communist Hungary and Poland.[13]

Article 20 of the agreement required all parties to respect the independence, territorial integrity and neutrality of Laos and Cambodia. The Communists continued to use these two countries for sanctuaries, bases, stockpiles, staging areas and infiltration routes. Fighting in Cambodia continued unabated. North Vietnam's troops were not withdrawn from Laos as required. Within days after the North Vietnamese army marched into Saigon, they completed the takeover of Laos and Cambodia.[14] The dominos in all of Indochina had fallen.

Hanoi's Plans to Overthrow the South

Hanoi's intentions to complete the takeover of South Vietnam were clearly evident by its massive buildup in the South and by numerous resolutions and directives. At a meeting of high ranking cadres of the Military Region 5 in May 1973, a delegate of the Communist Central Party of North Vietnam made the following revelation about the Peace agreement:

> The signing of the cease-fire agreement in the South is not a major move aimed at settling the war but only a strategy of the Central Party to turn the revolution in the South from a temporary military struggle into a political struggle. The objective of the party is to be loyal to the strategy initiated by Ho Chi Minh.[15]

At a meeting in southern Laos in August 1973, attended by the high level officials of Hanoi and the NLF, the strategy for the conquest of South Vietnam was reaffirmed:

The revolution in the South cannot be realized in any way other than the one pointed out in Ho Chi Minh's testament, i.e., "to fight the Americans and overthrow the Republic of [South] Vietnam's government." The United States has now withdrawn. We must continue the second step of overthrowing [the government] and seizing power in the South.[16]

In a speech before the North Vietnamese Congress on February 20, 1973, Premier Pham Van Dong reread Ho Chi Minh's testament to emphasize the fact that the new mission of the North Vietnamese is "to push forward with determination the struggle for the building of socialism in the North, achieve the national and democratic revolution in the South, advance towards reunification of the country, and completely realize Ho Chi Minh's strategy of consolidating the North and liberating the South."[17]

Just before and soon after the signing of the Paris Agreement, the Communists issued the following directives:

1. Directive dated January 19, 1973:
   - Use the Agreement as a tool for struggle.
   - Use the people's violence to smear the RVN's reputation.
   - Build and develop the armed forces and infrastructures in temporarily controlled areas.
   - Build base areas and stationing areas and launch operations to encroach on RVN territory.
   - Increase the developments of forces in all areas in accordance with the new situation.

2. Directive dated March 30, 1973, directed the Communist armed units to develop maximum strength and pointed out the three tasks of carrying out armed, political and military struggles.

3. Resolution No. 48 of the NLF gave orders to their forces to seize land, capture people, and if possible, to take the land piece-by-piece in areas the RVN neglects

to control. With regards to towns and cities, attention must be paid to the building of infrastructural units in order to promote political struggles and to cause military incidents.

4. The Spring 74 Resolution issued by the Communists put units in combat readiness for a probable general offensive on the occasion of the Lunar New Year...[18]

In the spring of 1974, a conference of high ranking North Vietnamese military staff and Communist Party officials was convened in Hanoi to review the Central Committee's 21st Plenum resolution. The army commanders considered the instructions given at the conference by the Party's First Secretary, Le Duan, and President Ton Duc Thang as orders for the entire army to "surge forward...." The party provided the following guidance for the conduct of the war:

> Faced with this situation [in the South], the party Central Committee's 21st Plenum held in October 1973 set forth the method of combining the political, military and diplomatic struggles and pointed out: The path of the revolution in the south is the path of revolutionary violence. No matter what the situation, we must firmly grasp the opportunity and the strategic offensive line and effect flexible leadership to advance the southern revolution. True revolutionary strength is both urgent and a basic requirement in the new situation....
>
> The southern revolution must firmly grasp the concept of strategic offensive. We must resolutely counterattack and attack the enemy, and we must firmly maintain and develop our active position in all respects. The spirit of the 21st Plenum resolution is that since the enemy fails to implement the agreement and continue to pursue Vietnamization [All U.S. troops were withdrawn from Vietnam by March 1973!]—which is actually a neocolonialist war—in an attempt to seize all the south, we have no alternative but to conduct a revolutionary war to destroy and liberate the South.[19]

Immediately following the 21st Plenum conference in Hanoi, the North Vietnamese General Staff began formulating strategic combat plans and organizing forces for the large-scale offensive that was to be launched everywhere in 1975. Orders were issued to the field armies to step up activities, conduct offensive and uprising operations and seize the initiative in preparation for the coming large scale offensive. Between April and October 1974, attacks were stepped up throughout the South, and according to General Dung, the Communists repeatedly and rapidly won "ever greater victories."[20]

In the fall of 1974, the increased strength of Communist forces in the South, complemented by the weakening of the South Vietnamese forces, brought about by the decrease in support by the United States, led the Communists to believe that the time was approaching for a new offensive in the South. In October 1974, North Vietnamese General Tran Van Tra, the Deputy Commander of all forces in the South, traveled to Hanoi to seek approval to launch a new offensive, with the ultimate objective of capturing all of South Vietnam during the dry season in 1976. He traveled north via what was now a modern highway complete with rest and service areas, fuel tanks and repair shops, all protected by antiaircraft gun batteries. He received approval for part of his plan, and in January 1975 the North Vietnamese launched a major attack on the province of Phuoc Long, approximately 75 miles north of Saigon. The attack was successful and by January 6, 1975, the Communists had seized Phuoc Binh, the provincial capital of Phuoc Long province.[21] According to the late William Colby, former Director of the CIA, this offensive was a test to determine how the South Vietnamese and Americans would react to the attack. The South Vietnam government was unwilling to risk its limited resources to defend the province, and more significantly, the United States did not take any action to enforce the Paris Agreement.[22] Colonel Bui Tin recalls that "we tested [President] Ford's resolve by attacking Phuoc Long. When Ford kept American B-52s in their hangers, our leadership decided on a big offensive against South Vietnam."[23]

The Phuoc Long offensive gave North Vietnam confidence that they could overcome the weakened South Vietnamese forces, and most importantly, they would not have to worry about the United States coming to the rescue of its ally.[24] Le Duan concluded, and rightly so, that political conditions at home would not permit the United States to send forces back into Vietnam. Hanoi also took notice that the reduction of U.S. aid made it impossible for South Vietnam to carry out combat operations and build up its forces. General Dung observed, "In fiscal year 1972-73 the United States had given the puppet troops [South Vietnam] $2,168 million in military aid. This aid was reduced to $964 million in fiscal 1973-74 and to $700 million in 1974-75." As a consequence he saw the capabilities of South Vietnam's armed forces in serious decline:

> Nguyen Van Thieu was forced to fight a poor man's war. Enemy firepower had decreased by nearly 60 percent because of the bomb and ammunition shortages. Its mobility was also reduced by half due to lack of aircraft, vehicles and fuel. Thus, the enemy had to shift from large-scale operations and heliborne deep-thrust and tank mounted attacks to small-scale blocking, nibbling and searching operations....thus bringing the balance of forces to a step further in favor of the revolution.[25]

A conference of the North Vietnamese Political Bureau held from December 18, 1974 to January 8, 1975 was hailed as "of historic significance." Considering the actual situation in the South, the Political Bureau stressed the need to more vigorously launch offensives earlier than planned. Le Duan concluded that:

> Never before have military and political conditions been more propitious and never have strategic opportunities been so favorable for achieving a people's national democratic revolution in the south and advancing toward a peaceful reunification of the fatherland now that the movement of the three Indochina countries is launching a strong offensive and winning ever greater victories.[26]

The original determination by the Political Bureau called for a 2-year, 1975-1976 strategic plan for the final conquest of South Vietnam. Widespread, large scale surprise attacks were to be launched in 1975 setting the stage for the general offensive in 1976. However, the determination of the Political Bureau included an important strategic contingency: "If the opportunities presented themselves early or late in 1975, South Vietnam had to be liberated that year."[27]

The drastic cutbacks in support of South Vietnam by the U.S. Congress had a major impact on the combat capabilities and morale of the South Vietnamese armed forces. Shortages of military supplies including fuel, ammunition, artillery shells, grenades, and even food severely limited the effectiveness of the South Vietnamese armed forces. Fuel shortages reduced the number of tanks, armored personnel carriers and vehicles available for combat by one half. Only a limited number of helicopter gunships and troop carriers were available to support combat operations. Shortages in fuel and spare parts drastically reduced South Vietnam's air power, and 224 aircraft had to be put in storage. The loss of 300 aircraft in combat had not been replaced by the U.S. as promised. Fire support for troops in the field was severely limited. All of these factors greatly reduced South Vietnam's ability to fight a well equipped enemy that was superior in numbers. These circumstances had a demoralizing effect on South Vietnamese troops.[28]

While South Vietnam struggled to keep up the fight for its survival with dwindling support from the United States, China and the Soviet Union continued to pour tons of modern weapons and war materials into North Vietnam for use in the offensive in the South. According to the official history of the North Vietnamese Army, 823,146 tons of war materials were infiltrated into the South between the beginning of 1974 and the beginning of the final assault in April 1975. This was more than one and a half times the amount infiltrated into the South in the previous thirteen years combined.[29]

This gross disparity in the support of South Vietnam put our "ally" in an impossible, no-win situation. The decline in the combat capabilities in the South did not go unnoticed in Hanoi. In early March 1975, the final offensive of the war was launched with 20 divisions of North Vietnamese troops and armor storming South Vietnam from several directions. Valiant but weak resistance against overwhelming odds led to the rapid fall of key objectives such as Ban Me Thuot in the Central Highlands in just a few days.[30]

On 29 March 1975, Party Secretary Le Duan sent a message to the commander in the South. He began by saying, "The situation is developing quickly. The revolution in the South is entering a stage of development by leaps and bounds. Our large and repeated victories have inflicted very heavy defeats upon the enemy and taken them completely by surprise. The puppet regime is in imminent danger of rapid military and political collapse." He exhorted the battlefield commanders to divide the enemy and encircle Saigon.[31]

As the attacking North Vietnamese forces achieved more and larger victories, the schedule for completing the conquest of South Vietnam was stepped up. At a meeting on March 31, 1975, the Political Bureau heard a report by the Military Commission of the Party Central Committee on the status of the offensive during recent weeks which caused them to issue new directions for completing the takeover of the South. The orders for the final battle went out to all military commands in the following message to Generals Bay Cuong, Sau and Tuan at 1400 hours, 1 April 1975:

> It is the assessment of the Political Bureau that, from the standpoint of strategy, from the standpoint of military and political forces, ours is a position of overwhelming strength in this situation and that the enemy is in imminent danger of collapse and annihilation. The United States has shown itself to be completely powerless and cannot extricate the puppets from their situation, even if it provides them with additional aid. Not only has the revolutionary war in the South entered a stage of development by leaps and bounds, but the opportunity for launching a general offensive and uprising in Saigon-Gia Dinh has also ripened. The final, strategic battle of our armed forces and people begins now.
>
> Our country's revolution is developing as much in one day as it would normally take 20 years to achieve. Therefore, the Political Bureau has decided that we must seize this strategic opportunity, be determined to carry out a general offensive and uprising and bring the war of liberation to a victorious conclusion as quickly as possible. Ideally, we should begin and conclude this general offensive and uprising in April of this year, no later. Our actions must be bold, unexpected and taken with the speed of lightning. We must attack immediately, while the enemy is in disarray and weakened. Even

larger forces must be concentrated on the main targets on each front and at each point in time....

As has been decided, we must now act more rapidly, must quickly strengthen the forces to the west of Saigon, strategically isolate and encircle Saigon from that direction, completely cut Route 4 and build pressure on Saigon.

At the same time, we must rapidly concentrate forces to the east and southeast, attack and occupy important targets and encircle and completely isolate Saigon from the direction of Long Khanh and Ba Ria-Vung Tau.

In the Mekong Delta, we must urge our military and political forces to take bold and urgent action, expand the scope of attacks and uprisings, destroy the apparata of the subsectors and district seats, destroy large portions of the enemy's control network and rapidly expand the liberated zone within key areas....

While the Central Department and the Regional Military Commission [of the Party Central Committee in Hanoi] will continue to perform the same duties, the Political Bureau has decided to establish the Saigon Front Command and Party Committee to unify and highly concentrate the leadership and guidance of this key battlefield. When [Generals] Sau and Tuan arrive, you are to discuss and immediately implement this decision.

Here in the North, the Political Bureau will bring together the various forces that provide guidance and has issued to the entire army, to all battlefields, sectors and levels the instructions necessary to insure total victory in this historic, decisive battle.

Determined To Win
Ba [Le Duan] [32]

In another message to military commanders in the South, Generals Tuan, Sau, Bay and Tan, sent at 1530 hours, April 22, 1975, new orders were issued by the Political Bureau in Hanoi. The message cited repeated defeats of South Vietnam's army and a new development, the resignation of South Vietnam's president Thieu. The message went on to urge battlefield commanders to take advantage of the new situation:

> The opportunity for launching the general military and political offensive on Saigon is at hand. We must launch new attacks every day. Taking action at this point in time is the surest guarantee of total victory. There is nothing to be gained either militarily or politically from waiting any longer.
>
> Immediately order your fronts to take prompt action; at the same time, instruct the Saigon-Gia Dinh Zone Party Committee to make preparations to mobilize the masses to stage uprisings in coordination with the attacks by our army. Coordinate the various fronts as well as the timing of attacks and uprisings in the course of your operations.
>
> If we seize this major opportunity, total victory will surely be ours
>
> I wish you good health.
Ba [Le Duan] [33]

On April 30, 1975, North Vietnamese tanks and troops rolled into Saigon and Colonel Bui Tin accepted the unconditional surrender of the Republic of South Vietnam.[34] On that day, the leaders in Hanoi sent a message of praise to the cadres and soldiers who participated in the "Ho Chi Minh" campaign:

> The Political Bureau of the Party Central Committee wholeheartedly praises the armed forces and people of Saigon-Gia Dinh, praises all cadres and soldiers, all party members and Youth Union members of the units

of the main force troops, local troops, special forces and militia and self-defense forces for having fought with extreme bravery, recorded brilliant feats of arms, annihilated and routed large enemy forces, forced the unconditional surrender of the Saigon puppet government, liberated the city of Saigon-Gia Dinh and brought the historic campaign that bore the name of the great Uncle Ho to total victory.

On behalf of the Political Bureau of the Party Central Committee

Le Duan[35]

The United States Congress and the Fall of Indochina

When the Paris Agreement was signed in January 1973, there were two critical factors that had to be in play for South Vietnam to survive against the aggression from the North: There had to be a real, credible threat to enforce the Paris Agreement in case it was violated by the Communists, and adequate military and economic support had to be provided to South Vietnam.[36] In persuading South Vietnam's President Thieu to accept the peace agreement negotiated by Kissinger, President Nixon made a solemn pledge to Thieu that if he signed the treaty "we will guarantee you that if the North Vietnamese do not comply with it, the United States will react with full force."[37] Thieu risked the fate of his nation when he accepted Nixon's pledge and signed the agreement. That would prove to be a grave mistake, for without congressional backing, Nixon could not uphold his promise. As described earlier, the antiwar critics in Congress had already made numerous attempts to legislate an end to the war.

Moreover, the antiwar militants were not ready to stop their efforts until all U.S. support for South Vietnam had ended Noted activist leaders like Sidney Peck, Jane Fonda and Tom Hayden vowed to promote action on several fronts, including the establishment of committees to keep watch on "American" compliance with the terms of the Paris agreement and complete termination of all American aid for South Vietnam.[38] According to the former Secretary of the Navy, James Webb, there was an organized effort by prominent democrats to cut off all congressional funding intended to help the South Vietnamese defend themselves. He cited a coalition of antiwar activists who were also working for the same outcome: "The Indochina Peace Coalition, run by David Dellinger and headlined by Jane Fonda and Tom Hayden, coordinated closely with Hanoi throughout 1973 and 1974 and barnstormed across America's campuses, rallying students to the supposed evils of the South Vietnamese government."[39] Not unexpectedly, no record can be found where any of these activists protested against North Vietnam when they began gross violations of the agreement nor when 20 North Vietnamese army divisions invaded in their final drive to take over the South. Congressional war critics were equally silent about North Vietnam's flagrant violations, but spurred on by the antiwar militants, they wasted no time in seeking to cut all aid to the government of South Vietnam, sealing its defeat.

When Congress came back into session in January 1973, armed with a democratic majority in both the House and Senate, there was an immediate rush to end all American participation and support of the war in Vietnam. On January 2, the House Democratic Caucus voted to cut off all funds for military operations in Indochina as soon as arrangements were made for safe withdrawal of American troops and return of our POWs. On January 4, the Senate Democratic Caucus passed a similar resolution. Had the Paris agreement not been close at hand, Congress was ready to legislate an end to U.S. involvement in the war.[40] As soon as our forces were withdrawn and POWs returned, Congress began an assault on the remaining operations in Indochina. In June 1973 Congress passed a bill cutting all funding for combat operations over or in Cambodia and Laos. The president vetoed this bill since it meant that our hands would be tied in helping South Vietnam to deal with the North Vietnam sanctuaries and staging bases in these two countries. It also undermined the administration's efforts to negotiate with Hanoi to withdraw the thousands of troops it had in Laos and Cambodia. This did not dissuade the liberal congressmen, and on July 1, 1973, Congress passed a bill which was much more restrictive. It prohibited direct or indirect combat activities over, on or near Laos, Cambodia, and all of Vietnam after August 15, 1973. General Davidson saw this as giving the Politburo a free hand to strike South Vietnam whenever it so desired.[41]

In October 1973 Congress passed the War Powers Act severely limiting the president's employment of armed forces without congressional approval. President Nixon vetoed this bill, but his veto was overridden and the bill became law in November 1973. President

Nixon saw this bill as an encroachment on the powers of the president. He also felt that "it would gravely undermine our ability to act decisively in an international crisis....[and] it also laid to rest any fears Hanoi might have had that another invasion of South Vietnam would provoke an American response."[42] One of the two elements mentioned earlier that were essential to South Vietnam's survival had been destroyed.

Next, Congress set out to deny the second element essential to South Vietnam's survival. Congress refused to replace unusable equipment and supplies as authorized by the Paris agreement and cut every aid package proposed by the administration. Congress cut funding for Fiscal Year 1974 to one half of the previous year, from $2,270 million in FY 73 to $1,010 million in FY 74. The proposed military assistance package for Fiscal Year 1975 also came under heavy attack by the antiwar Congress. The House and Senate first cut the $1.45 billion request to $1.00 billion and then only appropriated $700 million. From that amount they deducted shipping expenses, items not delivered from the previous year's program and $46 million for administration of the program. This left only $500 million for FY 75.[43]

General Murray, chief of the Defense Attaché Office in Saigon, called the congressional reductions catastrophic and warned that the aid cuts had left South Vietnam's army on a "starvation diet." Everything from ammunition to fuel for aircraft and vehicles had to be rationed. Medical supplies were in short supply, and helicopters were no longer available to airlift wounded soldiers from the battlefield. More died as a result. General Murray was angry and frustrated. He said, "The South Vietnamese are 'sacrificing blood for the lack of ammunition…'" In his view, "Congress was making a simple, immoral trade: saving American dollars by spending Vietnamese lives."[44] James Webb interviewed some of South Vietnamese troops who survived the final battles. They all had similar stories: "I had no ammunition." "I was down to three artillery rounds per tube per day." "I had nothing to give my soldiers." "I had to turn off my radio because I could no longer bear to hear their calls for help."[45] In effect, Congress had pulled out the last of the two legs that were essential to give South Vietnam a chance to fight off the Communists—military and economic assistance from the United States.

With close to 300,000 North Vietnamese troops in South Vietnam and a major assault on the province of Phuoc Long just 75 miles north of Saigon, President Ford made a last ditch appeal to Congress for an additional $300 million in military assistance for South Vietnam. President Ford made a passionate appeal at a Joint Session of Congress on April 10, 1975, some of which is quoted below:

> A vast human tragedy has befallen our friends in Vietnam and Cambodia. Tonight I shall not talk only of obligations arising from legal documents. Who can forget the enormous sacrifices of blood, dedication, and treasure that we made in Vietnam?
>
> Under five presidents and 12 Congresses, the United States was engaged in Indochina. Millions of Americans served, thousands died, and many more were wounded, imprisoned, or lost. Over $170 billion have been appropriated for the war by the Congress of the United States. And after years of effort, we negotiated, under the most difficult circumstances, a settlement which made it possible for us to remove our military forces and bring home with pride our American prisoners. This settlement, if its terms had been adhered to, would have permitted our South Vietnamese ally, with our material and moral support, to maintain its security and rebuild after two decades of war.
>
> The chances for an enduring peace after the last American fighting man left Vietnam in 1973 rested on two publicly stated premises: <u>first, that if necessary, the United States would help sustain the terms of the Paris Accords it signed 2 years ago, and second, that the United States would provide adequate economic and military assistance to South Vietnam.</u>[46]

President Ford described the unanimous agreement in the United States in late 1972 that we would provide adequate material support to South Vietnam if we could end our involvement. He cited the flagrant violations by North Vietnam including the illegal introduction of over 350,000 troops into South Vietnam. He continued:

> In the face of this situation, the United States—torn as it was by the emotions of a decade of war—was unable to respond. We deprived ourselves by law of the ability to enforce the agreement, thus giving North Vietnam assurance that it could violate that agreement with impunity. Next, we reduced our economic and arms aid to South Vietnam. Finally, we signaled our increasing reluctance to give any support to that nation struggling for its survival....
>
> The situation in South Vietnam and Cambodia has reached a critical phase requiring immediate and positive decisions by this Government. The options before us are few and the time is very short.
>
> On the one hand, the United States could do nothing more; let the Government of South Vietnam save itself and what is left of its territory, if it can; let those South Vietnamese civilians who have worked with us for a decade or more save their lives and their families, if they can; in short, shut our eyes and wash our hands of the whole affair if we can.[47]

The president then outlined the options open at the late date: obtain congressional authority to enforce the Paris accords with U.S. military action; approve his January request for $300 million in aid for economic and humanitarian aid; and increase his requests for emergency military and humanitarian aid which might enable South Vietnam to resist the onrushing invasion from the North. He referred to a report by General Weyand, U.S. Army Chief of Staff, whom he has recently sent to Vietnam to assess the situation, and from that cited the urgent need for $722 million in military aid to give South Vietnam a chance to defend itself. He concluded:

> I am mindful of our posture toward the rest of the world and, particularly, of our future relations with the free nations of Asia. These nations must not think for a minute that the United States is pulling out on them or intends to abandon them to aggression.

I have therefore concluded that the national interests of the United States and the cause of world stability require that we continue to give both military and humanitarian assistance to the South Vietnamese.

Assistance to South Vietnam at this stage must be swift and adequate. Drift and indecision invite far deeper disaster. The sums I had requested before the major North Vietnamese offensive and the sudden South Vietnamese retreat are obviously inadequate. Half-hearted action would be worse than none. We must act together and act decisively.

I am therefore asking the Congress to appropriate without delay $722 million for emergency military assistance and an initial sum of $250 for economic and humanitarian aid for South Vietnam. The situation in South Vietnam is changing very rapidly, and the need for emergency food, medicine, and refugee relief is growing by the hour.

Fundamental decency requires that we do everything in our power to ease the misery and the pain of the monumental human crisis which has befallen the people of [South] Vietnam. Millions have fled in the face of the Communist onslaught and are now homeless and are now destitute. I hereby pledge in the name of the American people that the United States will make a maximum humanitarian effort to help care for and feed these hopeless victims....

Members of the Congress, my fellow Americans, this moment of tragedy for Indochina is a time of trial for us. It is a time for national resolve.

We cannot, in the meantime, abandon our friends while our adversaries support and encourage theirs.

We cannot dismantle our defenses, our diplomacy, or our intelligence capability while others increase and strengthen theirs.

Let us put an end to self-inflicted wounds. Let us remember that our national unity is a most priceless asset. Let us deny our adversaries the satisfaction of using Vietnam to pit Americans against Americans. At this moment, the United States must present to the world a united front.

Above all, let's keep events in Southeast Asia in their proper perspective. The security and the progress of hundreds of millions of people everywhere depend importantly on us.[48]

Unfortunately, President Ford's compassionate appeal fell on mostly deaf ears. No more funds for South Vietnam or Cambodia were forthcoming. The attitude of some in Congress was unbelievable. The press quoted Senator Mansfield as saying, "Additional aid means more killing, more fighting. This has got to stop."[49] Senator McGovern, continuing to promote his antiwar agenda, stated on the floor of the Senate, "It is vital that Congress exercise its constitutional powers to end the further drain on American tax dollars now fueling the continued killing in Indochina. The time has come for healing, reconstruction and accommodation in Indochina. If these healing efforts are to get under way we must stop pouring in billions of dollars in American arms, oil and money to keep the war going."[50] In his book, *No More Vietnams*, President Nixon tells of antiwar senators and congressmen who argued that "our military assistance was 'fueling' the war and that reducing aid to Saigon would bring it to an end." He also cited one senator who said during the budget debate, "By limiting our military assistance, we do signal ally and adversary alike that it is time to negotiate."[51] Of course none of these pronouncements caused Hanoi to revise its plans. If anything, it was a clear signal that South Vietnam was theirs for the taking. It is astounding that some of our highest elected officials could be so naive. In removing the threat of U.S. intervention for violations by Hanoi and slashing military and economic aid for South Vietnam, there was nothing left for South Vietnam to negotiate. North Vietnamese

General Dung pressed on with the invasion of the South, and just 20 days after President Ford's appeal for emergency aid, North Vietnam raised its flag over Saigon.

Expressing his thoughts after the fall of South Vietnam, General William Westmoreland, who commanded the American forces in Vietnam for a large part of the war, made the point that "the United States had signed a solemn international agreement involving the fate of another country and in so doing had incurred a clear moral obligation to insure that the agreement was enforced." He put the blame for the failure of the United States to meet its obligation to assist South Vietnam on the Watergate scandal and the action by Congress forbidding any combat operations by U.S. forces after August 15, 1973. In his book, *A Soldier Reports,* General Westmoreland summed up his feelings about the way the United States ended its support of South Vietnam:

> Despite the long years of support and vast expenditures of lives and funds, the United States in the end abandoned South Vietnam. There is no other way to put it. We not only failed to react to the gross violations by the North Vietnamese of a solemn international agreement; we also failed to match the material support that the big Communist powers provided the North Vietnamese....[52]

General Davidson had the most profound comments about the failure of the United States to honor its obligations to our South Vietnamese ally. He focused on the lack of unity at home:

> The lack of unity was sharpened by ideological extremism, partisan politics, and personal ambition. The gap wore on, particularly after Nixon's election, which freed the liberal element of the Democratic Party from its loyalty to Lyndon Johnson and *his* war. Eventually, this chasm of national unity became so wide and so deep that in the end, the anti-war elements in Congress became the most powerful ally of the North Vietnamese Politburo.[53]

General Davison also saw that the news media played an important part in undermining support for the war. In his view, they misrepresented the war and had a bias against South Vietnam. Since the United States backed South Vietnam, the media were opposing their own country. General Davidson was convinced that the media, Congress and the American people were the target of a well orchestrated propaganda campaign by the North Vietnamese. In his opinion "the United States Government never clearly realized that the hearts and minds of the American people had become the critical battlefield and that it had to protect the nation here as surely as it did its armed forces in combat." The media, he felt, acted as an instrument of this battle: "The media, largely unknowingly, were effective practitioners of Giap's *dich van* [propaganda] program within the United States."[54]

President Nixon was probably in the best position to speak about the outcome of the war. In *No More Vietnams* he states:

> We won the war in Vietnam, but lost the peace. All that we had achieved in twelve years of fighting was thrown away in a spasm of congressional irresponsibility... .Congress proceeded to snatch defeat from the jaws of victory. Once our troops were out of Vietnam, Congress initiated a total retreat from our commitments to the South Vietnamese people. First, it destroyed our ability to enforce the peace agreement, through legislation.... Then it undercut South Vietnam's ability to defend itself, by drastically reducing our military aid.[55]

Thus far it has been shown that the Nixon administration, under pressure from Congress and the antiwar factions, signed a peace agreement that left South Vietnam in a very weak and untenable position politically and militarily. The antiwar Congress then dealt the final blows by drastically cutting aid to South Vietnam and forbidding U.S. forces from going to South Vietnam's aid when North Vietnam invaded. It is, therefore, obvious that in the end the antiwar movement had some influence in bringing the war to a close, as claimed by the antiwar critics. However, there is very strong evidence that the war could have ended several years earlier and with a different outcome had there been unity within the United States. The premise that the antiwar movement prolonged the war is the subject of the next chapter.

Chapter Twelve

Prolonging the War

It is fatal to enter any war without the will to win it.

—General Douglas MacArthur

    The antiwar movement has claimed credit for ending the war in Indochina. The antiwar factions deserve credit for driving Congress into a disastrous end to the war—condemning 20 million South Vietnamese to life under a brutal Communist totalitarian regime, absent of basic freedoms and liberties. However, as we shall see in this chapter, the undeniable truth is that the war was prolonged by the actions of the antiwar movement.

    At a conference at George Washington University in 1988, the role of Congress and the Indochina war was examined by a panel of distinguished scholars. It was the judgment of the panel that Congress bore some of the responsibility for the disastrous conclusion of the war in Vietnam. They saw a "direct road from the War Powers Act to the 'killing fields.'" The panel also concluded that "congressional action during the Vietnam War undermined our postwar deterrence strategy....[and] undercut our defense credibility both with our friends and our potential enemies."[1]

    Tragically for South Vietnam and the United States, the war could have been ended three to five years sooner, and with a much different outcome, had it not been for the encouragement given to the North Vietnam by the antiwar critics. This proposition is supported by many noted authorities, most of whom were in the forefront of the conflict and in a position to know. Moreover, the North Vietnamese who were in leadership positions during the war have given clear indications that they depended heavily upon the antiwar movement in the United States to deliver victory to their doorstep.[2]

The opportunities to bring about an end to the war began as early as 1968. The Tet offensive launched in January 1968 was a disastrous military defeat for North Vietnam, but turned out to be a great psychological victory for Hanoi. According to Colonel Bui Tin, North Vietnam's losses during Tet "were staggering and a complete surprise." He added, "Our forces in the South were nearly wiped out by all the fighting in 1968. It took us until 1971 to re-establish our presence... If the American forces had not begun to withdraw under Nixon in 1969, they could have punished us severely." General Giap, the military commander for the North Vietnamese army, told Bui Tin that "Tet had been a military defeat though it had gained the planned political advantages..."[3]

General Maxwell Taylor, former Chairman of the Joint Chiefs and Ambassador to South Vietnam, has written, "Ho Chi Minh lost the flower of his forces in the Tet offensive and subsequent operations of 1968. Out of 84,000 men who, we estimated, were committed to the immediate Tet offensive, over 30,000 were killed in the first two weeks of fighting. In the first six months of that year, the number of enemy killed in action approached 120,000."[4] The Institute for Strategic Studies in London analyzed the Tet offensive and concluded the following:

> The enormous losses incurred by North Vietnamese units during their major offensives of February and May 1968 destroyed the elite of North Vietnam's army. That army showed little sign of complete recovery during 1969....
>
> The effect on the size of Communist forces in South Vietnam was great enough....The effect on the morale of Communist forces was, if anything, even greater.
>
> Apart from the erosion of their political influence, the Viet Cong, by losing control of many of their "popular bases" in the countryside, had sacrificed much of the logistic organization which had permitted them to live off the land.[5]

North Vietnam was clearly on the ropes in 1968. As incredible as it might seem, North Vietnam's overwhelming defeat and tremendous losses during the Tet offensive were turned into a major defeat for the United States by the media and the antiwar critics. In *Following Ho Chi Minh,* Colonel Bui Tin wrote, "Thanks to the media, which exaggerated the damage caused by this [Tet] offensive, the American public was bedazzled..." [6] Walt Rostow, in *Diffusion of Power,* chronicled some of the media reactions to the Tet offensive, some of which are quoted below:

> On February 23, 1968, *The Wall Street Journal* concluded, "We think the American people should be getting ready to accept, if they haven't already, the prospect that the whole Vietnam effort may be doomed...."

> On February 27, 1968, some nine million Americans heard Walter Cronkite, after a visit to Vietnam, render his glum verdict: "To say we are mired in stalemate seems the only realistic yet unsatisfactory, conclusion."[7]

Information was available to correspondents in Vietnam clearly indicating that the Tet offensive had been a disaster for the enemy, and the VC/NVA in the South had been destroyed as a fighting force. Yet, the media grossly misrepresented the events in Vietnam and presented a picture of destruction and defeat of allied forces. This raises serious questions about the motivation of correspondents and the media. Even Walter Cronkite on return from a visit to Vietnam distorted the true situation in Vietnam after Tet. He declared, "It is increasingly clear to this reporter that the only rational way out...would be to negotiate."[8]

The impact of the distorted reports about the Tet offensive had far reaching effects on events surrounding the war. President Johnson declared that he would not seek a second term; negotiations were set in motion starting in May 1968, but made little progress; and North Vietnam used the lull in fighting and the bombing halt to recover from its defeat during Tet. Gene Kuentzler, writing in *Vietnam Veterans' War Stories,* gives us the most insightful look at the view from Hanoi right after Tet:

> According to [General] Giap, these distorted reports were inspirational to the North Vietnamese. They changed their plans from a negotiated surrender and decided instead, they only needed to persevere for one more hour, day, week, month, eventually the protesters in America would help them to achieve a victory they knew they could not win on the battlefield.[9]

Admiral Ulysses Grant Sharp, Jr., U.S. Navy (Ret), former commander of Pacific forces, including Vietnam, gives us one more view of what could have been the end of the war in 1968 if the administration had chosen to be resolute in the face of critics opposed to the war. In response to North Vietnam's actions to take advantage of the ongoing negotiations, Admiral Sharp's opinion was that the United States should have resumed offensive actions against the North, countering their buildup. He felt that "this could have significantly altered the whole course of the war from that point forward." He was convinced that the war could have been ended much sooner:

> It would have enabled us, in my view, to win a military victory by the end of 1968. However, there was a horror in Washington of doing anything that even breathed of escalation and, of course, the North Vietnamese took advantage of this attitude.[10]

As it turned out, we missed the opportunity to bring peace to Vietnam in 1968. In that year the number of American soldiers killed in action had reached approximately 28,000. In missing this chance to end the fighting, it can be said that every casualty that we or our allies sustained after that year can be attributed to the antiwar movement.

H.R. Haldeman, the White House second in command during the Nixon presidency, in the aftermath of major demonstrations, was convinced that "the two fall 1969 demonstrations 'prolonged the war three and one half years.'" He was confident that peace could have been achieved in the fall of 1969 if it had not been for the antiwar demonstrations which, in effect, "eliminated the possibility of a negotiated settlement." He was also convinced that "Hanoi's resolve was stiffened by the [antiwar] movement in October 1969."[11]

In January 1969, the doves had gained control of Congress, and opposition to the war was beginning to mount. In late 1969, Congress approved a resolution to restrict American operations in Laos and Thailand. The antiwar Congress, coupled with the increase in antiwar demonstrations, made it impossible for President Nixon to carry through with his ultimatum to North Vietnam to negotiate in good faith by November 1, 1969 or face an escalation in military operations.[12] Another opportunity to end the war passed, and with the continuation of the bombing halt which had been in effect since mid-1968, the North Vietnamese were free to pour thousands of troops and tons of supplies into the South in preparation for their next assault.

When negotiations reached another impasse in mid-December 1972, with Hanoi refusing to negotiate in good faith after more than three years of public and private talks, President Nixon's patience ran out. He lifted the pause in air strikes on the North and authorized attacks on North Vietnam's war making capabilities, including military targets such as logistics and supply centers, transportation and communications facilities, air bases, fuel storage areas, etc. This proved to be one of the most effective and successful uses of air power in the entire war. Admiral Sharp put it this way: "For the first time in this war we had used air power in a way that influenced their will to continue the aggression—we had convinced them that it was, in fact, becoming too costly. And so they began to negotiate in earnest."[13] Here was another opportunity to bring an end to the war. This proposition is born out by Sir Robert Thompson, a British counterinsurgency expert and former head of the British Advisory Mission to Vietnam during the war. He came to the following conclusion:

> In my view, on December 30, 1972, after eleven days of those B-52 attacks on the Hanoi area, you had won the war! They had fired 1, 242 SAMs; they had none left, and what would come in overland from China would be a mere trickle. They and their whole rear base at that point were at your mercy. They would have taken any terms....[14]

North Vietnam was again on the ropes, but the United States let another opportunity go by to bring the war to a close. Admiral Sharp saw it this way:

> Unfortunately, we failed to press home our advantage of the moment. The great public clamor in this country against our strong offensive stand caused the President to be reluctant to give the North Vietnamese more of the same when they once again slowed up the negotiations.... Even more unfortunate, our "signals" were so clear that the North Vietnamese almost certainly *knew* we would not take this kind of step again. They were therefore able to negotiate an agreement on *their* terms and in accordance with *their* long range goals.[15]

The three examples of lost opportunities presented above all had one thing in common: They were thwarted and undermined by the antiwar bloc in Congress, antiwar critics, and the press. In Chapter Ten we saw how the antiwar critics encouraged Hanoi to hold out for a better deal at the negotiating table, and in Chapter 11 it was clearly demonstrated that the antiwar Democrat majority in Congress undercut the administration's efforts to negotiate an acceptable end to the conflict by passing resolutions and legislation which took away nearly all of our negotiating leverage. This gave assurances to Hanoi that all they had to do was wait for Congress to hand them their long sought-after victory. Any lingering doubts that these actions contributed immensely to prolonging the war should be put to rest in the following pronouncements:

Presidents

Nixon. President Nixon was frustrated by the actions of the antiwar protesters for their unwillingness to recognize the real issues of the war and his genuine efforts to bring about a settlement. In his book, *No More Vietnams,* he expresses his concerns:

> I had mixed emotions about the antiwar protesters.... Whatever my view of their motives—and whatever their estimate of mine—the practical effect of their actions was to give encouragement to the enemy to fight on or refuse to negotiate a peace. That the brightest and the best in our great educational institutions could not

recognize that their peace protests prolonged the war is one of the tragic ironies of the Vietnam era.[16]

President Nixon was also disturbed by the drastic cuts for the war effort in Vietnam and Cambodia by Congress in the waning years of the war. He felt that the requests for military assistance were the minimum required to ensure survival of our allies. He commented:

> None of these events [congressional actions] went unnoticed in the North Vietnamese war councils. Hanoi's leaders could not believe their good fortune as the antiwar majority in Congress did their work for them.[17]

As opposition to the war at home increased and support for the war in Congress began to decline, Hanoi's willingness to compromise gave way to confidence in ultimate victory. President Nixon again voiced his frustrations with the antiwar movement:

> Unable to resolve the contradictions [preventing a settlement], Nixon began to see the source of his frustrations in American, not Vietnamese, realities. Not Hanoi but the American antiwar movement "destroyed whatever small possibility may still have existed of ending the war in 1969," he wrote in his memoirs. His critics' motives were in effect, treasonous. "North Vietnam cannot defeat or humiliate the United States. Only Americas can do that," he declared on November 3, 1969 in the "silent majority" speech....[18]

President Nixon and Henry Kissinger worried about Hanoi misinterpreting the dissent in American and they "saw Hanoi using American doves in all of their political and military activities, especially the Paris peace talks."[19] Nixon was certain of a connection between Hanoi's military strategy and American public opinion. This was confirmed by North Vietnamese Colonel Bui Tin, who in a conversation with the author, cited the intense interest that Hanoi had in the antiwar movement in the United States. President Nixon saw the disunity at home as a major impediment to the conduct of the war and negotiations. On several occasions he voiced his concern:

> If only the public would unite behind his programs, North Vietnam would be forced to negotiate in good faith. Henry Cabot Lodge, the chief negotiator in Paris, chimed in when he remarked in May [1969] that Hanoi was still waiting for a sign that "American public opinion is going to collapse."[20]

Johnson. President Johnson's opinion of the antiwar movement was similar to President Nixon's. In a television program in December 1967, President Johnson sought to convince the American people that "if the public got in line, Hanoi would be convinced that it could not win the war in American streets."[21] In 1966, President Johnson was quoted as saying, "This thing [antiwar movement] is assuming dangerous proportions, dividing the country and giving our enemies the wrong idea of the will of this country to fight."[22] Johnson was troubled by the disregard of civility and the disloyalty of some in the antiwar movement. In *Nixon, Johnson and the Doves*, Melvin Small gives us a clear picture of how President Johnson felt about the antiwar movement:

> Like many of his advisers, Johnson was exasperated with the antiwar movement since he was convinced that it had prolonged the war. He knew that all wars provoked some dissent. The dissent on the Vietnam War, however, had "passed the bounds of reasonable debate and fair discussion." Americans were "defeating ourselves," in 1968. By the time of the Tet offensive, he felt that the biggest foreign policy problem was "the divisiveness and pessimism at home."[23]

Congressmen

Senator Russell of Georgia. Addressing the Senate concerning American protesters prolonging the Vietnam War, Senator Russell had these strong words for the protesters:

> Mr. President, I regret that I have not heard all the statements made this morning on this subject, but I

cannot let this occasion pass without expressing my own profound contempt for these demonstrations, and my sickness of soul at the weakening of the body politic and the patriotism and spiritual life of this nation that these demonstrations indicate....

One sure effect of these campaigns and demonstrations will be to prolong the war in Vietnam. The prolongation will certainly increase the casualty lists of American boys who are being sent there to support this country and its flag. Every protest will cause the Communists to believe they can win if they hold on a little longer....

On yesterday afternoon I paid a visit to Walter Reed Hospital where I had an opportunity to talk to seven or eight battle casualties of the Vietcong who had been flown back to this country. Without exception, the first thing that each of these men mentioned was these demonstrations. They asked what Congress proposed to do about them. There is a great feeling of bitterness on the part of men who have been out there on foreign soil that American citizens without let [constraints] or hindrance, and without vigorous condemnation from the press and other media of communications, are permitted to take steps that will slow down the war and inspire the hopes of eventual victory in the mind of Ho Chi Minh....

It is sad, indeed, to think that so many foolish, misled young people who will themselves be caught up in the draft and may pay the penalty of their lives because their demonstrations have encouraged Ho Chi Minh and the Chinese to think that if they will just hold on a while longer, just carry on the war for a few more months or years, the American people will eventually weary of it and pull out....[24]

Senator Proxmire. Offering his support for Senator Russell's comments, Senator Proxmire had this to say:

Mr. President in an article published in the New York Times this morning, James Reston points out that one of the supreme ironies of recent years is that these protesters are inadvertently working against all the things they want, and are creating all the things they fear the most.

They are not promoting peace, because if there is any hope remaining in the hearts of the Vietcong and their leaders in Hanoi and Peiping, it is the distant wish that somehow the American people disapprove the Vietnam War and will make their disapproval felt, reverse our Vietnam policies and call our troops home.

It is this wish—this gross misreading of the attitude of t he American people—which more than anything else is keeping this war going, in spite of our immense power superiority and our solid military victories. It is this which is preventing peace.

And what is fostering the wish that keeps war going but the protests of the so-called peace marchers themselves. As Reston says, they are not persuading the President or the Congress, but deceiving Ho Chi Minh and General Giap into prolonging it.[25]

Congressman Dawson Mathis. Representative Mathis from Georgia submitted the following statement to the House Committee on Internal Security investigating travel to hostile countries:

Through my conversations with the returning prisoners of war, as well as the majority of my constituents, I find an overwhelming agreement that this most unfortunate and burdensome war was needlessly prolonged by individuals in this country who visited Hanoi and made public statements while in that country that were not only derogatory toward this country but perpetrated the false image that this country was succumbing to the peace movement....I would like to ask the distinguished Americans who visited Hanoi if they ever realized that their visits caused the Hanoi government to deter meaningful peace negotiations one extra day? How many POW's were put through senseless torture and humiliation, to pressure them to take pictures and tape interviews with these Americans self-appointed goodwill ambassadors? I wonder.[26]

Congressman L.A. "Skip" Bafalis. Skip Bafalis, Representative from Florida, submitted a statement to the House Committee on Internal Security which focused on antiwar critics prolonging the war through their travels to enemy areas. His statement was sharply critical of the impact on our POWs:

> Mr. Chairman, almost to a man, the prisoners of war released by the North Vietnamese and Viet Cong have complained bitterly about the Hanoi visits by antiwar activists.
>
> For the antiwar activists, the visits simply meant media exposure—a chance to stand before the television cameras and spout off. But for the POWs, the visits meant a prolonged war—and for them more beatings, more long days without decent food, more torture.
>
> For the anxious families of the POW's, it resulted in more loneliness, more days and nights of wondering whether husbands and fathers would ever be seen again.
>
> Every member of Congress hopes that Americans are never called on to fight a ground war like Vietnam again. But if we must, it is imperative that we keep the Jane Fondas and the Ramsey Clarks of this world from helping the enemy....[27]

Congressman G.V. Montgomery. U.S. Representative Montgomery from Mississippi, testifying before the Senate Judiciary

Committee investigating Communists infiltration and exploitation of the antiwar movement, expressed his concern about the impact of the antiwar activists' visits to Hanoi. Referring to the proposed legislation to restrict travel to enemy areas, he stated:

> And to get back to this legislation, it is necessary and needed, probably should have been passed two or four years ago, and I think there is no question about it that those who have gone into North Vietnam and have spoken out supporting the North Vietnamese have delayed the war and have caused other Americans to lose their lives.[28]

Congressman Louis Frey. Louis Frey, JR., U.S. Representative from Florida, saw that American travelers to Hanoi contributed to the intransigence of the North Vietnamese in agreeing to an end to the war, thus prolonging it. A short excerpt from his statement follows:

> The effect of the many unauthorized trips by American citizens to restricted countries since 1967 has been to: first, misrepresent American opinion to our adversaries; second, provide misinformation to the American public; third, provide propaganda ammunition and actual economic assistance to our adversaries; and fourth, to make the attainment of peace more difficult by interfering with private negotiations and other foreign policy activities.[29]

U.S. Military Leaders

General William C. Westmoreland, U.S. Army (Retired). General Westmoreland's speech, "Protests Encourage the Enemy," before the Associated Press was read into the Congressional Record on April 26, 1967 by Congressman Dorn of South Carolina. Here are just a few excerpts from this historic address:

> Yet, despite his [enemy's] staggering combat losses, he clings to the belief that he will defeat us. And through a clever combination of psychological and political warfare—both here and abroad—he has gained support

which gives him hope that he can win politically that which he cannot accomplish militarily....

But I am mindful that the military war in South Vietnam is, from the enemy's point of view, only part of a protracted and carefully coordinated attack, waged in the international arena. Regrettably, I see signs of enemy success in that world arena which he cannot match on the battlefield. He does not understand that American democracy is founded on debate, and he sees every protest as evidence of crumbling morale and diminishing resolve. Thus, discouraged by repeated military defeats but encouraged by what he believes to be popular opposition to our effort in Vietnam, he is determined to continue his aggression from the North. This, inevitably, will cost lives—American, Vietnamese, and those of our brave allies.[30]

In *A Soldier Reports*, General Westmoreland was very critical of those Americans who encouraged and gave the enemy hope. He wrote:

I can make no such accommodation for those who burned draft cards and their country's flag, besieged the Pentagon, paraded the enemy's flag in the streets, encouraged others to break the law, fled their responsibility, and in general went beyond the bounds of reasonable debate and fair dissention. None should escape the reality that his or her actions helped prolong the war.

Why should the enemy desist or even make concessions when Americans were falling over themselves to register their discontent and display how many concessions they themselves were prepared to make at whatever cost?....If nothing else, the dissenting voices of officials and legislators and the shouting in the streets provided a basis for North Vietnam propaganda and distasteful grist to be fed helpless American prisoners of war.[31]

Admiral U.S. Grant Sharp, U.S. Navy (Retired). Admiral Sharp was opposed to the bombing halts that were driven by the critics of the war in Congress and the antiwar activists. The following passages from his book, *Strategy for Defeat,* leave no doubt about his views about the bombing halts and their effect on the war effort:

> The psychological lift of freedom from attack and the recovery and reconstruction which are evident to the [enemy] population can only serve to fortify the will of the people of North Vietnam and give their leaders renewed confidence in the ultimate attainment of their objectives....
>
> The sum and substance of the situation is that continuation of the present restraints [bombing halt] in the absence of reciprocal moves by North Vietnam operates against us. Militarily it deprives us of our most important weapon to punish the enemy and to bring the war to the source of the support for continuing the war in the South....It invites even greater U.S. and Free World casualties through continued prolongation of the war in the South, through piecemeal application of our forces and resources that are available to the task. It prolongs the time until forces can be withdrawn and the larger fiscal outlays can be reduced.[32]

General Maxwell D. Taylor, U.S. Army (Retired). General Taylor testified before the Senate Foreign Relations Committee chaired by the antiwar critic, Senator Fulbright, in 1965. General Taylor expressed his belief that "Hanoi would eventually 'mend its ways' if the United States had the grit to persist." He went on to suggest that "the factor most likely to prolong the war would be opposition at home." One of the most rabid antiwar critics, Senator Wayne Morse, took exception to Taylor's comment about prolonging the war:

> *Morse:* You know we are engaged in a historic debate in this country, where there are honest differences of opinion. I happen to hold to the point of view that it

isn't going to be too long before the American people as a people will repudiate our war in Southeast Asia.

Taylor: That, of course, is good news to Hanoi, Senator.[33]

In *Swords and Plowshares*, General Taylor recounts that "North Vietnam proved to be incredibly tough in accepting losses which, by Western calculation, greatly exceeded the value of the stake involved." He also reveals that in the early years of the war, he and the Johnson administration did not "foresee in time that the conduct of the American war opponents at home would provide encouragement for the enemy to prolong the war."[34]

General Phillip B. Davidson, U.S. Army (Retired). In his role as the senior intelligence officer at Headquarters Military Assistance Command in Vietnam, General Davidson was in a unique position to analyze North Vietnam's strategy. He cites the enemy's *dich van* program, "aimed at shattering the support for the war by the American people," as being a critical element of the Communist's strategy. In his opinion, the program owed its success to its "unwitting American allies." According to General Davidson, "Giap's whole strategy after Tet 1968 was aimed at one decisive objective—to attack the greatest American vulnerability, its will to continue the struggle." In exploiting this American weakness, the North Vietnamese employed the following strategy:

> After 1968, Giap avoided direct attack on our forces in Vietnam, in favor of striking at the will of the American people. By this strategy he not only matched his strength against out weakness, but transferred the principal battlefield from the rice paddies of Vietnam to the streets of the United States....He forced the United States into a no-win strategic dilemma by these same attacks on the American home front....If the American leadership prosecuted the war forcefully, it risked losing domestic support to continue the war. If [it] attempted to assuage its war critics by restraining

military initiatives and measures, it had to forgo the hope of winning in Vietnam.

Eventually, this chasm of national unity became so wide and so deep that in the end, the antiwar elements in Congress became the most powerful ally of the North Vietnamese Politburo.[35]

American Prisoners of War

General Robinson Risner, USAF (Retired). In 1973 following his release from seven years as a POW in North Vietnam, Colonel Risner, an Air Force fighter ace, had harsh words for the antiwar protesters. He was convinced that the war protesters "kept us in prison an extra year or two." In addition to his comments about the antiwar movement prolonging the POWs' imprisonment, he said he felt anger not only toward the demonstrators, but also at those who berated the U.S. government and its policies. Risner confirmed what other POWs have said, that they were constantly subjected to anti-American propaganda, much of which was attributed to the antiwar activists.[36]

Colonel James Kasler, USAF (Retired). Soon after his release from a North Vietnamese POW camp, Colonel Kasler spoke out about the American antiwar protesters. He told of being tortured for refusing to meet with visiting protesters from the United States. He was adamant about one point: "We can thank the war protesters for prolonging the war. Their hands are stained with the blood of American GIs." Colonel Kasler was also critical of the officials and politicians who parroted enemy propaganda and undercut efforts to end the war.[37]

Testimony of Multiple POWs before the House of Representatives: Summing up the testimony of former POWs, Captain James Mulligan, USN, Commander Edwin Shuman III, USN, Lt. Commander Thomas Hall, USN, Lt. Commander David Wesley Hoffman, USN, and Air Force Captain Larry Corrigan, the House Internal Security Committee report of June 1973 stated:

> From their testimony one may conclude that the activities of many of our citizens who traveled to Hanoi without authority brought our men in the service only further

deprivation, mistreatment, and torture, increased the confidence of the enemy and prolonged the war.[38]

Central Intelligence Agency

A memorandum for the Director CIA, 30 November 1966, Subject: "View from Hanoi," reflects Hanoi's reliance on the U.S. domestic situation:

> In order to account for Hanoi's persistent determination to fight on, many Western observers have increasingly focused on the state of U.S. domestic and international opinion as the main prop in Hanoi's calculations....The standard estimate has been that Hanoi believes that a combination of US and international opinion will eventually force the US to offer important concessions to disengage from the war.[39]

American Statesmen

Dean Rusk. Former Secretary of State Dean Rusk, expressing his opinion a number of years after the war, remained firm in his convictions about the impact of the critics. He is quoted as saying, "The machinations of the press, the foolish protests, and all the demonstrations in the streets made the peace movement an unwitting ally of the North Vietnamese and stiffened their resolve to fight." According to author Thomas Schoenbaum, "He [Rusk] believes the North Vietnamese could not have taken the tremendous casualties inflicted upon them without suing for peace had they not become convinced by press accounts of the protests that politically the United States could not stay the course." Rusk also believed that dissent served Hanoi "because it gave the impression that American resolve was weak."[40]

Dean Rusk was asked in retrospect if the war in Vietnam could have been won. He responded, "I think so, if we could have maintained solidarity on the home front...But they [North Vietnamese] were encouraged to stick it out, and they eventually got it all....It wasn't until we pulled our forces out and Congress cut off supplies that North Vietnam overran the South."[41]

Henry Kissinger. As chief U.S. negotiator in Paris and former Secretary of State, Doctor Kissinger had faced the enemy numerous times across the conference table. This gave him exceptional insight into the thinking of the North Vietnamese. He described North Vietnam's view of negotiations as a "life and death" struggle. He interpreted their approach to negotiations in this way:

> To them the Paris talks were not a device for settlement but an instrument of political warfare. They were a weapon to exhaust us psychologically, to split us from our South Vietnamese ally, and to divide our public opinion through vague hints of obduracy of our government.... But to the extent that we maintained a firm position we were subject to domestic and bureaucratic pressures that gave Hanoi even more incentive to persevere in intransigence.[42]

Henry Kissinger agonized over what he felt were misguided antiwar student groups and young protesters, but he felt his obligation to his country outweighed his sympathy for them. Of the protesters, he stated, "They were, in my view, as wrong as they were passionate. Their pressures delayed the end of the war, not accelerated it: their simplifications did not bring closer the peace..." Referring to the opposition to the war in Congress, he felt that "Hanoi could only be encouraged to stall, waiting to harvest the results of our domestic dissent.[43]

W.W. Rostow. In *The Diffusion of Power*, Walt Rostow, National Security Advisor to President Johnson, cites a report he sent to the president in 1967 consisting of the results of an interrogation of an enemy defector. It left no doubt that Hanoi placed heavy reliance on the domestic front in America. The defector attended a meeting in July 1967 at which a resolution by the North Vietnamese Communist Party was briefed. The policy announced at that meeting was, "The longer the war continued, the stronger the U.S. doves would become and the VC were, therefore, dedicated to fight at least until the 1968 election." Rostow saw the forthcoming elections in 1968 as having an impact on Hanoi's position on negotiations. He suggested, "With at least one major Democratic candidate promising, if elected, to overthrow the GVN [government of South Vietnam], it was obviously in Hanoi's interest to postpone a settlement until after the November election."[44]

In August 1967, Walt Rostow reported to President Johnson on the situation in Vietnam. He stated, "All the evidence we have indicates that Hanoi does not now expect to win the war in the South on the battlefield. They are hanging on hoping that there will be a break in the will of the U.S. to continue the war."[45]

James Reston. Reston, speaking from the administrations viewpoint, made this assessment of the antiwar demonstrations: "They are not promoting but postponing it. They are not persuading the president or the Congress to end the war but deceiving Ho Chi Minh and General [Vo Nguyen] Giap into prolonging [it]...."[46]

H. R. Haldeman. Haldeman was convinced that the antiwar demonstrations stiffened Hanoi's resolve. He believed that the protesters prolonged the war by three and a half years.[47]

Winton M. Blount. Following a visit to South Vietnam, Winton Blount, Postmaster General during the Nixon Administration, at a White House news conference stated that he believed that "demonstrations are inspiring Hanoi to prolong the war and thus bring about more U.S. casualties." He added, "The troops in Vietnam don't understand the demonstrations and do not approve of them."[48]

Editorials and Reports

Robert Turner. As a distinguished scholar and historian, Robert Turner authored an extensive analysis of the antiwar movement in the United States. He cites a speech by the Premier of North Vietnam, Pham Van Dong, in August 1970 in which Dong placed a great deal of hope in the disunity in the United States. In that speech "Dong made it clear that Hanoi is placing great hope in the possibility of the United States being forced by domestic pressures to concede to the Communist victory it has thus far been denied them."[49]

A report emanating from a conference of 14 of American's foremost Asian scholars in late 1970 concluded that Hanoi was placing considerable confidence in the theory that the U.S. would give in as France did in 1954. The report states, "In this sense, the outcome is being decided on the streets and in the homes of America as much as in the jungles of Vietnam.[50]

After presenting a number of examples where the statements by American antiwar activists were essentially identical to the propaganda coming out of Hanoi, Turner asserted, "Further, through their antiwar protests these groups [antiwar activists] contribute substantially to the hope held by the North Vietnamese Communist leaders that the United States may be forced by internal pressure to withdraw from Vietnam. This may in fact serve to prolong the war, increasing casualties on all sides."[51]

Washington Security Council. In addressing the question about why the Communists refused to negotiate, the Council's *Washington Report* in January 1966 concluded that the Communists feel that "the political base for U.S. intervention will eventually crumble if only the war can be kept going." The report also made the point that "it is the supreme irony of the Vietnam war that those who call most loudly for 'peace' in Vietnam furnish Hanoi and Peking with almost their only good reason to continue the war."[52]

Time Essay. *Time Essay* article, "The Vietniks: Self-Defeating Dissent," October 29, 1969, concludes that "the fact is that the Vietniks, by encouraging the Communist hope and expectation that the U. S. does not have the stomach to fight it out in Viet Nam, are probably achieving what they would least like: prolonging the war and adding to the casualty list on both sides."[53]

Stars and Stripes. Vietnam Veterans for a Just Peace charged that antiwar activists "prolonged the war and brought additional pain to our POWs." They called upon Congress to investigate some of the leaders. The Veteran's group accused the antiwar activists of materially aiding our enemies and causing additional torture of our POWs.[54]

Washington Star. David Lawrence, in an article for the *Washington Star* in October 1965, expressed concern for the adverse publicity the demonstrations were getting around the world. He wrote, "The image conveyed abroad is that of a divided nation which soon will demand that there be a surrender and withdrawal of all military forces in Southeast Asia. This in turn encourages the Hanoi government in North Vietnam to continue the struggle, and thus more American lives are lost."[55]

The View from North Vietnam

General Giap. In his book, *How We Won the War,* General Giap, the general who led North Vietnam's army during the war, reveals how Hanoi had as an objective the cultivation of people around the world to support its cause. Giap said, "Most importantly, the Vietnamese reached out to the American people." He continued, "Politically, the Vietnamese always believed in the importance of the anti-war movement....They encouraged it as best they could, knowing that creating a climate of opinion hostile to the war would be one important way of ending it."[56]

Politburo. After their disastrous defeat during Tet 1968, the Politburo in Hanoi declared a shift in strategy. Following Lenin's philosophy, they decided on a "protracted war in order to gain time, to build up strength, to dishearten the enemy." It was also decided that the psychological war against the United States was to continue. Implementation of this strategy took on a familiar approach as indicated below:

> ...Giap and his colleagues were able to turn it [protracted strategy] into a grand strategy of the highest order: by prolonging the peace negotiations while at the same time killing American soldiers and airmen wherever and whenever they could, Hanoi eroded American public support for the war more and more.[57]

The Consequences

The evidence is overwhelming that the antiwar movement did not promote peace. The antithesis is true. The antiwar movement, collectively consisting of Congress, the media and activists, was influential in prolonging the war by several years. The movement encouraged and gave hope to the enemy; undermined our national unity and will; and persuaded Congress to cut off funds, ensuring the conquest of South Vietnam, Cambodia and Laos by the Communists. The cost of prolonging the war and handing North Vietnam a victory had three major consequences: it resulted in the death of thousands of American, South Vietnamese and allied soldiers; it resulted in the enslavement of millions of people under a totalitarian Communist regime; and it resulted in a bloodbath in South Vietnam and Cambodia. The next chapter will expound on this topic.

Chapter Thirteen

Aftermath

For every man who lives without freedom, the rest of us must face the guilt.

—Lillian Hellman

Justice would be partially served if those in America who protested and undermined our war efforts had to spend a few months living in "liberated" South Vietnam. Similarly, it is not likely that any of the antiwar activists would have enjoyed life under the Communist Khmer regime in Cambodia when it took over and murdered over two million of their countrymen. And how many of the antiwar activists would like to have lived in Laos after the brutal Communist regime came to power there?

The New Order

Lost Freedom. Thirty years after coming under the rule of the Communist regime in Hanoi, the people of South Vietnam are still awaiting the democracy, freedom, liberty and self-determination that Hanoi promised when the South was liberated and reunified with the Communist North. Tragically, what they got was repression of all basic freedoms and dire poverty.[1] Soon after Colonel Bui Tin accepted the surrender in Saigon, every man, woman and child in the South underwent a major upheaval in their lives. The new rulers relied on executions, re-education camps, thought reform, population resettlement, exile, surveillance, mandatory socialist education, and rigorous Communist indoctrination to create the new social order. The bloodbath that the antiwar factions belittled took an estimated

65,000 lives, while hundreds of thousands of former military officers, government officials, politicians, religious and labor leaders, scholars, intellectuals and lawyers, as well as critics of the new regime were ordered to "reeducation camps" where many of them perished. As late as 1982 there were still as many a 120,000 of these camps in operation in the South.[2] Families and relatives of those considered suspect were deprived of access to basic necessities of food, clothing, shelter and employment.[3]

Soon after the Communist victory "nearly two million South Vietnamese—1.1 million soldiers, 200,000 members of the police force, over 300,000 civil servants, and many thousands of [former] employees of U.S. agencies—found themselves out of a job and an income." Next came the campaign to eliminate "capitalist" tendencies, and with that another half-million people were put out of work.[4]

Re-education Camps. The use of re-education camps continued long after the initial conquest of South Vietnam, and these camps were still in use into the late 1980s and beyond. In the years following the initial incarceration of the military and other officials, these camps took on a new purpose. They were used to "incarcerate members of certain social classes in order to coerce them to accept and conform to the new social order." They were part of a broader effort to combat counterrevolution and resistance to the new socialist system. "Only those who 'deserved rehabilitation' (as opposed to those who deserved jail) were sent to the camps, where their political attitudes, work production records, and general behavior were closely monitored."[5]

The re-education camp system was developed to serve three levels of social control: short-term, long-term and permanent incarceration. The short-term camps were established near urban centers and were primarily to teach socialism and unlearn the old ways. They were primarily for southern proletarians and juvenile delinquents. These camps lasted for 30 days for some and for others from three to six months. The long-term camps were termed collective reformatories and had thought reform as their purpose. These camps were found in almost every province in southern Vietnam and processed at least 50,000 people. The third type of socialist-reform camp was intended for permanent incarceration and re-education involving indoctrination and forced labor. These camps were for southern Vietnamese such as "educators, legislators, province chiefs, writers, and supreme court judges...." As late as 1987 at least 15,000 people were still residing in these camps. Camp conditions were reportedly poor and there was a high death rate. In most cases, these prisoners were incarcerated without charges or trial.[6]

Boat People. Possibly as many as 1.5 million South Vietnamese took to the sea in a mass exodus to escape the persecution at the hands of the North Vietnamese conquerors. Many of the overcrowded boats were unseaworthy and posed great risk for the occupants. Several hundred thousand of these brave people went down with their rickety boats. Those who openly took to the sea were required to contribute gold to the Communist government. Those who were intercepted as they fled were stripped of all valuables. Property that was left behind was reallocated to the new ruling class.[7]

Population Relocation. A major part of the new social order was a massive relocation of the population in the former South Vietnam. This program, called the "state redistribution of labor program," began in 1976 and uprooted at least five million South Vietnamese people. The program's main purpose was to break up the existing social structure—"to help foster class struggle and turn the middle and upper class into social pariahs."[8]

Surveillance. This is the true model of Orwell's big brother. It is described in a Library of Congress study in the following way:

> Perhaps the most effective instrument of social control in the 1980s was the "revolutionary vigilance" surveillance system, commonly called "the warden method." In theory at least, every hamlet, city block, state farm, factory, school, state and party office had its own Revolutionary Vigilance Committee headed by a warden and made up of a team of neighbors, usually 25 to 40 households (120 to 300 persons)....Its purpose was to "help the government in all ways and aspects," specifically by monitoring the behavior of its members, reporting public opinion to higher authorities, and promoting various state and party policies and programs

locally. The committee's authority was shored up by the Ho Khau registration system, which required each individual to have an identity card and each family to have a family registration certificate or residence permit (listing the names of all persons authorized to live at one address). Both identification cards and family registration certificates were checked frequently by security cadres.[9]

More Social Controls. The 1980 Constitution created another mechanism of "control." The People's Organ of Control, as it is called, is a top down control mechanism from the Supreme People's Organ of Control to the lower levels of district and precinct organs of control. It functions in the following manner:

> These institutions function to "control the observance of the law by the ministries, armed forces, state employees and citizens; to exercise the right of public prosecution; and to insure strict and uniform observance of the law." Their purview is "any act encroaching upon the interests of the State, the collective, or the lives, property, freedom, honor, and dignity of citizens." The system is composed of many activities: physical control; re-education and reform; indoctrination, emulation, and motivation; and education. Its essence is organization and motivation, and in the hands of skilled cadres it could harness social pressure to induce new attitudes and ways of thinking.[10]

Human Rights. Basic human rights such as free speech, freedom of religion, freedom of press, the right to form free unions, freedom of association, etc. are still elusive for the people of Vietnam. The Socialist Republic of Vietnam's constitution guarantees freedom of religion–for the government "sanctioned" religions. Except for ordinary religious worship, churches must obtain official permission to conduct all other religious activities such as conferences, fund raising, promotion of senior clergy and new training institutions.[11]

The media in the Socialist Republic of Vietnam is controlled by the Vietnam Communist Party Central Committee's Propaganda and

Training Department which operates under guidelines established by the Ministry of Culture. The Party Congress "defines the media's role as being 'the voice of the party and the masses,' and identifies its task as being to 'propagate the party's lines and policies....'" In essence, the control over the media is to "ensure that it reflects the policies and positions of the party."[12]

The International Society for Human Rights (ISHR) has chronicled numerous instances of human rights violations in Vietnam. There are numerous reports of religious persecution and attacks on freedom of the press. According to ISHR reports, "journalists have to reckon with being sentenced to death, life imprisonment or up to 20 years imprisonment under the charge of 'propaganda against the Socialist Republic' or 'espionage.'" Journalists who make reports critical of the system are charged with being a threat to national security. Religious leaders can be arrested for acting as a priest without being authorized by the state. People are arrested and held for long periods without being charged. In one report, a journalist was held for two years without being charged or sentenced. They are often denied legal counsel, and visits by relatives are restricted to a few times a year. The wife of one journalist was allowed to see her husband only three times in 20 months. Some detainees are put in solitary confinement without books or writing materials. Mail to and from those in confinement does not always get through. In some instances, the family members of dissidents receive collective punishment. Expressing opinions that are unfavorable of the party or state are common reasons for arrest and incarceration.[13] Here are just a few examples of some of the recent human rights violations as reported by ISHR:

> The catholic priest Father Nguyen Van Ly was sentenced to 15 years imprisonment and five years of house arrest in a closed trial and without legal defense on 19 October 2001 for "sabotage of the solidarity policy..." The real reason is that Father Ly non-violently advocated religious freedom and the return of church property....Father Ly is restricted to a single visit from his sister or another relative every two months. They bring medication and food. Under surveillance, they are allowed to speak to Father Ly for up to one hour.... Father Ly is not allowed any writing material or books

in the cell. The vast majority of letters he was allowed to write to his family failed to arrive.[14]

In spring 2001, Siu Beng and Siu Be participated in demonstrations in the central Vietnamese highlands, when several thousands of Christians demanded the release of two pastors. The police brutally broke up the protests and arrested at least 200 people, amongst them 60 evangelical pastors and leaders of ethnic minorities (Montagnards). Afterwards the authorities closed nearly all churches in the region and used violent methods to force Christians to renounce their faith. [Siu Beng and Siu Be] were both sentenced to six and a half and three and a half years imprisonment in January 2002...[15]

Nguyen Vu Binh's case is typical. On 25 September 2002 he was arrested after having sent a human rights report to the US Congress. In the indictment, the prosecution accuses Binh of, amongst other things: applying to found a political party, publishing various articles with "negative contents," having contacts with "reactionary" Vietnamese in exile and receiving funds from abroad. The verdict...of 31 December 2003, sentencing him to seven years imprisonment and three years of house arrest was confirmed [in an appeal].[16]

The publicists Nguyen Khac Toan and Vu The Binh were arrested in Hanoi on 8 January [2002], because they had gathered information about farmers' demonstrations.[17]

The poet and journalist Bui Minh Quoc was put under house arrest for two years on 16 January [2002], because he had investigated the land concessions made to China in the border regions.[18]

Ms Nguyen Thi Hoa, Mr Nguyen Truc Cuong and Mr Nguyen Vu Viet were charged with "espionage" by the Vietnamese procuracy on 24 October [2002], because they had collected information about human rights violations against Buddhists and Catholics for a radio station and a human rights NGO [Non-Government Organization] in the United States.[19]

32-year old lawyer and journalist Le Chi Quang was arrested in Hanoi on 21 February 2002 because of "dissemination of documents agitating against the Vietnamese socialist state." In his publications he has advocated freedom of opinion and press as well as a pluralistic democracy....[20] On 8 November [2002]... Quang was sentenced in Hanoi to a total of seven years in prison and house arrest for "propaganda against the Socialist Republic of Vietnam."[21]

The Killing Fields

Another of the tragedies resulting from the abandonment of Indochina was the terror and mass genocide that took place in Cambodia following the withdrawal of U.S. forces and the termination of American assistance to that nation. Soon after the Khmer Rouge Communists seized power in Cambodia in 1975 with the assistance of North Vietnam, the systematic murder of an estimated 2.2 million Cambodians began. According to Dr. Gregory Stanton, Director of Genocide Watch and former law professor and Foreign Service Officer, "most former soldiers, government officials, doctors, teachers, and educated people were forced to dig pits and were then clubbed to death." Upon his return from a visit to Cambodia in 1980, Dr. Stanton, who at one time opposed the war, decided that the United States was right in trying to help defend South Vietnam and Cambodia from a Communist takeover. He stated, "I returned convinced the Congress's cutting off of assistance to fight the Khmer Rouge and to enforce the Paris Accords doomed millions of Cambodians and Vietnamese to unspeakable deaths." The horrors that took place in Cambodia changed Stanton's mind forever. He cited such things as a young boy being required to watch his mother and father disemboweled; seeing a tiny skeleton with a crushed skull; and smelling the rotting flesh in the mass graves.[22]

As brought out in the previous chapter, a panel of well known scholars reached the conclusion at a national security workshop in 1988 that Congress clearly shared the guilt for what took place in Cambodia.

They concluded that there is "a direct road from the War Powers Act to the killing fields." In addition to the War Powers Act, Congress doomed Cambodia with the passage of the Cooper-Church amendment in January 1971 which banned U.S. combat operations in Cambodia and dealt the final blow with the cut off of all military aid to Cambodia in August 1973.[23]

The Vietnam Syndrome

Former Secretary of State Henry Kissinger had serious misgivings about the impact of the United States withdrawing from Indochina and essentially abandoning our allies to the Communists. He was concerned with the damage to our credibility resulting from what appeared to be our unwillingness to stand by our allies. The cold war was in full force at that time and Kissinger worried about the impact on the alliances we had with the free world. He expressed his concern in the following passage from the *White House Years*: "For a great power to abandon a small country to tyranny simply to obtain a respite from our own travail seemed to me—and still seems to me—profoundly immoral and destructive of our efforts to build a new and ultimately more peaceful pattern of international relations."[24]

The damage to the United States' position in world affairs was manifested in the president's inability to mobilize public support to combat Communist expansionism beyond our borders. Knowing this, the Soviet Union and other Communist despots were encouraged to embark on adventures throughout the world. With Soviet backing, Cuba sent soldiers to Angola to help with the Communist insurgency in that country. Communist expansionism was also active in Ethiopia and Somalia. In Central America incursions by Communist guerrillas were active in El Salvador, Nicaragua and Grenada. The Soviets invaded Afghanistan, and our ally, the Shah of Iran was overthrown. All of these adventures by Communists were encouraged by the impression that the United States was a "crippled superpower" unable to act decisively. This malaise, called the "Vietnam syndrome" by some, became a constraint on U.S. foreign policy. President Reagan sought to overcome this syndrome, but even his efforts to combat the Communist revolutionaries were thwarted by Congress. The administration was barred from any involvement in Angola, giving the insurgents and Cuban military a free hand in that country, and Congress prohibited the use of any funds to help fight the Communist insurgency in Nicaragua.[25]

In their final judgment, the 15 members of the National Security Workshop cited earlier found that the victory of our adversaries in Indochina had profound effects on the postwar position of the United States as a world power:

> One [judgment] that seems fairly well established now is that congressional action during the Vietnam War has undermined our postwar deterrence strategy. Congressional pandering to neoisolationism and other irresponsible tendencies undercut our defense credibility both with our friends and our potential enemies. Whether this behavior had direct significant impact on the outcome of the war may be debated, but the postwar legacy is clear....
>
> A third judgment is that Congress used the Vietnam War to effect institutional change in U.S. foreign policy making. Congressional prerogatives now exist where they did not exist before. A steady congressional campaign, through the mechanism of the congressional hearing and other means, has diminished the foreign relations authority of the president.[26]

In *The Real Lessons of the Vietnam War*, Robert Turner and John Moore make a strong case that Congress, acting under strong pressures from the antiwar movement, handed South Vietnam, Laos and Cambodia to the Communist aggressors. They conclude that "in doing so, as Bill Colby and others have noted, Congress essentially snatched defeat from the jaws of victory."[27]

Chapter Fourteen

The Antiwar Legacy

If a house be divided against itself, that house cannot stand.

—The Bible, *Mark 3:25*

If there is one message that those who read this book should take with them it is that disunity at home leads to defeat abroad. In other words, *Divided We Fall.* Those who dissent are quick to claim that in the United States they have the right to oppose the policies and actions of their government. Those who have fought for their country are the first to defend this right, but while enduring the effects of dissent, they are also the ones who bear the consequences. The lessons of Vietnam teach us that actions have consequences which can be harmful to the nation and our servicemen. With free speech comes responsibility, and when that responsibility is ignored or obfuscated, the nation can be imperiled. It is justifiable to question the loyalty of those who place their country and armed forces in peril, especially when the nation is at war. Many of the acts of the antiwar activists meet the test of giving aid and comfort to the enemy—defined in the constitution as treason. In his book, *Aid and Comfort,* Henry Holzer makes a convincing case for treason by certain activists. Yet, no one has ever been prosecuted. No one has been held accountable for the consequences of the traitorous acts, summarized below, which provided incalculable aid to the enemy.

- As previously documented, Hanoi expressed appreciation and support on numerous occasions for the actions of the antiwar protesters in the United States. These actions encouraged the enemy and bolstered their morale (Chapter Five).

- As Colonel Bui Tin has attested, the antiwar activists who visited Hanoi gave the North Vietnamese confidence to hold out in the face of battlefield reverses. Hanoi saw the activists as the conscience of America and part of our war making capability, and the antiwar movement in the U.S. turned that power to Hanoi's favor (Chapter Six).

- Activists' visits to Hanoi caused greater hardship and suffering for American POWs held in Hanoi, and caused the POWs' families anguish and torment (Chapter Seven).

- The antiwar factions aided the enemy's worldwide propaganda campaign through their statements that often painted the United States as the imperialist aggressor and falsely accused the U.S. of deliberately bombing civilians and committing other atrocities (Chapter Six).

- Broadcasts from Hanoi by activists undermined the morale of United States and allied forces and the people of South Vietnam. Beamed to many other countries, these broadcasts undermined the United States' credibility in the eyes of the rest of the world (Chapter Eight).

- The antiwar activists sabotaged our war effort by mounting a massive campaign against the draft; they aided and encouraged young men to avoid service to their country by fleeing to other countries; they undermined the ROTC programs on campuses reducing the number of officers available for the armed forces; they obstructed draft boards and military recruiting efforts; they attempted to turn active military troops against their superiors and even encouraged desertion and sabotage; and the list goes on and on (Chapter Nine).

- They organized national and international protests against United States military operations that were designed to assist and protect our forces on the battlefield, including interdiction of enemy sanctuaries and staging bases in Laos and Cambodia (Chapter Eight).

- They opposed bombing of military targets in North Vietnam designed to stop the aggression in the South and aid U.S. and allied forces in defeating the enemy (Chapter Nine).

- They organized widespread demonstrations in an effort to force the United States to unilaterally withdraw its forces; to set a date for withdrawing all U.S. forces; to stop supporting South Vietnam; to stop bombing the North and the sanctuaries in Laos and Cambodia; and to end sending any additional troops to Vietnam. (Chapter Nine).

- They undermined the United States' and allied negotiating position by demanding unilateral concessions and insisting that the United States accept the terms of the enemy which amounted to surrender and abandonment of all of Indochina to the Communists (Chapter Nine).

- Congress, pressed by the antiwar movement, passed resolutions and legislation that undermined our war efforts and destroyed all of our leverage for negotiating with the enemy (Chapters Ten & Eleven).

- Following the withdrawal of U.S. forces, Congress guaranteed the fall of South Vietnam, Cambodia and Laos to the Communists by cutting off all but a trickle of military assistance while China and the Soviet Union pumped tons of modern war materials into North Vietnam (Chapter Eleven).

- All of the forgoing actions by the antiwar movement, including the media, Congress and the antiwar activists, aided our enemy, contributed to our defeat and handed the Communists victory over South Vietnam, Cambodia and Laos (Chapters Ten & Eleven).

- Collectively, the antiwar movement caused the war to be prolonged by several years, during which time as many as 30,000 to 40,000 American soldiers, sailors, airmen, and marines were killed in battle and thousands more were wounded and maimed. South Vietnamese and enemy casualties during that same time period were far greater (Chapter Twelve).

The question that reaches out from 30 years in the past is how any true American could carry out acts opposing their own government in wartime and give aid and comfort to an enemy who was killing their own countrymen. As a career military officer and Vietnam veteran, it is hard to comprehend how my own countrymen could have aided the enemy and put me and my comrades at risk while we were fighting for their freedom. We may never know the answer to this question, but one thing we know for certain, freedom is not free. Every American has the responsibility to defend that freedom. Many have given their lives for that cause. Giving aid and comfort to our enemies and other acts of disunity only serve to undermine that freedom.

This book has focused on the impact of disunity in the United States when we are engaged in armed conflict. The similarities between Vietnam and the Iraq War are all too real. Following the 1968 Tet offensive President Johnson was accused of misleading the American people on the progress of the war in Vietnam.[1] President Nixon was constantly hounded for allegedly lying to the public about having a plan to end the war in Vietnam and for prolonging the war with his Vietnamization program.[2] President Bush has come under similar attacks for his polices in Iraq. He has been dogged with charges that he misled the public on going to war; that he concocted the war for political reasons; and that he was sacrificing American blood for oil. Senator Kennedy charged that President Bush "told lie after lie after lie after lie."[3] In 2005 he called President Bush's policies on Iraq a catastrophic failure and asserted that the US Military in Iraq had become part of the problem, not part of the solution. He called for the president to set a timetable for withdrawal from Iraq.[4] Later that year he called the situation in Iraq an intractable quagmire with no end in sight.[5] In June 2005, the House Democratic leader Nancy Pelosi pushed an amendment that required President Bush to outline an Iraq exit strategy. She called the war in Iraq a war of choice and a grotesque mistake.[6] These comments are music to the ears of our enemies.

This open criticism by our own officials creates disunity and encourages our enemies. The terrorists who want to destroy us are bolstered by these irresponsible statements. It is obvious that the lessons of Vietnam have not been heeded. We are again being divided by those who place their personal agenda above the well-being of their country and the safety of our servicemen in harms way. Just as with Vietnam, the claims that the war in Iraq was a mistake and is unwinable leads the insurgents to believe that if they keep the pressure on and hold out a little longer, we will give up like we did in Vietnam.

Very few antiwar critics have come forward since the end of the war in Vietnam to accept the responsibility for the enslavement of 20 million South Vietnamese and the murder of over two million Cambodians. They give many excuses for their part in these tragedies. They claim that the war was a mistake, and we should not have interfered in this civil war. For those who might still believe it was a civil war, here is what the successor to Ho Chi Minh, Le Duan, had to say in 1975 in his victory speech: "Our party is the unique and single leader that organized, controlled, and governed the entire struggle of the Vietnamese people from the first day of the revolution." The North Vietnamese general Vo Ban said in an interview in 1983, "In May 1959 I had the privilege of being designated by the Vietnamese Communist Party [In Hanoi] to unleash a military attack on the South in order to liberate the South and reunify the fatherland."[7]

For those who say the war was a mistake, go back to Chapter Two and read what six American presidents said about defending the freedom-loving people of Vietnam and the rest of Southeast Asia from Communist aggression. There is a seventh president who thought the same way. In a speech on October 1980 Ronald Reagan made it clear that he, too, agreed with the six presidents who preceded him:

> It is time we recognized that ours was, in truth, a noble cause. A small country newly free from colonial rule sought our help in establishing self-rule and the means of self-defense against a totalitarian neighbor bent on conquest. We dishonor the memory of 50,000 young Americans who died in that cause when we give way to feelings of guilt as if we were doing something shameful, and we have been shabby in our treatment of those who returned. They fought as well and as bravely as any Americans have ever fought in any war. They deserve our gratitude, our respect and our continuing concern.[8]

Appendix A

National Security Action Memorandum No. 52, May 11, 1961

Source: Texas Tech University Vietnam Archive

~~TOP SECRET~~

THE WHITE HOUSE

WASHINGTON

May 11, 1961

NATIONAL SECURITY ACTION MEMORANDUM NO. 52

TO: The Secretary of State

The President today reviewed the report of the Vietnam Task Force, entitled "Program of Action to Prevent Communist Domination of South Vietnam." Subject to amendment or revisions which he may wish to make after providing opportunity for a further discussion at the next meeting of the National Security Council, now scheduled for May 19, the President has made the following decisions on the basis of this report:

1. The U.S. objective and concept of operations stated in the report are approved: to prevent Communist domination of South Vietnam; to create in that country a viable and increasingly democratic society, and to initiate, on an accelerated basis, a series of mutually supporting actions of a military, political, economic, psychological and covert character designed to achieve this objective.

2. The approval given for specific military actions by the President at the National Security Council meeting on April 29, 1961, is confirmed.

~~TOP SECRET~~

Declassified, MFD 4/9/76

3. Additional actions listed at pages 4 and 5 of the Task Force Report are authorized, with the objective of meeting the increased security threat resulting from the new situation along the frontier between Laos and Vietnam. In particular, the President directs an assessment of the military utility of a further increase in GVN forces from 170,000 to 200,000, together with an assessment of the parallel political and fiscal implications.

4. The President directs full examination by the Defense Department, under the guidance of the Director of the continuing Task Force on Vietnam, of the size and composition of forces which would be desirable in the case of a possible commitment of U.S. forces to Vietnam. The diplomatic setting within which the action might be taken should also be examined.

5. The U.S. will seek to increase the confidence of President Diem and his government in the United States by a series of actions and messages relating to the trip of Vice President Johnson. The U.S. will attempt to strengthen President Diem's popular support within Vietnam by reappraisal and negotiations, under the direction of Ambassador Nolting. Ambassador Nolting is also requested to recommend any necessary reorganization of the Country Team for these purposes.

6. The U.S. will negotiate in appropriate ways to improve Vietnam's relationship with other countries, especially Cambodia, and its standing in world opinion.

7. The Ambassador is authorized to begin negotiations looking toward a new bilateral arrangement with Vietnam, but no firm commitment will be made to such an arrangement without further review by the President.

~~TOP SECRET~~

8. The U.S. will undertake economic programs in Vietnam with a view to both short term immediate impact and a contribution to the longer range economic viability of the country, and the specific actions proposed on pages 12 and 13 of the Task Force Report are authorized.

9. The U.S. will strengthen its efforts in the psychological field as recommended on pages 14 and 15 of the Task Force Report.

10. The program for covert actions outlined on page 15 of the Task Force Report is approved.

11. These directions will be supported by appropriate budgetary action, but the President reserves judgment on the levels of funding proposed on pages 15 and 16 of the Task Force Report and in the funding annex.

12. Finally, the President approves the continuation of a special Task Force on Vietnam, established in and directed by the Department of State under Sterling J. Cottrell as Director, and Chalmers B. Wood as Executive Officer.

Signed
McGeorge Bundy

Information Copy to:
    Defense
    CIA
    USIA
    Treasury

(True copy, retyped for legibility, jr)

~~TOP SECRET~~

Appendix B

National Security Action Memorandum No. 111, November 22, 1961

Source: Texas Tech University Vietnam Archive

THE WHITE HOUSE
WASHINGTON

~~TOP SECRET~~ November 22, 1961

NATIONAL SECURITY ACTION MEMORANDUM NO. 111

TO: The Secretary of State

SUBJECT: First Phase of Viet-Nam Program

The President has authorized the Secretary of State to instruct our Ambassador to Viet-Nam to inform President Diem as follows:

1. The U.S. Government is prepared to join the Viet-Nam Government in a sharply increased joint effort to avoid a further deterioration in the situation in South Viet-Nam.

2. This joint effort requires undertakings by both Governments as outlined below:

    a. On its part the U.S. would immediately undertake the fol-[following] actions in support of the GVN:

    (1) Provide increased air lift to the GVN forces, including helicopters, light aviation, and transport aircraft, manned to the extent necessary by United States uniformed personnel and under United States operational control.

    (2) Provide such additional equipment and United States uniformed personnel as may be necessary for air reconnaissance, photography, instruction in and execution of air-ground support techniques, and for special intelligence.

    (3) Provide the GVN with small craft, including such United States uniformed advisers and operating personnel as may be necessary for operations in effecting surveillance and control over costal waters and inland waterways.

    (4) Provide expedited training and equipping of the civil guard and the self-defense corps with the objective of relieving the regular Army of static missions and freeing it for mobile offensive operations.

2

(5) Provide such personnel and equipment as may be necessary to improve the military-political intelligence system beginning at the provincial level and expanding upward through the Government and the armed forces to the Central Intelligence Organization.

(6) Provide such new terms of reference, reorganization and additional personnel for United States military forces as are required for increased United States military assistance in the operational collaboration with the GVN and operational direction of U. S. forces and to carry out the other increased responsibilities which accrue to the U.S. military authorities under these recommendations.

(7) Provide such increased economic aid as may be required to permit the GVN to pursue a vigorous flood relief and rehabilitation program, to supply material in support of the security efforts, and to give priority to projects in support of this expanded counter-insurgency program. (This could include increases in military pay, a full supply of a wide range of materials such as food, medical supplies, transportation equipment, communications equipment, and any other items where material help could assist the GVN in winning the war against the Viet Cong.)

(8) Encourage and support (including financial support) a request by the GVN to the FAO or any other appropriate international organization for multilateral assistance in the relief and rehabilitation of the flood area.

(9) Provide individual administrators and advisers for the Governmental machinery of South Viet-Nam in types and numbers to be agreed upon by the two Governments.

(10) Provide personnel for a joint survey with the GVN of conditions in each of the provinces to assess the social, political, intelligence, and military factors bearing

on the prosecution of the counter-insurgency program in order to reach a common estimate of these factors and a common determination of how to deal with them.

b. On its part, the GVN would initiate the following actions:

(1) Prompt and appropriate legislative and administrative action to put the nation on a wartime footing to mobilize its entire resources. (This would include a decentralization and broadening of the Government so as to realize the full potential of all non-Communist elements in the country willing to contribute to the common struggle.)

(2) The vitalization of appropriate Governmental wartime agencies with adequate authority to perform their functions effectively.

(3) Overhaul of the military establishment and command structure so as to create an effective military organization for the prosecution of the war and assure a mobile offensive capability for the Army.

McGeorge Bundy

Information Copies to:

The Secretary of Defense
Director of Central Intelligence
General Maxwell D. Taylor

Declassified September 20, 1971

(True copy. Retyped for clarity. Jr)

Appendix C

National Security Action Memorandum No. 273 November 26, 1963

Source: Texas Tech University Vietnam Archive

THE WHITE HOUSE
WASHINGTON

~~TOP SECRET~~

November 26, 1963

NATIONAL SECURITY ACTION MEMORANDUM NO. 273

TO: The Secretary of State
The Secretary of Defense
The Director of Central Intelligence
The Administrator, AID
The Director, USIA

The President has reviewed the discussions of South Vietnam which occurred in Honolulu, and has discussed the matter further with Ambassador Lodge. He directs that the following guidance be issued to all concerned:

    1. It remains the central object of the United States in South Vietnam to assist the people and Government of that country to win their contest against the externally directed and supported Communist conspiracy. The test of all U. S. decisions and actions in this area should be the effectiveness of their contribution on this purpose.

    2. The objectives of the United States with respect to the withdrawal of U. S. military personnel remain as stated in the White House statement of October 2, 1963.

    3. It is a major interest of the United States Government that the present provisional government of South Vietnam should be assisted in consolidating itself and in holding and developing increased public support. All U. S. officers should conduct themselves with this objective in view.

    4. The President expects that all senior officers of the Government will move energetically to insure the full unity of support for established U. S. policy in South Vietnam. Both in Washington and in the field, it is essential that the Government be unified. It is of particular importance that express or implied criticism of officers of other branches be scrupulously avoided in all contacts with the Vietnamese Government and with the press. More specifically, the

~~TOP SECRET~~   (page 1 of 3 pages)

TOP SECRET   November 26, 1963

President approves the following lines of action developed in the discussions of the Honolulu meeting of November 20. The offices of the Government to which central responsibility is assigned are indicated in each case.

5. We should concentrate our own efforts, and insofar as possible we should persuade the Government of South Vietnam to concentrate its efforts, on the critical situation in the Mekong Delta. This concentration should include not only military but political, economic, social, educational and informational effort. We should seek to turn the tide not only of battle but of belief, and we should seek to increase not only the control of hamlets but the productivity of this area, especially where the proceeds can be held for the advantage of anti-Communist forces.

(Action: The whole country team under the direct supervision of the Ambassador.)

6. Programs of military and economic assistance should be maintained at such levels that their magnitude and effectiveness in the eyes of the Vietnamese Government do not fall below the levels sustained by the United States in the time of the Diem Government. This does not exclude arrangements for economy on the MAP account with respect to accounting for ammunition, or any other readjustments which are possible as between MAP and other U. S. defense resources. Special attention should be given to the expansion of the import, distribution, and effective use of fertilizer for the Delta.

(Action: AID and DOD as appropriate.)

7. Planning should include different levels of possible increased activity, and in each instance there should be estimates of such factors as:

    A. Resulting damage to North Vietnam;
    B. The plausibility of denial;
    C. Possible North Vietnamese retaliation;
    D. Other international reaction.

Plans should be submitted promptly for approval by higher authority.

(Action: State, DOD, and CIA.)

8. With respect to Laos, a plan should be developed and submitted for approval by higher authority for military operations up to a

~~TOP SECRET~~ November 26, 1963

line up to 50 kilometers inside Laos, together with political plans for minimizing the international hazards of such an enterprise. Since it is agreed that operational responsibility for such undertakings should pass from CAS to MACV, this plan should include a redefined method of political guidance for such operations, since their timing and character can have an intimate relation to the fluctuating situation in Laos.

(Action: State, DOD, and CIA.)

9. It was agreed in Honolulu that the situation in Cambodia is of the first importance for South Vietnam, and it is therefore urgent that we should lose no opportunity to exercise a favorable influence upon that country. In particular a plan should be developed using all available evidence and methods of persuasion for showing the Cambodians that the recent charges against us are groundless.

(Action: State.)

10. In connection with paragraphs 7 and 8 above, it is desired that we should develop as strong and persuasive a case as possible to demonstrate to the world the degree to which the Viet Cong is controlled, sustained and supplied from Hanoi, through Laos and other channels. In short, we need a more contemporary version of the Jordan Report, as powerful and complete as possible.

(Action: Department of State with other agencies as necessary.)

McGeorge Bundy

cc:
Mr. Bundy
Mr. Forrestal
Mr. Johnson
NSC Files

DECLASSIFIED
Authority NSC memo 5/23/78
By MIE/LAJ, NARS, Date 9/16/83

(True copy. Retyped for clarity. Jr)

Appendix D

Text of an Address by President Lyndon B. Johnson on Viet-Nam, as Prepared for Delivery at Johns Hopkins University, Baltimore, Maryland, April 7, 1965

Source: Author's file of handout at USAF course

U.S. INFORMATION SERVICE
PRESS BRANCH

SPECIAL REPORT

特報ニュース

TEXT OF AN ADDRESS BY PRESIDENT LYNDON B. JOHNSON ON VIET-NAM
AS PREPARED FOR DELIVERY AT JOHNS HOPKINS UNIVERSITY BALTIMORE, MARYLAND, APRIL 7, 1965

My fellow Americans:

Last week 17 nations sent their views to some dozen countries having interest in Southeast Asia. We are joining these 17 countries in stating our American policy which we believe will contribute toward peace in this area.

Tonight I want to review once again with my own people the views of your Government.

Tonight Americans and Asians are dying for a world where each people may choose its own path to change.

This is the principle for which our ancestors fought in the valleys of Pennsylvania. It is the principle for which our sons fight in the jungles of Viet-Nam.

Viet-Nam is far from this quiet campus. We have no territory there, nor do we seek any. The war is dirty and brutal and difficult. And some 400 young men -- born into an America bursting with opportunity and promise -- have ended their lives on Viet-Nam's steaming soil.

Why must we take this painful road?

Why must this nation hazard its ease, its interest, and its power for the sake of a people so far away?

We fight because we must fight if we are to live in a world where every country can shape its own destiny. And only in such a world will our own freedom be finally secure.

This kind of a world will never be built by bombs and bullets. Yet the infirmities of man are such that force must often precede reason -- and the waste of war, the works of peace.

We wish this were not so. But we must deal with the world as it is, if it is ever to be as we wish.

The Nature of the Conflict

The world as it is in Asia is not a serene or peaceful place.

The first reality is that North Viet-Nam has attacked the independent nation of South Viet-Nam. Its object is total conquest.

Of course, some of the people of South Viet-Nam are participating in attack on their own government. But trained men and supplies, orders and arms, flow in a constant stream from north to south.

This support is the heartbeat of the war.

And it is a war of unparalleled brutality. Simple farmers are the targets of assassination and kidnapping. Women and children are strangled in the night because their men are loyal to the government. Small and helpless villages are ravaged by sneak attacks. Large-scale raids are conducted on towns, and terror strikes in the heart of cities.

The confused nature of this conflict cannot mask the fact that it is the new face of an old enemy. It is an attack by one country upon another. And the object of that attack is a friend to which we are pledged.

Over this war -- and all Asia -- is another reality: the deepening shadow of Communist China. The rulers in Hanoi are urged on by Peiping. This is a regime which has destroyed freedom in Tibet, attacked India, and been condemned by the United Nations for aggression in Korea. It is a nation which is helping the forces of violence in almost every continent. The contest in Viet-Nam is part of a wider pattern of aggressive purpose.

Why Are We in Viet-Nam

Why are these realities our concern? Why are we in South Viet-Nam?

We are there because we have a promise to keep. Since 1954 every American President has offered support to the people of South Viet-Nam. We have helped to build, and we have helped to defend. Thus, over many years, we have made a national pledge to help South Viet-Nam defend its independence.

I intend to keep our promise.

To dishonor that pledge -- to abandon this small and brave nation to its enemy -- and to the terror that must follow -- would be an unforgivable wrong.

We are also there to strengthen world order. Around the globe -- from Berlin to Thailand -- are people whose well-being rests, in part, on the belief they can count on us if they are attacked. To leave Viet-Nam to its fate would shake the confidence of all these people in the value of American commitment. The result would be increased unrest and instability, or even war.

We are also there because there are great stakes in the balance. Let no one think that retreat from Viet-Nam would bring an end to conflict. The battle would be renewed in one country and then another. The central lesson of our time is that the appetite of aggression is never satisfied. To withdraw from one battlefield means only to prepare for the next. We must say in Southeast Asia -- as we did in Europe -- in the words of the Bible: "Hitherto shalt thou come, but no further."

There are those who say that all our effort there will be futile -- that China's power is such it is bound to dominate all Southeast Asia. But there is no end to that argument until all the nations of Asia are swallowed up.

There are those who wonder why we have a responsibility there. We have it for the same reason we have a responsibility for the defense of freedom in Europe. World War II was fought in both Europe and Asia, and when it ended we found ourselves with continued responsibility for the defense of freedom.

Our Objective In Viet-Nam

Our objective is the independence of South Viet-Nam, and its freedom from attack. We want nothing for ourselves -- only that the people of South Viet-Nam be allowed to guide their own country in their own way.

We will do everything necessary to reach that objective. And we will do only what is necessary.

In recent months, attacks on South Viet-Nam were stepped up. Thus, it became necessary to increase our response and make attacks by air. This is not a change of purpose. It is a change in what we believe that purpose requires.

We do this in order to slow down aggression.

We do this to increase the confidence of the brave people of South Viet-Nam who have bravely borne this brutal battle for so many years and with so many casualties.

And we do this to convince the leaders of North Viet-Nam -- and all who seek to share their conquest -- of a simple fact:

We will not be defeated.

We will not grow tired.

We will not withdraw, either openly or under the cloak of a meaningless agreement.

We know that air attacks alone will not accomplish all these purposes. But it is our best and prayerful judgment that they are a necessary part of the surest road to peace.

We hope that peace will come swiftly. But that is in the hands of others besides ourselves. And we must be prepared for a long continued conflict. It will require patience as well as bravery -- the will to endure as well as the will to resist.

I wish it were possible to convince others with words of what we now find it necessary to say with guns and planes: armed hostility is futile -- our resources are equal to any challenge -- because we fight for values and a principle, rather than territory or colonies, our patience and determination are unending.

Once this is clear, then it should also be clear that the only path for reasonable man is the path of peaceful settlement.

Such peace demands an independent South Viet-Nam -- securely guaranteed and able to shape its own relationships to all others -- free from outside interference -- tied to no alliance -- a military base for no other country.

These are the essentials of any final settlement.

We will never be second in the search for such a peaceful settlement in Viet-Nam.

There may be many ways to this kind of peace: in discussion or negotiation with the governments concerned; in large groups or in small ones; in the reaffirmation of old agreements or their strengthening with new ones.

We have stated this position over and over again 50 times - and more - to friend and foe alike. And we remain ready -- with this purpose -- for unconditional discussions.

And until that bright and necessary day of peace we will try to keep conflict from spreading. We have no desire to see thousands die in battle -- Asians or Americans. We have no desire to devastate that which the people of North Viet-Nam have built with toil and sacrifice. We will use our power with restraint and with all the wisdom we can command.

But we will use it.

This war, like most wars, is filled with terrible irony. For what do the people of North Viet-Nam want? They want what their neighbors also desire: food for their hunger -- health for their bodies and a chance to learn -- progress for their country, and an end to the bondage of material misery. And they would find all these things far more readily in peaceful association with others than in the endless course of battle.

These countries of Southeast Asia are homes for millions of impoverished people. Each day these people rise at dawn and struggle through weary hours to wrestle existence from the soil. They are often wracked by disease, plagued by hunger, and death comes early, at the age of 40.

Stability and peace do not come easily in such a land. Neither independence nor human dignity will be won by arms alone. It also requires the works of peace.

The American people have helped generously in these works.

Now there must be a much more massive effort to improve the life of man in the conflict-torn corner of the world.

A Cooperative Effort for Development

The first step is for the countries of Southeast Asia to associate themselves in a greatly expanded cooperative effort for development. We would hope that North Viet-Nam will take its place in the common effort just as soon as peaceful cooperation is possible.

The United Nations is already actively engaged in development in this area. I would hope that the Secretary General of the United Nations could use the prestige of his great office -- and his deep knowledge of Asia -- to initiate, as soon as possible, with the countries of the area, a plan for cooperation in increased development.

For our part I will ask the Congress to join in a billion dollar American investment in this effort when it is under way.

And I hope all other industrialized countries -- including the Soviet Union -- will join in this effort to replace despair with hope, and terror with progress.

The task is nothing less than to enrich the hopes and existence of more than a hundred million people. And there is much to be done.

The vast Mekong River can provide food and water and power on a scale to dwarf even our own TVA.

The wonders of modern medicine can be spread through villages where thousands die for lack of care.

Schools can be established to train people in the skills needed to manage the process of development.

And these objectives, and more, are within the reach of a cooperative and determined effort.

I also intend to expand and speed up a program to make available our farm surplus to assist in feeding and clothing the needy in Asia. We should not allow people to go hungry and naked while our own warehouses overflow with an abundance of wheat and corn, rice and cotton.

I will very shortly name a special team of patriotic and distinguished Americans to inaugurate our participation in these programs. This team will be headed by Mr. Eugene Black, the very able former president of the World Bank.

In areas still ripped by conflict, development will not be easy. Peace will be necessary for final success. But we cannot wait for peace to begin the job.

The Dream of World Order

This will be a disorderly planet for a long time. In Asia, as elsewhere, the forces of the modern world are shaking old ways and uprooting ancient civilizations. There will be turbulence and struggle and even violence. Great social change -- as we see in our own country -- does not always come without conflict.

We must also expect that nations will on occasion be in dispute with us. It may be because we are rich, or powerful -- or because we have made mistakes -- or because they honestly fear our intentions. However, no nation need ever fear that we desire their land, or to impose our will, or to dictate their institutions.

But we will always oppose the effort of one nation to conquer another.

We will do this because our own security is at stake.

But there is more to it than that. For our generation has a dream. It is a very old dream. But we have the power and the opportunity to make it real.

For centuries nations have struggled among each other. But we dream of a world where disputes are settled by law and reason. And we will try to make it so.

For most of history men have hated and killed one another in battle. But we dream of an end to war. And we will try to make it so.

For all existence most men have lived in poverty, threatened by hunger. But we dream of a world where all are fed and charged with hope. And we will help to make it so.

Possibilities of Peace

The ordinary men and women of North Viet-Nam and South Viet-Nam -- of China and India -- or Russia and America -- are brave people. They are filled with the same proportions of hate and fear, of love and hope. Most of them want the same things for themselves and their families. Most of them do not want their sons to die in battle, or see the homes of others destroyed.

This can be their world yet. Man now has the knowledge -- always before denied -- to make this planet serve the real needs of the people who live on it.

I know this will not be easy. I know how difficult it is for reason to guide passion, and love to master hate. The complexities of this world do not bow easily to pure and consistent answers.

But the simple truths are there just the same. We must all try to follow them as best we can.

We often say how impressive power is. But I do not find it impressive. The guns and bombs, the rockets and warships, are all symbols of human failure. They are necessary symbols. They protect what we cherish. But they are witness to human folly.

A dam built across a great river is impressive.

In the countryside where I was born, I have seen the night illuminated, the kitchens warmed and the homes heated, where once the cheerless night and the ceaseless cold held sway. And all this happened because electricity came to our town along the humming wires of the rural electrification administration. Electrification of the countryside is impressive.

A rich harvest in a hungry land is impressive.

The sight of healthy children in a classroom is impressive.

These -- not mighty arms -- are the achievements which the American nation believes to be impressive.

And -- if we are steadfast -- the time may come when all other nations will also find it so.

We may well be living in the time foretold many years ago when it was said: "I call heaven and earth to record this day against you, that I have set before you life and death, blessing and cursing: therefore choose life, that both thou and thy seed may live."

- 10 -

This generation of the world must choose: destroy or build, kill or aid, hate or understand.

We can do all these things on a scale never dreamed of before.

We will choose life. And so doing we will prevail over the enemies within man, and over the natural enemies of all mankind.

***

Appendix E

Chronology of Second Tonkin Gulf Incident

Source: Office of the Assistant Secretary of Defense/ISA, Texas Tech University Archive

TONKIN GULF

Chronology of Second Tonkin Gulf Incident

Background

1. August 2 - We had earlier learned from an intelligence source of North Vietnamese plans to attack the Maddox. In accordance with those plans the attack was carried out in daylight. The attacking craft were clearly seen and were photographed. The launching of torpedoes and the torpedo wakes were observed. Machinegun fire from the attackers was observed, and one bullet was recovered. After the engagement Maddox was joined by the USS Turner Joy.

2. August 3 - 1900 (approx.) Tonkin Gulf time - Task Group Commander aboard Maddox reported to the Commander of the 7th Fleet as follows:

> "(a) Evaluation of info from various sources indicates that the DRV (Democratic Republic of Vietnam) considers patrol directly involved with 34A operations. DRV considers US ships present as enemies because of these operations and have already indicated readiness to treat us in that category. (b) DRV are very sensitive about Hon Me. Believes this is PT operating base and the cove there presently contains numerous patrol and PT craft which have been repositioned from northerly bases."

3. August 3 - At the direction of the President, a note of protest was sent to Hanoi. It concluded: "The US Government expects that the authorities of the regime in North Vietnam will be under no misapprehension as to the grave consequences which would inevitably result from any further unprovoked offensive military action against US forces."

4. August 4 - time unknown - CINCPAC sent a message saying that termination of the Desoto patrol after two days would be insufficient to demonstrate the US resolve "to assert out legitimate rights in these international waters." The message added:

"Accordingly, recommend following adjustments in remainder of patrol schedule. Provided paragraph T2, reference B in order to accommodate commander, US Military Assistance Commander in Vietnam. Request patrol ships remain north of latitude 19-10 north until 060600H--to avoid interference with 34A OPS. Four August patrol from points Delta to Charlie remaining north at 19-10 north."

"The above patrol will (a) clearly demonstrate our determination to continue these operations, (b) possibly draw NVM POMS (patrol boats) to northward away from the area of 34A operations, (c) eliminate De Soto patrol interference with 34A operations."

Second Incident - August 4

5. 2:30 a.m. EDT; 1430 Tonkin Gulf time - The Task Group Commander aboard the Maddox reported a suspected Red shadow 15 miles to the west and Skinhead radar on the same bearing.

6. 7:40 a.m. EDT; 1940 Tonkin Gulf time - Maddox and Turner Joy observed at least five contacts located about 36 miles northeast of the two destroyers.

7. Shortly after 9 a.m. EDT; 2100 Tonkin Gulf time - Maddox and Turner Joy held radar contacts approximately 14 miles to the east. These contacts were on course 160, speed 30 knots. At that time the two destroyers were approximately 60 miles from the North Vietnamese coast.

8. 9:20 a.m. EDT (approx.); 2120 Tonkin Gulf time - We received in Washington information from an intelligence source that North Vietnamese naval forces had been ordered to attack the patrol.

9. 9:39 a.m. EDT; 2139 Tonkin Gulf time - Maddox and Turner Joy opened fire on the approaching contacts when it became evident from their maneuvers that they were pressing in for attack positions. Range was about 6000 yards. Torpedo noises were then heard by the Maddox's sonar, and the destroyers took evasive action.

"A torpedo wake was then sighted passing abeam Turner Joy from aft to forward, approximately 300 feet to port on the same bearing as that reported by Maddox. This sighting was made by at least four of Turner Joy's topside personnel;" (McNamara testimony)

10. 10:24 EDT; 2224 Tonkin Gulf time -

"One target was taken under fire by Turner Joy. Numerous hits were observed on this target and it disappeared from all radars. The commanding officer and other Turner Joy personnel observed a thick column of black smoke from this target." (McNamara testimony)

11. 10:47 a.m. EDT; 2247 Tonkin Gulf time -
"Searchlight was observed by all signal bridge and maneuvering bridge personnel including the commanding officer of U.S.S. Turner Joy. The beam of the searchlight did not touch the ship, but was seen to swing in an arc toward Turner Joy and was immediately extinguished when aircraft from the combat air patrol orbiting above the ships approached the vicinity of the searchlight." (McNamara testimony)

12. 11 a.m. EDT (approx.) - Washington was informed that the destroyers had reported they were under attack.

13. Noon and afternoon, EDT - In his testimony on February 20, 1968 Secretary McNamara reported the following consultation with Secretary Rusk:

"The matter was so urgent and so important that I asked the Secretary of State to join me at the Pentagon before lunch, on August 4, which he did. We met there for a considerable time with representatives of the Chiefs. I say representatives because the Chairman was not then present, being out of the city, and subsequently the Secretary of State and I met with the President at the White House, and on several occasions during the day the Secretary of State and I directly or indirectly discussed our views with the President--indirectly only in the sense that we may have been on two telephones at the same time with the President."

14. Early afternoon EDT - National Security Council met. In his February 20, 1968 statement Secretary McNamara reported:

> "Shortly thereafter, having received the advice of the Joint Chiefs of Staff, we recommended to the President, and he approved, a response consisting of an air strike on the PT and Swatow boat bases and their associated facilities. During all of this time, the message reports of the engagement from the ships, plus other information of a very highly classified nature received during the attack, were being reviewed to eliminate any doubt that an attack on the destroyers in fact occurred."

15. 1:27 p.m. EDT; 0127 on August 5, Tonkin Gulf time - Commander of Task Group aboard <u>Maddox</u> reported:

> "Review of action makes many recorded contacts and torpedoes fired appear doubtful. Freak weather effects and over-eager sonarman may have accounted for many reports. No actual visual sightings by <u>Maddox</u>. Suggest complete evaluation before any further action."

16. Shortly thereafter - exact time unspecified - Secretary McNamara discussed the preceding message with CINCPAC by telephone and said:

> "We obviously don't want to carry out the retaliatory strike unless we are damned sure what happened."

17. 2:45 p.m. EDT (approx.); 0245 August 5 Tonkin Gulf time - Commander of Task Group aboard <u>Maddox</u> reported to CINCPAC that he was certain that "the original ambush was bona fide." (Quotation is from McNamara testimony of February 20, p. 58)

18. 5:23 p.m. EDT - CINCPAC called McNamara and stated that he was convinced the attack had occurred.

19. 6:07 p.m. EDT - CINCPAC called again and reiterated that he was fully assured that the attack took place. Secretary McNamara at that time authorized release of the execute order.

(True copy. Retyped for clarity. Jr)

Appendix F

"President's Message to Congress,
5 August 1964," Department of State
Bulletin, 24 August 1964, p. 261

Source: U.S. Department of Defense Pentagon Papers,
House of Representatives Edition

DOCUMENT FROM U.S. DEPARTMENT OF DEFENSE PENTAGON PAPERS
U.S. HOUSE OF REPRESENTATIVES EDITION
(Document declassified September 20, 1971)

<u>"President's Message to Congress, 5 August 1964," Department of State Bulletin, 24 August 1964, p. 261</u>:

* * *

"These latest actions of the North Vietnamese regime have given a new and grave turn to the already serious situation in Southeast Asia. Our commitments in that area are well known to the Congress. They were first made in 1954 by President Eisenhower. They were further defined in the Southeast Asia Collective Defense Treaty approved by the Senate in February 1955.

"This treaty with its accompanying protocol obligates the United States and other members to act in accordance with their constitutional processes to meet communist aggression against any of the parties or protocol states.

"Our policy in Southeast Asia has been consistent and unchanged since 1954. I summarized it on June 2 in four simple propositions:

"1. <u>America keeps her word</u>. Here as elsewhere, we must and shall honor our commitments.

"2. <u>The issue is the future of Southeast Asia as a whole</u>. A threat to any nation in that region is a threat to all, and a threat to us.

"3. <u>Our purpose is peace</u>. We have no military, political, or territorial ambitions in the area.

"4. <u>This is not just a jungle war, but a struggle for freedom on every front of human activity.</u> Our military and economic assistance to South Vietnam and Laos in particular has the purpose of helping these countries to repel aggression and strengthen their independence.

"The threat to the free nations of Southeast Asia has long been clear. The North Vietnamese regime has constantly sought to take over South Vietnam and Laos. This communist regime has violated the Geneva accords for Vietnam. It has systematically conducted a campaign of subversion, which includes the direction, training, and supply of personnel and arms for the conduct of guerrilla warfare in

South Vietnamese territory. In Laos, the North Vietnamese regime has maintained military forces, used Laotian territory for infiltration into South Vietnam, and most recently carried out combat operations -- all in direct violation of the Geneva agreements of 1962.

"In recent months, the actions of the North Vietnamese regime have become steadily more threatening. In May, following new acts of communist aggression in Laos, the United States undertook reconnaissance flights over Laotian territory, at the request of the Government of Laos. These flights had the essential mission of determining the situation in territory where communist forces were preventing inspection by the International Control Commission. When the communists attacked these aircraft, I responded by furnishing escort fighters with instructions to fire when fired upon. Thus, these latest North Vietnamese attacks on our naval vessels are not the first direct attack on armed forces of the United States.

"As President of the United States I have concluded that I should now ask the Congress, on its part, to join in affirming the national determination that all such attacks will be met, and that the United States will continue in its basic policy of assisting the free nations of the area to defend their freedom.

"As I have repeatedly made clear, the United States intends no rashness, and seeks no wider war. We must make it clear to all that the United States is united in its determination to bring about the end of communist subversion and aggression in the area. We seek the full and effective restoration of the international agreements signed in Geneva in 1954, with respect to South Vietnam, and again in Geneva in 1962, with respect to Laos."

* * *

(True copy. Retyped for clarity. Jr)

Appendix G

Gulf of Tonkin Resolution

Source: Texas Tech University Vietnam Archive

GULF OF TONKIN RESOLUTION
CONGRESSIONAL RESOLUTION

8/64

August 10, 1964

SOUTHEAST ASIA RESOLUTION[1]

Whereas naval units of the Communist regime in Vietnam, in violation of the principles of the Charter of the United Nations and of international law, have deliberately and repeatedly attacked United States naval vessels lawfully present in international waters, and have thereby created a serious threat to international peace; and

Whereas these attacks are part of a deliberate and systematic campaign of aggression that the Communist regime in North Vietnam has been waging against its neighbors and the nations joined with them in the collective defense of their freedom; and

Whereas the United States is assisting the peoples of southeast Asia to protect their freedom and has no territorial, military or political ambitions in that area, but desires only that these peoples should be left in peace to work out their own destinies in their own way: Now, therefore, be it

Resolved by the Senate and House of Representatives of the United States of America in Congress assembled, That the Congress approves and supports the determination of the President, as Commander in Chief, to take all necessary measures to repel any armed attack against the forces of the United States and to prevent further aggression.

SEC. 2. The United States regards as vital to its national interest and to world peace the maintenance of international peace and security in southeast Asia. Consonant with the Constitution of the United States and the Charter of the United Nations and in accordance with its obligations under the Southeast Asia Collective Defense Treaty, the United States is, therefore, prepared, as the President determines, to take all necessary steps, including the use of armed force, to assist any member or protocol state of the Southeast Asia Collective Defense Treaty requesting assistance in defense of its freedom.

SEC 3. This resolution shall expire when the President shall determine that the peace and security of the area is reasonably assured by international conditions created by action of the United Nations or otherwise, except that it may be terminated earlier by concurrent resolution of the Congress.

---

[1] Text of Public Law §3049S [H.J. Res. 1145]. 78 Stat. 384, approved Aug. 10, 1964.

Statement made

By President Johnson on the occasion of signing that joint resolution:

To any armed attacked upon our forces, we shall reply.

To any in Southeast Asia who ask our help in defending their freedom, we shall give it.

In that region, there is nothing we covet, nothing we seek–no territory, no military position, no political ambition. Our one desire–our one determination–is that the people of Southeast Asia be left in peace to work out their own destinies in their own way.

Appendix H

State Department White Paper, February 27, 1965

Source: Texas Tech University Vietnam Archive

"AGGRESION FROM THE NORTH":
STATE DEPARTMENT WHITE PAPER ON VIETNAM
February 27, 1965
(Department of State Bulletin, March 22, 1965)

South Vietnam is fighting for its life against a brutal campaign of terror and armed attack inspired, directed, supplied, and controlled by the Communist regime in Hanoi. This flagrant aggression has been going on for years, but recently the pace has quickened and the threat has now become acute.

The war in Vietnam is a new kind of war, a fact as yet poorly understood in most parts of the world. Much of the confusion that prevails in the thinking of many people, and even governments, stems from this basic misunderstanding. For in Vietnam a totally new brand of aggression has been loosed against an independent people who want to make their way in peace and freedom.

Vietnam is not another Greece, where indigenous guerrilla forces used friendly neighboring territory as a sanctuary.

Vietnam is not another Malaya, where Communist guerrillas were, for the most part, physically distinguishable from the peaceful majority they sought to control.

Vietnam is not another Philippines, where Communist guerrillas were physically separated from the source of their moral and physical support.

Above all, the war in Vietnam is not a spontaneous and local rebellion against the established government.

There are elements in the Communist program of conquest directed against South Vietnam common to each of the previous areas of aggression and subversion. But there is one fundamental difference. In Vietnam a Communist government has set out deliberately to conquer a sovereign people in a neighboring state. And to achieve its end, it has used every resource of its own government to carry out its carefully planned program of concealed aggression. North Vietnam's commitment to seize control of the South is no less total than was the commitment of the regime in North Korea in 1950. But knowing the consequences of the latter's undisguised attack, the planners in Hanoi have tried desperately to conceal their hand. They have failed and their aggression is as real as that of an invading army.

This report is a summary of the massive evidence of North Vietnamese aggression obtained by the Government of South Vietnam. This evidence has been jointly analyzed by South Vietnamese and American experts.

The evidence shows that the hard core of the Communist forces attacking South Vietnam were trained in the North and ordered into the South by Hanoi. It shows that the key leadership of the Vietcong (VC), the officers and much of the cadre, many of the technicians, political organizers, and propagandists have come from the North and operate under Hanoi's direction. It shows that the training of essential military personnel and their infiltration into the South is directed by the Military High Command in Hanoi. In recent months new types of weapons have been introduced in the VC army, for which all ammunition must come from outside sources. Communist China and other Communist states have been the prime suppliers of these weapons and ammunition, and they have been channeled primarily through North Vietnam.

The directing force behind the effort to conqueror South Vietnam is the Communist Party in the North, the Lao Dong (Workers) Party. As in every Communist state. the party is an integral part of the regime itself. North Vietnamese officials have expressed their firm determination to absorb South Vietnam into the Communist world.

Through its Central Committee, which controls the Government of the North, the Lao Dong Party directs the total political and military effort of the Vietcong. The Military High Command in the North trains the military men and sends them into South Vietnam. The Central Research Agency, North Vietnam's central intelligence organization, directs the elaborate espionage and subversion effort...

Under Hanoi's overall direction the Communists have established an extensive machine for carrying on the war within South Vietnam. The focal point is the Central Office for South Vietnam with its political and military subsections and other specialized agencies. A subordinate part of this Central Office is the liberation Front for South Vietnam. The front was formed at Hanoi's order in 1960. Its principle function is to influence opinion abroad and to create the false impression that the aggression in South Vietnam is an indigenous rebellion against the established Government.

For more than 10 years the people and the Government of South Vietnam, exercising the inherent right of self-defense, have fought back against these efforts to extend Communist power south across the 17th parallel. The United States has responded to the appeals of the Government of the Republic of Vietnam for help in this defense of the freedom and independence of its land and its people.

In 1961 the Department of State issued a report called A Threat to the Peace. It described North Vietnam's program to seize South Vietnam. The evidence in that report had been presented by the Government of the Republic of Vietnam to the International Control Commission (ICC). A special report by the ICC in June 1962 upheld the validity of that evidence. The Commission held that there was "sufficient evidence to show beyond reasonable doubt" that North Vietnam had sent arms and men into South Vietnam to carry out subversion with the aim of overthrowing the legal Government there. The ICC found the authorities in Hanoi in specific violation of four provisions of the Geneva Accords of 1954.

Since then, new and even more impressive evidence of Hanoi's aggression has accumulated. The Government of the United States believes that evidence should be presented to its own citizens and to the world. It is important for free men to know what has been happening in Vietnam, and how, and why. That is the purpose of this report...

The record is conclusive. It establishes beyond question that North Vietnam is carrying out a carefully conceived plan of aggression against the South. It shows that North Vietnam has intensified its efforts in the years since it was condemned by the International Control Commission. It proves that Hanoi continues to press its systematic program of armed aggression into South Vietnam. This aggression violates the United Nations Charter. It is directly contrary to the Geneva Accords of 1954 and of 1962 to which North Vietnam is a party. It is a fundamental threat to the freedom and security of South Vietnam.

The people of South Vietnam have chosen to resist this threat. At their request, the United States has taken its place beside them in their defensive struggle.

The United States seeks no territory, no military bases, no favored position. But we have learned the meaning of aggression elsewhere in the post-war world, and we have met it.

If peace can be restored in South Vietnam, the United States will be ready at once to reduce its military involvement. But it will not abandon friends who want to remain free. It will do what must be done to help them. The choice now between peace and continued and increasingly destructive conflict is one for the authorities in Hanoi to make.

Appendix I

Statement by Secretary of Defense Robert S. McNamara

Source: Author's File. Handout at USAF Staff Course

STATEMENT BY SECRETARY OF DEFENSE ROBERT S. MCNAMARA BEFORE THE SENATE FOREIGN RELATIONS COMMITTEE MARCH 3, 1966 AS REGARDS U. S. INVOLVEMENT IN SOUTH VIETNAM

Before responding to your questions, I should like to address myself to the ten major issues within my own area of competence as they have emerged in your deliberations over the past few weeks. Those ten issues are:

1. What is the true nature of the conflict in South Vietnam?

2. How long will the war last, and what reason do we have to believe that we can win?

3. How many more American troops will be required?

4. Shouldn't we limit our troop commitment to the present level and adopt the "enclave" strategy?

5. Why are we not using our full air and sea power to bomb the Hanoi regime into submission?

6. Are our troops in South Vietnam handicapped by shortages of equipment?

7. Are we not facing in Vietnam an unlimited, open-ended military commitment to a major land war in Asia?

8. Are we not facing an increasing risk of war with China?

9. Do not our political commitments in Southeast Asia and elsewhere exceed our economic ability to support them?

10. Has not the United States become stretched so thin militarily by our operations in Southeast Asia that we are not prepared to support our commitments elsewhere in the world?

The first issue, Mr. Chairman: What is the true nature of the conflict in South Vietnam?

Some, pointing to the fact that a numerical majority of the communist military personnel are from the South itself, have inferred that the war is a civil war, an "internal affair," in which the United States therefore should not be involved.

Any such conclusion is wholly unwarranted.

Indeed, it is belied by all we know and have learned about the nature of the war -- its origins, its development and its conduct -- over the years down to the present. Of course, many Viet Cong troops -- especially low-ranking troops and irregulars -- are from South Vietnam. But that fact reveals only one scrap of a much larger and quite different story. The controlling fact -- from which all else flows -- is that the North Vietnamese regime has, almost from the time the Geneva Accords of 1954 were signed, undertaken to do all that would be necessary to achieve a single aim: to overthrow the government of South Vietnam.

Immediately after 1954, pursuant to the opportunity provided by the accords for people to choose their side of the 17th parallel, 90,000 people moved North to communism while 900,000 trekked South to escape it. At that time, in direct violation of the accords, North Vietnam's communist party, which is for all practical purposes its government as well, directed thousands of militarily-trained leadership cadre to remain in South Vietnam. These troops were told to hide their weapons and supplies and to work against the fledgling government of South Vietnam. North Vietnam hoped that the new government in the South could be weakened and overthrown from within by propaganda, dissidence and subversion short of military force.

When it became clear in the late 1950's however, that South Vietnam could and would develop as a viable political and economic entity -- indeed, that South Vietnam was outpacing North Vietnam in economic improvements and in advances in health and education -- Hanoi directed its agents in the South to begin a program of terror and sabotage designed to destroy the developing allegiance of the people of South Vietnam to their government. Hanoi's "War of National Liberation" began.

The basic tactics of the approach are simple:

The approach aims, at first, not at destroying armies or winning territory. Rather it aims at cutting the tendons of the existing government and at exhausting the patience of the population. The tendons of a government are its ability to carry out economic and educational programs, to collect taxes, to raise military manpower and to develop a national spirit of unity and progress. Physical security is fundamental to the achievement of these things. Hanoi's first objective, therefore, has been to deny the government of South Vietnam the ability to provide that physical security.

Starting in the countryside, where law enforcement is weakest and slowest, there are assassinations and kidnappings. By focusing on local officials, the terrorists get triple returns: they demonstrate the government's inability to protect those who serve it, they destroy the government's official contact with the population, and they dramatize their own ruthlessness and total commitment -- a lesson that is not lost on those from whom they themselves demand service or taxes or information or silence.

As reports of their deeds spread, the guerrillas are able to use local agents relatively openly -- not unlike "protection racket" gangsters in United States cities in the 1920's -- to collect funds, to recruit, to propagandize, to inform on government activities. Thus a "shadow" administrative, political arms of the insurgency evolves, protected and supported by strong-arm guerrillas.

This is the process that Hanoi called down on the South. And, accidentally, it is the process we now see beginning in Thailand.

In South Vietnam, terrorism began in earnest in mid-1957 and grew steadily thereafter. In 1960, communist terrorists assassinated or kidnapped over 2,000 local officials and civilians. In 1965, an average of 20 civic officials were assassinated and 27 were kidnapped each month. And, aside from civic officials, 1665 South Vietnamese civilians were murdered and 10,275 were kidnapped in 1965. In terms of U.S. population, this is equivalent to 150,000 Americans murdered or kidnapped.

For nine years this intimidation and bleeding of the government structure in South Vietnam has gone on. It still goes on, selective and brutal as ever.

Statistics alone cannot convey the full meaning of this process. Thousands of pictures provide dramatic evidence of the communist technique aimed at destroying local administration, transportation and cooperation in the countryside.

The Viet Cong strike and run, usually at night. They assassinate a hamlet chief, overloading the police and making good administrators hard to recruit. They bomb a restaurant, causing all public places to be searched and protected. They sabotage one railroad bridge, forcing the government to guard them all. The government must tie down troops and police defending the most important people and facilities, and it must have quick-reaction forces in regional reserves, if it is to limit the guerrillas to hit-and-run attacks. Furthermore, to seek out and destroy and enemy who has no responsibilities to defend people or territory and thus can choose to evade battle, the government must invest great efforts in searching and encircling operations.

In such a conflict, a small, disciplined and determined guerrilla force can terrorize a nation. But depending on such tactics alone, the Viet Cong were losing in South Vietnam.

Realizing this, North Vietnam in 1960 undertook two new important programs that came to dominate the second chapter in its program of aggression against South Vietnam. First, Hanoi began to infiltrate into the South thousands of trained and expert military and other leadership personnel, drawing first on many of the 90,000 southerners who had fought against the French and had been ordered to North Vietnam by the communist leadership in 1954. In the intervening years, these men had been instructed and seasoned in the techniques of terror and guerrilla warfare. It is they who led the Viet Cong in the early 1960's as the war in South Vietnam was progressively enlarged by the communists. By the end of 1963 -- the end of North Vietnam's second chapter -- more than 36,000 infiltrators had entered South Vietnam from the North.

Second, in September 1960 North Vietnam's communist party directed the formation in the South of a "front organization" that would remain under the party's control but be used to draw together any political groupings in South Vietnam that would oppose the government there. Here lies the origin of the so-called National Liberation Front, the shadow organization that has no geographical seat and has never attracted a sole South Vietnamese national political group of stature. The true nature of the front is evidenced by a North Vietnamese document found on the body of a communist soldier as long ago as August 1961. Let me quote it:

"In implementation of the decision of the third congress of the Lao Dong party (the North Vietnamese communist party), the N. F. L. S. V. (the Front) was set up to unify the revolutionary struggle, to overthrow the U. S. - Diem regime, to establish a popular government of democratic union and bring about the peaceful reunification of the country. The revolution for the liberation of the South would never succeed if the party (i. e., the Lao Dong party) were not directing it."

But Hanoi's military program of infiltration and its political program resting on the National Liberation Front were not enough to achieve the overthrow of South Vietnam's government. North Vietnam apparently concluded during the winter of 1963 that the infiltration of former Southerners for the Viet Cong forces would not deliver the prize it sought. We now have persuasive evidence, in part from extensive interrogations of North Vietnamese soldiers captured in South Vietnam, that during the winter of 1963 and spring of 1964 Hanoi embarked on a major program to increase infiltration, including infiltration of regular units of the North Vietnamese army into South Vietnam through the Laos infiltration trails that had been used as early as 1960. Captured North Vietnamese military personnel repeatedly have declared that they began their infiltration and guerrilla warfare training in North Vietnam -- many were trained at the large Xuan Mai center near Hanoi -- during the spring of 1964 and that they began infiltrating through Laos into South Vietnam in the Summer of 1964. Regular combat units of the North Vietnamese 325th Division appeared in the South in the Fall of 1964. Lieutenant General Thai, former assistant chief of the North Vietnamese Joint General Staff, infiltrated in early 1964, and reportedly is the current commander of the Viet Cong armed forces. North Vietnamese Lieutenant General Luong, who may be in charge of political affairs for the central office for South Vietnam -- the highest communist headquarters in the country -- is also a 1964 infiltrator. Infiltration from North Vietnam reached almost 45,000 by the end of 1964. This was before U. S. combat forces were deployed to Vietnam. Our best estimate of infiltration as of the end of 1965 is 63,000.

We know from a study of our aerial photography that, concurrently, North Vietnam was completing the construction of a string of infiltration staging and supply points within its own territory and in Laos.

Bai Duc Thon, an area in southern North Vietnam some 24 miles from Mu Gia pass at the Laos border, was one of these.

Bai Duc Thon area was but one of many new installations. It represented a significant North Vietnamese effort to support their expanded infiltration southward and to enlarge the heavy truck transport capability required to maintain their increasing commitment in the South.

On December 30, 1963, a convoy of 19 camouflaged trucks heading South was detected near the town of Ban Nafilang. The trucks were observed in an open section of the road and represented the first of many such convoys detected during the next 26-month period. A convoy of 33 cargo trucks again was detected at Ban Nafilang heading North on 15 March 1964. Repetitive photographic coverage of this type confirmed the presence of other such convoys along these motorable routes during 1964.

In the Mu Gia pass area a North Vietnamese military camp and convoy check point was located by low level photography on May 24, 1964. A convoy of 29 cargo trucks and escorting armored vehicles was noted at this convoy check point. One of the trucks carried a large number of 55-gallon drums for support.

There was no question that in 1963 and 1964, before U. S. combat troops were deployed to Vietnam, there was a greatly expanded North Vietnamese commitment to the South.

Throughout 1965 we observed the extension of motorable routes southward. Most recently, for example, our reconnaissance has documented the systematic expansion of motorable routes deep into southern Laos. Segments observed have been constructed to within 15 miles of the tri-border area of Cambodia-Laos-South Vietnam, and clearing operations for this new road extends to within five miles of the border.

In short, what emerges is a picture of an enormous effort by North Vietnam, beginning more than a year before American combat troops were in South Vietnam, to develop supply lines and to transport supplies through Laos to South Vietnam.

It is estimated that 80 percent of Viet Cong weapons requirements must have been supplied from the outside. They are now bringing in additional quantities of heavy (120mm) mortars and anti-aircraft weapons, and have continued to supply the new family of 7.62mm individual weapons to additional units. Increased intensity of anti-aircraft fire against our aircraft indicates infiltration of large quantities of 12.7mm (about 50 caliber) machine guns and ample ammunition.

We have here in Washington a two-ton display of weapons captured by the American 1st Cavalry Division at Ia Drang valley in November 1965. Along with the weapons, documents, medical supplies and items of personal clothing were captured.

All of this newly captured material is manufactured in Bloc countries; some small arms ammunition is produced in North Vietnam; none is produced in South Vietnam.

I repeat that, during most of the period I have referred to, the American presence in South Vietnam was confined to an advisory and support role and was quite limited in numbers. At the end of 1961, when Hanoi's infiltration program was well under way and when its military force in the South -- the Viet Cong -- had been conducting guerrilla warfare for several years, there were only about 800 American military personnel in South Vietnam. At the end of 1963 there were some 16,000, and at the end of 1964 some 23,000. Our combat force buildup began in the spring of 1965, when the evidence of the critical involvement of North Vietnam's army had begun to accumulate.

In the remainder of my statement, I would like briefly to address the remaining nine questions.

The second question is: How long will the war last, and what reason do we have to believe that we can win?

We must bear in mind that victory for us and for South Vietnam is a limited objective. We do not seek to destroy North Vietnam, or even to maintain a base in South Vietnam. We win if North Vietnam leaves South Vietnam alone.

As for how long the war will last, I would very much like to provide a specific response. But no answer framed in terms of years or months can have validity because so much will depend on North Vietnam's estimate of our own determination and of the determination of the people of South Vietnam to sustain the integrated military, political and economic programs that are essential for success. Should the leaders of North Vietnam conclude for reasons of which we are unaware that they wish to end the conflict, they could act promptly -- almost overnight. But Hanoi may well persevere in its plan to take over South Vietnam by force. Then the people of South Vietnam and their armed forces, together with our own troops and those of other free world allies, will have no alternative but to continue the effort in South Vietnam to destroy the main force units of the North Vietnamese army and of the Viet Cong, and to protect the villages and hamlets from terror, sabotage and guerrilla attack.

We believe that we can win in the sense I indicated. First, we have every basis for believing that the people and the leadership of South Vietnam want and intend to persevere in their own defense: they believe -- as we do -- in the justice of their defense against aggression from the North. Second, assisted by the United States and other free world allies, the South Vietnamese forces have the will and the capability to defeat the efforts of Hanoi and the Viet Cong. Our existing and planned American military and economic strength, both within South Vietnam and elsewhere is clearly sufficient to achieve the objectives I have described.

The third question: How many more American troops will be required?

Here, too, no specific authoritative response can be given. As I have already indicated, deployments of American and free world forces to defend South Vietnam have been in direct response to the step up in the military activity by Hanoi and by the Viet Cong -- to the increased threat the enemy forces have posed. Our deployments have also been affected by the changing capability of the South Vietnamese to develop and train additional manpower from time to time. In a sense, therefore, future American deployments will be influenced in important respects by factors not entirely within our control.

It should be observed that we believe there exists a ceiling-- an upper range -- above which the Viet Cong and North Vietnam cannot generate additional forces and cannot adequately supply their forces in South Vietnam.

A major objective of our combat operations in South Vietnam is to attrite their forces, and a major objective of our air interdiction efforts in North Vietnam is to reduce the capacity of the supply routes as much as we can without running disproportionate risks of escalating the war in Southeast Asia. We estimate that North Vietnam has the capability to generate and infiltrate up to 4,500 combat troops monthly and that the Viet Cong have the capability of pressing into service some 3,500 South Vietnamese monthly. If these capabilities are fully exercised and if enemy losses continue to mount as South Vietnamese and U. S. forces intensify their operations, there could be in South Vietnam by the end of 1966 some 155 Viet Cong and North Vietnamese battalions, approximately 50 percent above the December 31, 1965 level. We believe our improved air interdiction efforts would prevent them from receiving much more than that amount.

It will have been necessary to have countered this enemy buildup during 1966 with an increase in South Vietnamese, American and other free world forces. We estimate that some 70,000 South Vietnamese troops will be added by the end of 1966, making a total of about 670,000.

United States forces there now total about 215,000 men. I cannot say at this time precisely how many additional American forces will be deployed.

We are in a position to deploy new forces as quickly as they can be efficiently employed against the enemy forces. The FY 66 supplemental appropriation and the Department of Defense FY 67 budget now being considered by Congress would permit the support and deployment in South Vietnam of additional American military personnel by the end of the year should they be required.

Additional free world allied forces are also expected to be deployed.

Fourth: Shouldn't we limit our troop commitment to the present level and adopt the "enclave" strategy?

These are really two separate questions.

The first deals with holding our forces at a fixed level -- the present level of about 215,000 in South Vietnam. That limit would bear no reasoned relation to the foreseeable increase in enemy capabilities that I have already described. Should the North Vietnamese and the Viet Cong deploy added forces, as they are in the process of doing, it simply would not be prudent for us to stand idly by while their strength grows. Our existing forces would increasingly be placed in jeopardy; our logistics and support areas would be exposed to greater hazards; our ability to come to the assistance of hard-pressed South Vietnamese forces would be gradually weakened. In short, the entire allied and South Vietnamese basic strategy of staying ahead of the anticipated enemy force build-up would be undermined.

More importantly, perhaps, is the fact that we have been unable, with our deployments thus far, to persuade North Vietnam and the Viet Cong that the prudent course for them is to enter into negotiations looking toward a peaceful and honorable settlement of the war. I believe that our ability to persuade would decrease markedly as the enemy's forces in South Vietnam grew and our own remained static at an arbitrarily fixed level.

With respect to the wisdom of the enclave strategy, General Taylor has described to you the flaring drawbacks of that course of military action. I concur in his assessments.

An enclave strategy would compel us to use American forces almost exclusively as security troops in static, defensive positions in and around their base areas. We would thus sacrifice the greatest advantages -- mobility and firepower -- that our forces presently have over the Viet Cong and North Vietnamese main force units.

The broader, and probably more important, effects of such a strategy would be to isolate the people of South Vietnam increasingly from their government as we and the South Vietnamese withdrew into circumscribed and limited areas. Large parts of the countryside, and the people residing there, would be openly written off and turned over to the enduring control of the military forces of the enemy. Our forces and those of the government of South Vietnam in the meantime would not be spared from enemy attacks. It is doubtful whether our casualties would be any less than under our existing strategy of energetically seeking out the enemy regular and main force units. Ultimately, we would be threatened with the destruction of the morale of our own forces; almost certainly the morale of South Vietnam's forces and population would be undermined and the government destroyed.

Fifth: Why are we not using our full air and sea power to bomb the Hanoi regime into submission?

The answer, in its most forthright and simplest form, is that such use of our air and sea power would be at odds with the underlying objectives of our military commitment to defend South Vietnam against aggression.

Our military actions in South Vietnam are designed to defeat the Viet Cong and North Vietnamese forces in their attempt to subvert and take over by force the people and the government of South Vietnam. We strive, in short, to afford the people of South Vietnam the fullest opportunity to shape their own political destiny and to choose freely the type of society in which they wish to live. We do not seek the destruction or the overthrow of the Hanoi regime; we seek no territory from North Vietnam, nor indeed any bases in or military alliance with South Vietnam once peace is restored.

Our military efforts are therefore directed primarily to actions within South Vietnam, with the air effort against North Vietnam fashioned as appropriate to assist in achieving our objectives in the South. That air effort in the North is -- as it should be -- mainly an effort to interdict the lines of communication and military traffic. Anything beyond that, short of destruction of the North Vietnamese nation, is not likely to make a significant military difference so long as Hanoi believes that in South Vietnam the war can be won.

Bombing aimed at the destruction of the North Vietnamese nation would carry with it very significant risks of enlarging the war in Southeast Asia. We believe we can achieve our limited objective without incurring such risks.

Sixth: Are our troops in South Vietnam handicapped by shortages of equipment?

The answer is no.

We have during the last five years greatly strengthened our military establishment for precisely this kind of a contingency. Excluding the extraordinary requirements for the large-scale military operations in Southeast Asia reflected in the FY 66 supplemental and the FY 67 budget, we had already added some 50 billion dollars of expenditures to the pre-FY 1961 level.

In the Army, the number of combat maneuver battalions will have increased from 141 on June 30, 1961, to 192 on June 30, 1966. The number of army aviation companies (primarily helicopter units) will have more than doubled during the same period, from 70 to 161.

In the Navy, the number of general purpose forces ships will have increased from 781 on June 30, 1961, to 912 on June 30, 1966, and the Navy general purpose forces ship construction program has virtually doubled.

In the Air Force, the number of tactical fighter wings will have increased from 16 to 21, and the number of tactical reconnaissance squadrons from 14 to 17.

Procurement of the kinds of equipment and consumables required for non-nuclear war was vastly increased in the FY 1962-65 period as compared with the four preceding fiscal years.

Finally, our airlift capability to Southeast Asia will have just about tripled between June 1961 and June 1966.

It was these increases in our military strength that made possible the tremendous feat of deploying to Southeast Asia within a matter of months a combat ready force of 300,000 men some 10,000 miles away and supporting them in combat -- without calling up the reserve forces, without a general extension of tours on an involuntary basis, and without invoking the usual economic controls.

But the question still remains: Why, if we had acquired what we needed, do we now have to increase our procurement so substantially in order to support our military effort in Southeast Asia? The answer to this question has three parts.

First, we are increasing the size of our active forces because we do not wish at this time to call up the reserve forces. These new forces must be equipped and supplied.

Second, we do not normally provide idle inventories of such major weapon systems as aircraft and ships in advance for combat attrition. Rather, we find that we can get far greater total effectiveness for the resources invested by providing active combat-ready forces in peacetime of sufficient size to allow for attrition at the beginning of a war, and then relying on new production to offset continuing attrition.

Third, we provide in our war reserve stocks only those quantities of combat consumables needed to tide us over until additional stocks can be acquired from new production. As we start to consume significant quantities of war reserve stocks in combat, we start to procure replacement stocks.

This is not to say that every one of the tens of thousands of Defense Department supply points is without a single "inventory shortage." Anyone who has had experience with large supply systems knows that somewhere, sometime, something will be lacking. This is true of private industry as well as government, and it is up to management at all levels to see to it that mistakes are held to a minimum and corrected promptly when discovered.

The acid test of our logistics system is the ability of our forces to take the field and engage in combat, an ability that has been demonstrated in full measure during the last six months. No shortages have impeded our combat operations in Southeast Asia or affected the morale or welfare of our men. This fact has been attested to by General Westmoreland, our commander in South Vietnam, by Admiral Sharp, our commander in the Pacific, and by General Wheeler, Chairman of the Joint Chiefs of Staff.

Seventh: Are we not facing in Vietnam an unlimited, open-ended military commitment to a major land war in Asia?

Before commenting on the military aspects of the issue, I would like to note that our military operations in South Vietnam are facing us with no more of a threat to an open-ended major land war in Asia than was expressly recognized by this committee in its report on the proposed treaty at that time.

My answer to the question is that I do not believe that we are facing in Vietnam an unlimited, open-ended commitment to a major land war in Asia if we keep our objectives limited and persistently make clear to all concerned-- friend, foe and neutral alike -- that our objectives are limited.

The risk of a major land war in Asia would increase significantly if our military strategy in Vietnam were such as to threaten the destruction of the North Vietnamese regime or the occupation of its territory. As I have already stated, this is not in any sense an objective of the United States policy in South Vietnam. On the contrary, our policy is essentially defensive -- to protect South Vietnam from attack, from aggression that is supported, directed and guided by North Vietnam.

Moreover, the war can be considered a limited one in a strictly military sense as well. As I have sought to point out we estimate that there is an upper range or limit for the enemy forces in South Vietnam that can be generated and supported by North Vietnam and the Viet Cong in the face of our intensive efforts to pursue the enemy, to interdict the enemy's supply lines, to destroy their base areas and to prevent their consolidation of control over large areas of South Vietnam.

In conducting the war in Vietnam as we have, it has been one of our basic objectives to persuade Hanoi to cease its aggression without changing the limited character of the war -- with respect to both geography and the parties involved. We have been successful thus far in keeping the war limited while blunting the communist drive; we expect to be successful in the months to come.

Eight: Are we not facing an increasing risk of war with China?

Here too the answer is basically the same. We have done everything humanly possible -- both militarily and diplomatically -- to make it unmistakably clear that there is no justification for communist China to involve itself in the war in Vietnam. Just as our policy in Vietnam is bottomed upon a disavowal of any intention to destroy the Hanoi regime or to seize its territory, our policy rests equally -- if not more so -- upon a rejection of any actions against China.

The United States would have no quarrel with a China -- even a communist China -- that would not seek to control the lives and the destinies of the nations and peoples on its borders. We would have no quarrel with a China that would devote its enormous energies to the betterment of the livelihood of its own people.

But communist China today and in recent years has not been such a nation. It has sought instead to foment revolutions against established governments, not only in such border lands as Thailand and South Vietnam but in Africa and Latin America as well. And it has engaged in conventional war -- in direct aggression and threat of aggression -- against India, the Republic of China and the Republic of Korea.

Given this history of militant aggressive actions by communist China, it would be irresponsible for me to say that we run no risk of war with China arising from our efforts to defend South Vietnam from aggression. But the risk is not created by our operations in South Vietnam; it was created by our treaty commitments. All of us must recognize that the United States did not assume this risk yesterday -- or simply as a result of what we are doing today in South Vietnam. That risk was inherent in every treaty the United States signed with small and freedom-loving countries of Asia who strive to chart their own national ways even though they lie in communist China's shadow. Thus, our bilateral treaties with Korea, with the Republic of China and with Japan engage us in a risk of war with China. So do our commitments under the ANZUS and SEATO treaties -- in particular our obligations to Thailand which is threatened today by a growing insurgency sponsored jointly from communist China and from North Vietnam. None of these treaties involves one bit of aggressive intent on our part. If communist China fears them, she need not.

I assure you that no efforts have been spared -- and none will be spared-- in direct and in indirect diplomacy, in public and in private -- to communicate to the leaders of communist China that America's limited objectives in Vietnam pose no threat to them. Our words on this matter are loud, clear and sincere. We urge the leaders of China to listen and understand.

Ninth: Do not our political commitments in Southeast Asia and elsewhere exceed our economic ability to support them?

The answer to this question is no. The relevant facts and figures should allay this concern.

At no time since World War II, indeed never before in history, has the United States been in a better economic position to fulfill its commitments abroad. To take a comparable period by way of illustration, during the Korean War our annual military spending rose from 4 percent of the Gross national product to 14 percent. In FY 66 and FY 67, military expenditures will approximate 7.7 and 7.8 percent of gross national product and less than in any one of the five years 1960, 61, 62, 63 and 64. In order to approach the Korean War figure of 14 percent it would be necessary for us to spend an additional 44 and 46 billion dollars in FY 66 and FY 67.

Tenth: Has not the United States become stretched so thin militarily by our operations in Southeast Asia that we are not prepared to support our commitments elsewhere in the world?

The answer is no.

We have today a total active duty military strength approaching three million men. U. S. forces now in Southeast Asia represent only about ten percent of that strength. Moreover, the three million figure does not include the organized reserve of about one million men receiving regular paid drill training in the reserve components of the armed forces. Nor does it include the other trained reserves and the vast civilian manpower resources of our nation.

In contrast to past military buildups, no mobilization has been decreed, partial or otherwise, no reserve forces have been ordered to active duty and, with the exception of relatively small numbers of men in the Navy and Marine Corps, no involuntary extensions of active duty tours have been imposed. In this respect, the Southeast Asia effort is unique in our military history.

The decision not to request a call up of the reserve forces and an unlimited extension of active duty tours do demand some special effort and ingenuity on the part of our military leaders to build up our forces as rapidly as required. But the task can be accomplished, while at the same time preserving our ability to meet contingencies elsewhere in the world. In fact, it will enhance our ability to do so since we will be leaving our reserve forces intact and available to meet new emergencies. Indeed, we have undertaken a number of measures to increase the strength and readiness of those reserve forces.

Including the three new division forces which are being added to the active force, we will have a total of 22-1/3 active division forces -- 18-1/3 Army and four Marine Corps. In addition, we will have ten high priority division forces in the reserve components, one Marine Corps and nine Army -- with six divisions and supporting forces manned at 100 percent. Including both the active and reserve division forces, we have today a substantial "central reserve" of ground forces upon which we would be able to draw to meet contingencies anywhere in the world, and we will have more in the future. Simply by calling up the reserves and extending tours we could make ready for deployment over approximately the next three months a total of nine additional combat ready division forces.

With regard to tactical air power, we now have a total of about 4,700 aircraft, including both the active and reserve forces of the Air Force, Navy and Marine Corps. Only a fraction of these have been committed to Southeast Asia. In an emergency, we could deploy into combat 4,300 tactical fighter and attack aircraft within 90 days, in addition to those now in Southeast Asia, Korea and Europe.

The major increase in our production and logistics base, achieved during the last six to eight months, will enable us to support combat forces considerably larger than now deployed. The gearing up of this production base was financed from the 700 million dollar supplemental added to the FY 65 budget last spring and the 1.7 billion dollars added to the FY 66 budget last August. The higher levels of production thus made possible are financed in the FY 66 supplemental and the FY 67 budget transmitted to the Congress this January.

It is clear therefore that, far from overextending ourselves, we have actually strengthened our military position. Our active duty forces are being expanded, our reserve forces are being strengthened and made more combat ready, and our production and logistics base is being vastly increased -- all without calling up the reserve forces, generally extending involuntarily active duty tours of military personnel or imposing price, wage and material controls on our economy. The very fact that we have not taken these steps means that we still have great untapped resources upon which we can quickly call to meet any other major contingencies which may confront us in the future.

It is essential that this point be clearly understood by friend and foe alike so that there may be no miscalculation as to our capabilities to meet our commitments anywhere in the world and to safeguard our national security and other vital interests.

Mr. Chairman, I have made three basic points.

First: The war in Vietnam was not and is not a civil war. It is a case of aggression "modern style" which calls on us to honor our treaty commitment.

Second: We are applying our power with restraint to fulfill our commitment and to achieve but a limited objective.

Third: We have sufficient power to achieve the limited objective without impairing our ability to support our commitments elsewhere and without increasing the risks in Southeast Asia accepted when the treaty obligation was undertaken.

In closing, I wish to say that, although all of the questions I have sought to answer relate to our military posture, I have considered the economic, social and political problems confronting them. Everything we do militarily in South Vietnam looks towards the prospect of free elections in South Vietnam. Our government is prepared to have such elections as soon as they can be arranged and to abide by the results of such elections, whatever they may be. I believe it would be a fair restatement on our military objectives in South Vietnam to say that we seek the removal of the obstacles that North Vietnam is imposing by force to the conduct on free elections in South Vietnam.

Appendix J

CIA Memo: International Communist Aid to North Vietnam

Source: Texas Tech University Vietnam Archive

CENTRAL INTELLIGENCE AGENCY
2 March 1968

INTELLIGENCE MEMORANDUM

Approved for Release
Date 13 April 1992

International Communist Aid to North Vietnam

Summary

The USSR continues to provide the overwhelming share of the increasing amounts of military aid being provided to North Vietnam and is willing to sustain this commitment at present or even higher levels. [   ] aid deliveries will increase even further in 1968. [   ] there is no quantitative limit to the types of the assistance that the USSR would provide with the possible exception of offensive weapons that would result in a confrontation with the US. [   ] the USSR cannot refuse to provide aid if it wishes to maintain its position in the socialist camp.

[   ] does not believe that the recent increase in aid deliveries reflects an awareness on the part of European Communist power that the Tet offensive was imminent.

[   ] the USSR has not been able to use its aid programs as a means of influencing North Vietnam's conduct of the war. [   ] the Chinese are a more influential power.

Finally, [   ] the USSR will use force to maintain access to the port of Haiphong. The evidence offered to support this statement conflicts sharply with the present judgment of the intelligence community and is undergoing extremely close scrutiny.

Soviet Military Aid to North Vietnam

1. The record of military aid deliveries to North Vietnam in 1967 and information on agreements for 1968 deliveries reflect the dominant role of the USSR as the main supplier of military equipment. Information [   ] indicates that military aid deliveries from North Vietnam's allies will increase even further in 1968. [   ] also makes it clear that there is no quantitative limit to the aid that will be provided to support North Vietnam's military effort and to offset the effects of bombing of the North or the material losses in South Vietnam.

Military Aid Deliveries in 1967

2. Our estimates of Communist military aid deliveries by quantity and value in 1965, 1966, and 1967 are shown in Tables 1 and 2. The value of military materiel delivered to North Vietnam in 1967 from the Soviet Union and Communist China increased to a total of about $660 million, from $455 million in 1966 and $270 million in 1965.

Of the total value of goods delivered in 1967 the Soviet Union supplied almost 80 percent—about the same percentage of the total supplied in 1965 and 1966. Communist China supplied the bulk of the remainder. Although East European countries supplied only negligible quantities of combat material in 1965 and 1966, the amounts increased during 1967 and will be even greater in 1968.

3. Soviet military aid has concentrated on air defense equipment including surface-to-air missiles, antiaircraft guns, radar, and fighter aircraft including MIG-21s. Chinese military aid has concentrated on the build-up of North Vietnamese ground forces and sustaining the military effort in South Vietnam. More recently, China has provided radar of increasing sophistication and apparently has supplied large quantities of MIG-17s in 1967—most of them being delivered in response to heavy losses in the latter part of the year.

4. Although we cannot make a confident judgment on levels of military deliveries at any particular time, there appear to have been erratic changes in the categories of military goods provided by some donors during 1967. Communist China delivered only eight MIG-15/17s during the two-year period 1965-66 but is believed to have delivered about 61 of these aircraft in 1967 with the bulk of them arriving in the latter part of the year. About 12 were delivered in late October and about 28 in December. The North Vietnamese armored vehicle inventory probably was increased substantially in the latter part of the year. Photography of October revealed at least 38 armored vehicles or self-propelled guns at Ping-hsiang China believed to be en route to North Vietnam from the Soviet Union. [these might well be a Czech-produced armored vehicle known as the TOPAS. This vehicle was specifically requested by the DRV delegation that negotiated 1968 deliveries in Prague during the fall of 1967. [

The 1967 Military Aid Agreements

5. During 5 August to 18 October 1967, representatives of the DRV concluded with 12 Communist countries* trade, aid, and technical-scientific agreements that were generally declared to be for strengthening the economic and national defense potential of the DRV. Details on the agreements are not available but public statements indicated that at least Communist China, North Korea, Bulgaria, Poland, USSR, Hungary and Rumania agreed to provide military assistance without charge to the DRV.

6. The 1967 agreements were also significant because for the first time the majority of the donor countries acknowledged that military as well as economic assistance was being provided to North Vietnam.

7. [ ] The negotiations with the European Communist countries were used, particularly by the USSR and Czechoslovakia, as an opportunity to encourage North Vietnam to give more public emphasis to its political rather than its military objectives. This approach on the part of the European Communist countries was reported to reflect their interest in a negotiated settlement of the war. The North Vietnamese rejected these approaches, partly on the belief that they can withstand present manpower losses "for a hundred years" and partly on the belief that North Vietnam is ruining the US and its economy.

8. Hanoi was able to obtain commitments for greater amounts of assistance but not to the levels it sought. The need for increased levels of military assistance is apparently regarded by the Communist countries as a logical result of the increased

---

*These 12 countries are the USSR, Communist China, Bulgaria, Poland, Hungary, Rumania, East Germany, Albania, Czechoslovakia, North Korea, Mongolia and Cuba.

damage caused by the bombing of the North and the war in the South. Generally, Hanoi's solicitations followed the pattern of previous years and [   ] revealed no intentions with respect to military strategy or North Vietnam's views of the phasing of the war. [   ] the North Vietnamese delegation stressed the need for accelerated deliveries in 1968 but gave no elaborations on the reasons. [   ] complaints on delays in deliveries, attributable in part to Chinese obstruction, have been chronic although abating somewhat in 1967.

9. [   ] attributed the more widespread acknowledgment that military assistance is being provided to North Vietnam as simply a ploy to preclude Chinese charges that European Communist countries are not helping their Communist ally.

Terms of the Agreements

10. The 1967 negotiations followed the pattern of previous years. Military aid is negotiated as a separate agreement whereas economic assistance is negotiated as annual protocols to long-standing agreements. All military assistance and much of the economic assistance is grant aid. Although some of the economic assistance is carried on the books as credits, [   ] reported that there was no expectation that these credits would be repaid. [   ] also indicated that all of the donor countries are aware that they will have to pick up much of the costs of North Vietnam's postwar reconstruction.

The Limits of Soviet Aid Programs

11. The public announcements about the 1967 aid agreements and information on the volume of goods being imported by North Vietnam all support an upward trend in military assistance from all donors, particularly the USSR. [   ] made several observations that confirm Soviet willingness to give North Vietnam almost unlimited military assistance.

-5-

12. Despite the fact that Hanoi's requests to Czechoslovakia in the 1967 negotiations were not fully met, the general impression among Czech official circles is that North Vietnam is provided essentially all the assistance it seeks. The outlook is that military aid will stay at least at its present high levels and if further assistance is required it will be provided. The USSR, [   ], feels that it cannot jeopardize its position in the socialist camp by refusing to meet demands for aid. He reported, moreover, that the volume and sophistication of the aid provided would have been even greater if it were not for the Chinese. [   ] a Soviet offer to provide more advanced equipment and technicians was refused by the North Vietnamese because the Chinese would object to a further influx of Soviet technicians. The Soviets apparently are not willing to provide this equipment without the accompanying technicians.

13. The only practical inhibition to Soviet willingness to provide aid at ever increasing levels is the desire to avoid a confrontation with the US. Thus [   ] the USSR would not, for example, provide short-range surface-to-surface missiles for use against targets in South Vietnam. [   ], however, [   ] they would provide such equipment if there were an invasion of North Vietnam.

14. The extent of the Soviet commitment to the North Vietnamese is illustrated by the source's report of the Soviet attitude toward a report that the US was considering the mining or a blockade of the port of Haiphong. [   ] the Czechoslovak minister of national defense was told by high Soviet military officials that if these measures were taken by the US that Soviet merchant ships would be provided armed escorts and would shoot their way through. The evidence offered [   ] to support this statement conflicts sharply with the present judgment of the intelligence community and is undergoing extremely close scrutiny.

Aid and Influence

15. Despite the significant role of the USSR in providing assistance to North Vietnam there is little evidence that the USSR exerts any influence or leverage on North Vietnam's conduct of the war. The North Vietnamese themselves have emphasized repeatedly that the strategic conduct of the war has been purely Vietnamese in origin and nature.

16. This situation is confirmed by [   ] The Soviets, for example, have had little success in influencing North Vietnam to negotiate a settlement of the war. Indeed, Soviet offers to increase the type and quantity of assistance have been refused. [   ] the large shadow of Communist China looms foremost in North Vietnam's attitude toward foreign Communist powers. Because of Chinese objections the North Vietnamese have refused both Czechoslovak and Soviet offers of military experts and have allowed only Soviet missile experts to maintain an extended presence in North Vietnam. This latter point to the best of our knowledge is true.

17. On balance [   ] if any power has an influence over North Vietnam's conduct of the war it is Communist China. [   ] the North Vietnamese may well have consulted with the Chinese before the Tet offensive. At any rate [ ] reading of Soviet and Czech reactions to the Tet offensive is that the high military officials in these countries had no prior knowledge of the event and took a rather sober view of the whole affair.

Table 1
Soviet Military Aid Deliveries to North Vietnam
1965-1967

	1965		1966		1967	
	Quantity (Units)	(Million US $) At Foreign Trade Prices	Quantity (Units)	(Million US $) At Foreign Trade Prices	Quantity (Units)	(Million US $) At Foreign Trade Prices
Total Value		210		360		505
SAM Missile Systems		72		77		136
Firing Battalions	15	66	30	44	5	22
Replacement Missiles	200	6	1,100	33	3,810	114
Aircraft	57	17	85	45	15	12
IL-28 light jet bomber	8	3				
MIG-21 jet fighter	12	9	26	21	15	12
MIG-15/17 jet fighter	32	4	42	6		
MI-6 Helicopter			6	12		4
MI-4 Helicopter	3	1	7	1		
U-MIG-15 jet trainer	3	Negl.				
AN-26 Medium Transport			3	3		
IL-18 Heavy Transport			1	2		
Armor	113	5	15	Negl.	123	5
T-54 medium tank	30	3			40	3
T-34 medium tank	25	1				
PT-76 amphibious tank	25	1	5	Negl.	10	1
BTR-40 armored personnel carrier	25	Negl.	10	Negl.	40	1

Table 1 (cont.)

	1965		1966		1967	
	Quantity (Units)	(Million US $) At Foreign Trade Prices	Quantity (Units)	(Million US $) At Foreign Trade Prices	Quantity (Units)	(Million US $) At Foreign Trade Prices
BTR-50 armored personnel carrier	8	Negl.			3	Negl.
ZSU-57 self-propelled gun						
SU-76 assault gun					30	Negl.
Artillery	1,430	38	2,830	50	2,230	53
100-mm AAA	100	5	100	5		
85-mm AAA	315	12	55	2	465	19
57-mm AAA	485	17	735	25	590	21
37-mm AAA	250	2	1,850	17	850	8
14.5-mm AAA	230	1	50	Negl.	100	Negl.
Field artillery (76-mm–152-mm)	50	1	40	1	225	5
Radar	23	2	160	17	89	9
Vehicles	650	3	400	2	850	1
Small arms and other infantry weapons		1		3		2
Ammunition (metric tons)	17,000	70	40,000	164	70,000	285

Table 2
Chinese Communist Military Aid Deliveries to North Vietnam
1965-1967

	1965		1966		1967	
	Quantity (Units)	(Million US $) At Foreign Trade Prices	Quantity (Units)	(Million US $) At Foreign Trade Prices	Quantity (Units)	(Million US $) At Foreign Trade Prices
Total Value		60		95		150
Aircraft	8	1	0	0	61	8
MIG-15/17 jet fighter	8	1			61	8
Naval craft	2	2	2	2	6	4
Shanghai-class fast patrol boat						
P-6 class motor torpedo boat	2	2	2	2		
Armor	25	1	0	0	6	4
T-34 medium tank	25	1			0	0
Artillery	320	6	140	4	645	8
57-mm AAA	100	4	100	4	100	4
37-mm AAA	200	2				
14.5-mm AAA					120	1
Field artillery (76-mm)	20	Negl.	40	Negl.	425	3
Radar	33	3	112	9	67	7
Vehicles	600	3	400	2	700	4
Small arms and other infantry weapons		10		35		22
Ammunition (metric tons)	8,000	33	10,000	41	24,000	98

Appendix K

MACV Policy on Handling Prisoners of War

Source: Handbook for US Forces in Vietnam, Headquarters Military Assistant Command, Vietnam April 1967.

HANDBOOK
FOR US FORCES IN VIETNAM

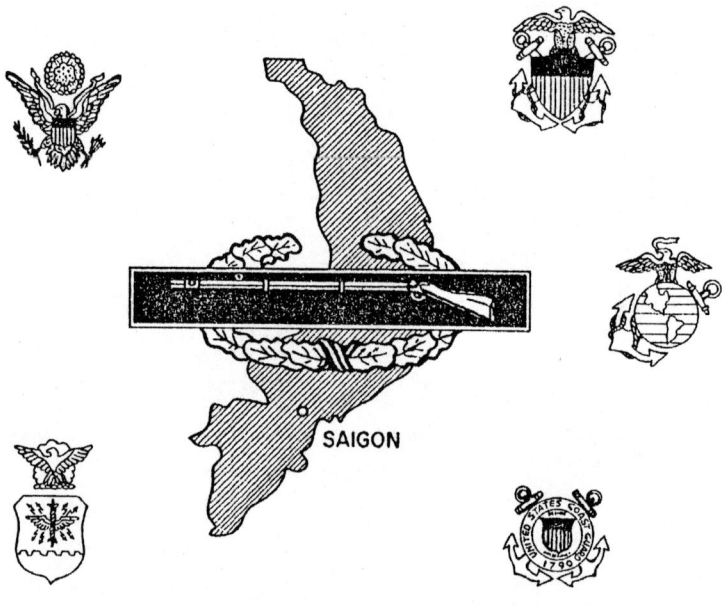

PUBLISHED BY MILITARY ASSISTANCE COMMAND, VIETNAM
APRIL 1967

HEADQUARTERS
UNITED STATES MILITARY ASSISTANCE COMMAND, VIETNAM
Office of the Commander
APO San Francisco 96222

FOREWORD

The enemy we face in South Vietnam today is challenging us with many old fighting techniques and a few new ones. We have shown that both his regular and guerrilla forces can and will be defeated.

This handbook summarizes certain basic techniques and procedures which have evolved out of several years of combat operations against the enemy. When followed, the guidance contained in the handbook will increase the effectiveness of our forces and preclude repetition of past mistakes.

The importance and value of the training given to each member of the Armed Forces prior to entering combat is demonstrated clearly in the results of every action. This handbook provides valuable lessons learned for incorporation into individual and unit training programs.

This handbook is not the last word. Each of us must continue to display imagination, resourcefulness and ingenuity in our combat actions.

W. C. WESTMORELAND
General, United States Army
Commanding

APPENDIX III

HANDLING PRISONERS OF WAR (PW)

1. General.

All members of the US military Forces must comply with the Geneva Prisoner of War Convention of 1949 to which the United States adheres. Under this convention:

    a. US Forces personnel will:

        (1) Disarm the prisoner

        (2) Immediately search the prisoner thoroughly

        (3) Require the prisoner to be silent

        (4) Segregate the prisoner from other prisoners

        (5) Guard the prisoner carefully

        (6) Take the prisoner to the place designated by the unit commander

    b. US Forces personnel cannot and must not:

        (1) Mistreat a prisoner

        (2) Humiliate a prisoner

        (3) Take any of the prisoner's personal effects which do not have significant military value

        (4) Refuse a prisoner medical treatment if required and available

2. Handling of PW.

    a. Handle PW firmly, promptly, but humanely. The prisoner must be disarmed, searched, secured and watched.

But he must also be treated at all times as a human being. He must not be tortured, killed, mutilated, or degraded, even if he refuses to talk. If the captive is a woman, treat her with all respect due her sex.

    b. Take the prisoner quickly to security. As soon as possible, evacuate the prisoner to a place of safety for interrogations, but the prisoner will keep his personal equipment, except weapons.

    c. Mistreatment of any prisoners is a criminal offense. Every soldier is responsible personally for the enemy in his hands. It is both dishonorable and foolish to mistreat a prisoner. It also is a punishable offense. Not even a beaten enemy will surrender if he knows his captors will torture or kill him. He will resist and make his capture more costly. Fair treatment of prisoners encourages the enemy to surrender.

    d. Treat the sick and wounded prisoners as best as you can. The prisoner saved may be an intelligence source. In any case, he is a human being and must be treated like one. The soldier who ignores the sick and wounded degrades his uniform.

    e. All detained persons, whether Prisoners of War or civilians, must be protected against violence, insults, curiosity and reprisals of any kind. Leave punishment to the courts and judges. The soldier shows his strength by his fairness, firmness and humanity to the persons in his hands.

3.   Key Phrases

ENGLISH	VIETNAMESE
Halt	Dung Lai
Lay down your gun	Buong sung xuong
Put up your hands	Dua tay len
Keep your hands on your head	Dua tay len dau

But he must also be treated at all times as a human being. He must not be tortured, killed, mutilated, or degraded, even if he refuses to talk. If the captive is a woman, treat her with all respect due her sex.

    b. Take the prisoner quickly to security. As soon as possible, evacuate the prisoner to a place of safety for interrogations, but the prisoner will keep his personal equipment, except weapons.

    c. Mistreatment of any prisoners is a criminal offense. Every soldier is responsible personally for the enemy in his hands. It is both dishonorable and foolish to mistreat a prisoner. It also is a punishable offense. Not even a beaten enemy will surrender if he knows his captors will torture or kill him. He will resist and make his capture more costly. Fair treatment of prisoners encourages the enemy to surrender.

    d. Treat the sick and wounded prisoners as best as you can. The prisoner saved may be an intelligence source. In any case, he is a human being and must be treated like one. The soldier who ignores the sick and wounded degrades his uniform.

    e. All detained persons, whether Prisoners of War or civilians, must be protected against violence, insults, curiosity and reprisals of any kind. Leave punishment to the courts and judges. The soldier shows his strength by his fairness, firmness and humanity to the persons in his hands.

3.   Key Phrases

ENGLISH	VIETNAMESE
Halt	Dung Lai
Lay down your gun	Buong sung xuong
Put up your hands	Dua tay len
Keep your hands on your head	Dua tay len dau

Appendix L

1. "North Vietnam Applauds Anti-war Demonstrations... Joint Publications Research Service, April 26,1971.

2. "Mme Binh Greets U.S. Anti-war Movement." Liberation Press Agency (Clandestine), April 21, 1971.

3. Madame Binh Sends Letter to Antiwar Americans. Paris Vietnam News Agency (VNA) to VNA Hanoi, April 20, 1971

Source: Texas Tech University Archive

NORTH VIETNAM APPLAUDS ANTI-WAR DEMONSTRATIONS IN WASHINGTON AND SAN FRANCISCO

[Editorial: "A Large and Powerful Demonstration Against Nixon's Policy of Aggression"; Hanoi, Quan Doi Nhan Dan, Vietnamese, 26 April 1971, pp 1, 4]

Yesterday, 25 April, more than a million persons from a number of states in the U.S. rallied at the capital, Washington, in a demonstration, holding banners high and thunderously shouting slogans against the war-mongering policies of Nixon, demanding an immediate end to the war of aggression in Indochina and immediate withdrawal of all forces from Vietnam.

Also on that day, in many large U.S. cities, there were numerous demonstrations of tens of thousands of people protesting Nixon's obstinacy in continuing, prolonging, and expanding the war of aggression against the countries of Indochina. In San Francisco, a major city in California, more that 500,000 people demonstrated. At the same time, in the capitals of England, France, West Germany, Belgium, Denmark, Holland, and Norway, outbursts in response to the American peace movement and supporting the people of Indochina against the U.S. aggressors were seen.

On the intense demonstrations across the U.S., on 24 April, the AP wrote, "This was one of the largest demonstrations, if not the largest, ever held in the U.S..." The BBC on 25 April affirmed, "This demonstration against the war was certainly the largest in the U.S. On 24 April the newspaper AFP also commented that these demonstrations were evidence that the American people want to end, once and for all, the nightmare of this war, the most offensive in the history of the U.S.

Panicking before the strong struggle being waged by all classes of people, Nixon had to put Federal troops on alert, and close the doors of public offices. The U.S. Congress cancelled its meetings, and Nixon himself went to Camp David in the state of Maryland to avoid the resistance and violence of the masses rising up strongly and steadily in the U.S. capital. Clearly this is the biggest struggle of the American people against the war of aggression and the largest crowd to shake the capital city of Washington, to shake the whole of the U.S., and to be heard throughout the world.

This demonstration of force was not only powerful but also a new stage of development in the movement of the American people against Nixon and his war of aggression in Vietnam.

In yesterday's huge demonstration nearly every class of American people was in Washington, the political center of the U.S.

Leading the group in the march which began at 0500 hours were thousands of U.S. enlisted men and officers who were veterans or in the service at that time from many bases throughout the U.S. Many of them, who had been wounded in the war of aggression in Indochina, used crutches to limp in the demonstration. They brandished the flag of the Democratic Republic of Vietnam [North Vietnam] and the flag of the [Democratic] Republic of South Vietnam [Viet Cong] and loudly shouted slogans: "Bring our brothers home now!," "We don't want your war!" (Nixon and his lackeys). These were the angry sounds and yells of numerous people; ever since then the U.S. authorities have reacted by making every effort to indoctrinate and confuse, and, in a vain attempt at using them as their tools of repression and aggression, pushed them into a bloody war of aggression for the selfish interests of the U.S. capitalistic monopolies.

There were tens of thousands of U.S. women whose husbands and sons have been captured or become cannon fodder in Vietnam. Many mothers with snow-white hair held banners saying: "My son has been killed in Vietnam. I want other mothers to avoid losing their sons!" Groups of people loudly shouted "Peace now!" in reply to the empty promise to "reduce casualties and withdraw from the war," which Nixon has often used to deceive the public.

Youths, students, and intellectuals . . .have made appearances in many struggles before this, and now again participate actively and strongly with various slogans, "Ho, Ho, Ho Chi Minh," "Stop the war now!" (aggression in Southeast Asia) "Nixon is a liar!" "Withdraw the military!"

Representatives from peace organizations, Catholics organizations, and unions. . .many Americans of African, Asian, Mexican, and Puerto Rican origin. . .people with white skin, black skin, and red skin, arm-in-arm waved high the flag of the anti-war forces and loudly shouted slogans opposing the policies of Nixon provoking the war, and in support of the people of the countries of Indochina and victory over our aggressors.

Many well-known U.S. congressmen and dignitaries also joined the demonstration. According to estimates of the American press, in support of this struggle were at 50 well-known dignitaries, such as the former U.S. Secretary of Defense Katzenbach, former U.S. Representative to the United Nations, Goldberg; the mayor of the city of San Francisco, and many congressmen of both the Democratic and Republican parties, including such people as the Republican Congressman Paul McClosky who is leading a "movement to overthrow Nixon."

The demonstration of 25 April was a highpoint in the "spring offensive" of the American people who plan to continue and prolong it into the middle of May. Even though Nixon and his lackeys sought every means to divide the people, they are becoming disorientated, are frightened and attacked by public opinion, and they still suffer a shameful defeat. Clearly this is not the "silent majority" that supported him, nor is it only an "extremist faction" against him, but the masses of the classes of American people opposing him, including numerous people in the U.S. Army, the U.S. Congress, the Republican Party, and forces which Nixon has long considered sources of support for the policies of prolonging and expanding the war of aggression in Vietnam and the countries of Indochina.

The strong growth of the opposition of the American people to the war-mongering policies and aggression of Nixon is a very logical development, one in harmony with the numerous recent failures of the U.S. imperialists on the battlefield in Indochina. Nixon promised and boasted loudly concerning his statements, "In my heart I want peace," and "The success of Vietnamizing the war" and "of his numerous stages of troop withdrawal." Yet in reality, his obstinacy continues to push the U.S. into the calamity of extending a bloody war and certain defeat.

Strong waves of resistance have flooded Washington and continue after the cruel defeat of the U.S. — puppets on Route 9 and other battlefields in Indochina are strong warnings to the Nixon warmongers. The more they, without regard for life or death, stubbornly charge head first into an unjust war of aggression and then are defeated on the battlefield, the more the people of the U.S. will violently oppose them, and the more cruelly isolated they will become.

The movement of the American people against the war of aggression in Indochina and against the warlike, obstinate lackies of Nixon, because of the interest of the American people in a peaceful would, is a strong development. It is also a valuable source of encouragement to the people of Indochina fighting a war for independence and freedom of their Fatherland, for peace and friendship among all peoples.

Standing firm on the front line against the U.S., our people and Armed Forces wholeheartedly welcome an support the struggle of the American people for peace, and a halt to the war of aggression in Indochina, Nixon's immediate withdrawal of U.S. forces to the U.S., an early end to the U.S. involvement in the ill-advised and drawn-out war, and the long cost to good people. With confidence and a firm belief in a final victory and the unifying strength of the war of our countries, with the cooperation and strong support of progressive people in the world, including the American people, our army and people our determined to stand shoulder to shoulder with the fraternal peoples of Laos and Cambodia, heighten their determination to win, steadfastly step up the struggle to gain greater victories and press forward to attack more strongly, attack the American pirates and completely defeat them for the independence and freedom of the Fatherland, and for peace, justice, and social progress of the people of the world.

8119
CSO: 3909-W   (True copy. Retyped for legibility. JR)

AVS:KUS/ANTI-HOST-0,GUER-B

MME BINH GREETS U.S. ANTI-WAR MOVEMENT

LIBERATION PRESS AGENCY (CLANDESTINE) IN ENGLISH TO EAST EUROPE AND THE FAR EAST 1555 GMT 21 APR 71 B

(TEXT) SOUTH VIET NAM APRIL 21 GPA—MME NGUYEN THI BINH, MINISTER FOR FOREIGN AFFAIRS OF THE REPUBLIC OF SOUTH VIET NAM, HEAD OF THE R.S.V.N. P.R.G. DELEGATION TO THE PARIS CONFERENCE ON VIET NAM, ON APRIL 19 SENT A LETTER OF GREETINGS TO THE PARTICIPANTS IN THE "SPRING OFFENSIVE" OF THE ANTI-WAR MOVEMENT IN THE UNITED STATES. THE LETTER SAID:

"MORE THAN EVER BEFORE, TO END THE WAR HAS BECOME AN URGENT DEMAND OF THE PEOPLES OF OUR TWO COUNTRIES, SO THE VIETNAMESE PEOPLE CAN BE RELIEVED OF SUFFERINGS AND MOURNINGS, REBUILD THEIR DEVASTATED COUNTRY, AND HEAL UP THE BLEEDING HEARTS, AND SO THE AMERICAN PEOPLE CAN CONCENTRATE THEIR ENERGY AND MATERIAL RESOURCES ON SOLVING THE URGENT QUESTIONS OF THEIR LIFE."

AFTER DENOUNCING THE VICIOUS AIMS OF NIXON'S "VIETNAMIZATION OF THE WAR" POLICY, URGING HIM TO SET A REASONABLE DATE FOR THE TOTAL WITHDRAWAL OF THE U.S. TROOPS FROM SOUTH VIET NAM, AND REITERATING THE FAIR AND REASONABLE PROPOSALS OF THE R.S.V.N. P.R.G. FOR A SOLUTION TO THE VIET NAM PROBLEM, MME NGUYEN THI BINH WROTE:

"I WISH TO TELL YOU THAT THE SOUTH VIETNAMESE PEOPLE ARDENTLY DESIRE TO LIVE IN PEACE AND FREEDOM AND TO HAVE FINE FRIENDLY RELATIONS WITH THE AMERICAN PEOPLE. IN THIS SPIRIT, WE HOPE TO REACH A CORRECT POLITICAL SOLUTION FOR THE SOUTH VIET NAM PROBLEM, TO BRING AN END TO THIS BRUTAL WAR, AND ESTABLISH NEW RELATIONS BETWEEN THE TWO COUNTRIES.

"HOWEVER, THE U.S. ADMINISTRATION, IN THE HOPE OF A MILITARY VICTORY AND IN PURSUANCE OF ITS PLAN OF ENSLAVING

OUR PEOPLE, HAS TAKEN NO INTEREST IN NEGOTIATIONS. THE FAIR AND REASONABLE PROPOSALS SE [SET] FORTH BY OUR SIDE FOR A SAFE WITHDRAWAL OF ALL U.S. TROOPS FROM SOUTH VIET NAM, A CEASEFIRE BETWEEN THE P.L.A.F. AND U.S. TROOPS, THE RELEASE OF CAPTURED ARMYMENT, AND A CORRECT SETTLEMENT OF THE POLITICAL PROBLEM IN SOUTH VIET NAM HAVE BEEN CONCEALED FROM THE BROAD PUBLIC OPINION IN THE U.S.A. BY THE NIXON ADMINISTRATION.

"THROUGH THE CALLEY CASE, THE AMERICAN PEOPLE HAVE FURTHER REALIZED THE EXTREMELY BRUTAL CHARACTER OF THE WAR. YOUR AMERICAN FRIENDS HAVE CLEARLY UNDERSTOOD THAT THE HONOR OF THE UNITED STATES DOES NOT LIE IN THE CONTINUATION OF THIS IMMORAL AND HOPELESS WAR BUT IN THE RESPECT OF FREEDOM, EQUALITY AND DIGNITY. THEREFORE, THE AMERICAN PEOPLE OF VARIOUS STRATA, INCLUDING MORE AND MORE PERSONALITIES OF U.S. POLITICAL CIRCLES, HAVE BEEN JOINING IN ANTIWAR ACTIVITIES ACROSS THE COUNTRY, FIRMLY VOICING THEIR LEGITIMATE DEMAND FOR AN END TO THE WAR, AND A DEADLINE FOR A TOTAL WITHDRAWAL OF U.S. TROOPS FROM SOUTH VIET NAM."

THE LETTER WISHED THE PARTICIPANTS IN THE "SPRING OFFENSIVE" MANY BRILLIANT SUCCESSES.

(True copy. Retyped for legibility. jr)

I. **MADAM BINH SENDS LETTER TO ANTIWAR AMERICANS**

(Paris VNA in Vietnamese to VNA Hanoi, 1331 GMT, 20 April 1971)

[Letter by Minister Nguyen Thi Binh to the American Friends who will Participate in the Spring Campaign——VNA Heading] [Monitored broadcast]

On 19 April 1971, Minister Nguyen Thi Binh sent the following letter to the American friends who will participate in the spring antiwar campaign in the United States in April and May 1971:

Dear American Friends,

I would like to extend my warmest greetings to all American friends of various circles and political and religious tendencies who will participate in the spring campaign.

Once again, you will gather in Washington, New York, San Francisco and other big U.S. cities to strongly express the voice of the authentic United States, (words indistinct) (?freedom and justice,) and to demand that your government put an end to the Viet-Nam war.

More than ever before, the end of the war has become an extremely pressing demand of our peoples so that the Vietnamese people may escape from sufferings and death, rebuild their ragged country, and heel the wounds in each person's feelings, and the American people may concentrate their resources and their strength on the pressing demands of life.

However, in the recent speech on 7 April 1971, President Nixon did not pay the slightest attention to the aspirations of the Vietnamese and American peoples.

While we demand him to end the war, Mr. Nixon answers that he will continue to implement "the Vietnamiztion" of the war, in other words, to prolong and expand the war. To justify this policy, Mr. Nixon has bragged about the victory of the Vietnamization, not only in Cambodia but also in Laos, in defiance of the obvious failure of the operation carried out by U.S. and puppet troops at Khe Sanh, in South Viet-Nam and southern Laos.

We demand that Mr. Nixon put forth a reasonable deadline for a total U.S. troop withdrawal so as to achieve a cease-fire between the liberation troops and U.S. troops and to discuss the question of insuring safety for the withdrawal of U.S. troops and the question of releasing (words indistinct) captured in the Viet-Nam war. Yet Mr Nixon has deliberately ignored the flexible proposals of the Provisional Revolutionary Government on this question (put forward on 17 September and 10 January 1970 (as received) and has ignominiously cheated the American people with the allegation that setting a deadline will make it impossible to bargain for the release of prisoners of war and insure the safety of U.S. troops.

The South Vietnamese people demand an administration which represents the people and stands for peace, independence, and neutrality. But Mr Nixon answers that he will not let down his bellicose and rotten "friends" Thieu, Ky and Khiem whom he has forced the South

Vietnamese people to accept. To soothe the American people who are certainly not satisfied with his speech, Mr Nixon has resorted to a series of fallacious allegations on peace, freedom, mutual respect, and so forth....

But Mr Nixon's attitude can only be explained by the fact that he refuses to end the war and to withdraw all U.S. troops from South Viet-Nam, in defiance of he sufferings and destructions suffered by the South Vietnamese people and the sufferings of scrupulous American people tortured by the towering crimes committed by U.S. troops in South Viet-Nam in the name of the United States.

Dear American friends of various segments, youths, students, women, workers, intellectuals, statesmen, religious men, businessmen, artists, and veterans of the Viet-Nam war.

I wish to tell you that the South Vietnamese people cherish peace and freedom and that they also want to have friendly relations with the American people.

With this spirit, we wan to achieve a satisfactory political solution to the South Viet-Nam problem in the hope of putting an end to this cruel war and building new relations between the two countries.

However, since the U.S. government is pursuing a military victory and plotting to rule our people, it has not been interested in negotiations at all.

The fair and reasonable proposals advanced by our side on a safe withdrawal of all U.S. troops from South Viet-Nam, a cease-fire between the South Viet-Nam People's Liberation Armed Forces and the U.S. troops, the question of releasing captured militarymen, and (?correct solutions to basic problems) in South Viet-Nm are all concealed by the (? U.S.) government from broad segments of the American public.

However, the American people of carious segments hold opposite views to those held by the U.S. government. Through the recent trial of Calley, the American people have recognized better the extremely cruel nature of this war. (? These friends) have increasingly recognized that the honor of the United States does not lie in the pursuit of this immoral and hopeless war but in the respect for the freedom, justice, and dignity of men. Therefore, the American people of various segments, including those in the U.S. political circles, have participated in an increasing number of antiwar activities throughout the United States, firmly expressing their sincere desire and demand that the U. S. government end the war and set a date for the rapid withdrawal of all U.S. troops from South Viet-Nam.

I wish you splendid victories in your spring activities movement and hope that the antiwar movement in the United States will further coordinate (? its activities) so that it will be effective in demanding that the Nixon administration seriously negotiate a political settlement in order to end the war and restore genuine and lasting peace in Viet-Nam.

(True copy. Retyped for legibility. jr)

Appendix M

List of Broadcasts from Hanoi

Source: House of Representatives Committee on Internal Security, Hearings Regarding H.R. 16742: Restraints on Travel to Hostile Areas.

7682

COMPILATION OF BROADCASTS PREVIOUSLY MADE OVER RADIO HANOI BY OTHER U.S. CITIZENS

September 6, 1972

TO: Donald G. Sanders
Chief Counsel

FROM: Joseph E. Thach
Research Analyst

RE: COMPILATION OF U.S. NATIONALS INVOLVED IN RADIO HANOI BROADCASTS, 1965-1972

This special memorandum has been prepared to provide a summary of Radio Hanoi broadcasts by U.S. nationals during the Vietnam conflict. Based on my compilation of data,

[sic] these now total some 82 broadcasts since 1965. Tapes prepared outside of North Vietnam are indicated with an asterisk. Multiple broadcasts within a given year are indicated in parentheses:

1965 - Robert Williams (3)*
Clarence C. Adams (2)*
Leo Taylor (2)
Herbert Adams

1966 - Robert Williams*
Elizabeth Stafford*
Ed Anderson*
"Radio Stateside" - Los Angeles Ca. (Steve Fisher and Joel Epstein)(3)*

1967 - Hugh R. Manes (2)
Charles Cobb
Stokeley Carmichael (5)
Dagmar Wilson (2)
Ruth Krause
Julius Lester
Thomas Hayden

7683

- 2 -

1968 - David Kirby and Mark Fulmer (joint broadcast)

1969 - Rennie Davis
　　　Linda Evans
　　　Richard J. Barnett and William Mayers (joint broadcast)
　　　James A. Johnson

1970 - Noam Chomsky, Douglas Dowd, and
　　　　　Richard Fernandez (joint broadcast)
　　　Eldridge Cleaver (4)
　　　Phillip Lawson (2)
　　　Robert Schaer
　　　■■■ Brown
　　　Hideko (Pat) Sumi
　　　Ann Froines
　　　Randy Rappaport
　　　Martha Westover
　　　Sydney Peck
　　　Mark Wefers
　　　Keith Parker
　　　David Ifshin

1971 - Katherine (Kay) Camp
　　　Theirrie Cook
　　　Joseph (Jay) Craven (2)
　　　Mark Wefers
　　　David Ifshin
　　　John Woodward
　　　Rev. Charles Koen

1972 - George Wald
　　　Pete Seeger
　　　Jane Fonda (21)
　　　Randy Floyd
　　　"American Deserters Committee - Sweden"

JET:alr

(True copy. Retyped for clarity. Jr)

Appendix N

Military Buildup Committee

Source: House of Representatives Committee on Internal Security Hearings, Investigation of Attempts to Subvert the United States Armed Forces, Part 3, 1972.

COMMITTEE EXHIBIT No. 59
[Solomon testimony 6/20/72]

OVERALL SUMMARY
AD HOC MILITARY BUILDUP COMMITTEE
APRIL 15, 1972

The Ad Hoc Military buildup Committee is a group of individuals from various anti-war organizations including G.I. organizing projects, the Vietnam Veterans Against the War, and the peace movement, which has been collecting information on the U.S. large-scale military buildup in Indochina since April 8, 1972. Information on the movement of men and material to the war zone and the placement of other men and material on alert for possible movement has been gathered through telephone contact with G.I. organizing projects (coffee houses, bookstores, and the like near military bases where active duty men and women, antiwar veterans, and civilians get together) around the United States and overseas. Contact was made with the staffs of these projects, who contacted active duty men on the bases near them for word of any alerts of movements, and then in turn reported these back to the ad hoc committee. We required two different G.I. sources or personal knowledge of the informant by a member of the committee to consider a story confirmed. Below is our summary of our findings to date. Included in the packet are summaries by service, a copy of an Associated Press Feature article on the Ad Hoc Committee, and the actual base by base stories we received with their sources, arranged by service and in a logical order within services. The Navy report includes a breakdown of the ship locations around the world that may have relevance to the current buildup.

OVERALL SUMMARY, ALL SERVICES, MILITARY BUILDUP

LEFT FOR INDCHINA:
    650 planes (390 on Air Craft Carriers); 37 ships (including 5 air craft carriers) 33,000+ men.

ON ALERT, STANDBY, OR FREEZE FOR POSSIBLE TRANSFER TO INDOCHINA:
    10 planes, 1 cruiser, 27,770 men.

TRANSFERRED TO/ARRIVED AT LOGISTICAL SUPPORT AREAS FOR INDOCHINA:
    138 planes; 1060 men.

GRAND TOTALS, INVOLVEMENT IN INDOCHINA MILITARY BUILDUP, ALL SERVICES:
    793 planes, 37 ships, 62,730+ men.

In short, the United States has dispatched a large-scale air and naval armada to Indochina. Furthermore, she has substantial numbers of ground troops, mainly marines, prepared to move if needed. There are also indications that the United States is making at least contingency preparations to possibly bomb very sensitive targets in North Vietnam, and to possibly mine Haiphong harbor from the air. The committee is no longer actively canvassing for information, but is continuing to accept calls which come in and to follow up important stories.

COMMITTEE EXHIBIT No. 56 –Continued

AIR FORCE   Compiled 4/15, 2 AM

LEFT FOR INDOCHINA

Tankers (KC135)	4	Westover
Fighter-bombers (F4, A6, F105)	160	Yokota, McConnell, Johnson
Bombers (B52)	11	March, Westover
Transport (C130, C141)	5	Johnson
	Total 180	

Men   1400 Hickam, Yokata, March, Beale,
                              McConnell, Johnson, Westover
                       Total 1400

TRANSFERRED TO/ARRIVED AT LOGISTICAL SUPPORT AREAS FOR INDOCHINA

Transport (C141, C5A)	138	Travis, Iwakuni
	Total 138	

Men   1060
                       Total 1060

ON ALERT/STANDBY/LIMITED CREW REST/FREEZE

Tankers (KC135)	4	Mather
Bombers (B52)	6	Mather
	Total 10	

Men   7770 Hickam, Iwakuni, Hamiliton,
                              Mather, Hanscom Field

(Units at) bases on above status: Iwakuni, Hickam, Clark, Travis, Hamilton, Norton, Mather, Offut, Shaw, Dover, Plattsberg, McGuire

UNUSUAL TRAFFIC

Tanker (KC135)	Hickam, Loring
Fighter-bomber (F4, A7)	Mountain Home
Bomber (B52)	Hickam
Transport	McGuire

GRAND TOTAL FOR AIR FORCE

   Aircraft 323   Men 10,230

Notes: 1. The grand total for aircraft is lower than earlier estimates. This reflects news that planes leaving Travis arrived at Iwakuni, which was not known earlier.
   2. Alerts, etc. may be off now. Time period covered is 4/5-4/12.
   3. Crew estimates: 1, A6; 1, F105; 2, F4; 6, C54; 6, KC135; 8, B52; 5, C141.

COMMITTEE EXHIBIT No. 59

AIR FORCE

HICKAM AFB, HAWAII

Monday, April 10, 1:00 P.M. Although the base went off red alert several days ago, men are still working 12 hours at a time. A vigil of several airmen watching the runaway has detected unusually large numbers of KC-135's taking off and landing. These four engine tankers are capable of refueling three jet fighters simultaneously. Obviously a lot of refueling is going on over this part of the Pacific.

300 men have been transferred to Japan, and many B-52's have been coming in and leaving, possibly enroute from the continental U.S. to the Far East.

Wednesday, April 12, 6:00 A.M. Jim Walkly of the "Liberation Barracks" reports that his old unit, the 548th Reconnaissance Group, has been drawing up target selection charts for Hanoi and Haiphong since last Thursday, April 6, 150 men from the 548th are on 6 hour alert for possibly temporary duty (TDY) to Thailand.

8 men from the 619th Support Group have already left for Thailand on TDY. From this unit an additional 300 men are on alert. Source: Steve Dilts, Gene Parker, and Jim Walkly of the "Liberated Barracks", 808-839-4855.

IWAKUNI MCAS, Japan.

Thursday, April 11, 2:30 A.M. Over 100 C-141's have landed at Iwakuni from bases in the U.S. (probably Travis AFB). It is suspected that they will be used to handle the increased flow of supplies and/or men to Indochina. The entire base of roughly 5000 men is on stand-by alert. Source: Ruth of Pacific Counseling Service, Tokyo, 269-5082

YOKOTA AFB, Japan.

Tuesday, April 11, 2:30 A.M. Many men have been transferred to Iwakuni to handle the large number of extra C-141's landing. Two squadrons of 36 fighter planes have definitely left for Viet-Nam. 20 to 26 of these were F-4 Phantoms and the rest A-6's. 250 crew members and maintenance personnel are going also.

Unless planes leaving Japan stop at some intermediate air field before landing in Viet-Nam, they violate the U.S.–Japanese security treaty. Normally planes on such flights touch down at the Philippines. Source: Ruth, PCS, Tokyo, 269-5082.

CLARK AFB, Philippines.

Tuesday, 11, 1:00 A.M. The entire flight line is on alert, including support maintenance crews. Since Nixon's visit to China in February, quite a few men have been sent to Taiwan on TDY. Source: Dale, Angeles City, Philippines, Phone 2888.

TRAVIS AFB, Fairfield, Cal.

Monday, April 10, 3:00 P.M. Four squadrons of C-141's, totaling 130 planes, have left for unknown destinations. Since these departures began on April 6, the number of C-141's has been reduced to only 10 left on the base. The C-141 transport can lift 100 men or carry supplies.

One clue to the unusual nature of flight activity on the base was the sudden recall of 2 planes loaded with ammunition that were all ready to take off. The cargo was removed from the planes, and they were sent off empty, presumably to pick up more important cargo elsewhere.

COMMITTEE EXHIBIT No. 59 --continued

AIR FORCE

TRAVIS AFB, cont'd.

One clue to the unusual nature of flight activity on the base was the sudden recall of 2 planes loaded with ammunition that were all ready to take off. The cargo was removed from the planes, and they were sent off empty, presumably to pick up more important cargo elsewhere.

One lieutenant commented, "Last Thursday evening this flight line was full of planes and by Friday they were all leaving." He called this highly unusual. This break in routine was confirmed by flight mechanics who said they were working 12 hour shifts last week.

In addition, 20 C-5A's have left Travis. This includes every one on base that is operable. The local maintenance squadron was on alert for four days until the planes had all left.

Source: Katherine Robert, 707-437-3636 and Nancy Hause 707-425-4955 or 422-0128.

HAMILTON AFB, Novato, Cal.

Monday, April 10, 2:00 P.M. From several men on base it was leaned that there have been several unusual alerts. This small base of only 2000 men is located near San Francisco. Airmen on emergency leave have suddenly fount it impossible to get extensions of leave.

Source: Alan Miller, Pacific Counseling Service, 415-479-5467.

MARCH AFB, Cal.

Sunday, April 9, Saturday 200 men were suddenly shipped to Viet-Nam.

Monday, April 10, 3:00 P.M. An undetermined number of B-52's and personnel have departed for undisclosed destination. However, at least three airmen who left last Wednesday have got word out that they are in Thailand on TDY. These three men are flight line mechanics, attached to the 33rd Communications Squadron.

Source: Robert Ratford, "Shelter Half Coffeehouse", 206-272-5227.

Statistics: 200 airmen shipped to Indochina, some of them to Thailand.

NORTON AFB, Cal.

Monday, April 10. The 63rd Military Air Command Airlift Unit is the back-up alert force for Travis AFB. Source: Terry Christian, Los Angeles S.O.S., former member U.S. Special Forces, 213-399-8697.

BEALE AFB, Marysville, Cal.

Monday, April 10, 9:30 P.M. 7 tactical reconnaissance photography specialists have been sent to Guam Friday night. Their job is to analyze photos of ground movements.

Source: Active duty personnel, does not want to be identified.

MATHER AFB, Cal.

Monday, April 10 This SAC base is on alert. There are 18 B-52 bombers, and 16 KC-135 tankers, of which 6 B-52's and 4 KC-135's of the 320th Bomb Wing are on alert. The unit is manned by 120 men. Source: Tim McAfee, 707-425-4950, 422-0128, 437-3636.

Monday, April 10 This SAC base is on alert. There are 18 B-52 bombers, and 16 KC-135 tankers, of which 6 B-52's and 4 KC-135's of the 320th Bomb Wing are on alert. The unit is manned by 120 men. Source: Tim McAfee, 707-425-4950, 422-0128, 437-3636.

MOUNTAIN HOME AFB, Idaho

Tuesday, April 11. There has been unusual cross-country fighter plane traffic in the last few days. Planes include many F-4 Phantoms equipped for long distance travel. Three of four A-7 fighter bombers were sighted Sunday landing, refueling and taking off. For the past two months airmen have been getting orders to Viet-Nam and Thailand. A large proportion of these

COMMITTEE EXHIBIT No. 59--Continued

AIR FORCE

MOUNTAIN HOME AFB, cont'd.
men work in radio, maintenance, and photo interpretation.
Source: Stan Richardson, "The Covered Wagon", 208-587-7474.

MCCONNELL AFB, Kansas.
Monday, April 10. 70 to 90 F-105 all weather fighter bombers are scheduled to leave for Viet-Nam in the next week. One squadron has left already. People on "mobility" are restricted to base.
Source: "The Covered Wagon", 208-587-7474

OFFUT AFB, Omaha, Neb.
Sunday, April 9, all "mobility teams" (mechanics, aircraft maintenance personnel) have been on alert since Saturday A.M. This base is the headquarters of the Strategic Air Command.
Source: "The Covered Wagon", 208-587-7474.
Monday, April 10, 6:00 P.M. The 55th Strategic Reconnaissance Wing is the major unit is the major unit still on alert.
Source: "The Covered Wagon"

SHAW AFB, South Carolina.
Sunday, April 9. Since Saturday the entire photo reconnaissance unit has been on alert for overseas duty.
Monday, April 10, 6:00 P.M. The 62nd Tactical Reconnaissance Squadron, the major unit of the base, is still on alert.
Source: Tom Spaulding, "The Covered Wagon", 208-587-7474.

SEYMOUR JOHNSON AFB, Goldsboro, N.C.
Tuesday, April 11, 12:15 A.M. 18 F-4 Phantom jets from each of 2 squadrons deployed for S.E. Asia earlier this week. The two squadrons, the 334th and 336th normally have 24 aircraft. On Wednesday the 335th squadron is scheduled to send out additional planes. No destination has been determined. 500 men have been deployed with the 2 squadrons. Thursday airmen boarded C-130's and C-141's with their equipment. 50 of the 60 men in the avionics section have been sent.
Source: Buddy Tiger, attorney, 919-485-5725
Statistics: 36 F-4 Phantoms (18 from each of the 2 squadrons) have left for unknown destinations. 1 additional squadron is scheduled to leave Wednesday. 500 crewmen and support personnel have departed.

DOVER AFB, Del.
Saturday, April 8. Last Thursday, April 6 there was an unusual practice alert at which the base commander made a rare appearance. A group at the NCO Club were informed that they could be sent to Viet-Nam. Source: Fred Breukblman, 302-658-0597

COMMITTEE EXHIBIT No. 59—Continued

AIR FORCE

MCGUIRE AFB, New Jersey.

Tuesday, April 11, 12:30 A.M., All flying squadrons (mostly transport) are on "limited crew rest" today, and must sign in and out of the base. Up until recently, most of the flights from this base have been to Europe. Nowm However, 90% of the traffic has been to S.E. Asia with supplies and ammunition.

Source: Lisa Schiller 609-723-4470.

PLATTSBURG AFB, New York.

April 10, 9:15 P.M. Crews for refueling KC-135s have been placed on alerts to be ready to go to work at a moment's notice. It is felt that some of these men may be transferred.

Source: Chuck Harrison, Potsdam, N.Y. 315-265-8571, 518-561-6842.

WESTOVER AFB, Chicapee, Mass.

Sunday, April 9, 10 B-52 crews and 11 KC-135 crews were sent to Guam, Okinawa, and Thailand on Thursday along with 310 personnel. Another 100 airmen, mostly plane crews, were being processed for shipment Saturday night and Sunday morning. An estimated 10 to 15 B-52's and KC-135's left the base Sunday.

Wednesday, April 12, 4:00 P.M. Of the planes that left the base over the week-end, it has now been learned that 10 were B-52's and 4 were KC-135's. Only a skeleton force of the 99th Bomber Wing remains for Strategic Air Command defense of the U.S.

Approximately 400 to 500 personnel have left for Guam, Okinawa, and Thailand. These men were aircraft crews and flight maintenance crews who make up "flight mobility teams". Unconfirmed reports indicate some of these men were shipped via commercial planes and "Air America" types.

Source: Fred Miller, Westover Action Project, 413-732-5880.

HANSCOM FIELD, Bedford, Mass.

75% of personnel have been put on a "freeze list" indicating possible overseas transfer. This kind of freeze has not happened within the memory of either source, one of whom has been at the base 2 years.

Saturday, April 8, Tom, Frank Neisser, LISP 617-492-5570.

LORING AFB, Caribou, Me.

Saturday, April 8, airmen have been notified of possible transfer to Thailand on TDY. The men include B-52 support and maintenance personnel. KC-135 tankers have been landing, refueling, and departing in large numbers with little or no time on the ground. Active duty contacts on base have been reluctant to give any more details since Sunday.

Monday, April 10, Maintenance and support crews now on 2 hour alert for TDY to Thailand.

Source: Jim Page, Caribou, Me. 207-496-7871.

COMMITTEE EXHIBIT No.—Continued

NAVY SUMMARY, April 15, 1972

LEFT FOR VIET-NAM:

Air Craft Carriers: 3 enrounte (Saratoga, Midway, Oriskany); 2 already arrived (Kitty Hawk and Constellation). These are added to the Ranger, the Coral Sea and the Hancock which were already there, which will make a total of 8 carriers when they all arrive, plus one Helicopter carrier which is already off Viet-Nam. Each has 4, 500-4,700 men; 75-80 planes.

Cruisers: 3 (the Albany, the Newport News, and an unidentified cruiser from San Diego). These join the Oklahoma City, already off Viet-Nam. Cruisers carry 1000 men.

Destroyers: 14 (Sarsfield, Stanly, Mullinix, Glennon, Wolfen, McCain, Summers, Engerthal, Brooks, Buckley, Hull, Davidson, Richard S. Edwards, identified last from Pearl Harbor) joining a large fleet of destroyers already there. Each destroyer carries about 250 men.

Destroyer Escorts: 13* (* 12 "Probably bound for S.E.Asia" from Pearl Harbor; plus the Roark from Subic Bay, Philippines.

Auxiliaries: 1 (AEO-4 "Detroit" from Norfolk).

Total ships enroute in current buildup: 33 (counts Constellation & Kitty Hawk already arrived & 12 "probable" destroyer escorts from Pearl Harbor)
Total planes on ships enroute: 390
Total men on ships enroute: 32,500

ON STANDBY ALERT;

E1 cruiser, the Columbus, on alert in Norfolk, Va. —1,000 men on it.

NAVAL TOTALS INVOLVED IN MILITARY BUILDUP:

37 ships, 390 planes, 33,500 men.

NAVAL POWER OFF THE COASTS OF VIETNAM WHEN ALL SHIPS ARRIVE:

8 carriers, 1 helicopter carrier, 4 cruisers, numerous destroyers, at least 13 destroyer escorts, at least one auxiliary, and an ammunition ship (Mount Katani).

COMMITTEE EXHIBIT No. 59—Continued

NAVY

<u>Mayport and Jacksonville, Fla.</u> -- The U.S.S. Saratoga (aircraft carrier) left Tuesday morning, April 11, 1972 for an unexpected 8 month deployment off the Vietnam coast. Two squadrons of jet fighters from Cecil Field (Jacksonville, Fla.) joined the ship. The Saratoga had formerly been scheduled to leave for the Mediterranean Sea May 1, 4700 sailors, 80 planes involved, including 50 attack jets.

The aircraft carrier was accompanied by the USS Albany, a Guided Missile cruiser. Lieutenant David Eisenhower is aboard the Communications Department on the "Albany". Also with the Saratoga from Jacksonville, Fla., are the destroyers USS Sarsfield and USS Stanley. The cruiser carries 1,000 men; the destroyers carry 250 men each.

<u>Norfolk Naval Base, Va.</u> -- The USS Millenix and the USS Glennon, both destroyers, left Norfolk on Tuesday, April 11, 1972, to join the Saratoga on the way to the coasts of Viet nam. The Newport News, a second fleet flagship—heavy cruiser with 8 inch guns, the most powerful shore bombardment cruiser the Navy has, is also on its way to Viet Nam this week, from Norfolk. The auxiliary ship carries 300 men. Still on alert at Norfolk is the Guided Missile Cruiser Columbus.
Source: David Jones, G.I. Office, Norfolk, Va. (703) 625 0802 (212) 924-8032

<u>Alameda, Calif.</u> -- The USS Midway (aircraft carrier) left Alameda Calif. Monday Morning, April 10, 1972, for Vietnam, at least a month ahead of schedule. It carried 4,500 sailors, 75 planes (these were armed with nuclear weapons, as is standard on this ship), and 200 marines, some 50 to guard bombs.
Source: Kent Hudson, Center for Servicemen's Rights, San Diego, Calif; (714) 263-4142 or 239-2119.

<u>San Diego-Long Beach, Calif.</u> -- The Air Craft Carrier Oriskany left San Diego on Monday, and Reuters reported it is going to the Tonkin Gulf. Also leaving San Diego and stopping at Long Beach presumably enroute for the Tonkin Gulf are the guided missile destroyers, Wolfen, McCain, Summers, Engerthal, Brooke, Buckley, and Hull, and an unidentified cruiser.
Source: Kent Hudson, Center for Servicemen's Rights, San Diego, 714-233-4142

<u>Pearl Harbor, Hawaii:</u> -- A squadron x of 3 destroyers including the USS Richard S. Edwards, the UsS Davidson, and a third, left Pearl Harbor on Monday, April 10, to join the carrier Midway on its route to Vietnam. 12 destroyer excorts also left with the destroyers, and these are "probably bound for South East Asia" to quote the Associated Press.
Source: Steve Diltxs, the "Liberated Barracks," Honolulu, 803-839-4855.

<u>Subic Bay, Philippines:</u> -- On Easter Sunday, the attack carrier "Kitty Hawk" cut short her normal port call at Subic Bay, Philippines in such haste that 300 men were left behind. The ship was supposed to stay in port at Subic Bay for three to four days, but received urgent orders to return to station of the Viet Nam coast. Also xat subic Bay, the destroyer escort USS Roard (DE1053) was given emergency orders to leave for Vietnam, and left.

COMMITTEE EXHIBIT No. 59—Continued

<u>Subic Bay, cont'd.</u>
Source: Kent Hudson, Center for Servicemen's Rights, San Diego (714) 283-4142; Dale, Angeles City, Philippines, phone: 2888 (Philippines)

Navy Update Monday, April 17, 8PM EST

The USS "nitro", an ammunition ship docked at Quonset Point, Rhode Island, will sail Wednesday, April 19, to Earl Ammunition Depot in New Jersey to load munitions before sailing for an unknown destination. Crew members believe that the ship is headed for the waters off Vietnam. A long-scheduled Mediterranean cruise has been cancelled.

Twenty of the 200-man crew have complained to Congressman Hastings Keith, describing excessive drill attributed to the new captain's desire to make rank, according to reliable sources. The source reported gripe letters from the crew slipped under the xxxxx cabin doors of the captain and the executive officer. The new sailing orders have inflamed feeling to the point of desperation. Twenty of the crew are considering jumping ship, according to reliable sources. One wife told her husband to start packing bags for Canada, stating, "There's no way I'm going to let you go to Vietnam."

The USS Nitro is normally associated with the carrier, USS Saratoga, which has cancelled a Mediterranean cruise to head for Vietnam, unexpectedly.

Source: George Stein, Mike Roche (Ad Hoc Military Buildup Committee) 617: 492-5570

USS MIDWAY UPDATE   2 AM   FRIDAY:

USS MIDWAY left without its full crew. It is reported that men are being flown to the Midway.
    John Powers took sanctuary in Berkley, Calif. He was greeted by the mayor and promised support.
    He then turned himself in with a CO application and was flown to the Midway.

Source: PCS, OAKLAND, CALIF. (Tom) (415) 836-1039

COMMITTEE EXHIBIT No. 59—Continued

MARINE CORPS SUMMARY   April 15, 1972

LEFT FOR VIETNAM:

Third Marine Air Wing, El Toro Marine Air Station---80 Aircraft. (One squadron definitely left, the other squadrons, are composed of fighter bombers and due to leave Monday April 10, 1972.

ON ALERT TO VIETNAM OR INDOCHINA:

1st Marine Division, Okinawa	15,000men
7th Marine Regiment, Camp Pendleton	4,000men
Elements, 2nd Marine Div., Camp Lejeune	?????
	19,000 + men

TOTAL MARINE INVOLVEMENT IN BUILDUP: 80 AIRCRAFT, 19,000 + men

ARMY SUMMARY:

Though some suspicious and exercises have been noted in the Army, we do not report large scale Army alerts or movements at this time.

COMMITTEE EXHIBIT No. 59—Continued

MARINE CORPS

KANEOHE BAY MARINE CORPS AIR STATION, Hawaii.
Monday, April 10, 6:00PM. Twelve hundred (1,200) Marines are leaving on an amphibious exercise, reportedly to be undertaken on one of the other islands in the Hawaiian Chain. These Marines have been on notice since Wednesday, April 5.
STATISTICS: 1,200 men on suspicious exercises.
SOURCE: Steve Dilts, "Liberated Barracks" (808) 839-4855.
This has been reliably confirmed.

CAMP PENDLETON, Calif.
The 7th Marine Regiment, stationed at Camp Pendleton, is on alert for possible transfer to Indochina. Several units at Camp Pendleton are reported to have been brought to full strength for the alert which is not usually done during a practice alert.
SOURCE: Terry Christian, Los Angelos "Support Our Soldiers" (213) 399-8697. From a report from an active duty Marine.

OKINAWA
Monday, April 10th, 5:00PM. The Marine Division on Okinawa has been on alert since early Sunday for shipment to Vietnam. This information was received from the mother of a man in the 1st Marine Division who talked with her son Sunday night. Her son had called her because he was upset about being placed on standby for Vietnam. The man is a member of H&S Co., H&S BN., Regiment Communications Center, 3rd FSR-FMF PAC at Camp Butler, Okinawa.
SOURCE: Mike Roache, Ad-Hoc Military Buildup Committee, 67 Winthrop St., Cambridge, Mass. (617) 492-5570

Congressman Paul McCloskey (REP., Calif.) has been contacted by at least three men from Okinawa Marine bases regarding this alert.
STATISTICS: One division (approx. 15,000 men) on alert for Vietnam.
SOUORCE: Lenny Spiegle, Pacific Counseling Service, Calif. (415) 322-4664

Thursday, April 13th, 6:00PM. New information on the story printed earlier: The men (a Marine) who contacted his mother and his Congressman regarding his pending shipment to Vietnam has been identified as Lance Corporal Edward Edewra. His mother, Mrs. Barbara Allen of Mountainview, Calif. (415) 964-1797 stated that her son said he "did not want to go to Vietnam" and this feeling is shared with many other Marines. This information has been confirmed after talking with his parents.
SOURCE: Mike Oliver, San Francisco Vietnam Veterans Against the War, (415) 861-7700. Mike Roache, Ad-Hoc Military Buildup Committee, Cambridge, Mass. (617) 492-5570

COMMITTEE EXHIBIT No. 59—Continued

MARINE CORPS cont'd

CONFIRMED Friday April 14th, 1:00AM. Up to 15,000 Marines of the 1st Marine Division on Okinawa are on alert.
SOURCE: Bill Marshall, 48 Davidson St., Vietnam Veterans Against The War, Detroit, Michigan.

EL TORO MARINE CORPS AIR STATION: Santa Ana, Calif.
Tuesday, April 11th 2:00AM. The Third Marine Air Wing has orders to Vietnam. This Air Wing has approximately 80 aircraft. One Squadron of photo reconnaissance left this morning (Monday, April 10th); the remaining squadrons, all composed of fighter bombers, were due to leave Monday afternoon.
SOURCE: Kent Hudson, Center for Servicemens Rights, San Diego, Calif. (714) 263-4142 or 239-2119

CAMP LEJUNE, North Carolina
Confirmed Tuesday, April 11th, 2:00AM. Elements of the 2nd Marine Division at Camp Lejune are on alert. These elements are composed of ground combat troops. The brass claim that this is normal. On this particular alert, members involved had participated in one just the week before.
SOURCE: Matt Renauldt, USAF, (212) 934-8032

ARMY

FT. BRAGG, North Carolina, 82nd Airborne Division.
Monday, April 10th 5:00PM. Through information obtained from an enlisted man at Ft. Bragg, 82nd Airborne Battalion, 82nd Airborne Division, it was leaned that the had been called back to the base by 15:00PM, Sunday, April 9th, to go to the field with Special Forces elements for field exercises.
This is unusual, due to the fact that they've recently returned from the field and were't due to go back.
During the maneuver exercises artillery elements went into heavy drills and all battlefield gear was thoroughly examined. It has been indicated that the men in this unit expect transfer to South East Asia.
SOURCE: Mike Buckley, 67 Winthrop St., Vietnam Veterans Against The War, Cambridge, Mass. (617) 492-5570.
Paul Coursetti, reporter for Record American, confirmed this report, stating that a friend of his, a captain in the Army at Ft. Bragg, N.C., is on standby.

Glossary

AAA	Antiaircraft Artillery
ARVN	Army of the Republic of (South) Vietnam
AKA	Also Known As
CINCPAC	Commander in Chief, Pacific
CMIC	Combined Military Integration Center
COMUSMACV	Commander, U.S. Military Assistance Command, Vietnam
COSVN	Central Office of South Vietnam (VC/NVA)
CPUSA	Communist Party of the United States of America
CSAP	Committee for Solidarity with American People
DGI	General Directorate for Intelligence (Cuban secret service)
DMZ	Demilitarized Zone
DRV	Democratic Republic of Vietnam (North Vietnam)
EIPJ	Entertainment Industry for Peace & Justice
FBIS	Foreign Broadcast Information Service
GMT	Greenwich Mean Time
GVN	Government of (South) Vietnam
ICC	International Control Commission
JCS	Joint Chiefs of Staff (U.S.)
JPRS	Joint Publications Research Service
JUSPAO	Joint US Public Affairs Office
LDP	Lao Dong Communist Party of North Vietnam
LPA	Liberation Press Agency (Clandestine)

LR	Liberation Radio (Clandestine)
MACV	Military Assistance Command, Vietnam
MDM	Movement for a Democratic Military
NCNA	New China News Agency (People's Republic of China)
NFLSV	National Front for Liberation of South Vietnam
Nhan Dan	Organ of the Central Committee of the Communist Party, Vietnam
NIE	National Intelligence Estimate
NIS	Naval Investigation Service
NLF	Same as NFLSV
NPAC	National Coalition against the War
NSAM	National Security Action Memorandum
NSC	National Security Council
NVA	North Vietnamese Army
PAVN	People's Army of (North) Vietnam
PCPJ	People's Coalition for Peace & Justice
PLA	People's Liberation Army (VC/NVA)
PLAF	People's Liberation Armed Forces (VC/NVA)
PLP	Progressive Labor Party (Communist USA)
PRC	People's Republic of China
PRG	Provisional Revolutionary Party (Communist front in SVN)
PRP	People's Revolutionary Party (South Vietnamese Communists)
RHN	Radio Hanoi
ROTC	Reserve Officer Training Corps
RVN	Republic of (South) Vietnam
SAC	Senior Agent in Charge (FBI)
SAM	Surface-to-Air-Missile
SANE	The National Committee for a Sane Nuclear Policy, Inc.
SEA	Southeast Asia
SEATO	Southeast Asia Treaty Organization
SDN	Saigon Daily News
SDS	Students for a Democratic Society

SNCC	Student Nonviolent Coordinating Committee
SWP	Socialist Workers Party
SRV	Socialist Republic of Vietnam (Current name for Vietnam)
SVN	South Vietnam
Tet	Vietnamese lunar new year
UCMJ	Uniform Code of Military Justice
VB	Venceremos Brigade
VC	Viet Cong
VNA	Vietnam News Agency (North Vietnam)
VNAF	Vietnamese (South) Air Force
VVAW	Vietnam Veterans against the War
WSP	Women Strike for Peace
WUO	Weathermen Underground Organization
YSA	Young Socialist Alliance (Youth arm of SWP)

Notes

Chapter One: The Second Front

1. Nicholas deB. Katzenbach, Under Secretary of State, memorandum to the President of the United States, subject: Vietnam, November 16, 1967, (Texas Tech University, Vietnam Center Archive).
2. Robert F. Turner, "How Political Warfare Caused America to Snatch Defeat from the Jaws of Victory in Vietnam," in *The Real Lessons of the Vietnam War*, ed. John Norton Moore and Robert F. Turner (Durham, N.C.: Carolina Academic Press, 2002), 235.
3. Ibid., 235-236.
4. Ibid., 236
5. "What's Holding Them Up?" *U.S. News and World Report*, 8 N9vember 1965, 1.
6. Stephen Young, "How North Vietnam Won the War," *Wall Street Journal*, 3 August 1995.
7. Colonel Bui Tin, interviewed by author at Texas Tech University, 24 October 2003.
8. "Answers to a Mystery Why North Vietnam Fights on," *U.S. News & World Report*, August 9, 1971, 41.
9. "The American People Are Increasingly Angry," *Nhan-Dan*, February 2, 1967.
10. Larry Berman, *Lyndon Johnson's War: The Road to Stalemate in Vietnam* (New York: W.W. Norton & Company., 1989), 57.
11. Dean Rusk as told to Richard Rusk, *As I Saw It*, ed. Daniel S. Papp (New York.: W.W. Norton & Company, 1990), 472.
12. Ibid.
13. Douglas Pike, *PAVN: People's Army of Vietnam* (Novato, CA: Presidio Press, 1986), 233-234.
14. Ibid., 236-245.
15. Ibid., 239.
16. Ibid., 239
17. Phillip B. Davidson, *Vietnam at War* (Novato, CA: Presidio Press, 1988), 28.

18. AIRGRAM, A-579, w/enclosure text of Viet Cong document 15 June 1966, American Mission Saigon to Department of State, 4 April 1967, (Texas Tech University, Vietnam Center Archives.), 1.
19. Ibid., 7-8, 13-16.

Chapter Two: Why Vietnam

1. W.W. Rostow, *Diffusion of Power* (New York: The Macmillan Co., 1972), 501.
2. Winston S. Churchill, *The Second World War: The Gathering Storm*, (Boston: Houghton Mifflin Company, 1948), 304.
3. United States Information Service, *Hanoi's Strategy for Conquest—the 'Liberation Front'* (American Embassy, Tokyo, June 1965), 1, TTU Vietnam Archive.
4. Ibid.
5. United States Information Agency, *Ho Chi Minh and the Communist Movement in Indo-China, A study in the Exploitation of Nationalism* (Washington D.C., August 1953), 4, TTU Vietnam Archive.
6. United States Information Agency, *Background on Communism, North Vietnam and the Threat in Southeast Asia* (Washington D.C., USIA Bulletin No. 61-SM-14, October 1961), 2-4, TTU Vietnam Archive.
7. Ibid.
8. United States Information Agency, *Ho Chi Minh and the Communist Movement in Indo-China*, 6.
9. Ibid.
10. United States Information Agency, *Background on Communism*, 4.
11. Ibid., 2.
12. United States Information Agency, *Ho Chi Minh and the Communist Movement in Indo-China*, 10.
13. Ibid., 10.
14. Ibid., 11-12.
15. Ibid., 12-13.
16. United States Information Agency, *Background on Communism*, 4-5.
17. Ibid., 5.
18. Ibid., 2-3.
19. Richard M. Nixon, *No More Vietnams* (New York, Arbor House, 1985), 29.

20. Department of State, *Why We Fight in Vietnam* (Washington D.C., Office of Media Services, Bureau of Public Affairs, Vietnam Information Notes No.6 June 1967), 1-2, TTU Vietnam Archive.
21. Ibid.
22. Ibid.
23. Ibid.
24. Foreign Affairs Division to Honolulu, Joseph B. Tydings, subject: Position of the Administration and Views of the Administration and Views of Critics on Vietnam, Library of Congress, Washington D.C., September1, 1967, TTU Vietnam Archive; and Robert F. Turner, "Public Opinion and the War at Home: How Political Warfare Caused America to Snatch Defeat from the Jaws of Victory in Vietnam," in *The Real Lessons of the Vietnam War*, ed. John Norton Moore and Robert F. Turner (Durham, NC: Carolina Academic Press, 2002), 233-234.
25. Admiral U.S. Grant Sharp, *The Strategy for Defeat, Vietnam in Retrospect* (Novato, CA.: Presidio Press, 1998), 9.
26. Senate Hearings, *The Heart of the Problem...Secretary Rusk, General Taylor Review Vietnam Policy*, in Department of State Bulletin, DOS Pub 8054, March 7, 1966, 4, TTU Vietnam Archive.
27. Ibid., 4-5
28. Ibid., 4-5
29. Department of State, *A Threat to the Peace, North Vietnam's Effort to Conquer South Vietnam, Part I* (Washington D.C., November 1961), 3, (TTU Vietnam Archive); and United States Information Service, *The World's Stake in Vietnam, (Saigon, July 1964*, 4, (TTU Vietnam Archive).
30. Senate Hearings, *The Heart of the Problem*, 2-3; and Secretary of State Dean Rusk, *The Winds of Freedom,* Selections from Speeches and Statements by Dean Rusk, January 1961-August 1962.
31. Secretary McNamara, *Communist Strategy,* April 26, 1965, 1, TTU Vietnam Archive.
32. Secretary Of Defense, Robert S. McNamara, *Helping Vietnam*, address at the Forrestal Memorial Awards Dinner in New York City, March 26, 1963, 9, TTU Vietnam Archive.
33. General Maxwell D. Taylor, *Swords and Plowshares* (New York: W.W. Norton & Company, Inc., 1972), 16.
34. Senate Committee Hearings on Foreign Relations, *The Vietnam Hearings* (New York: Random House, 1966), 169.
35. Ibid.

36. "Mr. Calwell Dismisses Threat of Communist China," *The Australian League of Rights 4,* no.2, (June 2003), 7, on-line, Internet, June 26, 2003, available at http://www.alor.org.
37. Ibid., 3.
38. Senate Hearings, *The Heart of the Problem*, 12.
39. House Armed Services Committee, *Partial Text of Statement by Robert S. McNamara, U.S. Secretary of Defense,* February 18, 1965, in U.S. Information Service Special Report, American Embassy, Tokyo, 7, TTU Vietnam Archive.
40. National Archives and Records, Harry S. Truman Library and Museum, Independence, MO, *A Factual Summary Concerning The American Mission for Aid to Greece,* June 15, 1948, 1.
41. *Truman Doctrine, President Harry S. Truman's Address before a Joint Session of Congress,* March 12, 1947, The Avalon Project, Yale Law School, 7, on-line, Internet, February 17, 2004, available at http://www.yale.edu/lawweb/avalon/trudoc.htm.
42. Norman A. Graebner, "The Scholar's View of Vietnam, 1964—1992," in *An American Dilemma, Vietnam, 1964—1973,* ed. Dennis E. Showalter and John G. Albert (Chicago, Imprint Publications, 1993), 13.
43. Ibid.
44. Ibid.
45. Admiral U. S. Grant Sharp, *Strategy for Defeat,* 7.
46. Dean Rusk as told to Richard Rusk, *As I Saw It, Roots of American Commitment* (New York: W.W. Norton & Co., 1990), 424.
47. Norman A. Graebner, *The Scholar's View of Vietnam,* 14.
48. George N. Katsiaficas, *Vietnam Documents* (Armonk, NY: M. E. Sharpe, July 1992), 33-34.
49. United States Information Service, *Why Vietnam* (Washington D.C.: Government Printing Office, 1965), 1, TTU Vietnam Archive.
50. Ibid., 2.
51. Department of State, *A Summary of the United States Commitment to Assist South Vietnam* (Washington D.C., Bureau of Publications, 1967), 2, TTU Vietnam Archive.
52. United States Information Service, *Why Vietnam,* 2-3.
53. John M. Newman, *JFK and Vietnam* (NY: Warner Books, 1992), 83.
54. *A Synopsis on America's Stake in Vietnam (*New York: American Friends of Vietnam [now defunct], 1956), 10-11, TTU Vietnam Archive.
55. Dean Rusk, *As I Saw It, 429-430.*
56. Department of State, *National Security Action Memorandum No. 52* (Washington D.C., The Secretary of State, May 11, 1961), n.p., TTU Vietnam Archive.

57. The White House, *National Security Action Memorandum No. 111* (Washington D.C., November 22, 1961), 419, TTU Vietnam Archive.
58. United States Information Service, *Why Vietnam*, 3.
59. Dean Rusk, *As I Saw It*, 435.
60. Dean Rusk, *As I saw It*, 442.
61. The White House, *National Security Memorandum No. 273* (Washington D.C., November 26, 1963), 1-3, TTU Vietnam Archive.
62. United States Information Service, *Three Presidents Demonstrate Continuity of U.S. Policy on Vietnam* (Washington D.C., 1964), 2-4.
63. United States Information Service, "Text of an Address by President Lyndon B. Johnson on Vietnam, as Prepared for Delivery at Johns Hopkins University, Baltimore, Maryland, April 7, 1965." (Washington D.C., Special Report, 1965), TTU Vietnam Archive.
64. Stanley Karnow, *Vietnam, a History* (New York: Penguin Books, 1983), 381-383.
65. Bui Tin, *Following Ho Chi Minh, the Memoirs of a North Vienamese Colonel* (Honolulu, University of Hawaii Press, 1995), 133.
66. Stanley Karnow, *Vietnam, a History*, 389.
67. Department of Defense, *Tonkin Gulf Chronology of Second Tonkin Gulf Incident* (Washington D.C., Office of International Security Affairs, May 1968), 3-4, TTU Vietnam Archive.
68. Ibid.; and *Pentagon Paper, vol. 3, The Defense Department History of United States Decision Making On Vietnam,* The Gravel Edition (Boston, Beacon Press, no date), 184-186.
69. Department of State, *President's Message to Congress, August 5, 1964* (Washington D.C., Department of State Bulletin, August 1964), 261, TTU Vietnam Archive.
70. The White House, *National Security Memorandum No. 343* (Washington D.C., March 1966), 1-2, TTU Vietnam Archive.
71. *Pentagon Papers,* Gravel Edition vol. 4, 429-430.
72. "President Lyndon B. Johnson's Address to the Nation Announcing Steps to Limit the War in Vietnam and Reporting His Decision Not to Seek Reelection," Lyndon Baines Johnson Library and Museum, March 31, 1968, 10, on-line, Internet, February 23, 2004, Available at http://www.lbjlib.utexas.edu/johnson/archives.hom/speeches.hom/680331.asp.
73. Admiral U.S. Grant Sharp, *Strategy for Defeat*, 227.
74. *President Lyndon B. Johnson's Address to Nation*, 10.
75. Richard Nixon, *No More Vietnams* (New York: Arbor House, 1985), 45-46.
76. President Nixon, "Address to the Nation on Vietnam, May 14, 1969," The Richard Nixon Library & Birthplace, 2, on-line, Internet, February

23, 2004, available at http://www.nixonfoundation.org/Research_Center/Nixons/speeches.

77. Richard Nixon, "Address to the Nation on the War in Vietnam," November 3, 1969 (Washington D.C., White House Press Office, November 1969), 5, 9.

78. Ibid., 2.

79. Richard Nixon, "President Nixon's Address to the Nation Announcing Conclusion of Agreement on Ending the War and Restoring Peace in Vietnam," January 23, 1973, The Richard Nixon Library & Birthplace, 9, on-line, Internet, February 23, 2004, available at http://www.nixonfoundation.org/Research_Center/Nixons/speeches.

80. Admiral U.S. Grant Sharp, *Strategy for Defeat*, 262-263.

81. Gerald R. Ford, "Address to Joint Session of Congress, August 12, 1974," 7, Gerald Ford Library & Museum, on-line, Internet, February 24, 2004, available at http://www.presidency.ucsb.edu/site/docs/pppus.php?admin.

82. Admiral U.S. Grant Sharp, *Strategy for Defeat*, 263-265.

83. Gerald Ford, "Address before a Joint Session of Congress, April 10, 1975," 5, Gerald Ford Library & Museum, on-line, Internet, February 23, 2004, available at http://www.presidency.ucsb.edu/site/docs/pppus.php?admin.

84. Ibid., 3-4.

85. Ibid., 5.

86. Ibid., 5.

87. Admiral U.S. Grant Sharp, *Strategy for Defeat*, 264.

Chapter Three: Hanoi's Grand Facade

1. Department of State, *Why Vietnam* (Washington D. C., U.S. Government Printing Office, 1965), 5, 9; and United States Information Service, *Opening Statement by Secretary Rusk Concerning Vietnam*, March 6, 1962, 1-2, Texas Tech University (TTU) Vietnam Archive.

2. United States Mission, Saigon, *Hanoi's Direction and Support of the Communist Effort in South Vietnam*, July 28, 1967, 1, TTU Vietnam Archive.

3. Ibid.

4. Department of State, *Aggression from the North, White Paper on Vietnam*, 1965 (Washington, D.C. Department of State Bulletin, March 22, 1965), n.p.

5. Secretary of Defense, Robert McNamara, Statement by Secretary of Defense Robert S. McNamara before the Senate Foreign Relations Committee March 3, 1966 as Regards U.S. Involvement in South Vietnam, Washington, D.C., March 3, 1966.
6. House of Representatives, *U.S. Policy in Southeast Asia,* Address by Honorable Douglas Mac Arthur II, Assistant Secretary of State for Congressional Relations, for the record, June 30, 1965, 1, TTU Vietnam Archive.
7. "On Target," *The Australian League of Rights* 4, no.2, June 26, 2003, 2, on-line Internet, June 26, 2003, available at http://www.alor.org.
8. Department of State, *Hanoi's Strategy for Conquest—the "Liberation Front,"* (American Embassy, Tokyo, June 2, 1965), A3706, TTU Vietnam Archive.
9. William Colby with James McCarger. *Lost Victory* (Chicago & NY, Contemporary Books, 1989), 53; and Hammond M. Rolph, *The Viet Cong: Politics at Gunpoint* (reprint, Communist Affairs 4, no. 4, 1966), 3-4.
10. Captain and Mrs. Fredric A. Wyatt (USNR Ret), "We Came Home," P.O.W Publications, January 30, 1997, n.p., on-line, Internet, April 7, 2004, available at http://www.pownetwork.org.
11. United States Information Agency, *Ho Chi Minh and the Communist Movement in Indo-China, a Study in the Exploitation of Nationalism,* August 1953, 17-18, TTU Vietnam Archive.
12. Ibid., 4.
13. Ibid., 4.
14. United States Information Agency, *The Viet Cong Front Technique* (Washington D. C.: Office of Policy and Research, April 1997), 7, TTU Vietnam Archive.
15. United States Information Agency, *The Viet Cong: Patterns of Communist Subversion* (Washington D.C., January 1966), 10, TTU Vietnam Archive.
16. Ibid.
17. P.J. Honey, *North Vietnam's Model of Strategy and Tactics for Revolutions* (Studies on the Soviet Union, 1966), 12.
18. *The Role of North Vietnam in the Southern Insurgency,* RAND Report RM-4142-PR, Prepared for the U.S. Air Force, (Santa Monica, CA: RAND, July 1964), 32, TTU Vietnam Archive.
19. RAND Report RM-4142-PR, *The Role of North Vietnam,* 34.
20. Phillip B. Davidson, *Vietnam at War, the History: 1946-1975* (Novato, CA, Presidio, 1988), 280.

21. United States Information Service, *Hanoi and South Vietnam's "Liberation Front"* (Washington D.C. September 1967), 10, TTU Vietnam Archive.
22. Ibid.
23. Department of State, *A Threat to the Peace, North Vietnam's effort to Conquer South Vietnam, Part I* (Washington D. C. December 1961), 46-47, TTU Vietnam Archive.
24. *Infiltration of Communist Armed Elements and Clandestine Introduction of Arms from North to South Vietnam* (Republic of Vietnam, Ministry of Foreign Affairs, Saigon, June 1967), Introduction, TTU Vietnam Archive.
25. United States Information Service, *Hanoi and the "Front"* (Washington D.C., February 1967), 1, TTU Vietnam Archive.
26. United States Information Service, *The Viet Cong* (Washington D.C., 1960), 1, TTU Vietnam Archive.
27. Ibid.
28. United States Information Service, *The 'Liberation Front' in South Vietnam: Hanoi's Political Façade* (Washington D.C., January 1966), 3, TTU Vietnam Archive.
29. *Hanoi's Strategy for Conquest,* 3.
30. National Liberation Front, "Five point Statement on a Vietnam Settlement" (Library of Congress Legislative Research Service, Washington D.C., March 1965) LRS 83, TTU Vietnam Archive; and Central Intelligence Agency, *Evolution of Communist Position Concerning Negotiations* (Washington D.C.: Office of the Deputy Director Intelligence, June 1965), 1, TTU Vietnam Archive.
31. Roger Swearingen, *The Vietnam Critics in Perspective* (reprint from Communist Affairs, May-June 1966), 3, TTU Vietnam Archive; and Jack A. Smith, "Students Plan New War Protests," National Guardian, May 1, 1965., TTU Vietnam Archive.
32. "The Role of the Democratic Republic of Vietnam in South Vietnam" (Selected Vietnamese Communist Documents, December 1968), 24, TTU Vietnam Archive.
33. Ibid.
34. "Hanoi and the Front," 1.
35. "Hanoi's Strategy for Conquest," 3.
36. A Background Paper, "Hanoi's Central office for South Vietnam (COSVN)" (U.S. Mission In Vietnam, Saigon, July 1969), 1, TTU Vietnam Archive; and Department of State, Bureau of Public Affairs, *Vietnam Information Notes* (Washington D.C., Office of Media Services, May 1967), 2-3, TTU Vietnam Archive.

37. "Hanoi and South Vietnam 'Liberation Front,'" 19-20
38. Ibid.
39. "Hanoi and the Front," 2-3.
40. Merle L. Pribbenov, "North Vietnam's Master Plan," *Vietnam Magazine*, August 1999, 8.
41. Colby, 55-56.
42. Department of Defense, "Fact Sheet, Ho Chi Minh Trail," February 1971, 3. (TTU Vietnam Archive).
43. "Hanoi's Direction and Support of the Communist Effort in South Vietnam" (U.S. Mission, Saigon, July 1967), 15; and "Infiltration of Communists" (Republic of Vietnam, Ministry of Foreign Affairs, Saigon, June 1967), 9-10, TTU Vietnam Archive.
44. United States Information Agency, *Infiltration of Military and Technical Personnel from North to South Vietnam,* 3 December 1964, 4-5, Document is now declassified, TTU Vietnam Archive.
45. "Hanoi's Direction and Support," 15.
46. Bui Tin, *Following Ho Chi Minh* (Honolulu, HI, University of Hawaii Press, 1995), 47.
47. Ibid., 47-48.
48. Davidson, 738.
49. Republic of Vietnam Ministry of Foreign Affairs, "Infiltration of Communists," 8.
50. Lewis Sorley, *A better War* (A Harvest Book, San Diego, NY, 1999), 50-51.
51. Davidson, 737-738.
52. Republic of Vietnam Ministry of Foreign Affairs, "Infiltration of Communists," 9-12.
53. Military Assistance Command, Vietnam (MACV), U.S.Element CMIC, letter, subject: The 70th Rear Service Group, Prisoner Interrogation, 19 October 1970.
54. Davidson, 738.
55. Department of State, *A Threat to the Peace, North Vietnam's Effort to Conquer South Vietnam, Part I* (Washington D.C. November 17 1961), 39; and *The North Vietnamese Military Adviser in Laos, a First Hand Account,* RAND RM-5688-ARPA (Santa Monica, CA: RAND July 1068), 5, TTU Vietnam Archive.
56. Pribbenov, Sidebar 1-2.
57. Pribbenov, 3-4.
58. RAND RM-5688-ARPA, The *North Vietnamese Adviser in Laos,* 5.
59. Central Intelligence Agency, *Construction of Roads Will Make Possible the Strengthening of Communist Forces in South Vietnam and*

Southern Laos (Washington D. C., October 1965), 1, TTU Vietnam Archive.
60. Department of State, *A Threat to the Peace, 8.*
61. Ibid.
62. Department of State, *Why We Fight in Vietnam* (Washington D.C., Bureau of Public Affairs, Vietnam Information Notes, no. 6, June 1967), 3-4, TTU Vietnam Archive.
63. Ibid., 4.
64. Department of State, *The International Control Commission and North Vietnam's Violations of the Geneva Accords* (Washington D. C., U.S. Information Agency, December 1961), 1, TTU Vietnam Archive.
65. Department of State, *Hanoi Still Denying Involvement in the South* (Washington D. C., U.S. Information Agency, December 1968), 1, TTU Vietnam Archive.
66. *The War in Vietnam, Liberation or Aggression?* A White Paper, (Saigon, Republic of Vietnam, Ministry of Foreign Affairs, 1968), 22, TTU Vietnam Archive.
67. Ibid., 23.
68. Ibid., 24-25.
69. David Lawrence, "Moscow and Peking Pay for Hanoi's War" *Washington Star*, December 21, 1966, F1, TTU Vietnam Archive.
70. Central Intelligence Agency. *International Communist Aid to North Vietnam* (Washington D.C., March 1968), 4, TTU Vietnam Archive.
71. "Soviet Party Leader: The Soviet Union Continues Assisting North Viet Nam Against U.S. Aggression," *North Vietnam News Service*, November 6, 1967, 1, TTU Vietnam Archive.
72. "Brezhnev Repeats Support for Democratic Republic of Vietnam, Peoples Revolutionary Government Cites Aid Agreement," Moscow, *Tass International Service* in English, November 29, 1970, 1-2, TTU Vietnam Archive.
73. CIA, *International Communist Aid, 1, 3.*
74. Jon M. Van Dyke, *North Vietnam's Strategy for Survival* (Palo Alto, CA, Pacific Books, 1972), 225.
75. Paul Wohl, "Red Bloc Steps Up Hanoi Aid," *Christian Science Monitor*, January 1967, 1, TTU Vietnam Archive.
76. MACV, US Element CMIC. *Report of a Hoi Chanh* [North Vietnamese defector], *Corporal Duong Cao, 24, Ha Bac Province*, December 1967.
77. "The Flow of Red Arms U.S. is Trying to Halt," *U.S. News and World Report*, May 22, 1972, 1; and Central Intelligence Agency, *The*

Soviet Role in North Vietnam's Offensive (Washington D. C. Vietnam Bulletin, April 1972), 21, TTU Vietnam Archive.
78. "Li Shaoqi and Le Duan, Beijing, 8 April 1965," n.p., on-line, Internet, *Cold War International History Project, Woodrow Wilson International Center for Scholars*, November 28, 2003, available from http://cwihp.si.edu.
79. "Chinese Assure NLF, PRG of Continuing Support," P*eking New China News Agency,* 19 December 1971, 1-2.
80. Chen Tse-ming, *The Chinese Communist's Role in the War in Vietnam* (Asia People's Anti-Communist League, Republic of China (Free China), Taipei, Taiwan, China, December 1965), 13-18, TTU Vietnam Archive.
81. Ibid., 19-21.
82. Van Dyke, 219; and Central Intelligence Agency, *Chinese Communist Military Presence in North Vietnam* (Washington D.C., Director of Intelligence, February 1966), 1-2, TTU Vietnam Archive; Intelligence Information Cable TDCS DC 315/03145-66, Central Intelligence Agency, to EXO, DDI, OSI, 28 October 1966, TTU Vietnam Archive; and Central Intelligence Agency, *Presence of Chinese Communist Troops in North Vietnam in October 1965* (Washington D.C., February 1967), 1-5, TTU Vietnam Archive.
83. Central Intelligence Agency, *Communist Military and Economic Aid to North Vietnam, 1970-1974,* (Washington D.C., March 1971), 1-2, TTU Vietnam Archive.
84. "Chinese Army men Celebrate North Vietnam's Downing of 2,000 U.S.," *New China News Agency, Peking,* June 12, 1967, 1-4, TTU Vietnam Archive.
85. "Full Combat Units Offered by Castro if Asked by Hanoi," *Washington Post*, July 27, 1966, A10, TTU Vietnam Archive.
86. "A Splendid Development of South Vietnam-Cuba Militant Solidarity," *Vietnam Courier*, July 10, 1967, 1, TTU Vietnam Archive.
87. Ibid.
88. Michael Benge, "Cuban War Crimes Against American POWs During Vietnam War," June 20, 1996, 3, on-line, Internet, April 6, 2004, available from http://ww.pownetwork.org; and "Testimony of Michael D. Benge before the House International Relations Committee," November 1999, 1-6, on-line, Internet, April 4, 2004, available from http://www.pownetwork.org.
89. "Weathermen Underground Summary," *Federal Bureau of Investigations Electronic Reading Room*, August 20, 1971), 120-126, on-line, Internet, April 12, 2004, http://FOIA.fbi.gov/room.htm.

90. Lewis Sorley, *A Better War* (San Diego, CA, NY, London, A Harvest Book, Harcourt Inc., 1999), 357-358.
91. Department of State, *The 1973 Paris Agreement—A Scorecard of Noncompliance* (Washington D.C., Bureau of Intelligence and Research, July 1987), 1, TTU Vietnam Archive.
92. Sorley, 363-364.
93. Sorley, 372.
94. "Senior General Van Tien Dung, 'Great Spring Victory' Part I 'Revolutionary Violence,'" *Nhan Dan*, April 1976, 1, in Foreign Broadcast Information Service, FBIS Vol. IV, No 110, Supp 38, 7 June 1976, 1, TTU Vietnam Archive.
95. Ibid., 2.
96. Ibid., 4-5.
97. Ibid., 5-8.
98. Sorley, 376.

Chapter Four: The Rise of the Second Front

1. Richard Helms, Director Central Intelligence Agency, memorandum for The President of the United States, subject: International Connections of US Peace Movement, Top Secret, Sensitive, 15 November 1967, 7-9, TTU Archive, Document now declassified.
2. Senate, *Extent of Subversion in Campus Disorders: Hearings before the Subcommittee to Investigate Security Act and Other Internal Security Laws, Committee on the Judiciary*, 91st Cong., 1st sess., 1969, 142-143.
3. Ibid., 122.
4. James H. Webb, Jr., "Sleeping With the Enemy, Peace, Defeat, What Did the Vietnam War Protesters Want? *The American Enterprise Institute*, May/June 1997, n.p., on-line, Internet, June 6, 2004, Jameswebb.com.
5. "President Ho Chi Minh Replies to American Peace Fighters, Hanoi November 14, 1965," *Vietnam Courier*, December 2, 1965, 1, TTU Archive.
6. Senate Concurrent Resolution 65, 89th Cong., 1st sess.,1965, XII, 17.
7. Ibid., XII.
8. "Teach-Ins and PSY War," *Washington Report, American Security Council* (Defunct now), June 21, 1965, TTU Archive.
9. Senate, *Extent of Subversion in Campus Disorders*, 4.
10. Ibid., XIV, XV.

11. House, *Intellectuals and Vietnam*, Honorable Elford A. Cederberg, quoting Stewart Alsop in *Saturday Evening Post*, May 27, 1965, 1, TTU Archive.
12. Federal Bureau of Investigation, *The Organized Opposition of the American Left to U.S. Policy on Vietnam*, (Washington D. C., 1965), 1, TTU Archive.
13. Ibid., 1.
14. Ibid., 1-2.
15. FBI, *The organizational Opposition of the American Left*, and House, *Anatomy of a Revolutionary Movement: Students for a Democratic Society*, Report by the Committee on Internal Security, 91st Cong., 2nd sess., October 6, 1970, H.R. 91-1565, 1.
16. House, *Anatomy of a Revolutionary Movement*, 1.
17. House, *Investigation of Students for a Democratic Society, Part 1-A*, (Georgetown University), Hearings before the Committee on International Security, 91st Cong., 2nd sess., 1969, 127.
18. Ibid., 6.
19. Ibid., 128
20. Ibid., 132-133.
21. W. W. Rostow, *The Diffusion of Power* (New York: The Macmillan Co., 1972), 486.
22. Senate, *Extent of Subversion in Campus Disorders*, 28.
23. Tom Hayden, *Trial* (New York: Holt, Rinehart and Winston, 1970), 33.
24. Ibid., 139-141.
25. Federal Bureau of Investigation, *Students for a Democratic Society/ Worker Student Alliance, Formerly Known as Students for a Democratic Society, Characterization of Subversive Organization Internal Security* (Washington D.C.: July 1974), 1-2.
26. F.S Putnam, Federal Bureau of Investigation, memorandum to Mr. W. R. Wannall, Federal Bureau of Investigation, subject: Weathermen Bombings, Explosives and Incendiary Devices; Sabotage, August 13, 1974, 1-2.
27. Ibid., 2.
28. Acting SAC Chicago, memorandum to Director, Federal Bureau of Investigation, *subject: Weathermen Underground Organization (WUO) Formerly Weathermen*, (Chicago, IL: FBI, 1976), 2.
29. Ibid., 8-9.
30. Ibid., 41, 178-185.
31. Ibid., 38.
32. Ibid., 38.

33. Ibid., 41.
34. Ibid., 39, 42-43.
35. Ibid., 40.
36. Ibid., 120.
37. Central Intelligence Agency, *Situation Information Report, Venceremos Brigade Update* (Washington D.C.: 1969) 1-2.
38. Acting SAC Chicago, *Weathermen Underground,* 127-128.
39. Ibid., 121-122.
40. Ibid., 125-126.
41. Ibid., 132.
42. Ibid., 333.
43. FBI, *The Organized Opposition of the American Left,* 3.
44. Laurence Feinberg, "Dissent Called a 2nd War Front," *Washington Post*, October 25, 1967, 1, TTU Archive.
45. Jim G. Lucas, "POW Wives Show Ire," *Washington Daily News*, February 5, 1970, 1, TTU Archive.
46. Thomas Powers, *The War at Home* (New York: Grossman Publishers, 1973) 166-167.
47. House, *Communist Origin and Manipulation of Vietnam Week (April 8-15, 1967),* Report by the Committee on Un-American Activities, 90th Cong., 1st sess., March 31, 1967, 6-7.
48. Ibid., 28-29.
49. Ibid., 5.
50. Ibid., 53-54.
51. House, *Subversive Involvement in the Origin, Leadership, and Activities of the New Mobilization Committee to End the War in Vietnam and its Predecessor Organizations,* Staff Study by the Committee on Internal Security, 91st Cong., 2nd sess., 1970, VI, TTU Archive.
52. Ibid., VII.
53. Ibid., VII.
54. Ibid., VII.
55. Ibid., VII-VIII.
56. Ibid., 29.
57. Ibid., 30.
58. Ibid., 30-31.
59. Ibid., 31.
60. Ibid., 31-34.
61. House, *National Peace Action Coalition (NPAC) and Peoples Coalition for Peace and Justice (PCPJ),* 91st Cong., 1st sess., 1971, 1445-1446.
62. Central Intelligence Agency, *Special Information Report,* (Washington D.C.: February 17, 1971), 1, TTU Archive.

63. Ibid., 2.
64. House, *National Peace Action Coalition*, 1446.
65. Captured Enemy Document 16 July 1971, No. 33/VP/TD, "Circular on Antiwar Movements in the U.S., Hoai Huong District Party Committee, VC Binh Tuy Province, VC Region 6, 1, TTU Archive.
66. Ibid., 2-3.
67. Ibid., 3.
68. Central Intelligence Agency, *Situation Information Report,* (Washington D.C.: June 9, 1971) 1, TTU Archive.
69. Ibid., 3.
70. Central Intelligence Agency, *Situation Information Report* (Washington D.C.: July 23, 1971), 1, TTU Archive.
71. From (Censored), FBI, memorandum to E.S. Miller, FBI, subject: Vietnam Veterans Against the War, Internal Security – New Left, November 24, 1971, 1 and enclosure, TTU Archive; and Mackubin Thomas Owens, 'Vetting the Vet Record," *National Review Online,* January 17,2004, 6, on-line, Internet, February 28, 2004, 1, 6.
72. SAC Springfield, memorandum to Director FBI, subject: Vietnam Veterans Against the War (VVAW), Internal Security-New Left, November 8, 1971, 1-2, TTU Archive.
73. Senate Committee on Foreign Relations, *Testimony of Lieutenant John Kerry before the Foreign Relations Committee on Behalf of the Vietnam Veterans Against the War,* 92nd Cong., 2nd sess., April 22, 1971, 4-5.
74. Ibid., 9.
75. Ibid., 11-13.
76. Ibid., 16.
77. FBI memorandum to E.S. Miller, subject: *VVAW,* 1; and "Key Points,' *WinterSoldier.com*, May 21, 2004, 3, on-line, Internet, May 21, 2004, available at www.wintersoldier.com.
78. FBI memorandum to E.S. Miller, subject: *VVAW,* 3.
79. Guenter Lewy, *America in Vietnam* (New York: Oxford University Press, 1978) 317.
80. "KEY Points," *WinterSoldier,* 2, and "Time Line," *WinterSoldier. com,* May 21, 2004, 10, on-line, Internet, May 21, 2004, available at www.wintersoldier.com.
81. H.G. Burkett, *Stolen Valor* (Dallas, TX: Variety Press, Inc., 1998), 81 and 111; and Mackubin Owens, 5.
82. "Time Line," *WinterSoldier, 3-4.*
83. Ibid., 5.

Chapter Five: From Hanoi with Love

1. "Premier Pham Van Dong Thanks the American 'Spring Mobilization Committee,'" *Vietnam Courier,* (Hanoi, Ministry of Foreign Affairs), April 1967, 107, TTU Archive.
2. "Message to the American People," in *Writings of Ho Chi Minh on the U.S., December 23, 1966,* 137-138, TTU Archive.
3. "We Stand by Your Side," *Vietnam Courier,* (Hanoi, Ministry of Foreign Affairs), March 1966, 52, TTU Archive.
4. Seymour Topping, "Asian Reds Say Protests Prove U.S. Will Withdraw, Communists are Thankful," *New York Times,* Hong Kong, October 19, 1965, 1, TTU Archive.
5. John Hughes, "Hanoi Keys Appeal to U.S. Mood," *Christian Science Monitor,* Hong Kong, October 17, 1969, TTU Archive.
6. "Madam Binh Sends Letter to Antiwar Americans," *Paris VNA to VNA Hanoi,* 1331 GMT, April 20, 1971.
7. "Madam Binh Telephones Harrisburg Peace Rally," *Liberation Radio* (Clandestine), 1900 GMT, April 3, 1972, 1-2, TTU Archive.
8. "Vietnam Committee for Solidarity with American People, October 16, 1967, 1-3, TTU Archive.
9. "Solidarity Committee Writes to U.S. People," *Hanoi VNA International News Service,* 1556 GMT, October 20, 1968, TTU Archive.
10. "South Vietnam Solidarity Committee Thanks Progressive Americans," *Hanoi VNA,* September 14, 1968, TTU Archive.
11. "U.S. Demonstrations for End to War Praised," *Liberation Press Agency,* 1514 GMT, January 17, 1969, TTU Archive.
12. "Ho Thu Acclaims U.S. Antiwar Demonstrations," *Liberation Radio* (Clandestine in South Vietnam), 1000 GMT, April 27, 1971, TTU Archive.
13. "Mass Organizations Back U.S. Antiwar Efforts," *Liberation Press Agency,* 1533 GMT, December 2, 1969, TTU Archive.
14. "Antiwar Letters Sent to U.S. Peace Groups," *Liberation Press Agency,* October 8, 1969, TTU Archive.
15. "Vietnam Organizations Laud American Antiwar Campaign," *Hanoi VNA International News Service,* 1621 GMT, April 21, 1971, FBIS, TTU Archive.
16. "Huang Minh Giam Supports U.S. Antiwar Activists," *Hanoi VNA International News Service,* 1557 GMT, April 17, 1971, FBIS, TTU Archive.
17. "Black Panther Party Offers Volunteers to RSVN, NFLSV," *Hanoi VNA International News Service,* 0546 GMT, October 20, 1970, TTU

Archive; and "PLAF Deputy Commander Replies to Black Panther Troop Offer," *Liberation Press Agency,* 1610 GMT, November 14, 1970, TTU Archive.

18. "Americans Attend Hanoi Solidarity Meeting," *Hanoi VNA International News Service,* 1633 GMT, April 26, 1971, 8-10, TTU Archive.

19. "Our Wishes for Your Victory in the 1971 Fall Offensive, Letter from Mr. Hothu to American People" *Vietnam Courier,* October 10, 1971, 1-2, TTU Archive.

20. Joint Publications Research Service, "Hanoi Students Send Telegram Supporting Antiwar Activities," *Nhan Dam,* Hanoi, Vietnam, November 14, 1969, TTU Archive.

21. "Women Support U.S. Strike for Peace," *Vietnam News Agency,* Hanoi, 1428 GMT, April 20 1962, TTU Archive.

22. "Women, Youth Send Letter to Groups in U.S.," *VNA International News Service,* Hanoi, 1608 GMT, February 11, 1968, FBIS February 15, 1968, TTU Archive.

23. "NLF Women's Union Condemns Treatment of Angela Davis," *Liberation Press Agency,* 1613 GMT, December 23, 1970, TTU Archive.

24. "Saigon Women Appeal to U.S. Senate Committee for End to War," *Liberation Press Agency,* 1512 GMT, May 17, 1971, TTU Archive.

25. "Nguyen Thi Binh Sends Letter to U.S. Congress," *Paris VNA,* 0540 GMT, April 26, 1972, FBIS, TTU Archive.

26. "Peking Hails Protests in U.S. on Vietnam, Has Own Rally," *Washington Star,* March 1966.

27. "Vietnam Solidarity Committee Writes to American People," *Vietnam News Agency,* Hanoi, 0734 GMT, February 8, 1973, 1, FBIS, TTU Archive.

28. "Hanoi's Efforts to Buildup the PRG," May 1974, 1, TTU Archive; and United States Information Agency, "Communists Admit PRG is 'Tool of Party,'" (Saigon: December 16, 1969, 1, TTU Archive.

29. Stephen Young, "How North Vietnam Won the War," *Wall Street Journal,* August 3, 1995, A10.

Chapter Six: The Collaborators

1. Stephen Young, "How North Vietnam Won the War," *Wall Street Journal,* August 3, 1995.

2. House, Committee on Internal Security, *Report, Restraints on Travel to Countries or Areas Engaged in Armed Conflict with the United States,* 93 Cong., 2nd sess., 1973, 3.

3. House, *Hearings Regarding H.R. 16742: Restraints on Travel to Hostile Areas, Hearings before the Committee on Internal Security*, 92 Cong., 2nd sess., 1972, 7642-7643.
4. "Jane Fonda Says Nixon 'Is Betraying America,'" UPI, July 22, 1972, TTU Archive.
5. House, *Hearings Regarding H.R. 16742*, 7672-7675.
6. Ibid., 7679.
7. "Fonda Dike Story a Lie, Pilots Say," *Stars & Stripes*, August 13, 1972, TTU Archive.
8. "Defense of the Bombing," *Stars & Stripes*, September 22, 1972, TTU Archive.
9. "VNA Cites Ramsey Clark's Call for End to Bombing," *Hanoi VNA International News Service*, 0726 GMT, August 6, 1972, TTU Archive.
10. Hanoi Radio in Mandarin to Southeast Asia, 0530 GMT, August 16, 1972, TTU Archive.
11. Lewis Sorley, *A Better War* (San Diego, CA: A Harvest Books, Harcourt, Inc., 1999), 321-322.
12. "Statement in Bangkok," Hanoi Radio to American Servicemen Involved in Indochina War, 1300 GMT, August 16, 1972, TTU Archive.
13. Hanoi in English to American Servicemen Involved in the Indochina War, 1300 GMT, August 15, 1972.
14. "Remarks in San Francisco," Hanoi in English to Europe, Africa and Middle East, 2000 GMT August 15, 1972, TTU Archive.
15. "Clark: Bombing of North Inhuman," *CDN/T,* Tokyo, August 13, 1972, TTU Archive.
16. Tim O'Brien, "Ramsey Clark Airings Called 'Contemptible,'" *Washington Post*, August 1972, TTU Archive.
17. Ibid., 1.
18. Ibid., 1.
19. Central Intelligence Agency, *Special Report, Vietnam Veterans Against the War,* July 7, 1972, TTU Archive.
20. "Nguyen Duy Trinh Receives U.S. Antiwar Veteran," *Hanoi VNA International News Service,* 1501 GMT, March 27, 1972, TTU Archives.
21. Department of Justice, FBI, *VVAW Regional Coordinating and National Steering Committee Meeting, November 15, 1971, Kansas City, MO.,* 1-2.
22. Message, Director FBI to the President, Vice President and Secretary of State, "VVAW Confidential (declassified)," 11:50 AM, November 11, 1971, 2-3, TTU Archive.

23. Senate, *A Staff Study for Subcommittee, Committee on the Judiciary, The Anti-Vietnam Agitation and the Teach-in Movement: the Problem of Communist Infiltration and Exploitation*, 91st Cong., 1st sess., 1971, 7618.
24. Hanoi, *VNA International News Service*, 1633 GMT, August 31, 1971, TTU Archive.
25. "Premier's Interview with U.S. Peace Fighters," Hanoi, *VNA International News Service*, 0212 GMT January 28, 1966, TTU Archive.
26. "Akahata Interviews U.S. Singer Baez in Hanoi," *Akahata, Tokyo*, December 24, 1972, TTU Archive.
27. "Peck Describes Antiwar Movement in the United States," Hanoi in English to American Servicemen in South Vietnam, 1300 GMT, November 18,1970, 10-12, TTU Archive.
28. "Quakers Begin Dramatic Voyage to Haiphong, NVN," *Fellowship, Peace Information Edition*, March 1967, TTU Archive.
29. "PRG Paris Delegates Confer with U.S. Peace Group," *Paris VNA to Hanoi VNA*, 0740 GMT, March 8, 1971, 23, TTU Archive.
30. "American Antiwar Delegation Arrives in Hanoi," *Hanoi Domestic Service*, 1430 GMT, November 5, 1972, TTU Archive; and "Pham Van Dong Receives American Antiwar Delegation," *Hanoi VNA International News Service*, 0240 GMT, November 12, 1972, TTU Archive.
31. Stanley Karnow, *Vietnam: a History* (New York: Penguin Books, 1997), 662-666.
32. "Antiwar Delegation Visits Northern Region of DRV," *Hanoi Domestic Service*, 0430 GMT, November 14, 1972, 10, TTU Archive.
33. Ibid., 10.
34. Ibid., 10-11.
35. "Pham Van Dong Receives Two U.S. Antiwar Delegations," *Hanoi International News Service*, 1557 GMT, August 26, 1971, TTU Archive.
36. Joint Publications Research Service (JPRS), "American Visitors Give Impressions of Anti-U.S. Struggle: 'How did the Americans Speak of Vietnam,'" Hanoi Lao Dong, October 21, 1970, 45-46, TTU Archive.
37. Douglas Pike, "The Viet-Cong Strategy of Terror," (U.S. Mission, Vietnam, 1970), 82, TTU Archive.
38. Acting Senior Agent in Charge (SAC), Chicago, memorandum to the Director FBI, Subject: Foreign Travel and Contacts with Representatives of Foreign Governments which Influenced the WHO, in Weather Underground Summary dated August 20, 1976, 64-66, FOIA.
39. Ibid., 66.
40. Ibid., 68.
41. Ibid., 68.

42. Ibid., 70-71.
43. Ibid., 92-93.
44. Ibid., 92-93.
45. Ibid., 208
46. Ibid., 264.
47. Ibid.,283.
48. Ibid., 284-286.
49. Ibid., 285-286.
50. Ibid., 203-204.
51. Ibid., 204-205.
52. "Foreign Visitors to the South Vietnam Liberated Areas this Year," *Hanoi Bao Tan Viet Hoa,* December 20, 1973, 17-18, TTU Archive.
53. Ibid.

Chapter Seven: Band of Tritors

1. Craig Howes, *Voices of Vietnam POWs* (New York, Oxford University Press, 1993), 35.
2. Smith Hempstone, "The Hanoi Tourists, POWs and Reality," *Washington Evening Star,* April 7, 1973, TTU.
3. "Hanoi Jane: Yesterday's Fiery Communist Revolutionary," *U.S. Veteran Dispatch,* October-December 1996 Issue, 1-4, on-line, Internet, February 5, 2004, available from http://www.usvetdsp.com/story8.htm.
4. House, *New Mobilization Committee to End the War in Vietnam. Part 2: Hearings before the House Committee on Internal Security,* 91st Cong., 2nd sess., 1970, 4190.
5. George E. Day, Colonel USAF Ret., *Return With Honor* (Mesa, AZ: Champlin Museum Press, 1991), 104.
6. House, *Report, Restraints on Travel to Countries or Areas Engaged in Armed Conflict with the United States,* 93d Cong., 1st sess., 1973, H.R. 93-248, 4.
7. Stuart I Rochester and Frederick Kiley, *Honor Bound* (Washington D. C.: Historical Office, Office of the Secretary of Defense, 1998), 180.
8. Sam Johnson and Jan Winebrenner, *Captive Warrior* (College Station, TX: Texas A&M University Press, 1992), 153.
9. House, *Hearings on Restraints on Travel to Hostile Areas: Hearings before the Committee on Internal Security,* 93d Cong., 1st sess, 1973, 3-4.
10. Ibid., 6-7.
11. Ibid., 4-5.
12. Ibid., 5-6.

13. Ibid., 8-10.
14. Ibid., 32-33.
15. Ibid., 9-10.
16. Ibid., 10-11.
17. Ibid., 12
18. Ibid.
19. Ibid., 13-14.
20. Ibid., 18-19.
21. Howes, *Voices of the Vietnam POWs*, 56.
22. House, *Hearings on Restraints on Travel*, 16.
23. Ibid., 17.
24. Ibid., 17-18.
25. House, *American POWs in Southeast Asia, Hearings before Committee on Foreign Affairs*, 1971, 6.
26. Ibid., 20.
27. House, *Extracts from an Interview with a Vietcong Returnee, Hearings before the Committee on Foreign Affairs*, 1970, 1.
28. Douglas Pike, "Treatment of Prisoners of War by the Vietcong/DRV 1962-1972," U.S. Mission, Saigon, 1972, 144, TTU.
29. Ibid.
30. Ibid., 161.
31. Ibid., 162.
32. Ibid., 155.
33. Ibid., 152.
34. Ibid., 150.
35. Ibid., 151.
36. Ibid., 150.
37. Ibid., 147.
38. Ibid., 148.
39. Ibid., 95.
40. Ibid., 93.
41. Michael Benge, "Cuban War Crimes Against American POWs During Vietnam War, *POW Network*, June 20, 1996, n.p., on-line, Internet, April 6, 2004, http://www.pownetwork.org/bios.
42. Douglas Pike, "Treatment of Prisoners," 141.
43. Sam Johnson, *Captive Warriors*, 250.
44. John Norton Moore & Robert F. Turner, *The Real Lessons of the Vietnam War* (Durham, NC: Carolina Academic Press, 2002), 227-228.
45. Robert P. Hey, "Two Camps Heard," *Christian Science Monitor*, November 13, 1969; "Representative Lowenstein Backs D.C. March," *Washington Post*, November 7, 1969; and "U.S./ Assailed on Vietnam

Policy Before 17,000 at a Garden Rally," *New York Times*, June 9, 1965, TTU.
46. Douglas Pike, "Treatment of Prisoners," 92.
47. John Moore and Robert Turner, *The Real Lessons of the Vietnam War*, 229.
48. House, *Communist Harassment of Vietnam Servicemen's Kin*, Congressional Record, June 22, 1965, 1.
49. House, *New Mobilization Committee to End the War*, 4188-4189, and House, *Report, Restraints on Travel*, 8.
50. House, *New Mobilization Committee to End the War*, 4191-4206.
51. Ibid., 4206-4215.
52. House, *Hearings on Restraints on Travel to Hostile Areas*, 26-28

Chapter Eight: Assault on the Troops

1. House, *Hearings Regarding H.R. 16742: Restraints on Travel to Hostile Areas: Hearings before the Committee on Internal Security*, 92d Cong., 2d sess., 1972, 7642-7643, 7682-7683.
2. Ibid., 7688.
3. Ibid., 7666-7671.
4. Michael Lind, Vietnam *the Necessary War* (New York: Simon & Schuster, 1999), 152-153.
5. House, *Restraints on Travel*, 7658.
6. Ibid., 7689-7691.
7. Ibid., 7690-7691.
8. Ibid., 7692.
9. Ibid., 7692.
10. Ibid., 7693.
11. House, *Restraints on Travel to Countries or Areas Engaged in Armed Conflict with the United States, Report by the Committee on Internal Security*, 93 Cong., 1st sess., report No. 93-248, 3-4.
12. House, *Investigation of Attempts to Subvert United States Armed Service, Part 1, Hearings before the Committee on Internal Security*, 92d Cong., 1st sess., *October 20-28, 1971*, USGPO 1972, 6382-6283, 6386.
13. Ibid., 6382.
14. Ibid., 6382.
15. Ibid., 6384.
16. Ibid., 6384, 6487-6489.
17. Ibid., 6489-6492.

18. House, *Investigation of Attempts to Subvert United States Armed Services, Part 3, Hearings before the Committee on Internal Security*, 92d Cong., 2nd sess., 1972, 7353.
19. House, *Investigation of Attempts to Subvert, Part 1*, 6481.
20. Ibid., 6623-24.
21. House, *Investigation of Attempts to Subvert, Part 3*, 7348-7350, 7500.
22. Ibid., 7349-7350.
23. House, *Investigation of Attempts to Subvert, Part 2*, 7099-7101.
24. Ibid., 7104-7105.
25. House, *Investigation of Attempts to Subvert, Part 1*, 6406.
26. Ibid. 6422, 6426, 6457.
27. House, *Investigation of Attempts to Subvert, Part 3*, 7222-7226.
28. Ibid., 7338-7340.
29. Ibid., 7340-7345.
30. Ibid., 7375.
31. Ibid., 7479, 7480, 7486, 7488.

Chapter Nine: Sabotaging the War Effort

1. Clark Dougan and Samuel Lipsman, *A Nation Divide* (Boston, MA, Boston Publishing Company, 1984), 170.
2. General William C. Westmoreland, *Report of the Chief of Staff of the United States Army* (Washington D.C. Department of the A, 1977), 49, 72-73.
3. House, *Anatomy of a Revolutionary Movement: Students for a Democratic Society Report by the Committee on Internal*, 91st Cong., 2d sess., 1970, 93.
4. Tom Wells, *The War Within* (Berkley, CA, University of California Press, 1994), 406-407, 421.
5. Ibid., 421.
6. Colonel Bui Tin, "How North Vietnam Won the War", *Wall Street Journal*, August 3, 1995, A10.
7. Tom Wells, 425.
8. House, Investigation of Students for a Democratic Society, Part 1-A, Georgetown University, Hearings before the Committee on Internal Security, 91st Cong., 1st sess., 1969, 212-213.
9. Ibid., 207-208.
10. Lewis Sorley, *A better War* (San Diego, Harvest, Inc., 1999), 303, and "Statistics About the Vietnam War," *The History Channel,* 8, on-line, Internet, April 20, 2003, http://www.historychannesl.com.

11. Nancy Zaroulis and Gerald Sullivan, *Who Spoke Up* (Garden City, NY, Doubleday & Company, Inc., 1984), 367.
12. House, *Investigation of Attempts to Subvert the United States Armed Services, Hearings before the Committee on Internal Security,* 92d Cong., 2nd., 1972, 7125-7131.
13. Nancy Zaroulis, 73.
14. Flyer, "Peoples Blockades of Arms for Indochina, A Project of Americans Friends Service Committee," July 1972, TTU Archive.
15. James Haskins, *The War and the Protest: Vietnam* (Garden City, NY, Doubleday & Company, Inc., 1971) 64, TTU Archive.
16. House, *Anatomy of a Revolutionary Movement*, 32-33.
17. Ibid., 44-45.
18. Ibid., 45.
19. Ibid., 46.
20. Ibid., 46.
21. Ibid., 50.
22. Clark Dougan, 174.
23. Nancy Zaroulis, 235.
24. Clark Dougan, 174.
25. Nancy Zaroulis 230.
26. Ibid., 235.
27. Arlo Tatum, ed., *Handbook for Conscientious Objectors* (Philadelphia, PA, Central Committee for Conscientious Objectors, 1966), n.p., TTU Archive.
28. "Fellowship of Reconciliation," *Fellowship,* Peace Information Edition, January 1, 1968.
29. "Upright with the Draft," Central Committee for Conscientious Objectors, (reprinted with permission of War Resisters League, New York, December 1967), n.p., TTU Archive.
30. "The Military Draft and 1969 Draft Lottery," 15th Field Artillery Regiment, 1917-2004, Vietnam Troop Levels, *Congressional Quarterly* n.d., n.p., on-line, Internet, July 7, 2004, available at www.landscaper.net/draft.htm; and "What Border? U.S.-Canada History," *The National,* n.d., n.p., on-line, Internet, July 12, 2004, available at http://www.tv.cbc.ca/national/pgminfo/border/waves.html; and *Handbook for Conscientious Objectors,* n.p.
31. Ibid., n.p.
32. "1960s Draft Dodgers Group—Toronto Anti-Draft Programme," Radical Middle Newsletter, n.d., n.p., on-line, Internet, July 5, 2004, available at http://www.radicalmiddle.com/fadp.htm.

33. "American Deserters Committee," Flyer, n.d., n.p., FBI/FOIA, on-line, Internet, July 5, 2004, available at http://Foia.fbi.gov/adc.htm.
34. Message, American Deserters Committee, Moscow Vietnam News Agency to Vietnam News Agency Hanoi, 1743 GMT, December 1971, TTU Archive.
35. Michael Lind, *Vietnam: the Necessary War* (New York, Simon & Schuster, 1999), 192-193; and Stanley Karnow, *Vietnam, a History* (New York, Penguin Books, 1993), 414, 648; and Richard Nixon, *No More Wars* (New York, Arbor House, 1985), 138-139.
36. Stanley Karnow, 648.
37. Richard Nixon, 139.
38. "Vietnam Insider Urges Others to Leak Secrets," *Colorado Springs Gazette*, July 12, 2004.

Chapter Ten: Peace Initiatives

1. *Webster's New Explorer Dictionary of Quotations* (Springfield, MA: A Division of Merriam-Webster, Inc., 2000), 439.
2. James Webb, "Sleeping with the Enemy," n.d., n.p., on-line, Internet, December 5, 2003, available at www.James%20webb.htm.
3. United States Information Service, *Special Report, Text of an Address by President Lyndon B. Johnson on Vietnam Prepared for Delivery at Johns Hopkins University, Baltimore, MD, April 7, 1965* (Washington, D.C., April 7, 1965), 5-6, TTU Archives.
4. Walter W. Rostow, Special Assistant for National Security Affairs, White House, memorandum to the President, subject: Peace Initiatives, March 30, 1967, 1 of atch. TTU Archives.
5. Ibid., 1 of atch.
6. Ibid., 1 of atch.
7. Ibid., 1 of atch.
8. Dean Rusk, as told to Richard Rusk, Edited by Daniel S. Sharp, *As I Saw It* (New York: WW Norton & Company, 1990), 466.
9. Walter W. Rostow, Peace Initiatives, 2 of atch.
10. Ibid.
11. Ibid.
12. Ibid.
13. Ibid.
14. Ibid.
15. Ibid., 3 of atch.

16. Department of State, *Vietnam Peace Bids Chronology, March-September, 1967* (Washington, D.C., State Department Bulletin 162, October 1967), 4, TTU Archives.
17. Ibid., 4.
18. Henry Kissinger, *White House Years* (Boston/Toronto, Little Brown and Company, 1979), 234.
19. "Chronology of Events," *CRN Special*, January 29, 1968, TTU Archive.
20. "Chronology of Events," and Stanley Karnow, *Vietnam, A History*, (New York, Penguin Books, 1984), 580-581.
21. Walter W. Rostow, 4.
22. Walter W. Rostow, 4, and Department of State, *US Reply to 17 Nation Appeal on Vietnam, April 8, 1965* (Washington, D.C., Department of State Bulletin, April 26, 1965), 610-612, TTU Archives.
23. Walter W. Rostow, 4.
24. Ibid., 4.
25. Ibid., 5.
26. Ibid., 5.
27. Ibid., 6-7.
28. "Chronology of Events."
29. Henry Kissinger, 236-237.
30. U.S. Mission, Saigon, *Vietnam: The Pursuit of Peace*, January 1966, 2.
31. Vietnam Peace Bids, 2.
32. Dean Rusk, 475-477.
33. Stanley Karnow, 580-581.
34. Admiral U.S. Grant Sharp, USN Ret., *Strategy for Defeat* (Novato, CA.: Presidio Press, 1998), 214.
35. Dean Rusk, 472.
36. Peter MacDonald, *Giap* (New York: W.W. Norton and Company, 1993), 324.
37. Defense Document Center, Defense Supply Agency, *Hanoi on War and Peace* (Santa Monica, CA.: RAND, December 1967), 37, TTU Archives.
38. Henry Kissinger, 254-255.
39. Ibid., 237.
40. U.S. Mission, Saigon, *Paris Talks, the Allied Side*, October 1970, 2, TTU Archives.
41. Ibid.
42. President Richard M. Nixon, "Vietnam Peace Initiatives," Televised Report to the Nation on the War In Vietnam, May 14, 1969, TTU Archive.

43. Department of State, "The Paris Peace Talks," *Vietnam Information Notes*, no. 15, (November 1969), 3, TTU Archives.
44. Ibid., 1.
45. Ibid., 3.
46. U.S. Mission, Saigon, *Excerpt from a Letter to the Central Office for South Vietnam from Le Duan, First Secretary of the Lao Dong Party* (Captured Enemy Document, by U.S. Forces in Vietnam, January 1967), n.p., TTU Archive.
47. Henry Kissinger, 443.
48. Ibid., 444.
49. Ibid., 260-261.
50. Ibid., 290-291.
51. Ibid., 452-453.
52. Ibid., 505-513.
53. Ibid., 970-971.
54. Ibid., 983.
55. Ibid., 989-1002.
56. Ibid., 1012.
57. Ibid., 1020.
58. Ibid., 1037.
59. Ibid., 1038-1039.
60. Ibid., 1044.
61. Kissinger, 1097-1098, 1109-1011, and Karnow, 655.
62. Kissinger, 1190-1191, 1195-1197.
63. Ibid., 1170.
64. Karnow, 666.
65. Kissinger, 1373-1375.
66. Ibid., 1434-1435.
67. Karnow, 667.
68. Kissinger, 1454-1455.
69. Karnow, 668.
70. Kissinger, 1468-1469.
71. U.S. Information Service, *Talking Points: Some Thoughts on the Current Vietnam Debates* (USIS Saigon, April 1972) 1, TTU Archive.
72. Ibid.
73. "Liberation Press Agency Cites Varied Antiwar Sentiment in America," *Liberation Press Agency* (Clandestine) FBIS 1545 GMT, July 15, 1970, 1, TTU Archive.
74. "Congressional, Other Opposition against Indochina War Reported" *Hanoi Vietnam News Agency, International Service*, FBIS 1552 GMT, June 12, 1971, n.p., TTU Archive.

75. "Commentary Applauds U.S. Antiwar Fall Offensive," *Hanoi Domestic Service*, FBIS 1430 GMT, October 18, 1971, n.p., TTU Archive.
76. "Javits Statement," *Moscow Domestic Service*, FBIS 1400 GMT, November 22, 1965, n.p., TTU Archive.
77. "War of Aggression in Vietnam Deepens U.S. Political Division," *Hanoi Domestic Service*, FBIS 1430 GMT, May 17, 1971, 1-2, TTU Archive.
78. USIS *Talking Points*, 1.
79. Dennis E. Showalter and John G. Albert, ed., *An American Dilemma, Vietnam, 1964-1973* (Chicago, IL.: Impact Publications, 1993), 195.
80. "Fed up by Those Who'd Peril GIs in Viet-Laird," *Stars and Stripes*, Washington Bureau, April 26, 1972, n.p., TTU Archive.
81. Senate Committee on Judiciary, *The anti-Vietnam Agitation and the Teach-in Movement, A Staff Study for the Subcommittee to Investigate the Administration of the Internal Security Act and Other Internal Security Laws*, 89 Cong., 1st sess., 1965, S Doc. 72, 7619.
82. "Beg, Don't Bomb," *Stars & Stripes*, July 1, 1972.
83. "Saving Face or Saving Lives, McGovern Diagrams Plan for Peace," *Stars & Stripes*, October 12, 1972.

Chapter Eleven: Sellout

1. Dean Rusk as told to Richard Rusk, *As I Saw It* (New York: W.W. & Company, 1990), 490-491.
2. Liberation Radio (Clandestine), 2200 GMT 20 September 1974, "It's the Same Vicious Circle of the Nixon Doctrine," L4, (Foreign Broadcast Information Service), TTU Archives.
3. Hanoi VNA 1627 GMT 30 March 1974, "Text of Le Duc Tho Recorded Speech to Stockholm Conference," K4, (Foreign Broadcast Information Service), TTU Archives.
4. "Paris Peace Accords," *All POW-MIA*, 8, on-line, Internet, August 17, 2004, http://www.aiipowmia.com/sea/ppal1973.hrml.
5. Admiral U.S. Grant Sharp, U.S. Navy (Ret), *Strategy for Defeat, Vietnam in Retrospect* (Novato, CA: Presidio Press, 1998), 260.
6. All POW-MIA, 1.
7. Phillip B. Davidson, *Vietnam at War* (Novato, CA: Presidio Press, 1988, 738; and Arnold R. Isaacs, *Without Honor* (Baltimore, MD, Johns Hopkins University Press, 1983), 317.
8. All POW-MIA, 3.

9. Embassy of Vietnam, *One Year of Implementation of the Paris Agreement on Ending the War and Restoring Peace in Vietnam* (Washington, D.C., Vietnam Information Office, March 19, 1974), 8, TTU Archive.
10. Department of State, *The 1973 Paris Agreements—a Scoreboard of Noncompliance,* Washington, D.C., Secretary of State, INR Analysis, July 21, 1987), 3, TTU Archive.
11. Office of the White House, *Protocol: The Agreement on Ending the War & Restoring Peace in Vietnam* (Washington, D.C.: Office of the Press Secretary, January 1973) Chapter IV, 4, TTU Archive.
12. Department of State, *The 1973 Paris Agreements—a Scoreboard of Noncompliance,* 3.
13. Ibid., 3.
14. Ibid., 3-4.
15. Embassy of Vietnam, 6.
16. Ibid., 6.
17. Ibid., 6-7.
18. Ibid., 7.
19. Sen. Gen Van Tien Dung, "Great Spring Victory," Asia & Pacific, Daily Report Supplement, no.1, (FBIS-APA-76-110, June 7, 1976): 38, TTU Archive.
20. Ibid., 1-2.
21. Stanley Karnow, *Vietnam, a History* (New York: Penguin Books, 1984), 677-678.
22. William Colby with James Gregory, *Lost Victory* (New York: Contemporary Books, 1989), 349-350.
23. Colonel Bui Tin, "How North Vietnam Won the War," *Wall Street Journal,* August 3, 1995, A10
24. Stanley Karnow, 350.
25. Sen Gen Dung, 4-5.
26. Ibid., 8.
27. Ibid., 8.
28. Arnold R. Isaacs, 316-317.
29. Lewis Sorley, *A Better War* (San Diego, CA, New York: Harcourt, Inc., 1999), 372-373.
30. Ibid., 376.
31. Foreign Broadcast Information Service (FBIS), *Southeast Asia Report, Vietnam TAP CHI CONG SAN, No. 4, April 1985,* JPRS-SEA-85-103, July 1, 1985, 10, TTU Archive.
32. Ibid., 11-13.
33. Ibid., 14.

34. Lewis Sorley, 380.
35. FBIS, *Southeast Asia Report*, 15.
36. Richard Nixon, *No More Vietnams* (New York: Arbor House, 1985).
37. Ambassador William Colby, "Turning Points in the Vietnam War", keynote speech before the 2nd Triennial Vietnam Symposium, Texas Tech University, The Vietnam Center, April 18, 1996, 6, TTU Archive.
38. Nancy Zaroulis and Gerald Sullivan, *Who Spoke Up* (New York: Doubleday & Company, Inc., 1984), 405.
39. James Webb, "Sleeping with the Enemy", 6, on-line, Internet, December 5, 2003, available at www.james%20webb.htm.
40. Richard Nixon, 169-170.
41. Phillip B. Davidson, 741.
42. Richard Nixon, 181.
43. LTC Stuart A. Harrington, *Peach with Honor* (Novato, CA: Presidio Press, 1983), 120; and Arnold R. Isaacs 314-315.
44. Arnold R. Isaacs, 315
45. James Webb, 2.
46. President Gerald R. Ford, address before a Joint Session of Congress, National Archives, Washington, D.C., April 10, 1975, 2.
47. Ibid., 2-3.
48. Ibid., 4-6.
49. General William C. Westmoreland, *A Soldier Reports* (Garden City, NY: Doubleday & Company, Inc., 1976), 409.
50. Senate, *Additional Military Aid to Vietnam is Ill Advised*, 93rd Cong., 2d sess., 1974, 1.
51. Richard Nixon, 189-190.
52. William C. Westmoreland, 408.
53. Phillip B. Davidson, 809.
54. Ibid., 810, 744.
55. Richard Nixon, 165.

Chapter Twelve: Prolonging the War

1. Douglas Pike, *Congress and the Indochina War*, A National Security Workshop, (George Mason University Review, Fall 1988), 128, TTU Archive.
2. John Norton Moore and Robert F. Turner, ed., *The Real Lessons of the Vietnam War* (Durham, NC: Carolina Academic Press, 2002), 239, 256; and Maxwell Taylor, *Swords and Plowshares* (New York: W.W. Norton & Company, Inc., 1972), 408.

3. Stephen Young, "How North Vietnam Won the War," *Wall Street Journal,* August 3, 1995, A10.

4. Maxwell Taylor, *Swords and Plowshares* (New York: W.W. Norton & Company, Inc., 1972), 383.

5. W.W. Rostow, *The Diffusion of Power* (New York: Macmillan Company, 1972), 468-469.

6. Bui Tin, *Following Ho Chi Minh* (Honolulu: University of Hawaii Press, 1995), 62.

7. W.W. Rostow, 519.

8. Dennis E. Showalter and John G. Albert, *An American Dilemma, Vietnam 1964-1973* (Chicago: Imprint Publications, 1993), 29.

9. Gene Kuentzler, "Tom Hayden, Jane Fonda, Hanoi Hanna," *Vietnam Veterans' War Stories*, 4, on-line, Internet, July 2, 2003, available at www.war-stories.com.

10. Admiral U.S. Grant Sharp, U.S. Navy (Retired), *Strategy for Defeat, Vietnam in Retrospect* (Novato, CA.: Presidio Press, 1998), 232.

11. Melvin Small, *Johnson, Nixon and the Doves,* (New Brunswick, NJ: Rutgers University Press, 1988), 185-186.

12. Ibid., 179, 186.

13. Admiral Sharp, 240-258.

14. Ibid., 255.

15. Ibid., 255.

16. Richard Nixon, *No More Vietnams* (NY.: Arbor House, 1985), 127.

17. Ibid., 194.

18. Arnold R. Isaacs, *Without Honor, Defeat in Vietnam and Cambodia* (Baltimore: Johns Hopkins University Press, 1983), 494.

19. Melvin Small, 180-181

20. Ibid., 181.

21. Ibid., 122.

22. Ibid., 81.

23. Ibid., 151-152.

24. Senate, *American Protesters Prolong Vietnam War*, October 18, 1965, 26298, TTU Archive.

25. Ibid., 26295.

26. House, *Restraints on Travel to Hostile Areas: Hearings before the Committee on Internal Security*, 93d Cong., 1st sess., 1073, 68.

27. Ibid., 66.

28. Senate Committee on Judiciary, Subcommittee to Investigate the Administration of the Internal Security Act and the Internal Security Laws, *Staff Study, Anti-Vietnam Agitation and the Teach-in Movement*, 89th Cong., 1st sess., 1965, 7612.

29. Ibid., 7619.
30. House, *Extension of Remarks of Hon. W.J. Bryan Dorn, General Westmoreland, Protests Encourage the Enemy,* April 26, 1967, A2055-A2056, TTU Archive, TTU Archive.
31. General William C. Westmoreland, *A Soldier Reports* (Garden City, NY.: Doubleday and Company, Inc., 1976), 413-414.
32. Admiral Sharp, 235.
33. Thomas Powers, *The War at Home* (NY.: Grossman Publishers, 1973), 113.
34. Maxwell Taylor, 401.
35. General Phillip B. Davidson, U.S.Army (Retired), *Vietnam at War* (Novato, CA.: Presidio Press, 1988), 808-809.
36. "Protesters Prolonged Our Captivity-Risner," *Stars & Stripes*, March 1, 1973, TTU Archive.
37. "Peaceniks and PWs," *New York Times*, March 9, 1973, TTU Archive.
38. House Committee on Internal Security, *Report: Restraints on Travel to Countries or Areas Engaged in Armed Conflict with the United States*, 93d Cong., 1st sess., 1973, 4.
39. Central Intelligence Agency, Memorandum for the Director, CIA, Subject: The View from Hanoi, November 30, 1966, 21, Secret, now declassified.
40. Thomas J. Schoenbaum, *Waging Peace and War* (New York: Simon and Schuster, 1988), 439, 496.
41. Dean Rusk as told to Richard Rusk, *As I Saw it* (New York: W.W. Norton & Company, 1990), 493.
42. Henry Kissinger, *White House Years* (Boston: Little, Brown and Company, 1979), 260.
43. Ibid., 510.
44. W.W. Rostow, 516, 562.
45. Larry Berman, *Lyndon Johnson's War, the Road to Stalemate in Vietnam* (New York: W.W. Norton & Company, 1988), 1989, 57.
46. Thomas Powers, 88.
47. Melvin Small, 185-186.
48. "Anti-war Riots Killing American Soldiers: Blount," *Stars & Stripes,* November 20, 1969, TTU Archive.
49. Robert Turner, "The Anti-war Movement in the U.S.," 1972, 6, TTU Archive.
50. Ibid., 6.
51. Ibid., 16.
52. Fred J. Johnson, "Perspective on Vietnam," *American Security Council Washington Report*, January 31, 1966, 6-F, TTU Archive.

53. "The Vietniks: Self-Defeating Dissent," *Time Essay*, October 15, 1965, 45, TTU Archive.
54. "Seek Probe of Antiwar Leaders," *Stars & Stripes*, April 9, 1973, TTU Archive.
55. David Lawrence, "Moscow, Student Protest Link Seen," *Washington Star*, October 29, 1965, TTU Archive.
56. Peter Macdonald, *Giap, the Victor in Vietnam*, (New York: W.W. Norton & Company, 1993), 323-324.
57. General Vo Nguyen Giap, *How We Won the War* (Philadelphia: Recon Publishers, 1976).

Chapter Thirteen: Aftermath

1. Viet Dinh, "How We Won the War In Vietnam," *Policy Review*, 9, on-line, Internet, July 6, 2004, available at www.policyreview.org/dec00/ding_print.html.
2. "Vietnam after 1975," *Library of Congress Country Studies*, December 1987, 3, on-line, Internet, September 12, 2004, available at http://lcweb2.loc.gov/frd/cs/cshome.html.
3. Viet Dinh, 2.
4. Le Manh Hung, "Problems & Prospects since Reunification," *Vietnam Perspectives*, May 18, 1990, n.p., TTU Archive.
5. "Vietnam: Re-education Camps," *Library of Congress Country Studies*, December 1987, 2, on-line, Internet, September 9, 2004, available at http://lcweb2.loc.gov/frd/cs/cshome.html.
6. Ibid., 1-2.
7. Bui Tin, *Following Ho Chi Minh*, Honolulu, University of Hawaii Press, 1995), 101-102; and Lou Morano, "Vietnam: The Trail Not Taken," *Jewish World Review*, May 24, 2002, 5, on-line, Internet, July 9, 2000, available at www.jewishworldreview.com.
8. "Vietnam: Population Relocation," *Library of Congress Country Studies*, December 1987, 1, on-line, Internet, September 9, 2004, available at http://lcweb2.loc.gov/frd/cs/cshome.html.
9. "Vietnam: Surveillance," *Library of Congress Country Studies*, December 1987, 2, on-line, Internet, September 9, 2004, available at http://lcweb2.loc.gov/frd/cs/cshome.html.
10. "Vietnam: Social Control," *Library of Congress Country Studies*, December 1987, 2, on-line, Internet, September 9, 2004, available at http://lcweb2.loc.gov/frd/cs/cshome.html.

11. "Vietnam Country Brief," *Department of Foreign Affairs and Trade, Government of Australia*, July 2004, 26, on-line, Internet, September 12, 2004, available at http://www.dfat.gov.au/geo/vietnam/vietnam_brief.hrml.
12. "Vietnam: The Media," *Library of Congress Country Studies*, December 1987, 4, on-line, Internet, September 2, 2004, available at http://lcweb2.loc.gov/frd/cs/cshome.html.
13. "Vietnam: Free Press is State Enemy No.1," *Press Release, International Society for Human Rights*, November 13, 2002, 2, on-line, Internet, July 3, 2003, available at http://www.ishr.org/press; and "Vietnam: Father Ly Must Not Be Forgotten," *Press Release, International Society for Human Rights*, May 13, 2004, 2, on-line, Internet, September 13, 2004, available at http://www.ishr.org/press.
14. "Vietnam: Father Ly Must Not Be Forgotten, 1-2.
15. "Vietnam: ISHR Demands Release of Prisoners Imprisoned for Religious Reasons," *Press Release, International Society for Human Rights*, February 11, 2004, 1, on-line, Internet, September 13, 2004, available at http://www.ishr.org/press.
16. "Vietnam: Journalist Sentenced to Ten Years Imprisonment and House Arrest for Publishing 'Negative Articles,'" *Press Release, International Society for Human Rights*, May 5, 2004, 2, on-line, Internet, September 13, 2004, available at http://www.ishr.org/press.
17. "Vietnam: Free Press is State Enemy No.1," 1-2.
18. Ibid., 1.
19. Ibid., 2.
20. "Vietnamese Are Not Even Allowed Freedom of Opinion on the Internet," *Press Release, International Society for Human Rights*, September 26, 2002, 2, on-line, Internet, July 3, 2003, available at http://www.ishr.org/press.
21. "Vietnam: Free Press is State Enemy No.1, 2.
22. John Norton Moore & Robert E. Turner, ed., *The Real Lessons of the Vietnam War* (Durham, NC: Carolina Academic Press, 2002), 449-454.
23. Douglas Pike, *Congress and the Indochina War*, a National Security Workshop (George Mason University Law Review, Fall 1988), 127-130, TTU Archive.
24. Henry Kissinger, *White House Years* (Boston: Little, Brown and Company, 1979), 228.
25. Paul Elliot, *Vietnam: Conflict and Controversy* (London: Arms and Armour Press), 178-179.
26. Douglas Pike, 128.
27. John Norton Moore, 482.

Chapter Fourteen: The Antiwar Legacy

1. Lewis Sorley, *A Better War* (San Diego, CA: Harvest Book Harcourt, Inc. 1999), 12; and Melvin Small, *Johnson, Nixon and the Doves* (New Brunswick, NJ: Rutgers University Press, 1989), 129, 134.
2. David S. Broder, "Muskie, McGovern Attack Viet Policy," *Washington Post*, April 14, 1972; and "Kennedy Hits Nixon Policy in Vietnam," *Washington Post*, April 8, 1972; and "Congressional, Other Opposition against Indochina War Reported," *Vietnam News Agency*, June 12, 1971.
3. Steve Le Blanc, "Kennedy Says Case for Iraq War Was Fraud," *AOL News*, September 18, 2003, n.p., on-line, Internet, September 20, 2003, available at http://aolsvc.news.aol.com; and "Kennedy to Assail Bush over Iraq War," *Boston Globe Archives*, October 16, 2003, n.p., on-line, Internet, November 26, 2003, available at www.boston.com/news/archives.
4. Senator Edward M. Kennedy, "America's Future in Iraq," address, Johns' Hopkins School of International Studies, Baltimore, MD, January 27, 2005.
5. "Rumsfeld Brushes Aside Call for Resignation," *Fox News*, June 23, 2005, 3, on-line, Internet, June 23, 2005, available from www.foxnews.com.
6. "Pelosi: 'This War in Iraq is a Grotesque Mistake; It is Not Making America Safer,'" *Press Release*, June 20, 2005, 2, on-line, Internet, June 22, 2005, available from www.house.gov/pelosi/press/release; and "Pitch Battle for Troop Withdrawal," *Fox News*, June 20, 2005, 2, on-line, Internet, June 22, 2005, available from www.foxnews.com.
7. David Bender & Bruno Leone, series ed., William Dudley & David Bender, book ed., *The Vietnam War* (San Diego, CA: Greenhaven Press, Inc., 1984), 99.
8. Ibid., 99.

Bibliography

Books

Ashmore, Harry S., and William C. Baggs. *Mission to Hanoi.* New York: G.P. Putnam's Son 1968.

Berman, Larry. *Lyndon Johnson's War: the Road to Stalemate in Vietnam.* New York: W.W. Norton & Company, 1989.

Braestrap, Peter. *Big Story: How American Press and TV Reported and Interpreted the Crisis of Tet 68.* New Haven: Yale University Press, 1983.

Burkett, B. G., and Glenna Whitley. *Stolen Valor: How the Vietnam Generation Was Robbed of Its Heroes and Its History.* Dallas: Variety Press. Inc., 1998.

Califano, Joseph A. Jr. *The Triumph and Tragedy of Lyndon Johnson: the White House Years.* New York: Simon & Schuster, 1991.

Chandler, David P. *The Tragedy of Cambodian History.* New Haven: Yale University Press, 1991.

Charen, Mona. *Useful Idiots.* Washington D.C.: Regnery Publishing, Inc., 2003.

Charlton, Michael, and Anthony Moncrieff. *Many Reasons Why: The American Involvement in Vietnam.* New York: Hill and Wang, 1978.

Colby, William. *Lost Victory.* Chicago: Contemporary Books, 1989.

Churchill, Winston S. *The Second World War: The Gathering Storm.* Boston: Houghton Mifflin Company, 1948.

Davidson, General Phillip B. *Vietnam at War: The History: 1946-1975.* Novato, CA: Presidio Press, 1988.

Day, Colonel George E. *Return with Honor.* Mesa, AZ: Champlin Museum Press, 1989.

DeBenedetti, Charles. *An American Ordeal: The Antiwar Movement of the Vietnam Era.* New York: Syracuse University Press, 1990.

Denton, Admiral Jeremiah A. and Ed Bramdt. *When Hell Was in Session.* New York: Readers Digest Press, 1976.

Dougan, Clark, and Samuel Lipsman. *A Nation Divided.* Boston: Boston Publishing Company, 1984.

Drameci, John A. *Code of Honor.* New York: W. W. Norton, 1975.
Dudley, William, and David Bender, eds. *The Vietnam War: Opposing Viewpoints.* San Diego: Greenhaven Press, Inc., 1990.
Eisenhower, Dwight D. *Waging Peace 1956-1961.* Garden City, NY: Doubleday & Company, Inc., 1965.
Elliot, Paul. *Vietnam: Conflict and Controversy.* London: Arms and Armour, 1996.
Evans, Rowland and Robert Novak. *Lyndon B. Johnson: The Exercise of Power.* New York: The New American Library, Inc., 1966.
Gaiduk, Ilya V. *The Soviet Union and the Vietnam War.* Chicago: Ivan R. Dee, 1996.
Garfinkle, Adam, and Stephen E. Ambrose. *Telltale Hearts: The Origins and Impacts of the Vietnam Antiwar Movement.* New York: St. Martin's Press, 1995.
Giap, General Vo Nguyen. *How We Won the War.* Philadelphia: RECON Publications, 1976.
Gottlieb, Sherry Gershon. *Hell No We Won't Go.* New York: Viking Penguin Books USA, Inc., 1991.
Haldeman, H. R., and Joseph D. Mona. *The Ends of Power.* New York: New York Times Book Company, Inc., 1978.
Haskins, James. *The War and the Protests in Viet Nam.* Garden City, NY: Doubleday & Company, Inc., 1971.
Hayden, Tom. *Trail.* New York: Hold, Rinehart and Winston, 1970.
Heineman, Kenneth J. *Campus Wars.* New York: New York University Press, 1994.
Herrington, LTC Stuart A. *Peace with Honor.* Novato, CA: Presidio Press, 1983.
Howes, Craig. *Voices of the Vietnam POWs.* New York: Oxford University Press, 1993.
Isaacs, Arnold R. *Without Honor: Defeat in Vietnam and Cambodia.* Baltimore: The Johns Hopkins University Press, 1983.
Isaacson, Walter. *Kissinger: A Biography.* New York: Simon & Schuster, 1992.
Jensen, Jay R. *Six Years in Hell: A Returned POW Views Captivity, Country and the Nation's Future.* Orcutt, CA: Publications of Worth, 1989.
Johnson, Sam, and Jan Winebrenner. *Captive Warriors.* College Station, TX: Texas A&M University Press, 1992.
Karnow, Stanley. *Vietnam: A History.* New York: Penguin Books, 1997.
Katsiaficas, George. *Vietnam Documents: American and Vietnamese Views of the War.* Armok, NY: M. E. Sharpe, Inc., 1992.

Kissinger, Henry. *Crisis: The Anatomy of Two Major Foreign Policy Crises*. New York: Simon & Schuster, 2003.

Kissinger, Henry. *The White House Years*. Boston: Little, Brown and Company, 1979.

Lake, Anthony. *Legacy of Vietnam*. New York: New York University Press, 1970.

Lane, General Thomas A. *America on Trial*. New Rochelle, NY: Arlington House, 1971.

Lewy, Guenter. *America in Vietnam*. New York: Oxford University Press, 1978.

Lind, Michael. *Vietnam: The Necessary War*. New York: Simon & Schuster, 1999.

Lindley, Ernest K, ed., *The Winds of Freedom*. Boston: Beacon Press, 1963.

Luce, Phillip Abbott. *The New Left*. New York: David McKay Company, Inc., 1966.

Lynd, Alice. *We Won't Go*. Boston: Beacon Press, 1968.

Macdonald, Peter. *Giap: The Victor in Vietnam*. New York: W.W. Norton & Company, 1993.

McConnell and Schweitzer. *Inside Hanoi's Secret Archives: Solving the MIA Mystery*. Simon & Schuster, 1995.

McNamara, Robert S. *In Retrospect: The Tragedy and Lessons of Vietnam*. New York: Times Books, 1995.

Miller, Merle. *Lyndon: An Oral Biography*. New York: G.P Putnam's Sons, 1980.

Moore, John Norton, and Robert F. Turner, eds. *The Real Lessons of the War*. Durham, NC: Carolina Academic Press, 2002.

Mulligan, Captain James A. *The Hanoi Commitment*. Virginia Beach, VA: RIF Marketing, 1981.

Nasmyth, Spike. *2355 Days: A POW's Story*. New York: Orion Books, 1991.

Newman, John M. *JFK and Vietnam*. New York: Warner Books, 1992

Nicosia, Gerald. *Home to War*. New York: Crown Publishers, 2001.

Nixon, Richard. *In the Arena*. New York: Simon & Schuster, 1980.

Nixon, Richard. *No More Vietnams*. New York: Arbor House, 1985.

Nixon, Richard. *The Real War*. New York: Warner Books, 1980.

O'Neill, John E, and Jerome R. Corsi. *Unfit for Command*. Washington D.C.: Regnery Publishing, Inc., 2004.

O'Neill, Robert J. *General Giap: Politician & Strategist*. New York: Frederick A. Praeger, Inc., 1969.

Pike, Douglas. *PAVN People's Army of Vietnam.* Novato, CA: Presidio Press, 1986.
Pike, Douglas. *War, Peace, and the Viet Cong.* Cambridge, MA: The M.I.T. Press, 1969.
Powers, Thomas. *The War at Home: Vietnam and the American People, 1964-1968.* New York: Grossman Publishers, 1973.
Risner, General Robinson. *The Passing of the Night: My Seven Years as a Prisoner of the North Vietnamese.* Duncanville: World Wide Printing, 1999.
Rochester, Stuart I, and Frederick Kiley. *Honor Bound: The History of American Prisoners of War in Southeast Asia, 1961-1973.* Washington D.C.: Historical Office of the Secretary of Defense, 1998.
Rostow, Walt W. *The Diffusion of Power: An Essay in Recent History.* New York: Macmillan Company, 1972.
Rusk, Dean. *As I Saw It.* New York: W.W. Norton & Company, 1990.
Sharp, Admiral U.S. Grant, U.S. Navy (Retired). *Strategy for Defeat: Vietnam in Retrospect.* Novato, CA: Presidio Press, 1998.
Showalter, Dennis E., and John G. Albert, eds. *An American Dilemma: Vietnam, 1964-1972.* Chicago: Imprint Publications, 1992.
Small, Melvin. *Covering Dissent.* New Brunswick, NJ: Rutgers University Press, 1994.
Small, Melvin. *Johnson, Nixon, and the Doves,* New Brunswick, NJ: Rutgers University Press, 1989.
Sorley, Lewis. *A Better War.* San Diego, CA: A Harvest Book Harcourt, Inc., 1999.
Students for a Democratic Society. *The Port Huron Statement.* Chicago: Charles H. Kerr Publishing Company, 1962.
Summers, Colonel Harry G. Jr. *On Strategy: The Vietnam War in Context.* Carlisle Barracks, PA: Strategic Studies Institute, U.S. Army War College, 1981.
Tang, Troung Nhu. *A Vietcong Memoir.* New York: Vintage Books, 1986.
Taylor, General Maxwell D. *Swords and Plowshares.* New York: W.W. Norton & Company, Inc., 1972.
Tin, Colonel Bui. *Following Ho Chi Minh: The Memoirs of a North Vietnamese Colonel.* Translated by Judy Stowe and Do Van. Honolulu: University of Hawaii Press, 1995.
Tin, Colonel Bui. *From Enemy to Friend.* Annapolis, MD: Naval Institute Press, 2002.
Van Dyke, Jon M. *North Vietnam's Strategy for Survival.* Palo Alto, CA: Pacific Books, 1972.

Victory In Vietnam: The Official History of the People's Army of Vietnam, 1954-1975. Translated by Merle L. Pribbenow. Lawrence, KA: University Press of Kansas, 2002.

The Vietnam Hearings. Introduced by William J. Fulbright. New York: Random House, 1966.

Warner, Dennis. *Certain Victory: How Hanoi Won the War.* Kansas City, MO: Sheed Andrews and McMeel, inc., 1977.

Warner, Roger. *Back Fire: The CIA's Secret War In Laos and Its Links to the War in Vietnam.* New York: Simon & Schuster, 1995.

Wells, Tom. *The War Within.* Berkley, CA: University of California Press, 1994.

Westmoreland, General William C. *Report of the Chief of Staff of the United States Army: 1 July 1968 to 30 June 1972.* Washington D.C.: Department of the Army, 1977.

Westmoreland, General William C. *A Soldier Reports.* Garden City, NY: Doubleday & Company, Inc., 1976.

Wirtz, Jamaes J. *The Tet Offensive.* Ithaca, NY: Cornell University Press, 1991.

Zaroulis, Nancy, and Gerald Sullivan. *Who Spoke Up.* Garden City, NY: Doubleday & Company, Inc., 1984.

Congressional Documents

U.S. Congress. House. Committee on Internal Security. *Anatomy of a Revolutionary Movement: Students for a Democratic Society. Report by the Committee on Internal Security.* 91st Cong., 2nd sess., 1970. H.R. 1565.

U.S. Congress. House. Committee on Internal Security. *Restraints on Travel to Countries or Areas Engaged in Armed Conflict with the United States. Report by the Committee on Internal Security.* 93rd Cong., 1st sess., 1973. H. R. 93-248.

U.S. Congress. House. Committee on Un-American Activities. *Communist Origin and Manipulation of Vietnam Week. Report by the Committee on Un-American Activities.* 90th Cong., 1st sess., 1967. H.R. 186.

U.S. Congress. House. *Hearings Regarding H.R. 16742: Restraints on Travel to Hostile Areas. Hearings before the Committee on Internal Security.* 92nd Cong., 2ne sess., 1972.

U.S. Congress. House. *Hearings on Restraints on Travel to Hostile Areas H.R. 1594. Hearings before the Committee on Internal Security.* 93rd Cong., 1st sess., 1973.

U.S. Congress. House. *Investigation of Attempts to Subvert the United States Armed Services. Hearings before the Committee on Internal Security, Part 1.* 92nd Cong., 1st sess., 1971.

U.S. Congress. House. *Investigation of Attempts to Subvert the United States Armed Services. Hearings before the Committee on Internal Security, Part 2.* 92 Cong., 2nd sess. 1972.

U.S. Congress. House. *Investigation of Attempts to Subvert the United States Armed Services. Hearings before the Committee on Internal Security, Part 3.* 92nd Cong., 2nd sess., 1972.

U.S. Congress. House. *National Peace Action Coalition (NPAC) and Peoples Coalition for Peace & Justice (PCPJ), Part 1. Hearings before the Committee on Internal Security.* 92nd Cong., 1st sess., 1971.

U.S. Congress. House. *New Mobilization Committee to End the War in Vietnam, Part 1. Hearings before the Committee on Internal Security.* 91st Cong., 2nd sess. 1970.

U.S, Congress. House. *New Mobilization Committee to End the War in Vietnam, Part 2. Hearings before the Committee on Internal Security.* 91st Cong., 2nd sess., 1970.

U.S. Congress. House. *Investigation of Students for a Democratic Society, Part 1-A. Hearings before the Committee on Internal Security.* 91st Cong., 1st sess., 1969.

U.S. Congress. House. *Student Views Toward United States Policy in Southeast Asia. Hearings before the Ad Hoc Committee of Members of the House of Representatives.* 91st Cong., 2nd sess., 1970.

U.S. Congress. House. *Subversive Involvement in the Origin, Leadership, and Activities of the New Mobilization Committee to End the War in Vietnam and Its Predecessor Organizations. Staff Study by the Committee on Internal Security.* 91st Cong., 2nd sess., 1970.

U.S. Congress. House. *Vietnam-Cambodia Conflict. Report Prepared at the Request of the Subcommittee on Asian and Pacific Affairs Committee on International Relations.* 95th Cong., 2nd sess., 1978.

U.S Congress. Joint Resolution. *Southeast Asia Resolution. Gulf of Tonkin Resolution.* August 10, 1964.

U.S. Congress. Senate. *An Amendment to End the War, Referred to the Committee on Armed Services.* 91st Cong., 2nd sess., 1970. H.R. 17123.

U.S. Congress. Senate. Committee on the Judiciary. Subcommittee to Investigate the Administration of the Internal Security Act and

Other Internal Security Laws. *Staff Study on The Anti-Vietnam Agitation and the Teach-In Movement.* 89th Cong., 1st sess., 1965. S. Doc. 72.

U.S. Congress. Senate. Concurrent Resolution 65. *The Anti-Vietnam Agitation and the Teach-In Movement.* 89th Cong., 1st sess., 1965.

U.S. Congress. Senate. *Extent of Subversion in Campus Disorders. Testimony of Ernesto E. Blanco. Hearings before the Subcommittee to Investigate Administration of the Internal Security Act and Other Internal Security Laws, Part 1.* 91st Cong., 1st sass., 1969.

U.S. Congress. Senate. *Extent of Subversion in Campus Disorders. Testimony of Max Phillip Friedman. Hearings before the Subcommittee to Investigate Administration of the Internal Security Act and Other Internal Security Laws, Part 2.* 91st Cong., 1st sess., 1969.

U.S. Congress. Senate. *Extent of Subversion in the "New Left." Testimony of Robert J. Thomas. Hearings before the Subcommittee to Investigate Administration of the Internal Security Act and Other Internal Security Laws, Part 1.* 91st Cong., 2nd sess., 1970.

U.S. Congress. House. *The Viet Cong, the Anti-War Movement and POW'S.* Extracts form an Interview with a Vietcong Returnee. Washington, D.C. House Foreign Affairs Committee Hearings. March 1970. Texas Tech University Vietnam Archive.

U.S, Congress. Senate. *Vietnam Commitments, 1961. A Staff Study Based on the Pentagon Papers Prepared for the Use of the Committee on Foreign Relations. Study No. 1.* 92 Cong., 2nd sess., 1972.

Presidential Documents and Addresses

Eisenhower, Dwight D. *Address April 4, 1959, Gettysburg College, Gettysburg, PA.* Enclosure to Letter from Mr. David Martin, Office of Senator Dodd, April 1, 1965. Texas Tech University Vietnam Archive.

Ford, Gerald R. *Address to a Joint Session of Congress.* August 12, 1974. 7. Gerald Ford Library and Museum. On-line. Internet. February 24, 2004. Available at www.ford,utexas.edu/library/speeches/htm.

Ford, Gerald R. *Address before a Joint Session of Congress Reporting on the United States Foreign Policy.* April 10, 1975. 11. Gerald Ford Library. On-line. Internet. August 24, 2004. Available at www.ford,utexas.edu/library/speeches/htm.

Johnson, Lyndon B. *Annual Message to Congress on the State of the Union.* January 12, 1966. 13. LBJ Library. On-line. Internet. February 8, 2004. Available at www.lbjlib.utexas.edu/johnson/archives.hon/speeches.

Johnson, Lyndon B. Annual Message to the Congress on the State of the Union, January 17, 1968. 12. LBJ Library. On-line. Internet. February 23, 2004. Available at www.lbjlib.utexas.edu/johnson/archives.hon/speeches.

Johnson, Lyndon B. *Annual Message to the Congress on the State of the Union and Farewell Address, January 14, 1969.* 9. LBJ Library. On-line. Internet. February 23, 2004. Available at www.lbjlib.utexas.edu/johnson/archives.hon/speeches.

Johnson, Lyndon B. *Order by Johnson Reaffirming Kennedy's Policy on Vietnam. Excerpt from National Security Action Memorandum 273, November 26, 1963.* Texas Tech University Vietnam Archive.

Johnson, Lyndon B. *The Pursuit of Peace. Statement by the President on January 31, 1966.* Texas Tech University Vietnam Archive.

Johnson, Lyndon B. *Special Message to Congress on U.S. Policy in Southeast Asia.* August 5, 1964. Texas Tech University Vietnam Archive.

Johnson, Lyndon B. *The Strategic Stakes in Southeast Asia. Message to Congress, May 4, 1965.* 1. Texas Tech University Vietnam Archive.

Johnson, Lyndon B. *Test of an Address by President Lyndon B. Johnson on Vietnam as Prepared for Delivery at John's Hopkins University, Baltimore, MD, April 7, 1965.* U.S. Information Service Press Branch, April 4, 1965. Texas Tech University Vietnam Archive.

Kennedy, John F. *Address by Senator Kennedy to a Symposium on America's Stake in Vietnam, September, 1956.* Enclosure to Letter from Mr. David Martin, Office of Senator Dodd, April 1, 1965. Texas Tech University Vietnam Archive.

Nixon, Richard M. *Address to the Nation: Vietnam Peace Initiatives, May 14, 1969.* Texas Tech University Archive, No. 230607004.

Nixon, Richard M. *Address to the Nation on the War in Vietnam,* November 3, 1969. 9. On-line. Internet. February 14, 2004. Available at www.nixonfoundartion.org/Research_Center/Nixons/speeches/Vietnam/Address.shtml.

Nixon, Richard M. *Nixon Announces the Invasion of Cambodia, April 30, 1970, on National Television.* 6. On-line, Internet. December

5, 2003. Available at www.file://A:\Nixon%20Announces%20Cambodian%20Invasion.htm.

Nixon, Richard M. *"Peace with Honor" Radio-Television broadcast, President Nixon re: Initialing of the Vietnam Agreement.* January 23, 1973. 3. On-line. Internet. August 8, 2004. Available at http://oll.temple.edu/hist249/course/Documents/peace_with_honor.htm.

Harry S Truman. *A Factual Summary Concerning the American Mission for Aid to Greece, June 15, 1948.* 3. Truman Presidential Museum & Library. On-line. Internet. February 17, 2004. Available at http://www.trumanlibrary.org/whiltlestop/study_collection/doctrine/large folder9/tdi01-3.

Harry S. Truman. *Truman Doctrine. President Harry S. Truman's Address before a Joint Session of Congress, March 12, 1947.* 7. The Avalon Project at Yale Law School. On-line. Internet. February 17, 2004. Available at http://www.yale.edu/lawweb/avalon/trudoc.htm.

White House Memoranda

White House. *U.S. Policy on Viet-Nam: White House Statement, October 2, 1963.* Washington, D.C.: Department of State Bulletin, October 21, 1963. Texas Tech University Vietnam Archive.

White House. *National Security Action Memorandum No. 52.* Washington, D.C.: May 11. 1961. Texas Tech University Vietnam Archive.

White House. *National Security Action Memorandum No. 111.* Washington, D.C.: November 22, 1961. Texas Tech University Vietnam Archive.

White House. *National Security Action Memorandum No. 273.* Washington, D.C.: November 26, 1963. Texas Tech University Vietnam Archive.

White House. *National Security Action Memorandum No. 388.* Washington, D.C.: March 17, 1964. Texas Tech University Vietnam Archive.

White House. *National Security Action Memorandum No. 343.* Washington, D.C.: March 28, 1966. Texas Tech University Vietnam Archive.

U.S. Government Departments and Agencies
Central Intelligence Agency
Central Intelligence Agency. *Attitudes of Ho Chi Minh and Le Duan Toward the War in Vietnam.* Washington, D.C.: Office of Current Intelligence. 11 April 1966. Document is now declassified.

Central Intelligence Agency. *CIA Special Report on South Vietnam.* Washington, D.C.: January 1964. Document is now declassified. Texas Tech University Vietnam Archive.

Central Intelligence Agency. *Bloc Support of the Communist Effort against the Government of Vietnam.* Washington, D.C.: 5 October 1964. Document is now declassified.

Central Intelligence Agency. *Communist Deliveries to Cambodia for the VC/NVA Forces in South Vietnam December 1966 – April 1969.* Washington, D. C.: Directorate of Intelligence. December 1970. Document is now declassified.

Central Intelligence Agency. *Communist Objectives,* Capabilities and Intentions in Southeast Asia (Including Indochina). CIA Report (NIE 10-62), Washington, D. C.: February 21, 1962. Document is now declassified. Texas Tech University Vietnam Archive.

Central Intelligence Agency. *The Current Status of PAVN Infiltration to South Vietnam.* Washington, D. C.: Office of Current Intelligence. 9 April 1966. Document is now declassified. Texas Tech University Vietnam Archive.

Central Intelligence Agency. *Intelligence Memorandum: Hanoi's View of the War.* Washington, D. C.: Office of Current Intelligence. 14 December 1965. Document is now declassified. Texas Tech University Vietnam Archive.

Central Intelligence Agency. *Intelligence Memorandum: International Communist Aid to North Vietnam.* Washington, D.C.: 2 March 1968. Document is now declassified. Texas Tech University Vietnam Archive.

Central Intelligence Agency. *Memorandum for the Director: The View from Hanoi.* Washington, D.C.: 30 November 1966. Document is now declassified.

Central Intelligence Agency. *Memorandum for the President: International Connections of US Peace Groups.* Washington, D. C.: Director CIA. 15 November 1967. Document is now declassified. Texas Tech University Vietnam Archive.

Central Intelligence Agency. *North Vietnamese Intentions and Attitudes Toward the War.* Washington, D. C.: Director of Intelligence. 25 July 1966. Document is now declassified.

Central Intelligence Agency. *Special National Intelligence Estimate. The Outlook from Hanoi: Factors Affecting North Vietnam's Policy on the War in Vietnam.* Washington, D. C.: SNIE 14.3-70. U.S. Intelligence Board. 5 February 1970. Document is now declassified.

Central Intelligence Agency. *The Soviet Role in North Vietnam's Offensive.* Washington, D.C.: Vietnam Bulletin April 20, 1972. Texas Tech University Vietnam Archive.

Central Intelligence Agency. *Viet Cong/North Vietnamese Tactics and Strategy for the Tet General Offensive.* Washington, D.C.: February 20, 1968. Document is now declassified. Texas Tech University Vietnam Archive.

Central Intelligence Agency. *The Vietnamese Communists Debate Military Strategy.* Washington, D.C.: Directorate of Intelligence. 25 August 1966. Document is now declassified.

Defense Department

Defense Department. *Communist Strategy: Interview with Secretary McNamara.* 26 April 1965. Texas Tech University Vietnam Archive.

Defense Department. *Communist Strategy as Reflected in Lao Dong Party and COSVN Resolutions, SRAP 1569.* Military Assistance Command Vietnam. Saigon. Strategic Research & Analysis Division (SRA), Directorate of Intelligence. Texas Tech University Vietnam Archive.

Defense Department. *Fact Sheet, Ho Chi Minh Trail.* Washington, D.C.: Defense Department. February 1971. Texas Tech University Vietnam Archive.

United States Army. *Images of a Lengthy War.* Washington, D. C. Center of Military History. 1986.

Defense Department. *Statement by Secretary of Defense Robert S. McNamara before the Senate Foreign Relations Committee March 3, 1966 as Regards U. S. Involvement in South Vietnam.* Washington, D. C. March 3, 1966.

Westmoreland Report: Enemy Organization for the Conduct of the War in South Vietnam. July 1, 1968.

Federal Bureau of Investigation

Federal Bureau of Investigation. *Memorandum for the Director. Communist Infiltration of the Students for a Democratic Society.* May 25, 1965. Document is now declassified.

Federal Bureau of Investigation. *Memorandum to the Director: Vietnam Veterans Against the War (VVAW) IS – New Left.* SAC Springfield. November 8, 1971. Document is now declassified.

Federal Bureau of Investigation. *Memorandum: Vietnam Veterans against the War (VVAW) Internal Security – New Left.* Washington, D.C.: November 24, 1971. Document is now declassified. Texas Tech University Vietnam Archive.

Federal Bureau of Investigation. *Memorandum: Weather Bombings, Explosives and Incendiary Devices; Sabotage.* Washington, D.C.: August 13, 1974. Document is not declassified.

Federal Bureau of Investigation. *Memorandum: Weatherman Underground Organization.* Chicago, IL. August 20, 1980. Document is now declassified.

Federal Bureau of Investigation. *Memorandum: Vietnam Veterans against the War (VVAW) Internal Security – New Left.* Washington, D.C.: November 24, 1971. Document is now declassified. Texas Tech University Vietnam Archive.

Federal Bureau of Investigation. *Vietnam Veterans Against the War Regional Coordinators and National Steering Committee Meeting, Weekend November 12-15, 1971, Kansas City MO.* Washington, D.C.: November 24, 1971. Document is now declassified. Texas Tech University Vietnam Archive.

Foreign Broadcast Information Service

Foreign Broadcast Information Service. *Asia & Pacific. General Giap, Dung Article on 1975 Spring Victory in South Vietnam.* FBIS-A&P-75-134. 11 July 1975. Texas Tech University Vietnam Archive.

Foreign Broadcast Information Service. *Asia & Pacific. Sen Gen Van Tien Dung Article: "Great Spring Victory" [Volume I and II].* FBIS-APA. 7 June 1976. Texas Tech University Vietnam Archive.

Foreign Broadcast Information Service. *Southeast Asia Report: Vietnam Tap Chi Cong San No. 4, April 1985.* JPRS-SEA-85-103. 1 July 1985. Texas Tech University Vietnam Archive.

State Department

State Department. *Aggression from the North: The Record of North Viet-Nam's Campaign to Conquer South Viet-Nam.* Washington, D.C.: Department of State Publication 7839. February 1965. Texas Tech University Vietnam Archive.

State Department. "Aggression from the North." *White Paper on Vietnam*. Washington, D.C.: February 27, 1965. Department of Stated Bulletin, March 22, 1965.

State Department. *Address by William P. Bundy, Assistant Secretary for Far Eastern Affairs...May 27, 1965. "A Perspective on U. S. Policy in Viet-Nam."* Washington, D.C.: Department of State Bulletin. June 21, 1965. Texas Tech University Vietnam Archive.

State Department. "Communist-Directed Forces in South Viet-Nam." *Viet-Nam Information Notes*. Department of State Number 3. May 1967. Texas Tech University Vietnam Archive.

State Department. *The Heart of the Problem...Secretary Rusk, General Taylor Review Viet-Nam Policy in Senate Hearings*. Department of State. February 18, 1966.

State Department. *INR Analysis: The 1973 Paris Agreements – A Scorecard of Noncompliance*. Department of State/INR. July 21, 1987.

State Department. "Legal Basis for U.S. Military Aid to South Viet-Nam." *Viet-Nam Information Notes*. Department of State. Number 10. August 1967. Texas Tech University Vietnam Archive.

State Department. *Letter from Assistant Secretary MacArthur to Senator Fulbright, August 2, 1965: The U.S. Commitment to Assist South Vietnam*. Texas Tech University Vietnam Archive.

State Department. *Memorandum for the President: Viet-Nam*. Washington D.C.: The Under Secretary of State. November 16, 1967. Document is now declassified.

State Department. *North Vietnamese Involvement in the South*. Bureau of Intelligence and Research. July 16, 1968. Texas Tech University Vietnam Archive.

State Department. "South Viet-Nam: Reality and Myth." *Foreign Affairs Outline*. Department of State, Bureau of Public Affairs. 1965. Texas Tech University Vietnam Archive.

State Department. "A Summary of the United States Commitment to Assist South Viet-Nam." *Public Information Series*. Bureau Of Public Affairs. April 4, 1967. Texas Tech Vietnam Archive.

State Department. *A Threat to the Peace: North Viet-Nam's Effort to Conquer South Viet-Nam, In Two Parts*. Department of State. November 17, 1961. Texas Tech University Vietnam Archive.

State Department. *The North Vietnamese Role in the Origin, Direction, and Support of the War in South Vietnam*. Draft of State Department Study. 1967 Texas Tech University Archive.

State Department. "The Paris Peace Talks." *Viet-Nam Information Notes.* Department of State. Number 15, November 1969. Texas Tech University Vietnam Archive.

State Department. "President's Message to Congress, 5 August 1964." *Department of State Bulletin.* 24 August 1964. Texas Tech University Vietnam Archive.

State Department. *Rusk Cites Record of Communist Aggression in Vietnam.* Washington D.C.: Department of State Release No. 211-61. December 9, 1961. Texas Tech University Vietnam Archive.

State Department. "The Search for Peace in Viet-Nam." *Vietnam Information Notes.* Department of State. Number 2, February 1967. Texas Tech University Vietnam Achieve.

State Department. "Viet Cong Terror Tactics in South Viet-Nam." *Viet-Nam Information Notes.* Department of State. *Number* 7, July 1967. Texas Tech University Vietnam Archive.

State Department. *Viet-Nam in Brief.* Department of State. Publication 8173. Washington, D.C.: Government Printing Office, 1966. Texas Tech University Vietnam Archive.

State Department. *Viet-Nam: The Struggle for Freedom.* Department of State. Publication 7724. Government Printing Office, 1964.

State Department. *Vietnam Peace Bids Chronology March-September, 1967.* Department of State. Bureau of Research. October 1967. Texas Tech University Vietnam Archive.

State Department. *Vietnam in Perspective: An Address by Secretary of State William P Rogers.* Department of State. April 21, 1969. Texas Tech University Vietnam Archive.

State Department. "Wars of National Liberation." *Viet-Nam Information Notes.* Department of State. Number 12, June 1968. Texas Tech University Vietnam Archive.

State Department. "Why We Are in Viet-Nam." *Public Affairs Series.* Department of State. Bureau of Public Affairs. July 1965. Texas Tech University Vietnam Archive.

State Department. "Why We Fight in Viet-Nam." *Viet-Nam Information Notes.* Department of State. Number 6, June 1967.

United States Information Service/Agency

United States Information Agency. *Dikes, Dams, and Propaganda in North Vietnam. USIA* Office of Policy and Research, Research Service. August 11, 1968. Texas Tech University Vietnam Archive.

United States Information Service. *Excerpts from an Address by General Maxwell D. Taylor Former U.S. Ambassador to the Republic of Viet-Nam before the Association of the United States Army Washington, October 27, 1965.* American Embassy – Tokyo. October 1965. Texas Tech University Vietnam Archive.

United States Information Service. *The Free World's Stake in Viet-Nam.* USIS Saigon. July 1964. Texas Tech University Vietnam Archive.

United States Information Service. *Hanoi Exercises Overall Control of Viet Cong Insurgency.* American Embassy - Tokyo. February 15, 1965.

United States Information Service. *Hanoi – and South Vietnam's "Liberation Front."* Washington, D.C.: 1962. Texas Tech University Vietnam Archive.

United States Information Services. *Hanoi Still Denying Involvement in South.* Washington, D.C.: December 1968. Texas Tech University Vietnam Archive.

United States Information Services. *Hanoi's Strategy for Conquest – The 'Liberation Front.'* American Embassy – Tokyo. June 21, 1965. Texas Tech University Vietnam Archive.

United States Information Service. *Ho Chi Minh and the Communist Movement in Indo-China.* Washington, D.C.: August 1953. Texas Tech University Vietnam Archive.

United States Information Service. *Lao Dong Decision to Escalate War: 1953.* Washington, D.C.: January 1, 1963. Texas Tech University Vietnam Archive.

United States Information Service. *Lao Dong History: Late 1950's, early 1960's.* Washington, D.C.: January 1, 1960. Texas Tech University Vietnam Archive.

United States Information Agency. *North Viet-Nam and the Threat to Southeast Asia. Backgrounder on Communism.* Washington, D.C.: No. 61-SM-14. October 1961. Texas Tech University Vietnam Archive.

United States Information Service. *North Vietnamese Politburo Foresaw GVN-US Response to Invasion of South.* Principal Reports from Communist Sources. Number 11. USIS Saigon. 10 August 1972. Texas Tech University Vietnam Archive.

United States Information Service. *Partial Text of Statement by Robert S. McNamara, U.S. Secretary of Defense before the Armed Services Committee House of Representatives, February 18,*

1965. American Embassy – Tokyo. 1965. Texas Tech University Vietnam Archive.

United States Information Service. *Secretary Rusk says U.S. Actions in Viet-Nam in Consonance with International Law; Condemns Communist Concept of "Wars of Liberation."* USIS Saigon. April 27, 1965. Texas Tech University Vietnam Archive.

United States Information Service. *Three Presidents Demonstrate Continuity of U. S. Policy on Viet-Nam.* Washington, D.C.: August 1964. Texas Tech University Vietnam Archive.

United States Information Service. *U. S. Can Document NLF Ties with Hanoi.* Washington, D.C.: December 15, 1967. Texas Tech University Vietnam Archive.

United States Information Agency. *The Viet Cong Patterns of Communist Subversion – R-8-66.* Research and Reference Service. Washington, D.C.: January, 1966.

United States Information Agency. *The Viet Cong: The Front Technique.* R-13-67. Washington, D.C.: Office of Policy & Research. April 20, 1967. Texas Tech University Vietnam Archive.

United States Information Agency. *Why Hanoi Wants a 'Front' in Saigon. Backgrounder on Communism.* Washington, D.C.: No. 66-SM-51. May 1966. Texas Tech University Vietnam Archive.

US Mission Vietnam

US Mission Vietnam. *Hanoi's Central Office for South Vietnam (COSVN), A Background Paper.* Saigon. July 1969. Texas Tech University Vietnam Archive.

US Military Assistance Command, Vietnam. *Handbook for US Forces in Vietnam.* MACV April 1967.

US Mission Vietnam. *Hanoi Control of the Viet Cong under General Nguyen Chi Thanh.* March 18, 1967. Texas Tech University Vietnam Archive.

US Mission Vietnam. *Hanoi's Direction and Support of the Communist Effort in South Vietnam.* Captured Enemy Document. July 28, 1967. Texas Tech University Vietnam Archive.

US Military Assistance Command, Vietnam. *Hanoi and the "Front." Hanoi Calls for the Formation of the "Front."* Saigon. MACV/ CED. February 2, 1967. Texas Tech University Vietnam Archive.

US Mission Vietnam. "NLF Thoughts on Peace Negotiations, World Policies – A Cadre's Notes on a High Level 1967 Reorientation Course." *Viet-Nam Documents and Research Notes.* Saigon. JUSPAO. Document No. 14. January 1968. Texas Tech University Vietnam Archives.

US Mission Vietnam. *Pham Van Dong's Speech on the 25th Anniversary of the Founding of the Democratic Republic of Viet-Nam.* Saigon. September 1970. Texas Tech University Archive.

US Mission Vietnam. "The Position of North Viet-Nam on Negotiations." *Viet-Nam Documents and Research Notes.* Saigon. JUSPAO. Document No. 8. October 1967.

US Mission Vietnam. *Relationship between Hanoi and the "NLFSV."* Saigon. JUSPAO. January 28, 1967. Texas Tech University Vietnam Archive.

US Mission Vietnam. *Press Release: Release of Captured Enemy Document.* Saigon. August 18, 1967. Texas Tech University Vietnam Archive.

US Mission Vietnam. *Translation of a letter dated March 1966 Written by Le Duan, First Secretary of the Lao Dong Party Central Committee...* Document Captured by 173d Airborne Brigade, January 21, 1967. Texas Tech University Vietnam Archive.

US Mission Vietnam. *Viet Cong Foreign Affairs and Propaganda Activities.* Saigon. JUSPAO. April 11, 1967. Texas Tech University Vietnam Archive.

US Mission Vietnam. *Press Release: Viet Cong Units Directed to Intensify Struggle to Take Advantage of U.S. Peace Movement.* Saigon. November 20, 1969. Texas Tech University Vietnam Archive.

US Mission Vietnam. "World Situation and Our Party's International Mission As Seen from Hanoi, 1960-1964." *Viet-Nam Documents and Research Notes.* December 1963. Texas Tech University Vietnam Archive

Republic of South Vietnam

Republic of Vietnam. *Communist Aggression against the Republic of Viet-Nam.* Saigon. July 1964. Texas Tech University Vietnam Archive.

Republic of Vietnam. *Infiltration of Communist Armed Elements and Clandestine Introduction of Arms from North to South Vietnam.* Republic of Vietnam. Saigon. Ministry of Foreign Affairs. June 1967. Texas Tech University Vietnam Archive.

Republic of Vietnam. *One Year of Implementation of the Paris Agreement on Ending the War and Restoring Peace in Viet-Nam.* Washington, D.C.: Embassy of Viet-Nam. March 19, 1974. Texas Tech University Vietnam Archive.

Republic of Vietnam. *The War in Vietnam: Liberation or Aggression?* Republic of Vietnam. Ministry of Foreign Affairs. Saigon. 1968. Texas Tech University Vietnam Archive.

Democratic Republic of (North) Vietnam (DRV)

DRV. *Appeal by President Ho Chi Minh of the Democratic Republic of Vietnam.* Hanoi. July 17, 1966. Texas Tech University Vietnam Archive.

DRV. *Commentary on Implementation of Ho's Letter.* Liberation Radio. September 12, 1967. Texas Tech University Vietnam Archive.

DRV. *Circular on the Concentration of all Forces to Coordinate with the Diplomatic Offensive and Promote the Movement.* People's Revolutionary Party of Vietnam. July 5, 1971. Texas Tech University Vietnam Archive.

DRV. *Directive about the Propaganda Plan Relating to the Establishment of the Provisional Revolutionary Government of the Republic of South Viet-Nam.* Captured Enemy Document. June 1969. Texas Tech University Vietnam Archive.

DRV. DRV Government Statement on Formation of P.R.G. Hanoi Domestic Service in Vietnamese. June 12, 1969.

DRV. *On Foreign Policy.* Hanoi, Vietnam News Agency. April 18, 1958. Texas Tech University Vietnam Archive.

DRV. *Hanoi Calls for the Formation of the Front.* Captured Enemy Document. December 20, 1966. Texas Tech University Vietnam Archive.

DRV. *LPA Hails Soviet Support.* Hanoi. Liberation Press Agency. April 12, 1971. Texas Tech University Vietnam Archive.

DRV. *Le Duc Tho on Strategy in South: Official Notes Unity of Communist Camp.* Hanoi, VNA, January 14, 1961. Texas Tech University Vietnam Archive.

DRV. *Mme. Binh Greets U.S. Anti-War Movement.* Liberation Press Agency. April 21, 1971. Texas Tech University Vietnam Archive.

DRV. "Premier Pham Van Dong of North Viet-Nam: Policy Declaration." *New York Times.* April 14, 1965. Texas Tech University Vietnam Archive.

DRV. *NLF Acknowledges Chinese Assistance.* Hanoi. Liberation Press Agency. January 1, 1971. Texas Tech University Vietnam Archive.

DRV. *Station Commentary: The Indochina War and Nixon's Increasingly Isolated Position in U.S. Political Circles.* Hanoi Domestic Service. April 1971. Texas Tech University Vietnam Archive.

DRV. *Vietnam Committee for Solidarity with American People*. Viet-Nam Committee for Solidarity with American People. Hanoi, DRV. Texas Tech University Vietnam Archive.

DRV. *The Vietnamese People's Great Victory*. Foreign Language Press. Peking. 1975. Texas Tech University Vietnam Archive.

Miscellaneous Sources

Colby, Ambassador William. "Turning Points in the Vietnam War." Keynote Speech, 2nd Triennial Vietnam Symposium. Vietnam Center, Texas Tech University. April 18,1996. 8. On-line. Internet. November 27, 2003. Available at file://A:\\Ambassador%20William%20Colby,%20"Turning%20Points%20in%20the%20.

"From Geneva '54 to Paris '69 Have Words Lost All of Their Meanings." Speech by Mr. Tran Chanh Thanh, Minister of Foreign Affairs, 10 March 1969, Saigon. Council on Foreign Relations. Texas Tech University Vietnam Archive.

Gelb, Leslie H. "The Essential Domino: American Politics and Vietnam." *Foreign Affairs, April 1972*. Texas Tech University Vietnam Archive.

"Gromyko at U.N. Repeats Soviet Support of PRG Proposals." *Tass International Service*. Moscow. October 21 1970. Texas Tech University Vietnam Archive.

Gurtov, Melvin. "Hanoi on War and Peace." Research Report, RAND Corporation, Santa Monica, CA. December 1967. Texas Tech University Vietnam Archive.

"The Party Central Committee Holds its 15th Plenum." *Hanoi History of 15th Plenum*. May 1959. Texas Tech University Vietnam Archive.

"Hanoi's Organization of Control in the South." SEATO. October 1972. Texas Tech University Vietnam Archive.

Johnstone, William C. "The Political-Strategic Significance of Vietnam." *Current History*. 56, no. 330. (February, 1969): [1-70]. Texas Tech University Vietnam Archive.

Langer, Paul, and Joseph J. Zasloff. "The North Vietnamese Military Adviser in Laos: a First Hand Account." Research Report. RAND RM-5688-ARPA. Santa Monica, CA. July 1968. Texas Tech University Vietnam Archive.

"The 'Liberation Front' in South Vietnam: Hanoi's Political Façade." January 1966. History of the Vietnam War on Microfilm. Texas Tech University Vietnam Archive.

"Mao Zedong and Pham Van Dong, Hoang Van Hoan; Beijing. 5 October 1964." *Cold War International History Project.* Woodrow Wilson International Center for Scholars. 4. On-line. Internet. July 21, 2003. Available at http://wwics.si.edu/index.cfm?fuseaction=topics.home8topic_id=1409.

Pike, Douglas. "A National Security Workshop: Do We Have an 'Imperial Congress.'" George Mason University Law Review. Vol. No. II. (Fall 1988): [119-131]. Texas Tech University Vietnam Archive.

Pike, Douglas. "Hanoi/Viet Cong View of the Vietnam War. *Vietnam War Internet Project.* October 11, 1990. 23. On-line. Internet. February 2, 1999. Available at http://www.vwip.org/topictop.html. Texas Tech University Vietnam Archive.

Rolph, Hammond M. "The Viet Cong: Politics at Gunpoint." Communist Affairs. 4, no. 4 (July-August 1966): [1-34]. Texas Tech University Vietnam Archive.

Turner, Robert. "The Anti-War Movement in the U.S." January 1, 1972. History of the Vietnam War on Microfilm. Texas Tech University Vietnam Archive.

A Symposium on America's Stake in Vietnam. American Friends of Vietnam. New York: Carnegie Press, Inc. September 1956. Texas Tech University Vietnam Archive.

Weiss, Joseph H. "How Hanoi Controls the Vietcong." *Focus on Vietnam.* Reprint no.7 (January 1968): [n.p.]. Texas Tech University Vietnam Archive.

"Why Vietnam: The Roots of Commitment." U.S. Government Printing Office, 1965 0-785-527. August 20, 1965. Texas Tech University Vietnam Archive.

Zasloff, Joseph J. "The Role of North Vietnam in the Southern Insurgency." Research Report RAND RM-4140-PR. Santa Monica, CA. July 1964. Texas Tech University Vietnam Archive.

Index

A

Abzug, Bella 119, 293
Ad Hoc Military Buildup Committee 236, 237, 238, 438
Air defense 69, 70, 71, 72, 300
Alden, Major Gary 162
American Deserters Committee 256, 257, 259, 260
American Friends Service Committee 250, 255
American Immigrants Employment Service 256
American Servicemen's Union (ASU) 226
An Loc 61
Antiaircraft artillery (AAA) 72, 74
Anti-draft 222, 251, 252, 254, 256, 260
  campaign 251
  movement 144, 150, 151, 152, 169, 170, 176, 180, 181, 186, 189, 208, 209, 236, 251, 263, 271, 293, 294, 295, 296, 300, 305, 318, 319, 320, 322, 325, 326, 330, 334, 335, 337, 339, 349, 351, 352
  Union 222
Antiwar
  activists 3, 9, 94, 95, 105, 119, 120, 127, 153, 155, 169, 172, 181, 182, 183, 184, 201, 206, 207, 215, 216, 217, 221, 223, 238, 243, 245, 260, 264, 300, 310, 329, 330, 332, 334, 338, 341, 350, 351, 352
  activities 98, 103, 109, 128, 141, 174, 196, 233, 242, 290
  acts 136, 138
  agenda 316
  and anti-administration 85
  and anti-American 74, 180, 201, 217, 231
  and Communist Party 227
  and pro-Communist 191
  campaign 129, 140, 141
  conferences 110
  Congress 312, 318, 323, 324
  critics 34, 38, 46, 56, 268, 271, 271, 273, 283, 284, 287, 290, 310, 312, 318, 319, 321, 324, 329, 332, 354
  demonstrations 3, 4, 135, 138, 154, 271, 283, 291, 295, 322, 323, 337
  dissenters 6
  doves 206, 264
  drive 119
  efforts 118, 119, 139, 147, 226
  elements 45, 334
  factions 80, 216, 217, 225, 233, 241, 242, 251, 253, 318, 319, 341, 351
  groups 80, 81, 83, 87, 105, 110, 114, 120, 126, 128, 133, 135, 141, 174, 196, 197, 207, 227, 237, 250, 336
  leaders 119, 154
  legacy 350, 351, 352, 353, 354
  militants 310, 311
  movements ix, x, 1, 3, 4, 8, 9, 80, 81, 83, 85, 87, 107, 109, 116, 117, 118, 119, 120, 128, 133, 135, 137, 143, 144, 150, 151, 152, 169, 170, 176, 180, 181, 186, 189, 208, 209, 226, 236, 251, 263, 271, 293, 294, 295, 296, 318, 319, 320, 322, 325, 326, 330, 334, 337, 339, 349, 351, 352
  movies 229
  objectives 204, 205
  organizations 118, 120, 140, 167, 175, 236

people 133, 201
politicians 184
protesters 72, 184, 288, 324, 334
protests 290, 338
resolutions 283
senators 294, 316
sentiments 110, 139, 257
seven 172
shows 216
tactics 119
veterans 166, 237
zealots 264
Aptheker, Herbert 168
Army of (South) Vietnam (ARVN) 5
Australia 17, 23, 68

B

Baez, Joan 169, 184
Bafalis, L.A. 329
Ban Me Thuot 306
Beijing 17, 50, 70, 86
Benge, Michael 182
Berrigen, Daniel 253
Berrigen, Phillip 253
Binh, Mme. Thi Nguyen 119, 120, 123, 126, 132, 133, 150, 163, 170, 171, 172, 181, 259, 304, 346, 427, 431, 432, 433, 434
Black Panthers 98, 113, 142, 255
Boat People 343
Bombing dikes 156, 162, 164, 197, 198
Bombing halts/pauses 37, 38, 136, 137, 266, 270, 271, 272, 283, 288, 321, 323, 332
Bombing North Vietnam 37, 38, 70, 96, 123, 156, 157, 158, 159, 160, 162, 163, 164, 165, 169, 172, 173, 176, 197, 198, 220, 231, 239, 265, 266, 267, 268, 269, 270, 271, 272, 283, 284, 288, 289, 290, 295, 296, 321, 323, 332, 351, 352
Bratislava meeting 175

Brezhnev, Leonid 68, 110
Broadcasts from Hanoi viii, 155, 156, 157, 161, 183, 184, 201, 202, 216, 217, 218, 220, 221, 223, 224, 225, 351, 435
  by Clark 163, 164, 165
  by Fonda 155, 156, 157, 161, 217, 218, 220, 221, 225
  by others 435, 436, 437

C

Calvert, Greg 92
Cambodia 7, 9, 10, 11, 14, 18, 22, 23, 26, 41, 42, 44, 45, 46, 50, 51, 58, 61, 62, 68, 75, 121, 144, 145, 149, 154, 204, 217, 245, 268, 272, 274, 277, 279, 284, 285, 286, 287, 301, 311, 313, 314, 316, 325, 339, 340, 341, 347, 348, 349, 352
  killing fields 23, 45, 319, 347, 348
  sanctuaries 9, 245, 249, 272, 283, 284, 285, 301, 311, 351, 352
  staging bases 9, 311, 352
Campus disorders 93
Canada 64, 110, 251, 255, 256, 257, 258, 260, 268
Carmichael, Stokely 167, 184, 223
Carrigan, Captain Larry 191
Castro, Fidel (Premier) 72, 73, 181
Central Committee, Lao Dong Party 6, 53, 54, 56, 57, 58, 70, 76, 100, 145, 177, 206, 224, 254, 282, 307, 308, 309, 310
Central Highlands 287, 306
Central Intelligence Agency (CIA) viii, 63, 69, 72, 80, 98, 118, 119, 121, 124, 166, 260, 261, 304, 305, 335
Central Office for South Vietnam (COSVN) 6, 7, 58, 59
Che Guevara 82, 89
Chiang Kai-Shek 14, 18
Chicago 8 224

Chicago Seven 208
Chinese 8, 12, 13, 14, 18, 20, 22, 24, 61, 69, 70, 71, 72, 151, 169, 233, 327
Chinese People's Republic (CPR) 169
Chomsky, Noam 223
Chou En-Lai 20, 70, 233
Christian Science Monitor 131
Churchill, Winston S. 11, 24
CINCPAC *See* Commander in Chief Pacific
Clark, Ramsey 154, 162, 163, 164, 165, 182, 183, 184, 198, 205, 296, 329
Cleaver, Eldridge 221, 229
Coffeehouses 216, 227, 229, 230, 231, 238
Colby, William 304, 349
Cole, Lewis 178
Commander in Chief Pacific 33, 34, 322
Committee for Peace and Freedom 255
Committee for Solidarity with American People 133, 135, 136, 137, 138, 139, 140, 141, 144, 145, 151, 166, 451
Committee of Liaison 104, 105, 183, 208, 209, 211, 212, 213, 214
Communist Fronts 54, 110, 133, 136, 137, 138, 139, 142, 145, 147, 148, 166, 168, 176, 181, 267, 270
Communist Party of USA (CPUSA) 81, 167, 223
Congressional ix, 4, 9, 34, 116, 265, 283, 286, 288, 295, 310, 311, 312, 314, 318, 319, 325, 349
   doves 4, 38, 206, 264, 265, 289, 323, 325, 336
   hearings 89, 106, 108, 155, 156, 185, 213, 224, 233, 436
   resolutions 264, 283, 285, 286, 287, 294, 301, 324, 352
Conscientious objector 216, 224, 228, 251, 254
COSVN *See* Central Office for South Vietnam
Cronkite, Walter 321
Cuba 19, 52, 68, 72, 73, 74, 95, 97, 98, 99, 100, 101, 154, 167, 180, 181, 206, 227, 295, 348

D

Dau tranh 5
Davidson, Carl 92, 252
Davidson, General Phillip B. 6, 333
Davis, Rennie 177, 208, 212, 213
Day, Colonel George 183
Declaration of Honolulu 35, 36
Dellinger, David 105, 208, 311
Demilitarized Zone (DMZ) 61, 62, 70, 269, 287, 299
Democratic Convention 272, 296
Democratic Party 136, 157, 264, 282, 317
Democratic Republic of Vietnam (DRV) 52, 68, 137, 163, 218, 220, 299 *See also* North Vietnam
Democrats 105, 201, 206, 289, 295
Demonstrations 3, 8, 87, 106, 107, 109, 115, 116, 117, 118, 131, 135, 136, 137, 140, 154, 184, 228, 229, 244, 249, 252, 271, 283, 291, 294, 295, 322, 323, 327, 335, 337, 338, 346, 352
Department of Defense (DOD) 231, 243, 384
Department of State (DOS) 383
Deserters 256, 257, 258, 259, 260
Dien Bien Phu 14, 202
Dikes 156, 162, 164, 197, 198, 218
Dish van 5, 6
Dissent 91, 111, 191, 243, 252, 283, 325, 326, 335, 336, 350
Disunity ix, 38, 216, 274, 326, 337, 350, 353
DMZ *See* Demilitarized Zone

Dohrn, Bernadine 95, 97, 178
Domino Theory 23
Doss, Lt. Commander Dale Walter 211
Doss, Martha Shaw 211
Dowd, Douglas 82, 109
Draft 86, 106, 110, 172, 197, 219, 222, 229, 242, 251, 252, 253, 254, 255, 256, 257, 260, 290, 327, 331, 351
   board 251, 252, 253, 351
   evaders 255, 256, 257
   files and records 251, 254
   resisters 252, 256
Dung, Senior General Van Tien 33, 75

E

Easter offensive 164, 237
Eisenhower, Dwight D. (President) 22, 23, 24, 25, 30, 34
Elections 15, 16, 17, 52, 116, 118, 178, 253, 273, 277, 278, 280, 287, 296, 336
Ellsberg, Daniel 260
Entertainment Industry for Peace & Justice (EIPJ) 231
Espionage 236
Evans, Linda Sue 179

F

Federal Bureau of Investigation (FBI) v, x, 87, 89, 91, 94, 95, 96, 97, 98, 101, 103, 106, 115, 120, 124, 137, 158, 167, 175, 176, 178, 222, 272
Fernandez, Reverend Robert 208, 212, 223
Fifteenth Plenum 53
Fonda, Jane 120, 122, 126, 154, 155, 156, 157, 158, 159, 160, 161, 162, 183, 184, 198, 205, 217, 218, 220, 221, 225, 230, 231, 232, 310, 311, 329
   antiwar activist 172, 175
   broadcasts 155, 156, 157, 161, 217, 218, 220, 221, 225
Ford, Gerald R. (President) 41, 42, 44, 45, 304, 312, 313
Foreign Broadcast Information Service (FBIS) 158, 222
Foreign Policy, U.S. 87, 296, 326, 330, 348, 349
Fragging 227
France ix, 2, 5, 7, 11, 12, 14, 17, 22, 178, 255, 337
French War in Vietnam 11, 12, 13, 14, 15, 18, 22, 24, 52, 166, 181, 202, 220, 267, 271
Frey, Louis 295, 330
Frishman, Lieutenant Robert 183, 209
Froines, Ann 174, 223
FTA 230, 231, 232
Fulbright, William J. 75, 288, 332
Fulbright-Allen Amendment 75

G

General Directorate of Intelligence, Cuba (DGI) 101, 102
Geneva Accords 1554 7, 9, 10, 11, 14, 18, 22, 23, 26, 27, 34, 35, 41, 42, 46, 50, 51, 60, 61, 62, 63, 68, 75, 121, 144, 145, 149, 204, 217, 245, 272, 274, 277, 279, 283, 284, 285, 286, 287, 293, 301, 311, 323, 339, 341, 349, 352
Geneva Convention 123, 206
GI Movement 218, 225, 226, 227, 237
Giap, General Vo Nguyen 13, 14, 20, 33, 46, 58, 272, 318, 320, 322, 328, 333, 337, 339
Gold, Theodore 180
Gore, Albert 283
Great Britain 7, 11, 14, 17
Gregory, Dick 122
Gruening, Ernest 206

Gulf of Tonkin viii, 32, 34, 35, 157, 287, 379 *See also* Tonkin Gulf Incident
Gulf of Tonkin Resolution viii, 33, 35, 283, 287 *See also* Tonkin Resolution

H

Haiphong 169, 171, 238, 239, 288, 289
Hall, Lt. Commander Thomas, Jr. 190, 334
Handbook for Conscientious Objectors 254
Hanoi Hilton 183, 194, 176, 198, 209, 212
Hanoi Radio 47, 163, 164, 169, 217, 218, 220, 221, 223, 266, 290, 297
Harvard 87, 223
Havana 86, 95, 97, 98, 99, 100
Hayden, Thomas
  antiwar propagandist 172
  Chicago Seven 208
  conspiracy 8 179, 229
  founder of SDS 168, 172
  Port Huron Statement 90, 93
  president of SDS 90, 93
  testimony before House 90
  travel to North Vietnam 168
Hearings, House/Senate 89, 106, 108, 155, 156, 185, 213, 224, 233
Hegdahl, Seaman Douglas 183, 209
Ho Chi Minh x, 3, 11, 12, 13, 14, 16, 18, 22, 33, 50, 52, 54, 59, 61, 62, 63, 83, 129, 221, 266, 267, 285, 301, 302, 309, 320, 321, 327, 328, 337, 354
  in Moscow 11, 13, 68, 86, 288
  on revolutionary intent 11, 13, 20, 50, 54, 56, 57, 75, 85
Ho Chi Minh Trail 59, 61, 62, 285
  infiltration routes 62, 63, 301

staging bases 9, 311, 351
Hoffman, Abby 224
Hoffman, Lt. Commander David W. 186, 200, 201, 202, 334
Hoover, J. Edgar 89, 90
House Armed Services Committee 457
House Committee on Internet Security 89, 90, 108, 115, 155, 156, 183, 209, 211, 213, 217, 224, 225, 328, 329
House Internal Security Committee 109, 114, 217, 221, 223, 224, 228, 233, 249, 334
Hubbard, Al 125, 126, 166, 167
Human rights 206, 344, 345

I

Ichord, Richard 115, 185, 199, 200
Imperialism 3, 52, 71, 72, 73, 82, 95, 96, 97, 98, 99, 100, 101, 111, 142, 143, 151, 168, 174, 180, 181, 221, 231, 253, 257, 258, 259, 260, 262
Imperialists 3, 6, 8, 20, 46, 47, 68, 73, 96, 143, 231, 281, 298
Indochina ix, 2, 6, 10, 11, 13, 14, 17, 22, 23, 24, 42, 45, 50, 52, 120, 121, 144, 160, 163, 170, 172, 220, 221, 237, 238, 250, 285, 289, 290, 291, 292, 294, 296, 297, 301, 305, 310, 311, 313, 315, 316, 319, 347, 348, 349, 352
  defense of 10, 11, 17, 22, 23, 24, 42, 45, 313, 315, 316
  strategic importance 22
  U.S. aid 76, 305
  U.S. policy 87, 107
Infiltration 35, 43, 50, 53, 59, 60, 62, 63, 75, 79, 81, 178, 266, 299, 300, 301, 330

Insurgency 9, 10, 19, 21, 46, 47, 52,
	53, 56, 58, 59, 62, 67, 74, 76,
	348, 349
International Commission for Control
	and Supervision (ICCS) 301
International Control Commission
	(ICC) 35, 64, 66
International Society for Human
	Rights (ISHR) 345
Interrogation 46, 62, 72, 73, 193, 195,
	199, 336

J

Jaffe, Naomi Esther (aka Naomi
	Safier) 178
Javits, Jacob 293
Johnson administration 264, 267, 271,
	333
Johnson, Lyndon B. (President) 1, 3,
	4, 29, 30, 32, 33, 34, 35, 36, 37,
	38, 47, 73, 91, 119, 128, 130,
	131, 136, 137, 265, 266, 267,
	268, 269, 317, 321, 326, 336,
	337, 353, 368
Johnson, Sam 184, 205, 206
Joint Chiefs of Staff (JCS) 260

K

Kasler, Colonel James H. 195
Katzenbach, Nicolas deB 1
Kennedy, Edward 272, 283, 292, 353
Kennedy, John F. 4, 10, 20, 25, 27, 28,
	29, 38, 91, 177, 179, 216, 295
Kerry, John F. 122, 123, 124, 125
	member of VVAW 125
	testimony before Senate 122, 124
Khe Sanh 61, 62
Khmer Rouge 284, 347
Khrushchev, Nikita 29
Kiley, Colonel Frederick 184
Killing fields 45, 319, 347
Kissinger, Henry x, 172, 260, 267,
	282, 286, 287, 288, 289, 295,
	320, 335, 336, 348
Klonsky, Michael 92
Kosygin, Alexi 110, 111

L

Lane, Mark 122, 126
Lao Dong Party 46, 54, 55, 56, 57, 58,
	66, 67, 70, 75, 76, 104, 153, 169
Laos 7, 9, 10, 11, 14, 18, 22, 23, 26,
	27, 34, 35, 41, 42, 46, 50, 51,
	60, 61, 62, 63, 68, 75, 121, 144,
	145, 149, 204, 217, 245, 272,
	274, 277, 279, 283, 284, 285,
	286, 287, 293, 301, 311, 323,
	339, 341, 349, 351, 352
	Geneva Accords 1954 37, 49, 52,
		64, 279
	sanctuaries 285, 287, 351, 352
Lawson, Reverend 223
Le Duan 33, 52, 53, 54, 55, 56, 57, 63,
	70, 280, 303, 304, 305, 306,
	308, 309, 310, 354
Le Duc Tho 57, 172, 282, 288, 297
Levine, Major Stephen 162
Liao Cheng-chih 151
Liberated Barracks 238
Liberation Press Agency, clandestine
	137, 139, 142, 148, 149, 291
Liberation Radio, clandestine 138,
	217
Lin Pao, Marshal 20
Lin Shaoqi 70
Lodge, Henry Cabot 273, 326
Lowenstein, Allard 206
Ly, Father Nguyen Van 345

M

MacArthur, Douglas II 49, 50
Mansfield Amendment 286, 287
Mao Tse-tung 14, 19, 20, 50, 51, 70,
	72, 89
Maoist 5, 263
Marxism-Leninism 13

Marxist 52, 56, 57, 80, 82, 93, 94, 95, 103, 106, 168, 233, 234, 235, 260
Mathis, Dawson 328
May 2 Movement (M2M) 87
May Day Collective 118, 119
McCain, John III 51
McCarthy, Eugene 206, 272
McGovern, George 119, 206, 263, 272, 290, 291
McGovern-Hatfield Amendment 284, 291
McNamara, Robert S. viii, 19, 48, 80, 394
Meacham, Stewart 208
Media ix, 6, 12, 206, 207, 283, 284, 285, 286, 287, 288, 290, 318, 321, 327, 329, 339, 344, 345, 352
Mekong Delta 308
Military Assistance Command, Vietnam (MACV) 61, 123, 333, 421
Military Buildup Committee viii, 236, 237
Military Counseling Service 228
Military Law Project 228
Montgomery, G.V. 195, 329
Morse, Wayne 206, 332
Movement for a Democratic Military (MDM) 223, 226, 228, 233
Mulligan, Captain James 334
Murray, Major General John 312
Muste, A.J. 105

N

National Front for the Liberation of the South (NFLSVN) 56, 57, 270 *See also* National Liberation Front
National Liberation Front (NLF) 56, 71, 73, 74, 76, 104, 109, 110, 142, 145, 147, 150, 152, 153, 176, 179, 206, 259, 267, 272, 273, 277
National Mobilization Committee to End the War in Vietnam 107, 136, 137
National Peace Action Coalition (NPAC) 114, 115, 116, 117, 119, 120, 174
National Security Action Memorandum (NSAM) vii, 27, 35, 355, 359, 363
National Security Council (NSC) 21
Naval Investigative Service (NIS) 125
Negotiations 12, 13, 22, 39, 44, 55, 56, 103, 150, 153, 263, 264, 265, 266, 267, 268, 272, 273, 274, 276, 279, 280, 281, 282, 283, 284, 286, 288, 292, 295, 296, 297, 300, 321, 322, 323, 324, 326, 329, 330, 336, 339
New Guy Village 194
Newton, Huey 142, 143, 229
New Left 85, 89, 91, 97, 99, 252
New Mobilization Committee to End the War in Vietnam 107, 108, 109, 139, 170, 208
New Zealand 17, 23, 68
Nguyen Ai Quoc 11 *See also* Ho Chi Minh
Nguyen Van Thanh. 11 *See also* Ho Chi Minh
Nhan Dan 13, 75
Nixon, Richard M. 38, 39, 40, 41, 114, 117, 118, 119, 131, 132, 133, 139, 140, 141, 145, 146, 149, 150, 151, 156, 160, 169, 170, 173, 174, 179, 218, 220, 232, 242, 259, 261, 273, 274, 282, 283, 284, 287, 288, 289, 290, 291, 292, 293, 294, 295, 296, 310, 311, 312, 316, 318, 320, 322, 323, 324, 325, 326, 337, 353
  Address May 14, 1969 39
  Address November 3, 1969 40

Paris Agreement 41
Vietnamization 40, 114, 133, 150, 166, 245, 259, 284, 285, 287, 291, 303, 353
North Vietnam viii, ix, x, 2, 3, 4, 5, 6, 8, 9, 11, 13, 14, 16, 17, 18, 30, 32, 36, 37, 38, 39, 40, 41, 42, 43, 46, 47, 48, 49, 54, 55, 56, 57, 58, 59, 60, 61, 62, 63, 64, 65, 66, 67, 69, 70, 71, 72, 73, 74, 75, 76, 77, 95, 104, 110, 123, 128, 129, 130, 131, 132, 133, 136, 137, 142, 146, 152, 154, 156, 157, 160, 162, 163, 164, 165, 166, 167, 168, 169, 170, 171, 172, 174, 175, 176, 177, 178, 179, 181, 182, 184, 185, 190, 192, 195, 197, 201, 202, 203, 204, 206, 208, 209, 217, 218, 220, 221, 223, 224, 227, 238, 239, 242, 259, 264, 265, 266, 267, 268, 269, 270, 271, 272, 273, 275, 276, 277, 278, 280, 282, 284, 288, 289, 290, 295, 296, 297, 299, 300, 301, 304, 306, 311, 313, 314, 317, 318, 319, 320, 321, 322, 323, 325, 326, 330, 331, 332, 333, 334, 335, 336, 337, 338, 339, 347, 352
North Vietnam's Air Defense System 69, 70, 71, 72, 300
North Vietnamese Army (NVA) 2, 3, 58, 59, 60, 61, 142, 143, 153, 154, 166, 177, 187, 188, 301, 306, 311, 320, 321

O

Overly, Colonel Norris 202

P

Pacific Counseling Service 228, 232, 238

Pakistan 17
Paris Agreement on Ending the War and Restoring Peace in Vietnam 1973 41, 42, 61, 62, 74, 75, 152, 181, 298, 299, 302, 304, 310, 321, 322
Paris Conference 133, 170, 288
Paris Peace Accords 297
Paris Peace Talks 116, 265, 325
Party Central Committee, Lao Dong 6, 53, 54, 56, 57, 58, 70, 76, 100, 145, 177, 206, 224, 254, 282, 307, 308, 309, 310
Pathet Lao 27, 62, 63, 68, 166
Peace activists 182, 183, 184, 207
Peace envoys 182, 183, 212, 266
Peace initiatives 263, 264, 273
Peace proposal 145, 161, 171
Peck, Sidney 105, 223, 310
Peking *See* Beijing
Pentagon Papers 118, 260, 261, 262, 384
People's Army Defense Committee 228
People's Army of (North) Vietnam (PAVN) 5, 51, 59, 63, 65, 228
People's Blockade of Arms to Indochina 250
People's Coalition for Peace and Justice (PCPJ) 114, 115, 116, 117, 118, 119, 133, 172, 174
People's Liberation Army Forces (PLAF) 58, 72, 143
People's Organ of Control 344
People's Peace Treaty 223
People's Republic of China (PRC) 70, 71
People's Revolutionary Party (PRP) 57, 58, 59
Pham Van Dong 13, 47, 128, 129, 167, 168, 172, 174, 270, 302, 337
Philippines 6, 17, 19, 23, 26, 219, 231, 241, 268
Phuoc Binh 304
Phuoc Long 304, 312

Pike, Douglas 4, 5
Plenum 53, 75, 303, 304
Politburo 47, 52, 53, 58, 264, 282, 311, 317, 334, 339 *See also* Political Bureau
Political Bureau 73, 82, 104, 123, 133, 155, 164, 167, 179, 181, 182, 183, 184, 185, 198, 199, 200, 201, 202, 203, 204, 205, 206, 207, 208, 209, 212, 229, 274, 284, 286, 287, 290, 292, 296, 297, 311, 329, 334, 338
Political warfare 1, 2, 5, 6, 330, 336
Population relocation 343
Port Huron Statement 90, 93
Potsdam Agreement 12
POW wives 104, 105, 184, 209
POWs *See* Prisoners of War
Prisoners of War 155, 182, 183, 191, 198, 209, 210, 273, 278, 296, 328, 329, 331
Progressive Labor Movement (PLM) 85, 87
Progressive Labor Party (PLP) 93, 94, 105, 234, 235
Propaganda 1, 6, 7, 8, 9, 50, 58, 59, 84, 85, 104, 106, 107, 110, 117, 122, 128, 152, 155, 165, 166, 177, 184, 187, 191, 196, 197, 200, 202, 203, 211, 215, 223, 224, 225, 226, 228, 231, 254, 258, 290, 301, 318, 330, 331, 334, 338, 345, 347, 351
Psychological Warfare 85, 113, 155, 225
Pyongyang 223

R

Reagan, Ronald (President) 354
Recruiting 64, 81, 101, 243, 252, 351
Re-education camps 341, 342
Republic of (South) Vietnam (RVN) 17, 25, 28, 36, 46, 52, 68, 81, 133, 137, 142, 145, 170, 218, 220, 297, 299, 300, 302, 309, 344, 347
Republican convention 120, 124, 294
Reserve Officer Training Corps (ROTC) 242, 243, 244, 245, 246, 247, 248, 251, 351
Reston, James 328, 337
Revolutionary Union (RU) 233
Revolutionary Youth Movement (RYM) 94
Risner, Colonel Robinson 334
Rogers, William (Secretary of State) 165
Rope treatment 186, 200
Rostow, Walter W. 4, 91, 321, 336, 337
ROTC *See* Reserve Officer Training Corps
Rowe, Major Nick 206
Rudd, Mark 92, 97
Rusk Dean 4, 28, 267, 271, 297, 335
Ruskin, Eleanor 95
Rutter, Colonel George 162

S

Saigon x, 2, 4, 7, 12, 22, 52, 58, 67, 72, 76, 149, 164, 178, 277, 282, 286, 287, 289, 291, 298, 301, 304, 307, 308, 309, 310, 312, 316, 317, 341
SAM *See* Surface-to-Air Missile
Sanctuaries 9, 245, 249, 272, 283, 284, 285, 301, 311, 352
Scheer, Robert 223
SDS *See* Students for a Democratic Society
SEATO *See* Southeast Asia Treaty Organization
Second Front vii, ix, 1, 3, 5, 7, 9, 80, 81, 83, 85, 87, 89, 91, 93, 95, 97, 99, 101, 103, 104, 105, 107, 109, 111, 113, 115, 117, 119, 121, 123,

125, 127, 216
Selective Service System 110, 248, 251, 253
Senate Foreign Relations Committee 33, 48, 122, 282, 332
Senate Internal Security Committee 108, 109, 114, 217, 221, 223, 224, 228, 230, 233, 234, 237, 238, 249, 334
Senate Judiciary Committee 329
Sharp, Admiral Ulysses Grant 34, 322, 323, 332
Shuman, Sue Allen 209, 213
Silent Majority speech 40, 170, 325
Social controls 344
Socialist Republic of Vietnam (SRV) 46, 300, 344, 347
Socialist Workers Party (SWP) 81, 85, 89, 105, 108, 114, 115, 226, 233
South Korea 6, 18, 22, 68
South Vietnam *See* Republic of Vietnam (RVN)
Southeast Asia 9, 10, 11, 12, 17, 20, 22, 23, 24, 26, 27, 29, 30, 32, 34, 35, 36, 37, 50, 51, 52, 73, 81, 82, 86, 91, 122, 124, 138, 159, 163, 216, 217, 224, 225, 228, 236, 237, 238, 240, 242, 249, 261, 265, 266, 268, 292, 296, 316, 333, 338, 354
Southeast Asia Treaty Organization (SEATO) 17, 36, 261
Soviet Union 14, 18, 19, 20, 21, 42, 51, 52, 67, 68, 69, 70, 76, 99, 110, 118, 306, 348, 352
Spock, Benjamin 83, 135
Spring Mobilization to End the War in Vietnam 105, 107, 128, 129
Stockholm Conference 109, 110
Students for a Democratic Society (SDS) 88, 89, 90, 91, 92, 93, 94, 95, 98, 99, 119, 168, 172, 175, 177, 178, 179, 180, 181, 244, 245, 251, 252, 253, 255

Subversion 18, 20, 25, 34, 53, 56, 74, 85, 224
Sumi, Hideko 223
Surface-to-Air Missile (SAM) 62, 70, 71, 181, 300
Surveillance 27, 28, 341, 343, 345
Sutherland, Donald 231

T

Taylor, General Maxwell D. 20, 27, 320, 332, 333
Teach-ins 83, 84, 85, 87, 245
Tet Offensive 6, 66, 94, 250, 266, 269, 271, 320, 321, 326, 333, 339, 353
Thailand 17, 19, 20, 23, 26, 31, 50, 51, 68, 121, 164, 268, 323
Than, Nguyen Chi 47
Thang, Ton Due 303
Thieu, Nguyen Van 123, 148, 156, 219, 259, 277, 287, 289, 290, 291, 292, 305, 309, 310
Thompson, Fletcher 165
Tonkin Gulf Incident 32, 34, 157, 378
Tonkin Resolution viii, 33, 34, 35, 283, 386
Toronoto Anti-draft Programme 256
Torture 9, 123, 175, 182, 183, 184, 189, 194, 195, 196, 204, 205, 207, 329, 335, 338
Treason 1, 94, 109, 165, 173, 350
Trinh, Nguyen Duy 166, 221
Trotskyite 108, 114, 115, 119, 226
Truman Doctrine 21
Truman, Harry S. (President) 21
Tuner, Robert F. 207, 337, 347, 349

U

U.S. Army 6, 168, 232, 236, 244, 314, 330, 332, 333
U.S. House of Representatives 88, 116, 134, 185, 206, 285, 334, 384

U.S. Military Assistance Advisory Group (USMAAG) 22, 24, 27
U.S. Senate 17, 33, 34, 48, 49, 81, 84, 86, 93, 116, 122, 123, 124, 149, 184, 206, 207, 264, 282, 284, 285, 286, 287, 290, 293, 294, 295, 311, 312, 316, 326, 329, 332
UN Secretary General 265, 266, 268
Uniform Code of Military Justice (UCMJ) 121, 228, 232
United Nations (UN) 15, 16, 206, 269
University of Michigan 84, 87

V

Vancouver Committee to Aid American Objectors 256
Venceremos Brigade 74, 98, 99, 100, 102, 103, 227
Viet Cong 2, 4, 5, 47, 49, 53, 54, 57, 58, 62, 85, 86, 94, 97, 98, 103, 118, 119, 123, 126, 132, 142, 161, 167, 180, 181, 182, 206, 230, 271, 320, 329
Viet-Minh 5, 12, 13, 14, 63
Vietnam Courier 73
Vietnam Day Committee 224
Vietnam News Agency 66, 68, 132, 135, 136, 156, 162, 165, 259, 291
Vietnam syndrome 348
Vietnam Veterans 120, 122, 124, 125, 126, 238, 321, 338
Vietnam Veterans Against the War (VVAW) 120, 161, 166, 167, 237, 240
Vietnam Week 106, 107
Vietnamization 40, 114, 133, 150, 166, 245, 259, 284, 285, 287, 291, 303, 353
VVAW *See* Vietnam Veterans Against the War

W

Wald, George 223
War Powers Act 41, 311, 319, 348
Wars of National Liberation 17, 19, 20, 21
War Resisters League 255
Washington Security Council 338
Washington Star 151, 338
Weather Underground (WUO) 95, 96, 97, 98, 180
Weathermen 94, 95, 97, 98, 181 *See also* Weather Underground
Webb, James H., Jr. 82, 263, 310, 312
Weiss, Cora 104, 181, 183, 208, 210, 214
Westmoreland, General William C. 243, 317, 330, 331
White House 11, 84, 118, 162, 260, 274, 322, 337, 348
Wilson, Dagmar 103
Winter Soldier Investigation 122
Women Strike for Peace (WSP) 103, 104, 147, 183, 192, 208
Workers Student Alliance (WSA) 94
Workers World Party 85

Printed in the United States
50599LVS00004B/277-369